1ST   12 -

D0983990

*Speaking of Literature
and Society*

THE WORKS OF LIONEL TRILLING

UNIFORM EDITION

LIONEL TRILLING

SPEAKING OF LITERATURE AND SOCIETY

Edited by Diana Trilling

New York and London

HARCOURT BRACE JOVANOVICH

Copyright © 1980 by Diana Trilling and James Trilling
Copyright © 1979, 1980 by Diana Trilling

All rights reserved.
No part of this publication
may be reproduced or transmitted in any form or
by any means, electronic or mechanical, including
photocopy, recording, or any information storage
and retrieval system, without permission in
writing from the publisher.

Printed in the United States of America

Material in this book is copyright © 1968 by Lionel Trilling;
copyright © 1924, 1939, 1940, 1941, 1945, 1948, 1956, 1958, 1964 by
the Estate of Lionel Trilling; copyright © 1942, 1952, 1968, 1969,
1970, 1973, 1976 by Diana Trilling and James Trilling; copyright © 1949,
1951 by Diana Trilling as Executrix of the Estate of Lionel Trilling,
copyright renewed 1977, 1979; copyright © 1978 by Diana Trilling;
copyright © 1944, 1953, 1955, 1957 by The New York Times Company
(reprinted by permission).

Library of Congress Cataloging in Publication Data

Trilling, Lionel, 1905–1975.
Speaking of literature and society.

(The Works of Lionel Trilling)
1. Literature, Modern—19th century—History and criticism—
Addresses, essays, lectures. 2. Literature, Modern—20th century—
History and criticism—Addresses, essays, lectures.
I. Trilling, Diana. II. Title.
III. Series: Trilling, Lionel, 1905–1975. Works.
PN761.T7 1980 809'.03 80-7944
ISBN 0-15-184710-X

First edition

B C D E

Editor's Foreword

SPEAKING OF LITERATURE AND SOCIETY is a selection from the previously uncollected critical writings of Lionel Trilling. It is the twelfth and final volume in the Uniform Edition of his work. There was very little my husband wrote—a few speeches; notes for classroom use; some journals—that wasn't published in his lifetime, usually close to the occasion of its composition, but far from all of his critical writing was gathered in books. Indeed, although he himself put together four essay collections—*The Liberal Imagination* (1950), *The Opposing Self* (1955), *A Gathering of Fugitives* (1956), and *Beyond Culture* (1965)—to which this edition has added two further critical volumes, *Prefaces to The Experience of Literature* and *The Last Decade*, the latter a group of major essays dating from the last ten years of his life, more than half a million words were still available to me from which to select the contents of the present volume.

By twentieth-century standards this is an impressive productivity even without taking into account the fact that writing was in effect a second profession for my husband, always forced to take a subsidiary role to his teaching, and that he also engaged in such consuming activities as the preparation of college texts and the supervision, along with Jacques Barzun and W. H. Auden, of two book societies, The Readers' Subscription and The Mid-Century. And it draws attention, I think, to certain aspects of his life and character which are intimately connected with his work but which, to my knowledge, have not previously been recorded. I take license to speak of them here from the several places in this collection where he remarks on the usefulness and naturalness of our acquainting ourselves with an author not merely as a writer but also as a person.

The first of my two personal statements will no doubt be the more startling, even to people who knew Lionel fairly well: throughout his lifetime he had serious difficulty in putting words on paper. His problem was not precisely of the sort we usually have in mind when we say of a writer that he suffers from a "block." A true block is a wholly calamitous thing, incapacitating a writer so that he produces nothing. It can last for years and even terminate a literary career. The difficulty under which my husband worked was happily not this ultimate. He was always, finally, able to meet his commitments. But at what cost in pain and perseverance! There were periods when he could spend day after interminable day trying to write a single satisfactory sentence. It was an inconsistent phenomenon: exacerbated at one moment, at the next it could suddenly and with no apparent explanation disappear. His book on E. M. Forster, for example, was written in a short six weeks while he was teaching four full courses (or was it five that year?), and his long essay, "Freud: Within and Beyond Culture" —it was first called "Freud and the Crisis of Our Culture" and was delivered as the Freud Anniversary Lecture of the New York Psychoanalytic Society—was done in less than two weeks. Yet the brief critical prefaces to *The Experience of Literature,* which read as if they had been tossed off between tea and dinner in the enviable way that English men of letters are reputed to get their work done, were the product of extended agonizing efforts of will.

I do not use the word "will" by accident: it is a signal word throughout Lionel Trilling's writing. No more is it by accident that I cite Forster and Freud in discussing my husband's problems in composition. For both Forster and Freud, though in quite different ways, the concept of will was central to their thought. His critical study of Forster was the second book that Lionel wrote; it was published in 1943. As he got older, or perhaps as Forster got older, Lionel lost some of his earlier pleasure in Forster's mind —I think he became tired of the famous "relaxed will" of the author of *A Passage to India* as it came to guide, or misguide, Forster's judgment in all areas of opinion. Lionel's admiration for Freud never diminished; on the contrary. And it was an admiration that referred as strongly, or even more strongly, to Freud's character as to his doctrine, because Lionel saw the character of the man *in* the doctrine, indeed at its core. For the great innovating intelligence of the founder of psychoanalytical thought, the whole precarious structure of civilization rested on the proper definition and disposition of will, and this was a view that my husband concurred in. Will, as it refers to either the ego or the superego, is not attractive to the modern mind, and for sound reason, since it has increasingly come to associate itself with power—power, that is to say, not as the organizing principle of the personal life but as a public and political manifestation. The will that kept Lionel at his desk day after day confronting his blank sheet of paper was not the will of imposition. It was the will of freedom and individual affirmation, the will that mobilizes itself against all despotisms, even those of our own temperaments.

The second of my personal reports is similarly relevant to the nature of Lionel's work, as I see it. It has been my experience that most people happen upon their professions through the conjoined operations of choice and chance. Had the circumstances been different the doctor might have been a writer, the lawyer a naturalist, the architect a banker, the banker a violinist. But there was never a possibility that Lionel could have been anything but what he was, a writer and teacher of literature. While it never excluded the enjoyment of music, ballet, movies, television, fishing, and the companionship of friends, his dedication to reading was the nearest thing to an absolute in his character. It defined his being and thus had a direct bearing on the view he had of literature as an influence in our moral lives and as a living force in society, both the image and the creator of our humanity. To believe, in the current critical mode, that the meaning of a literary text was to be discovered only in isolation from the society in which it had appeared and in which it was now read would, for him, have been to condemn himself to exile from the human race and the knowable universe. Among seeming paradoxes, perhaps none that concerns my husband is more pleasing to me than that this man whose life was so much lived in books, far from confusing life with literature, found in books a first and enduring means of entry into a very wide world.

Yet these personal statements which I adumbrate here, while germane, I think, to the contents of this volume, must of course not be read as having generated the principle by which I chose the pieces in *Speaking of Literature and Society.* As any anthologist will understand, in the process of fixing on my selections I con-sulted many principles and then, in the end, none. Lionel was born in 1905. The material available to me spanned more than half a century: it began when he was a Columbia undergraduate between 1921 and 1925 and ended only with the end of his life in 1975. I had impossible ambitions: I wanted to trace his intellectual evolution over those years; I wanted to suggest at least some few of the significant changes in the literary culture of our century and some of the ways in which Lionel responded to those changes; I wanted to tell young readers about the hard complex history of decades of which they had had no direct experience and how this was reflected in our literary culture; especially I wanted the young reader to glimpse something of the form in which the Stalinization of the American intellectual classes announced itself, also the shape and location of the dissent from it; I wanted to remind older readers of conflicts they had perhaps forgotten and of reputations gained and lost with none of us taking sufficient heed. I wanted very much to get down at least the dim outline of a personal narrative: Lionel's failed search for "a Jewish identity" in his early writing for *The Menorah Journal;* his failed search in Marxism for an answer to the social and economic questions raised in the wake of the stock market crash of 1929. And not only were these desires to be balanced against each other. I wanted as well to balance formal and informal critical enterprises and allot adequate space to his purely academic writings—all of this while still choosing only his best work in any category.

As I say, in the long run all these criteria had to be discarded: the directives were too many. Consciousness ceded to instinct: I chose the pieces, long or short, which for whatever unstatable reason impressed me as being interesting, and decided to include, for biographical purposes, an Appendix reprinting the memoir "Lionel Trilling: A Jew at Columbia." Of John Dos Passos's *U.S.A.*, which Lionel reviewed on its publication in the late Thirties, he wrote, "His book *tells* more than it *is*." In putting together this volume there came the point when, even as I reminded myself to remind its readers that Proust, Mann, Joyce and Lawrence weren't yet the great literary "masters" of our century but were all still alive and working in Lionel's young manhood—in fact, Lionel at 22 reviewed Proust's *Cities of the Plain,* which had just appeared in English—I also urged upon myself the self-contradictory hope that *Speaking of Literature and Society is* more than it *tells* us of social and cultural history.

I acknowledge with gratitude the receipt of a Chairman's Grant from the National Endowment for the Humanities which, at my husband's death, made it possible for his much-tumbled papers to be sorted and catalogued for deposit in the Columbia University Library, and the unceasing cooperation that has been given me by Mary Boone Bowling, who made this Archive, and Kenneth Lohf, the Librarian for Rare Books and Manuscripts Libraries of Columbia University.

Without the help, the patience and the devoted personal support of Barbara Crehan, it would quite simply have been impossible for me to produce any of the new volumes in this Uniform Edition. It is chiefly through her skillful and persistent sleuthing that many items not mentioned in a previous bibliography have now come to light.

But surely my largest debt is to William Jovanovich, who not only conceived this Uniform Edition but also sustained it at every stage of its perilous growth, putting all the resources of his gifted designing and editorial staffs at my disposal. For such an act of serious publishing in a time like ours there can be no sufficient expression of thanks.

New York
February 1980   Diana Trilling

Editorial Note

THE contents of this volume are presented in chronological order. The copy used and the dates supplied are those of first publication; in the few instances in which this rule could not be followed, the departure is indicated. Wherever possible the original titles of the pieces have been retained but if for some necessary reason a title has been supplied by the Editor, this information appears in a footnote. The texts conform exactly to the original printings except that, other than within quotations, English spellings have been Americanized.

D. T.

Contents

Contents

Contents

Speaking of Literature
and Society

The Poems of Emily Brontë

[*The Morningside*,[1] 1924]

A TALL Irishman, incredibly handsome, forsook the farm-
land of his ancestors for the divinity books of Cambridge;
he married a lady with a neat little mind and a mim little
mouth and got himself made incumbent of the little living of
Haworth, somewhere on the surly moors of Yorkshire. The lady
and the Irishman, whose name was Patrick Brontë and who, in
moments of exuberant exasperation, was given to firing pistols
through the back door and to stuffing the hearth-rug into the fire to
enjoy the stinking smoke, contrived between them to propagate
one of the most famous of literary families. In a few years, for
none of that family lived to be forty, they flashed upon the world
to delight, shock, and surprise it.

In the National Portrait Gallery there is a group of the three
famous sisters, done by their infamous, red-headed brother, Patrick
Branwell. Branwell was to die, a young abomination, of drink,
vanity, drugs, and decayed intellect; his artistic talent is slight
enough, his training negligible, yet he has managed, at least, in the
frequently mentioned picture, to set down the intimate knowledge
derived from close companionship. To the right stands Charlotte,
Jane Eyre, plain-faced with a square chin, a practical, kindly mouth,
and a thick-set, kindly nose. To the left is Anne in shadow, pensive,
wistful, conventionally passionate, a blessed damozel. Emily Jane

---

[1] *The Morningside* was an undergraduate literary magazine of Columbia College.
(D.T.)

is brave between the two, thoughtful and full-lipped, humorous and very sad, a cursed damozel if there ever was one. Ten years later, Branwell painted her again, this time in profile, dressed in a low, Italianate gown. The bravery is still there, the mouth is set a trifle bitterly, the lips are compressed, the eyes are trying to be steadfast. This is the Emily that died at twenty-nine longing very intensely for something she will not define and never got. This was the Emily that, pale and scared, had bullied and beaten her savage dog into obedience; that had died standing up in the parlor, refusing to go to bed and clinging to a table for support; that had written one of the great novels of England in a manner never before known, full of a black, crazy beauty.

Her fame as a novelist is dimmed by her older sister's; her merit as a poet is eclipsed by her own as a novelist. Of the family of versifiers, the father's numbers are laughable, and Charlotte's are poor, for Jane Eyre, the common-sense heroine, cannot turn couplets. Branwell writes like a conceited, talented pup, and Anne as one would expect of a blessed damozel. But Emily accomplishes a very difficult thing. Her métier is obviously the novel, and when she sets her hand to verse, she must convey her meaning through a tough crust of triteness and by an idiom of poetic imagery worn to almost meaningless abstraction. In her ability to break through lies her achievement, for, more often than not, she reveals herself freshly and directly. The poetic jargon that she uses is the language of a bad poetry. She had read Milton, Shakespeare, Pope and Byron, but she had been lamentably influenced by Thomson, Campbell, Southey and the poorer Wordsworth. Lacking the clear, crisp, unrestricted dialect of Emily Dickinson, whose turn of thought her own closely resembles, the charm of the poetic mind most surely hers is not immediately apparent. We resent the world of turrets, guitars, eastwinds, moors, graves, and minster-walls that she offers us, yet the conquering of that resentment is the indication of her power. But there is not always resentment, and certainly none caused by these lines with their flavor of her more skillful namesake.

> Hope was but a timid friend;
>   She sat without the grated den,
> Watching how my fate would tend
>   Even as selfish-hearted men.
>
> She was cruel in her fear;
>   Through the bars, one weary day,
> I looked out to see her there,
>   And she turned her face away. . . .

Or by these—

> The old clock in the gloomy hall
>   Ticks on from hour to hour;
> And every time its measured call
>   Seems lingering slower and slower.
>
> And, oh, how slow that keen-eyed star
>   Has tracked the chilly gray;
> What, watching yet! how very far
>   The morning lies away. . . .

Her art at its best is of great accuracy and precision; at its worst, it is never insipid, only unhappily and dully presented. And it is always put to brave uses, for Emily Jane never shrank from the facts as she saw them. She loved her brother dearly, yet she had always been the mystically religious and moralistic member of the family and at his death she wrote

> Vain as thou wert, and weak as vain,
> The slave of Falsehood, Pride and Pain,
> My heart has nought akin to thine,
> Thy soul is powerless over mine. . . .

and then, sternly relenting—

> Do I despise the timid deer
> Because his limbs are fleet with fear?
> Or would I mock the wolf's death howl
> Because his form is gaunt and foul?
> Or hear with joy the leveret's cry
> Because it cannot bravely die? . . .

Yearning passionately for something, it is no romantic posturing that she indulges in, but a very actual and sincere emotion. We never learn what that longing is for—whether for an actual lover with black hair, or, like the other Emily, for a closer communion with their Papa above, for surcease from her constant domestic sorrows, or for a deeper realization of Emily Jane herself. She had seen

> . . . how hearts could hide
> Their secret with a lifelong pride
> And then reveal it as they died. . . .

She understood that "strange courage and strange weakness, too" but hers was only the courage.

A Study of
Terror-Romanticism

[A review of *The Haunted Castle: A Study of the Elements of English Romanticism* by Eino Railo. *New York Evening Post*, December 10, 1927]

THERE is no word in the critical vocabulary that has so many meanings—and consequently so little meaning—as "romantic." Yet it is somehow a necessary word and critics use it unsparingly. It remains one of the liveliest problems of scholarly criticism to determine a proper use for the word—that is to say, a restricted use. At present the mutations of its significance are endless and a mere listing of its divergencies would require many pages; we are indeed very confused about it. To this confusion Eino Railo brings an immense erudition and assiduity but no resolution. True, he does not undertake to define the idea of romanticism, yet the explanatory part of his title, "a study of the elements of English Romanticism," seems to indicate that he chooses to describe terror-romanticism because by the pathologically exaggerated member he intends to explain the more normal manifestations of the main branch of romanticism.

The academic assumption in the study of the "Romantic Movement" is that the movement was an entirely new thing, a sudden, doctrinated, theorized creation. This assumption is, of course, in part true; there certainly were doctrine and theory. There was, however, no creation, but only return. This academic assumption is made for convenience' sake to indicate the schism with a regnant literary tradition which we call "classical." But it should easily be seen that the Romantic Movement of the late eighteenth century is exactly a return to the more characteristic accent and tone of English literature. With the conscious readaptation of the old tone (which we may call—but with an understanding of the precariousness of doing so—romantic) the bloated *genre* of the terror-novel was born. This was a fifth-rate sort of writing—romanticism on a spree. It was new in one way: writers had never before taken for their sole province the production of shudders; it was new, therefore, in its proportions. But in kind it was not new. Writers before Lewis, Beckford and Maturin had sought to terrify, though not exclusively.

But Mr. Railo seems not to recognize this, and he is pitifully betrayed by his naïvely genealogical scholarship. To Mr. Railo, romanticism (and especially terror-romanticism) is entirely new. But by the tenets of his sort of scholarship there is nothing really new, and everything in literature has a "source." So romanticism is a new thing and not a new thing. Everything happens because something happened before it. Terror-romanticism is fond of bells ringing and of knocking upon gates. This it got from the porter scene in *Macbeth*. But people knock on the door with good effect in Chaucer. Terror-romanticism preferred night to day and drew the preference from *Il Penseroso*. (Mr. Railo has created a monster whom he calls "Shakespeare-Milton.") But what of the night in *Agamemnon?* Terror-romanticism was interested in bats; so, we may point out, was John Webster, and what of it? Terror-romanticism uses the theme of the haunted castle and got its clue from *Hamlet*. But why not from *Beowulf?* And if from *Beowulf,* why does not every villain, every hero, every monster, every gloom and every struggle come from *Beowulf?* And why is not every piece of literature a manifestation of a solar myth? By Mr. Railo's way of thinking, Chaucer could not have made Griselda (nor, certainly, Boccaccio before him) had it not been for Alcestis.

The ridiculousness of this sort of scholarship is almost charming when it speculates on the "sources" of the helmet in *The Castle of*

Otranto. Did Pallas Athene's helmet give the hint, or King Arthur's, or the helmet of Mambrinus, famed in tales of chivalry? But it is most ridiculous when its exercise indicates its uselessness. For the fact is that Romanticism did not start with Walpole, nor with Gray, nor with Macpherson, nor with Young but with the very beginning of the literature—and before. The problem terror-romanticism presents is not where it got its properties and themes but what was the intellectual and emotional climate that fostered it, and upon this Mr. Railo scarcely touches. Yet his book will be useful for its compendiousness; it describes well and explicitly, and its usefulness will be increased when a new edition gives it an index.

Cities of the Plain

[A review of *Cities of the Plain* (*Sodome et Gomorrhe*) by Marcel Proust, translated by C. K. Scott Moncrieff. *New York Evening Post*, January 21, 1928]

PAUL VALÉRY, in an essay on Proust, writes: "Unconsciously we lend the characters of a novel all the human lives which exist in us potentially, for our faculty of living implies that of giving life. As much as we lend them, so much is the novel worth." How the quantity of this loan is to be measured is, with many novelists, a very difficult problem. With Proust it is the least difficulty. Our loan of life to his people may not be made with such obvious fervor as that of the London ladies to Richardson's when they stormed his house to learn sooner about Pamela, nor as that of the Petersburg readers to Tolstoi's who sent to the printer inquiring after Anna Karenina. Yet to a group of Proust's admirers one will enter and announce: "Mme. Verdurin has become the Duchess of Guermantes"; and the astonishment, the disgust, the deep and actual sorrow that follow are almost comic, so closely do they approximate in degree the emotions the same event in "actual life" would cause.

That so large a part of his concern with the section of the novel called *Cities of the Plain* must be this of "What happens?" is scarcely fortunate for the reviewer. It is forced upon him by the fact that the entire novel, *Remembrance of Things Past*, is too far advanced to permit further comment or explication of its method, and not enough advanced in translation to allow discussion of the whole design. Yet such a concern in this case cannot be so supererogatory as it usually is, for here events are so material in themselves that Proust was in considerable doubt whether to call his production a novel or a work of memoirs.

The action of this book, then, may very roughly and with some arbitrariness be divided into three parts not at all coincident either with chapter divisions or chronology. One of these, and in a painful book perhaps the most painful, is that which recounts the revolution which raises Odette Swann and Mme. Verdurin to their desired pinnacles. It is, of course, painful to see Swann (whom, in *The Guermantes Way,* we know to be slowly dying) with his cheeks spotted blue and eaten away with disease; there are, however, certain things that we accept with sorrow and without rebellion. It is somewhat painful that "I," the narrator, now a friend of the Duchess, no longer finds her the comprehensive symbol of beauty and strangeness, but we understand disillusion and Proust has been teaching us its further subtleties for six preceding volumes. But when we see Odette, the stupid Lesbian and courtesan for whom Swann had so injured his brilliant social position, become a person of more consequence than he, a person to whose eminence his characteristics, eccentricities, and loyalties contribute while they sink him, we are shocked and depressed. When we perceive the crescendo of that hymn to vulgarity and hypocrisy, Mme. Verdurin and her "clan," we are helplessly enraged, powerless before the forces of unworthiness.

A second part deals with the growing importunity of the affair of "I" with Albertine. Its former slow and tortuous course, about to be completed in boredom, is continued and hastened by the increasingly certain suspicion that Albertine has been having homosexual relations with Mlle. Vinteuil and her infamous friend, as well as with Bloch's sister and cousin. The end of the present two volumes finds "I" removing Albertine from Balbec to Paris to prevent her further meeting with any of these women.

The third part and the largest is that which undertakes the Baron de Charlus, his homosexual proclivities and his romance with Charlie Morel, the violinist. Our first hint of his inversion was given in *The Guermantes Way* with his defeated attempt upon "I" and the magnificent scene between them in his library. The significance of the incident had been hidden from "I"; now he sees from a window the flirtation and meeting of Charlus and Jupien, the tailor. From this episode we follow the proud and clever Baron through the tortures of his love, which, corrosive, attacks not only his peace (as might the most heterosexual passion) but his assurance, his integrity, his freedom, his pride, and works upon every component of his apparent and accepted character to belie and change him. It is no pretty spectacle to watch, this alchemic transmutation of the proudest man in France into a cunning, wary, deviously explanatory and self-justifying suitor of a vulgar violinist, son of a valet.

Once before, in *Swann's Way,* Proust treated homosexuality. But there he saw and treated it as a curious and horrible event, entirely isolated, while the affair of Charlus has endless social and emotional connotations. The famous comparison of the invert and the Jew as social phenomena producing much the same patterns of social idiosyncrasies early defines what use is to be made of the Charlus material. Nevertheless, in the light of the influence which the more popular scientific writings on the subject have had (Havelock Ellis', for example) and in the light of the tone and the quite calm acceptance of (say) André Gide's works, there is something puzzling in Proust's concern about the "indecency" of his book and in the moralizing air which, every now and then, becomes apparent. This latter in the case of Albertine is understandable; it is seldom obtruded when Charlus is being concretely considered; when, however, the subject of inversion is under abstract investigation it is likely to appear.

There is, of course, nothing necessarily wrong artistically in this, yet it is somehow surprising. It is also surprising when we know that Proust preferred titles "quite simple, quite colorless," that he should have chosen so explicit a name for these volumes. It emphasizes the restrictive and moralizing attitude (his inverts are, for example, identified with the justly destroyed cities of the plain, but emphatically denied any kinship with the Greek and Roman votaries of the same Eros); it also gives the harmful impression that the book is a treatise.

Besides that melancholy induced by the triumph of unworth over worth, and besides the melancholy pervasive through the whole novel, there begins, in this section of it, a new melancholy caused by the immediacy of life to the hero. It is "that melancholy which we feel when we cease to obey orders which, from one day to another, keep the future hidden, and realize that we have at last begun to live in real earnest, as a grown-up person, the life, the only life that any of us has at his disposal." And it may be that this sad sense of the onliness of life, this sense of the future which must, to some degree, negate that past which has been so real to him from extremest youth, this knowledge of the need for action which the diminution of futurity demands (all of them things sharply understood only at the accession to adulthood) have had their effect upon the writing.

For, though the greater ease in reading these tremendous sentences of his (not probings and penetrations, as Pierre-Quint will have them, but each one a long and anguished travail) may be the result of the training of the six previous volumes, it is more likely that the style itself is really more "open" and easier.

It is, of course, accurately consonant with the hero's growth from adolescence to adulthood that he lose some of his old fila-mental sensitivity of every sense. Yet as no sooner do we pass with relief from the malaises of adolescence than we begin to recall them with regret, so must we regret that old, actionless (but never pas-sive) leisured suffering of "I." With the addition of the full-length portrait of Charlus, we have a complete gallery of Proust's heroes and may understand the single quality that, with Proust, constitutes the hero. There are two kinds of heroes—the hero morally and the hero technically. The technical hero—that is, the hero from the novelist's point of view—is simply the man who, by some inner necessity, is set off from the crowd. Since he is set off from the crowd he must be against the crowd as the melody in a generally unmelodic musical composition is set off from the piece and is "against" it. He need have no more moral significance than that melody. In Proust there are several such heroes. "I" is a hero twice over, once as an invalid, once as an observer and artist. The others are Charlus, the invert, and Swann, the Jew. (Vinteuil, the musician, and Elstir, the painter, might be included as artist-heroes, but Vinteuil is too vague, and Elstir is too indifferent to society; he is rather a serene demi-god than a hero.)

None of these men has qualities which make him a hero in the moral sense, save Swann when the Dreyfus affair forces upon him the need for a decision, and he chooses the more difficult way. But the others have no such occasions and partake in no way of any of the characteristics of the moral hero save endurance. The statement of the anti-social necessity of the hero is not startling, I think, nor are the implications of it anything but obvious. They are important, however. "Not only in early Greek times but throughout the whole of antiquity," writes Gilbert Murray, "the possibility of all sorts of absurd and atrocious things lay much nearer, the protective forces of society were much weaker. The strain on personal character, the need for real 'wisdom and virtue' were much greater than today." The removal of this need is indicated by the ethical indifference of Proust's novel, which makes his frequently ethical consideration of inversion so surprising. And the activity of the hero is now not the fight against evil *for* society, but a fight against society itself.

Also, it should be pointed out that the Proust heroine is not simply a female hero. Not Gilberte, not Albertine, not Rachel, not Oriane are heroines, but "I's" mother and grandmother. No disability, no maladjustment in a woman, Proust seems to be saying, but only the best arranged normality can set her apart and bring her heroism. And this, when it comes, is twofold: the novelist's heroism and the moralist's.

Proust's present American publishers have issued these two volumes abominably and inexcusably proofread. Both Mr. Holt and Mr. Seltzer did far better by their author and his readers. The translation of Mr. Scott Moncrieff continues excellent. His task is extraordinarily difficult but this difficulty is also its own consolation and facilitation to Mr. Scott Moncrieff, for it throws him and us, in a score of places, back to the French and keeps us constantly, though never irritatingly, mindful of an original—which, contrary to orthodox opinion, is what a translation should do.

Another Jewish Problem Novel

[A review of *The Disinherited* by Milton Waldman. *The Menorah Journal*, April 1929]

IN one of the few passages in which Mr. Waldman breaks the
woodenness of his prose with imagination, he says of his hero,
Walter Michaelson: "[He] resembled . . . a certain figure in
the representation of Titus' triumphant return from the sack of
Jerusalem on the arch which bears his name. Whether the figure
in question portrays one of the conqueror's captives or one of his
warriors it is impossible with certainty to say."

Michaelson himself, however, had never been conscious of any
question about his affiliation; nor had it ever been broached by the
warriors—the established, the accepted. There was no thought but
that this good, heavy man was one of the warriors. Then, as he
awaits the possible news that his son's illness may be fatal, and as
he realizes how much of his life will be ashes in his mouth should
the boy die, and from what insecure roots the sap of his life rises,
doubt begins to invade him. But it is still an unformulated doubt.
Though his son recovers, the doubt remains, made deeper in-
trenched by his wife's unconscious emotional withdrawal from him.

Soon, however, the doubt progresses toward formulation. Michaelson, a lawyer, is a leading citizen of a Middle Western city. His
partner is a Gentile. His wife is a Gentile with all the blond, lily
quality inevitable to Gentile women in Jewish novels. His social

circle is Gentile. His children are Gentile. If his grandfather, the peddler, had founded the city's first synagogue, he had also been one of the genitors of the city's great wealth. Michaelson, then, is indeed one of the conqueror's warriors. But some atavism makes him undertake the case of the contractor Lebsky, none too innocent, against the even more corrupt city administration. A swift concatenation of events moves him, first into a material, later into a spiritual consciousness of Judaism. His secretary's brother is kept from the local university by an intelligence test. An attractive Jewess, Esther Rhodes, has her suit for divorce put into his hands. A new rabbi, romantically named Abrabanel and talking the romantic Judaism of Zangwill and the Nineties, comes to town. Soon every facet of his neat life is touched by Judaism.

Then the touch, from mere contact, becomes pressure, and crushes the perfectly organized crystal. His political career is ruined by his espousal of Lebsky's cause. His wife objects to the new Jewish social connections. He resigns from his club when Abrabanel is blackballed. Scandal and his wife make impossible the increasingly important friendship with Esther Rhodes. Torn more and more completely from Gentile ground, he cannot, nevertheless, transplant into Jewish. The proud and pure Judaism which he espouses has no place in the councils of the city's Jewish leaders, and he is consistently unlucky in combatting their crass opportunism and their distrust of his ancestry and connections. So, bereft at all points, he leaves the country to travel abroad, to make quest, to see Jerusalem.

That Mr. Waldman uses the theme which has longest been identified with the spiritual histories of Jews is cause neither for blame nor praise. The theme, that the hero *comes* to Judaism, was first used for Moses, was found indispensable for Daniel Deronda and, latterly, for the hero of Mr. Lewisohn's *The Island Within*. It is the parallel—perhaps, indeed, the converse—of the folk fable theme of the scullion who is a prince by birth and who discovers his origin late by some sign or mark; it is patterned as rigidly and it may be discussed with the same scientific gravity that folklorists use. Its formula is that a man, usually of some importance among

Gentiles, either does not know or does not care that he is a Jew. Some circumstance makes him know or care; the fact that he is a Jew becomes important; frequently he suffers in material things because of it; almost always, immediately upon the recognition, he enters into full spiritual and intellectual maturity. The very age of this formula and its recurrence (among writers probably but half-conscious of the tradition behind it), argue for it both a dramatic and an actual truth which is hard to deny. Always, seemingly, and not only nowadays when Mr. Edman's Reuben Cohen stretches out a weary hand from rejection and environing chaos for the rest he thinks he will find in Judaism avowed, there has been, in the telling of the personal history of the Jew, the tendency, conscious or unconscious, to feel that Judaism is not a thing which the Jew is endowed with at birth, but a thing to which the Jew comes.

Mr. Waldman, then, is on pretty safe ground with his plot, one which seems well-rooted in a continued racial pattern. Yet the book, for all this foundation, for all it is honest, for all it has a certain socially critical intelligence, is far from important and even far from interesting. It moves along in heavy doggedness. It carries its pack to the end of the road and sets it down with a sigh. At only one incident does Mr. Waldman add to his socially critical intelligence a fictional intelligence, and make his story glow with drama—at the incident of Michaelson's renunciation of Esther Rhodes. He has seen in her a certain quality which his new Jewishness identifies as a Jewish quality, and one of which he has deep need. But the force of the very Jewishness in him, which has driven him toward her, manifests itself in another aspect, the patriarchal sense of the family, and so he is bound by Jewishness to all that is not Jewish. There is an irony in this which, for all the skimpiness of its exposition, undoubtedly succeeds. But the rest of the story is dull. Michaelson is an honest man but not interesting. It is a difficult fictional job to make a finely spiritual being develop out of one essentially good but heavy. Thomas Mann, in *The Magic Mountain,* succeeded with Hans Castorp, but Michaelson goes on his quest with much the same high-minded, intelligent, emotional aplomb that he must have used in his investigation of the civic administration.

All the novel's functional details are dull and dully used. Michaelson's Gentile activities are stuffy with court business, abortive political campaigns, administrative details, and bad conversation with practically non-existent people. His Jewish explorations are stiff with conventionality: the orthodox smell of a synagogue, the bad manners of a Russian-Jewish family and its food, the snobbery and social aggressiveness of Jewish men of wealth, the lack of true idealism in local charity boards and Jewish social centers, his own vague and yearning Jewish ideology gropingly discussed with Abrabanel. The incidental dialogue is empty and irritating in its effort after the colloquial ease and awkward velleity of American talk. All the characters move with difficulty; they live in a world as dull as a Sunday at home after dinner; they have all read the newspaper supplements; they have nothing to do. At last Walter Michaelson, more bored than the rest, takes a walk to the Zoo to look at the animals.

Yet it is not merely—and not even chiefly—a poor technical execution of his perfectly sound theme that makes Mr. Waldman's book so unsuccessful, so cabined and so cramped. It is rather the conventions and limits into which the modern Jewish novel has settled that garrote all the books' interest and significance. No one who has followed the Jewish novel can miss the mean qualities that almost inevitably characterize even the best of the genre—the crabbed pathos, the niggling heroics, the stuffiness, griminess, vexatiousness, the something that is almost sordid. These qualities are the result of a bad selection and of an unclever emphasis. As soon as the Jewish writer gets his hero to be a Jew, he wraps him up warm in a *talith* and puts him away. The hero's coming to Judaism is regarded as something equivalent to a mystical Christian conversion; the Jewish hero is lifted out of life and made to goggle his eyes in functionless ecstasy at the fact that he is a Jew. But though a Jew's coming to Judaism is perhaps just as dramatic as a mystical Christian conversion, it is certainly an experience more related to normal life and therefore an experience both more varied and more dangerous. Consequently, it must be stated in terms very different from those of the pious secular saints-legends that are now used for it.

Indeed, the whole complex of experiences that we call the Jewish problem presents a literary theme of such great importance and such fertile potentialities as to demand more than the mere honesty and simple earnestness which too easily have been permitted alone to characterize it. It demands poetry, passion, a little madness. It will support greatness. Its specialness does not bar it from greatness. Rabelais, Cervantes, Bunyan, all wrote specially and to limited purpose and, when that purpose lost point with time, there still remained a large residue of greatness, of beauty, of important meaning. And it may even be that the specialness of the theme is but seeming.

But certainly the Jewish novel will never have greatness, the Jewish problem will never be illuminated by the only instruments of illumination in fiction—poetry, passion, a little madness—until the limits of the Jewish novel are rearranged. To remove from the Jewish novel the mean qualities that now characterize it and to make the "Jewish problem" take on nobility and validity and, indeed, attractiveness, the problem itself must be transcended. Only by transcending the problem will it become illuminated. Only when the Jewish problem is included in a rich sweep of life, a life which would be important and momentous even without the problem of Jewishness, but a life to which the problem of Jewishness adds further import and moment, will a good Jewish novel have been written and something said about the problem.

Flawed Instruments

[A review of *Adam* by Ludwig Lewisohn and *Stephen Escott* by Ludwig Lewisohn. *The Menorah Journal*, April 1930]

MR. LEWISOHN'S play *Adam* is conceived in falsely simple terms and executed in the idiom of an outmoded theater. It is possible, however, to see in it an intention which might excuse and even justify its failure as a serious work. Mr. Lewisohn has assumed the honorable character of propagandist for the doctrine that affirmation of Judaism is necessary for fertile life as a Jew and as a modern man. In his propagandist capacity it is understandable that Mr. Lewisohn should attempt to affect every class of the Jewish people. Therefore, if *Adam* is a dilution of Mr. Lewisohn's feeling about Judaism put into direct and melodramatic form for presentation by synagogue drama leagues and collegiate Jewish societies, he is justified in sacrificing ultimate artistic merit to immediate emotional effect. Criticism may well stand off from a morality play intended for people of limited philosophy about Jews and allow Mr. Lewisohn's pragmatic intentions their full chance.

Adam is the tragedy of the son of a German rabbi, who, slighted at school because of his race, runs away to establish himself in the Gentile world. His life becomes a constant struggle to escape his Jewishness. Despite the enormous wealth he amasses, despite his entry into aristocratic English society, despite his beautiful Gentile wife and his tender Gentile mistress, he is frustrated and miserable. English society suspects him, his wife cannot fulfill him nor his mistress comfort him. He is a wanderer and a stranger, without home and fellow-men. In the last scene his valet and his airplane pilot discuss his misery. The valet thinks that his master is unhappy "because he don't practice his religion." Meanwhile Adam has jumped from the plane. As a contrast to this sterile tragedy of rejection, we are given an epilogue of two work-weary Palestinians in love.

It is very possible that for the purpose for which Mr. Lewisohn perhaps intended this play, the naïveté of the conception and the simple melodrama of the incidents will actually be an advantage. For amateurs, the silly, snobbish English people of the first scene, the coarse brother-in-law of the second, the pious rabbi and gentle mother of the fifth, and the humble valet of the seventh, will be easy to play. The other characters are but little less completely set in stereotype, and it may have been out of regard for the limitations of amateurs that Mr. Lewisohn never brings his hero on the stage but creates him by the conversation of others. As for the weakening and cheapening of his thesis by an elementary conception and technique, Mr. Lewisohn may have thought this worth risking for his purpose and may have relied on the greater strength of his previous works on the same subject to sustain this one.

So much of an excuse can be sincerely made out for *Adam*. But when *Stephen Escott* (undoubtedly a better, if only because a more difficult, work) presents essentially the same faults and suggests no pragmatic excuse for them, one is not so sure but that blame must be transferred from Mr. Lewisohn's intentions and set on Mr. Lewisohn's abilities. Moreover, one remembers *Don Juan* and *Roman Summer*.

It is clear, from both his precept and his practice, that Mr. Lewisohn conceives the novel as an instrument for moral teaching. In this conception he is thinking in a great tradition, not merely because all good novels illuminate some aspect of life and therefore make moral choice more possible, but because many of the greatest novels have definite doctrine to teach. The usual objection to moral purpose in art—that the morality perverts the art—is frequently irrelevant because the art is almost never perverted but bad to begin with. The real objection to the use of art for specific moral teaching is seldom given—that the art is likely to falsify the morality. This is what almost always happens in Mr. Lewisohn's moral novels, his insufficiencies as a novelist are constantly invalidating his strength as a moralist. It is no more possible for a sound moral idea to be convincingly presented by incomplete characters than for beautiful music to be interpreted on a flawed instrument.

In *Stephen Escott* Mr. Lewisohn intends the depiction and refutation of two extreme standards of marital sexual relationship. On the one hand, he puts the marriage of Stephen Escott and Dorothy, a marriage tragically ruined by Dorothy's puritanical feeling about sex. From marriage she wants many good things—home, children, position, peace, companionship—but none of the passionate things which have their roots in unashamed sexuality. Her husband is too weak and too ignorant to break down her inhibitions and finally she dies of them. On the other hand, the marriage of Paul Glover and Janet is sexually most complete. He is a poet and she potters at various careers. She fails at her artistic efforts and is bored, until, fortified by current doctrine of sexual freedom, she enters into a love affair. She still retains considerable affection for her husband but he, having made her the great fact in his life, is devastated by her action and kills her lover.

The deficiencies of Mr. Lewisohn as a novelist and his consequent deficiencies as a moralist do not appear so clearly in Stephen Escott's own story as they do in Paul Glover's. Escott's life is, on the whole, sufficient to carry the morality assigned to it. True, Stephen and his wife are not very vital people nor very interestingly presented, but the author's considerable, if rather abstract, knowledge of their marriage is sufficient to make the reader give credence to the story and therefore adherence to the morality. But one has only to recall how, in *Lady Chatterley's Lover,* D. H. Lawrence preached the importance of sex and denounced sterile prudery to understand just how much the novel can do as a pedagogic instrument and to see how Mr. Lewisohn's preaching, based on truth though it be, is washed out and made dim by a work that deals not only with truth but with people. One need not labor the point. Mr. Lewisohn's characters have the interest which the Mr. J. and Mrs. V. of the case histories always have. But they have no more than that. And it is, of course, in proportion to the interest and importance of the characters that the morality of a novel has force.

It may be worth a moment's divergence to speculate on the causes for Mr. Lewisohn's inability to create character. With concepts and institutions he is vivid and convincing. But even where, as in his autobiographies, he deals with real people, Mr. Lewisohn makes little more than an intelligent man's careful and pretty accurate judgments about them; he seldom succeeds in capturing their essence. In these autobiographies he often catches admirably the temper of a group of people, but individuals he seems to see in the patterns laid down by popular or artistic tradition. And it is exactly the novelist's function to break up these patterns.

Probably Mr. Lewisohn's alien complex, that carefully rationalized sense of personal and racial apartness which animates so much of his living and writing, is the cause of this. For one thing, it makes him think chiefly in terms of social forces and not of individual beings. For another, it drops between him and his fellows a thin but obscuring veil.

The story of Paul Glover is more interesting than Stephen Escott's, but for its purpose it is far weaker. Mr. Lewisohn betrays his position by a flagrant special pleading that has its eventual cause in this same inability to manage character. The failure in this case is a special pity, for the position which Mr. Lewisohn defends is one that is intelligently tenable and yet has not had any intelligent public defense.

It has been the contention of many modern moralists of sex (Bertrand Russell is the most obvious example) that the passionate love between husband and wife need not be disturbed by the casual extra-marital relations of either. However desirable such an ethic may be, there are at least two objections to it, one on the ground of its illogicality, the other on the ground of its naïveté. The adherents to this philosophy of love unanimously proclaim, on the one hand, the supreme importance of sex and base on it not only the artistic but the general moral impulses and the tender affections. On the other hand, they make it a matter of the supremest unimportance, declare it to be without significance or any use save relief—a completely puritanical way of thinking about sex. And they naïvely suppose, in support of the conflict of their two views, that even for sensitive people a sexual experience can be an entirely impersonal matter if one so wills it.

To consider the worth or unworth of the current modern belief, or of Mr. Lewisohn's conflicting one, is scarcely the purpose of this review. Certain fallacies in the former have been indicated only in an attempt to show that Mr. Lewisohn's opposition to the modern view has a very real basis and is not unintelligent because not modern. Unfortunately, however, Mr. Lewisohn in his attack arbitrarily puts so great a handicap on his opponents that his victory must be discredited. In Paul Glover he creates a rather admirable man, a poet, whose love for his wife is the motive of his existence, a thing which he cannot even separate from his genius and his work. But instead of giving him a wife who is his intellectual and moral equal, whose belief in the new sexual morality is considered and real, Mr. Lewisohn gives him an empty, canting girl, craftily adopting a theory to justify her lust. Instead of giving the woman a decent lover, Mr. Lewisohn gives her a slobbering whoremaster. How subtle, how utterly terrible would the story have been if, Paul's love being the same, his wife had been a good woman who truly loved him, and if the lover had been as good a man as Paul yet less important to the wife! As it now stands, it is merely a story of vulgar, old-fashioned adultery in which the wife besoils herself beyond sympathy, almost beyond pity. And Mr. Lewisohn spends himself disproving a proposition which is not the one the new moralists set.

Whether the sexual point of view which Mr. Lewisohn set out to uphold (and so unfortunately let down) is essentially a Jewish one, both passionate and common-sensible, recognizing the sensitivities of the body as equal with those of the mind, and opposed to a Gentile, Western view which is unpassionate and defeatist at bottom, is a question that may be broached but not answered. Mr. Lewisohn implies that it is, and as a contrast to the defeat of Escott and Glover he introduces the successful and fruitful love of the Jewish David and Ruth Sampson. But again his inability to think in personal terms defeats Mr. Lewisohn's purpose. Those of his Jews who are adjusted to their Jewishness are but animated mosaics carefully constructed of gems from the Talmud. They are as real as Orinooko the Noble Savage, or Voltaire's wise Orientals, or the omniscient Jews of the more benevolent nineteenth-century novel. We have need of idealism about Judaism and Jews; no tradition can exist without its idealization. But if this idealism is not based on a sound reality, it can but serve to inflate the vanity of the ignorant and make those who know turn away smiling.

The Promise of Realism

[A review of *Bottom Dogs* by Edward Dahlberg,
Pay Day by Nathan Asch, *Frankie and Johnnie*
by Meyer Levin. *The Menorah Journal*, May
1930]

ALL three of these novels are "realistic." However, it is not so
much this common character that aptly fits them for review together as the two distinct tendencies in realism
that they illustrate. For Mr. Levin's book, though it is a respectable
piece of work, indicates admirably the footless course of American
realism, while both Mr. Asch's and Mr. Dahlberg's suggest a course
that, one may reasonably predict, will land American writing somewhere.

We perceive nowadays that realism is a manner and a subject
rather than a virtue. We understand that it is a literary cant word
used to indicate a sort of literature that confines itself to an account
(simple rather than devious) of the pain of people (humble rather
than exalted) in a struggle with their environment. We know that
this manner and subject are not necessarily more "real" than any
other. And, indeed, by now we are certain that the limitations of
this manner and subject are likely to prevent an ambitious literature
or one that is spiritually important.

All this admitted to the belittlement of realism, the fact remains
that realism is necessarily the most relevant literature we are producing today. We are living in an environment of an impossible
strenuousness. But strenuousness is not terrible: we are living in
an environment that is befouling and insulting. Only the very

wealthy do not live in such an environment and only the very blind do not know it.

The first record of this life was, on the whole, not very satisfactory. It is difficult to recall a single realistic novel of the American Renaissance that truly performs what it implicitly promises. Protest lay in the conception of these books, but a curious thing happened to them. Fighting their environment, they became in time scarcely distinguishable from their foe. Perhaps the simplest and best reason for this seemingly mystic happening (one remembers the oracular tone of Nietzsche's aphorism which says in effect, "Be careful in fighting dragons a long time lest you yourself become a dragon") is that there was a lurking love for the foe these books were fighting. For Anderson and Dreiser and the literary aura that developed around them, America is pretty cruel, but cruel like a schoolboy who will grow into mature gentleness, or cruel with splendid magnificence and strong barbarism.

At bottom, these books were saying, there was something divine about America. And if it killed you, though it might do so ruthlessly, it killed you like a god—first making you do something for which it had the right to kill you. It was a fate, and you were involved in it—you with your little quota of Free Will which ought to do you some good but which quite surely wouldn't. You fought your god with a man's fight, and he did you in but you loved him. America was a tragedy all right—an American Tragedy—with all the fine, gaudy, consoling trappings of tragedy.

This is the tradition of the older realists and it is in this tradition that Mr. Levin writes. He is not entirely in this tradition because he lacks the fundamental, hidden faith in America they had, but he has all the literary values that faith evolved. For all its seemingly hard casualness, Mr. Levin's novel is touched by sentimentality. It tells the story of a boy and a girl, children of superior clerks. They are alive with a jerky energy in a world that is tawdry but not uncomfortable. They fall in love, have a surge of sweet emotionality, squabble and part. The book is a tiny footnote to American life, reliable but unimportant. No book about American life should stay so close to the surface of unhappiness. There is too much surface "normality" in *Frankie and Johnnie*. It is honest and solid enough. It says that American life is tawdry and difficult, and here are two young people in American life; they do not have a very good time. Well, this is very true. But if that is all the truth and if it is realism's function to tell only this truth, then realism is pretty useless. But this is not all the truth; there are many far darker things than Mr. Levin hints which make up the truth realism must tell.

Some years ago Mr. Ludwig Lewisohn had a hero, John Austen, who was an American but who tried to be an Englishman and a Jew and finally decided to be an American. He was a writer and, as a sign of this acceptance of being an American, he decided to write a realistic novel of America; he will write it in "good gray prose." This acceptance of America as a sort of diamond in the rough, this business of the novel in good gray prose is what made realistic writing about America so futile. There is only one way to accept America and that is in hate; one must be close to one's land, passionately close in some way or other, and the only way to be close to America is to hate it; it is the only way to love America.

And the only way to write about America is to leave swimming on the surface of good gray prose, however honestly, and to get down where it is hard to breathe—to leave the surface of normality, tawdry unpleasant normality though it be, and get to where there is insanity.

For at the bottom of America there is insanity. It is this insanity which Mr. Asch and Mr. Dahlberg catch and by catching it they write truly. They write of what D. H. Lawrence in his introduction to *Bottom Dogs* calls "consciousness in a state of repulsion"—which means neurasthenia, which means, eventually, insanity.

Bottom Dogs and *Pay Day* are amazingly the same, and (for realism not only allows but requires looking beyond the created world of the book into the actual world) their actual implications are equally terrible.

Mr. Dahlberg's Lorry starts in Kansas City, the son of a lady barber. He grows up, plays in the streets, is sent to an orphanage and eventually bums his way to the Coast. And as he grows up, the stink, the vulgarity, the dullness of the land bear in upon his not very sensitive soul until, still scarcely more than a boy, he walks through a street and hopes appallingly: "Anyhow if he got the clap he would go to the Los Angeles City Hospital; maybe, those enameled iron beds, the white sheets, the immaculateness of it all, might do something to him. Something had to happen; and he knew nothing would. . . ."

Lorry is an individual, however blurred. There is a touch of the pioneer still in him; to some degree he takes charge of his own life. But Mr. Asch's hero, Jim, is cast and stamped. He fights against the pattern that society has imposed on him, against the ideal pattern he thinks he should impose upon himself. He must exist in the social order and he must respect himself. And between the upper millstone of these two necessities and the nether millstone of his desire to live freely, his poor, foul mind is ground to a grit of worry and of nagging hate. He hates the well-dressed, he hates the intellectual, he hates the desirable women he cannot have, he hates the girl he goes out with, he hates himself.

As he goes about his heartbreaking evening of trying to assert himself and of trying to have a good time, Sacco and Vanzetti are being killed. Mr. Asch has been accused of a too obvious morality in introducing this motif of nobility and social protest to give ironic point to the degradation of Jim, but its use is, if sometimes forced, generally very effective. Dimly, as the news of the event comes to him through headlines and snatches of talk, the boy gets some sense of its significance. He cannot retain it, however, save to remember as he returns to his home at dawn, "Oh my God. They're dead."

Mr. Dahlberg's Lorry is a superior person to Jim. The touch of the pioneer and wanderer in him, the touch of the observer as he goes about and makes faint judgments of people, his effort to keep himself free, all give him a human decency. He seems to represent a time a little anterior to the time Mr. Asch's Jim lives in. But he breaks, and in a very real sense Jim is his spiritual son. And of Jim one is sure that, if one could get a record of the mind of a caged animal, it would be little different from his. He is little more than an irritable reaction—to the ball game, to the cop, to a small salary, to the success ads, to social inferiority. After the failure of one personal sexual incident, sex becomes an impersonal desire to humiliate and control another human. His fundamental movement is a pendulation between arrogance and self-contempt.

On the whole, Mr. Dahlberg's is the better book of the two. Its detachment and fine unsentimentality demand a greater credence than does Mr. Asch's dramatic method. Though the story seldom leaves Lorry for long, the boy is kept well in the background, and the nation, so admirably rendered in hard detail, is the true protagonist; the relation between the boy and his environment is always just and he never dominates the scene with his misery and defeat. Nor is the reader forced into a false relationship with him; he is seen as one of a crowd; our pity is not called upon; what we have, we give.

There is no real sentimentality in Mr. Asch's treatment of his hero but the dramatic method gives Jim a factitious hero-position and forces us into a false *rapport* with him. Sometimes Mr. Asch's detachment breaks down and the boy's self-pity becomes Mr. Asch's pity for him. In spite of this, the book remains hard and terrible. Nevertheless, it does not stand so much by itself and for itself as Mr. Dahlberg's.

In the essay in which he introduces *Bottom Dogs,* D. H. Lawrence finds the cause of the spiritual condition of America—the condition which a book like *Bottom Dogs* describes, or a book like *Pay Day,* or any true realistic novel—in the heart of the country being broken by the hard business of existence. The "blood-sympathy" between man and man is gone: only the will is left.

The deep psychic change which we call the breaking of the heart, the collapse of the flow of spontaneous warmth between man and his fellows, happens of course now all over the world. . . . It brings a people into a much more complete social unison, for good or evil. But it throws them apart in their private individual emotions. Before, they were like cells in a complex tissue, alive and functioning diversely in a vast organism composed of family, clan, village, nation. Now, they are like grains of sand, friable, heaped together in a vast inorganic democracy.

While the old sympathetic glow continues, there are violent hostilities between people, but they are not secretly repugnant to one another. Once the heart¹ is broken, people become repulsive to one another secretly, and they develop social benevolence. They smell in each other's nostrils. . . .

How alone these two boys are, Lorry and Jim! Democracy is all around them, the pack, the herd. But they are quite alone, not because there is some quality that sets them apart, but because they hate and fear their fellow creatures automatically; and are hated and feared automatically. Never once does either of them feel fellowship; only, sometimes, a blind yearning back to the mother. They are sure, very sure, that their world is against them. And they are right: their world is *for* nobody.

These two books cannot be read detachedly. They have been sneered at as sociological studies. If by that was meant that they deal with a class irrelevant to the class that makes and reads the studies, there is a self-defensive lie in the sneer. For, dodge as we may, these books are enormously relevant to everyone. There is no person in the United States, save he be a member of the plutocratic class, who is not in a direct line with this Lorry and this Jim, not one who is not tainted, a little or much, with the madness of the bottom dog, not one who is not in an asympathy of disgust and hate with his fellows. The emotions of the "terrible and brutal . . . failure that nourishes the roots of the gigantic tree of dollars" are the universally relevant emotions of America.

The implication behind the "sociological" sneer is that this sort of book is not "literature," and it illustrates admirably the blindness of "literary" critics. Realism is perhaps never productive of great art. But America must, by the conditions of its life, be committed to realism for a long time yet, for painful contact with environment will not soon cease, and we cannot in literature avoid the bases of our life. We want great writing. But the tendency is against it.

Well, then we must not put our hope for greatness in the tendency but in the individual. Someone will come along and by new technique and new passion will do great writing. He will raise realism to a new power; he will remove its limits—as Rembrandt did, as Dostoevski did, as Joyce did, all of whom began with "straight" realism. But—and the literary critics who were all for Thornton Wilder should realize this—he will not abandon realism. He will be above the tendency, but he will be rooted deep in it. He will find new meanings and new values in America. And we may be sure that his America will be the America that Mr. Dahlberg and Mr. Asch are exploring for him, an America of insanity and dissolving souls, of weariness and hate.

The Social Emotions

[A review of *The Nineteen* by A. Fadeyev. *The New Freeman*, July 16, 1930]

THE NINETEEN, a novel of revolutionary Russia, does a strange and exciting thing: it gives to the social emotions a new credibility and makes them instinctive and passionate. Out of the novel emerges a set of ethical and emotional values so fine that, if revolution be necessary to secure them, revolution becomes desirable. Just as Hemingway, merely by giving a glamorous credibility to sexual love and loyalty, considerably jolted a public comfortably settled in a literary convention of moral cynicism, Fadeyev startles by rehabilitating social love and loyalty.

The hero of *The Nineteen* is a tattered and half-starved regiment of irregular Soviet troops, mostly miners and laborers. The regiment is in a bad position, and the book is the story of its maneuvers to escape the Japanese forces and the harrying White troops of Kolchak. Under the leadership of Levinson, a little red-bearded Jew, a man of competence, courage, and tender insight, they make painful way through the forests. The trials of the march foster insubordination and almost mutiny, which Levinson quells. It is not merely his superb leadership, however, that forces the men on together, but an idea folded up in their usually stupid heads, an idea of their duty and of the virtue of their Revolution.

Though Levinson, together with Baklanov his lieutenant and the stoic scout Metilitsa represent for Fadeyev the highest development of communal man, the moral motifs of the book are carried by the two privates, Metchik and Morozka. Young Metchik is drawn obviously to represent the pre-revolutionary Russian, "sensitive," self-justifying, introspectively concerned with the outmoded emotion of insult-and-injury. He honestly strives for obedience and bravery, but his "sensitive" self-concern drags him always into shirking and cowardice. Morozka, his counterpart, is a simple young miner whose ignorance and high spirits lead him into a sort of wild individualism. But the idea of the Revolution and of communal duty serves him always as a vague but effective conscience. One of his proudest moments comes when he quiets a minor panic of peasants against his natural inclination to stir up the turmoil. After a quarrel with his unfaithful wife, the regimental nurse, his anger and humiliation fade before "the picture of the peasants' meeting, when he had missed being expelled from the company by the skin of his teeth."

So touching and so pure are the deeds and the motives in this novel that one almost distrusts it. One cannot imagine the American masses acting in any such way, and one cannot believe that so much difference exists between two peoples. Yet one remembers the difficulty and suffering with which the Revolution was kept alive, and one is sure that this could never have been done without some spiritual force, however obscured. Even if one applies the corrective of another book about the Revolution, such as Babel's *Red Cavalry,* to which one gives an easier credence if only because it contains more stupidity and cruelty, the spiritual dedication of a people remains a fact—though perhaps not so simple a fact as Fadeyev makes out.

Were it not for this simplification of Fadeyev's and the aura of romantic adventure which envelops *The Nineteen,* one might with much more confidence discover in it an important implication: that far from dehumanizing men into cogs of a communal machine, the communal ideal has given them a new and far stronger individualism. The drama and danger of war somewhat obscure this implication until one recalls that these men are not soldiers but workers, that their ultimate pride is in their working group, and that it is in their moments of peace and safety—while they are engaged in the consideration of justice, for instance—that they reach their greatest individualism. Communal force is always at work on them, but instead of standardizing them it seems to give direction to their actions and stimulus to their energies.

D. H. Lawrence:
A Neglected Aspect

[From *The Symposium*, July 1930[1]]

FROM a purely literary point of view, D. H. Lawrence lies a little beyond the grasp of our criticism. The form of his work cannot profitably be discussed, for both the poems and the novels generally have about as much form as a completed emotion—which is considerable—but no more. The qualities of his prose, the intensity of his poetic insight are entirely personal, the result of a personal manipulation of traditional means. They can be praised in the mass or quarreled with in detail but they elude the precision of definition, the abstractness, which, to deal with aesthetic experiment, modern criticism has developed.

For us Lawrence's deepest significance must be as a poet of rebellious social theory. Nothing could represent him more untruly than the prevalent feeling that he is devoted to the sexual individual in a social vacuum, a feeling which has been crystallized by Mr. Joseph Wood Krutch who says: "He had no political interests and no social program. It was only incidentally that he condescended to touch a detail of our system, as he did, for example, when he attacked the censorship, for he had repudiated it in toto and he saw no reason for meddling with it in detail." If there is

---

[1] Lawrence died on March 2, 1930. (D.T.)

one surely connecting thread running through all Lawrence's work, it is the thread of social interest. He did indeed repudiate our system as a way of life for himself. As a form of treacherous injustice, he kept it within constant reach of his castigating rod.

"The poet begins where the man ends." Thus writes the Spanish critic Señor Ortega as he describes the modern tendency which he calls the *dehumanization* of art.[2] One must recognize this tendency and one must admit its force. And as one recognizes it, one sees just how far from modernity Lawrence's literary practice was. In the preface to *New Poems* he differentiates three kinds of poetry: the poetry which carries us back to the past, the poetry which carries us forward to the future, and the poetry of the present moment. "The poetry of the beginning and the poetry of the end must have the exquisite finality, perfection which belongs to all that is far off." But the poetry of the present moment is a thing of flux: like the present moment itself it has "no perfection, no consummation, nothing finished."

This third kind of poetry is, of course, Lawrence's kind. Its purpose is to express what Lawrence called the *quick* of the universe, the quick of himself. If the dictum, "The poet begins where the man ends," has any meaning at all, for Lawrence it certainly had none. Lawrence the poet begins exactly at scratch with Lawrence the man. "Pure" and "abstract" art, devoid of human content, signifies nothing to him in itself. In the practice of it he can see only the index of a human condition. "I think all these tubes and corrugated vibrations are stupid enough for anything," he has his last hero say of an abstract painting. "They show a lot of self-pity, an awful lot of self-opinion, seems to me." He himself used his immense artistic gift never as a thing in itself but as an instrument to reproduce the flux and plasm of life. But it is not with any simple-hearted artist-joy that he concerned himself with this flux and plasm of life. He wrote of it frightened and angered by its misery. With a hard-headed commonsense he avoided with his anger the

---

2 "The Dehumanization of Art" by José Ortega y Gasset, *The Symposium*, April 1930.

metaphysical bases of life and struck square into the middle of the cause of all misery—the social order. In short, Lawrence's divergence from the tendency which would have the poet begin where the man ends was not merely an aesthetic manifestation. It is also the very nub of his social feeling.

Lawrence's refusal of the abstract in any manifestation, his excited, angry, loving interest in humanness, are rare among the talents of today. Even if we exclude the consciously "dehumanized" arts which Señor Ortega mentions—the anti-naturalism out of Mallarmé, the non-representational painting and the depersonalized music—and turn to examples of art which contain a considerable amount of human significance, we still find a sort of dehumanization operating. Works such as Joyce's or Thomas Mann's novels or Mr. Hart Crane's recent poem are deeply concerned with human significances which often they exploit with great success. But even when their human apperception is most keen, some veil comes between creator and creature—and we find we are dealing with human *values* rather than with human qualities.

The reason for this is fairly obvious. The organization of our social life becomes more and more complex and we delegate more and more functions to the social machine. The vital contacts of our living are less and less with our fellow men and more and more with the machine. To contact with a fellow man one responds—in whatever degree—with the whole of one's self. To contact with the social machine one responds with only some *value* of one's self: the particular value the machine is serving or attacking. Frequent response with the self deepens one's sense of the self. Frequent response with abstracted values makes these values more discrete, more separate from their possessor. Man begins to function with one value at a time. He begins to be a collection of values and finds fewer and fewer chances to respond with all of himself at once, integrally, completely.

Lawrence's revolt was against these forces of dehumanization, against the forces which had split the individual into a collection of values, and had set him into merely mental life. Sex was Lawrence's carryall for the weapons of this revolt. It was not the only vehicle: the struggle with nature for survival, the free expression of personal enmity, are (as in *Boy in the Bush*) equivalent to sex in efficacy to bring about liberation and fullness of life. Lawrence was seeking a symbol to express the salutariness of unrestrained contact with some sentient thing and in sex he found the symbol that was at once deepest and most universal.

His earliest novels employ sexual patterns which are repeated in his later ones; his first novel, *The White Peacock,* contains the ideological seeds and many of the characters of his last, *Lady Chatterley's Lover*. Already Lawrence sees his men as sexually disadvantaged, his women, still strong, misdirected by the weakness of the men. In these early novels he attempts no social interpretation; but as he carries on his exploitation of spiritual maladjustment, the social implications grow, until in *Lady Chatterley's Lover* they flower into explicitness, and passages of social theory intertwine with passages of sexual practice.

Though a poet of social theory, Lawrence is still a poet and the truth about him cannot be reached by systematizing his insights. Nevertheless, in *Fantasia of the Unconscious,* written in the very middle of his career, he himself attempts to articulate what he has arrived at sporadically and intuitively. This strange book, a mélange of psychology, physiology, physiognomy, ethics, and pedagogics, is almost medieval in its unabashed physical mysticism. Lawrence divides the body into two planes. In the lower plane lie the solar plexus and the lumbar ganglion. In these centers he finds the seats of self-perception—of the knowledge *I am I*. In the upper plane lie the thoracic ganglion and the cardiac plexus, the centers of world-perception—*you are you*. The lower centers generate the "dark" forces, self-assertion, masterfulness, pride, and joy. In the upper centers of objectivity are the urges toward pity and tenderness, the spiritual will. When there is a perfect polarity between all the centers, the individual is complete and full-functioning. But very seldom in our time does that perfect polarity occur. All emphasis of educational and social pressure is put upon the upper centers; these are trained and nourished; the lower centers are forced into atrophy.

It is obvious what agencies have created this condition: democracy and capitalistic industrialism must of their own necessity bring about the atrophy of the "dark" centers. These agencies cannot exist together with the virtues of pride and self-integration. Their virtues must be those of the upper centers—idealism, benevolence, dutiful submission—and these the rapacity of the modern politico-economic system succeeds in enforcing where Christianity failed. From the defeat of the virtues of the lower centers and the triumph of those of the upper, comes the messy sterility of modern life. Love with its demand for pity and tenderness, unbalanced by the self-integrating "dark" forces becomes a sterile combat of spiritual wills. For the human will, when it functions through the polarity of upper and lower forces, is a clean and apparent thing; even as it functions through the lower forces only, though it may be destructive, it is still clean and apparent; as it functions through the upper centers only it becomes the spiritual bullying which lies hidden in our notion of love, in our idealism, in our social benevolence.

The flat staleness of life, the loss of savor, the inability to feel in the body and in the nerves an irrefutable reason for living, have been the mournful subject of literature since the rise of democracy and industrialism. And though scores have given enlightening expression to the affliction, no one has been so downright, so simple-spoken about its cause as Lawrence. No one has said as he says: we are miserable and full of spleen because half of ourselves has been taken from us; our system has taken from us the body and its joy and knowledge. In the midst of a passage of love dalliance, Mellors, the hero of *Lady Chatterley's Lover*, declaims:

"Let's live for summat else. Let's not live ter make money, neither for us-selves, nor for anybody else. Now we're forced to. We're forced to make a bit for us-selves, an' a fair lot for th' bosses. Let's stop it! Bit by bit, let's drop the whole industrial life, an' go back. The least little bit o' money'll do." He paused and then went on:

"An' I'd tell 'em: Look! Look at Joe! He moves lovely! Look how he moves, alive and aware. He's beautiful! An' look at Jonah! He's clumsy, he's ugly, because he's never willin' to rouse himself. I'd tell 'em: Look! Look at yerselves! one shoulder higher than t'other, legs twisted, feet all lumps! What have yer done ter yerselves, wi' the blasted work? Spoilt yerselves. No need to work that much. Take yer clothes off an' look at yerselves. Yer ought ter be alive an' beautiful, an' yer ugly an' half dead. So I'd tell 'em. An' I'd get my men to wear different clothes: 'appen close red trousers, bright red, an' little short white jackets. Why, if men had red, fine legs, that alone would change them in a month. They'd begin to be men again, to be men! An' the women could dress as they liked. Because if once the men walked with legs close bright scarlet, and buttocks nice an' showing scarlet under a little white jacket: then the women 'ud begin to be women."

This is the simplest possible statement to simple people. But Lawrence, though himself of proletarian stock and a warm, unsentimental champion of the proletariat, is not writing at this class. He is directing himself at the sensitive middle class and at the rulers or those who are close to the rulers of the world. The heroes who carry his didactic burden are often proletarians who have been born into industrialism and who have escaped it to come into contact with Nature. But what they have to say is not for their class fellows. The proletariat may be crippled in body; it is not further diseased with the parasite of mind. The enslavement of the physical body to machines cannot be lifted by words; but there is some hope that the spiritual body enslaved to the sapping mind can be freed. After all, though the disease of this class is indubitably the result of the social order, it is in some part the result of an inertia which words may exorcise. To this class which lives by perception, Lawrence pleads the passionate perception of the body.

When humanity comes to its senses [he says in *Fantasia of the Unconscious*] it will realize what a fearful Sodom apple our understanding is. What terrible mouths and stomachs full of bitter ash we've all got. And then we shall take away our "knowledge" and "understanding," and lock them up along with the rest of poisons, to be administered in small doses only by competent people.

We have almost poisoned the mass of humanity with *understanding*. The period of actual death and race-extermination is not far off. We could have produced the same barrenness and frenzy of nothingness in people, perhaps, by dinning it into them that every man is just a charnel-house skeleton of unclean bones. Our "understanding," our science and idealism have produced in people the same strange frenzy of self-repulsion as if they saw their skulls each time they looked in the mirror. A man is a thing of scientific cause-and-effect and biological process, draped in an ideal, is he? No wonder he sees the skeleton grinning through the flesh.

On the rehabilitation of the body, on the reestablishment of the knowledge of the blood and nerves, Lawrence bases his faint hope of human salvation. But Lawrence may not be dragged into the untruths which a simpler man would have hurled himself into, having come to such conclusions. The importance he puts upon sex, for instance, is far from carrying him into the vulgar promiscuity of the ordinary "pagan." Sex is not for him a means of amusement or of "self-expression." The slippery facility of Bertrand Russell's sexual morality, arrived at by strict process of logic and calculated to destroy whatever meaning there is left to sex, is not Lawrence's.

Sex is a life-flame, a dark one, reserved and almost invisible. It is a deep reserve in a man, one of the core-flames of his manhood.
What, would you play with it? Would you make it cheap and nasty? Buy a king-cobra and try playing with that.

Again, it is often misconceived of Lawrence that he found in sex the ultimate activity of man. But in *Fantasia of the Unconscious* he makes clear the place of sex. "Men, being themselves made new after the act of coition, wish to make the world new. A new, passionate polarity springs up between men who are bent on the same activity, the polarity man and woman sinks to passivity. It is now daytime, and time to forget sex, time to be busy making a new world." "And," he continues, "I am sure that the ultimate, greatest activity of man in this desire for great *purposive* activity." Sexual activity as an end in itself, as an ultimate, he sees as anarchic: sexuality made the great center of life is the beginning of despair. But the two activities, sexual and purposive, feed each other. Starve one of the other and it becomes inevitably sterile and destructive.

Mr. Wyndham Lewis has attacked Lawrence as a denier of mind, as an exponent of the Feminine Principle and of the "child-cult." The attribution to Lawrence of a position such as this could only have been arrived at by Mr. Lewis by means of a false simplification. Lawrence is far from denying mind. When he attacks understanding he is attacking a thing which has been artificially grafted onto the ruck of mankind who cannot support it and whose life is sapped by it. "There are *few, few people* in whom the living impulse and reaction develops and sublimates into mental consciousness. There are all kinds of trees in the forest. But few of them indeed bear the apples of knowledge. So we go through the forest of humanity, cut back every tree, and try to graft it into an apple-tree. A nice wood of monsters we make by doing so."

As to Lawrence's subscription to the "child-cult," the following passage from *Lady Chatterley's Lover* indicates that Lawrence's understanding of it is as great as Mr. Lewis' and his disgust with it even greater. Clifford, the impotent husband of the heroine, deprived of his wife, falls into a perverse relation with his middle-aged nurse, in which he is "a child when he was a man."

The curious thing was that when this child-man, which Clifford was now and which he had been becoming for years, emerged into the world, it was much sharper and keener than the real man he used to be. This perverted child-man was now a *real* business-man; when it was a question of affairs, he was an absolute he-man, sharp as a needle, and impervious as a bit of steel. When he was out among men seeking his own ends and "making good" his colliery workings, he had an almost uncanny shrewdness, hardness and a straight sharp punch. It was as if his passivity and prostitution to the Magna Mater gave him insight into material business affairs, and lent him a certain remarkable human force. The wallowing in private emotion, the utter abasement of his manly self, seemed to lend him a second nature, cold, almost visionary, business-clever.

And finally, no reader of his novels can take seriously the accusation that Lawrence abased himself before the Female Principle.

Every one of his heroes is engaged in a frantic and bitter struggle against just this abasement. But Mr. Lewis wishes to broaden the accusation by identifying the Feminine Principle with flux and the Eternal Becoming with which Lawrence was confessedly concerned. Nevertheless, this concern is not the hidden intellectual evasion Mr. Lewis would have it. Lawrence does not chuck himself regardless into the stream of Becoming. If he does not seek to crystallize its drops into timeless perfection, he indeed confines them in a strong vessel of pertinent meaning.

The Problem of
the American Artist[1]

[A review of *Portrait of the Artist as American* by Matthew Josephson. *The Symposium*, October 1930]

THE body of this volume is devoted to an attempt to discover the social causes for the failure of literature in America during the amazing Gilded Age of post-Civil War expansion. On the whole, it must be accounted a thorough and intelligent social-literary history. If it is scarcely original in its conclusions, this is not entirely the author's fault, for the component stories of Mr. Josephson's history have, of late years, burned themselves deep into the consciousness of most literate Americans and have become sad and scaring myths in the American cosmology.

The history is tragically simple. In a civilization that was still pioneering, a few artists dared to raise their heads. The environment was brutal, fevered, insensitive, and material. It not only made the basic mechanics of life difficult for the artist but it afforded no scene that was worth treating—it had no variety, no depth, no color, no complexity. As a result of this condition, those who were brave enough to declare themselves artists were crushed or sent crippled from our shores, and American literature, which had such bright seeds of promise, withered to a regretful unfulfillment.

In the conclusions of this history, agreement with Mr. Josephson

[1] Title supplied by the editor of this volume.

is inevitable. At the door of a stupid, ruthless civilization must indeed be laid the mass of personal misery and crippled talent that marked our artistic life for so many years.

Further than this, however, one cannot go with Mr. Josephson, although in his Introduction he demands our company for longer. In this chapter, as an explanation for the failure of American literature even in the present day, Mr. Josephson blames the continuation of the same conditions which blighted our early efforts. And if these conditions have changed at all, it is only in the direction of increased intensity. Where once the artist was shoved aside by ruthless personal enterprise, he is now made to fall in line by an equally ruthless mechanical enterprise. The flatness of life has become a mightier and more active thing: it has become the Mob with its demand to legislate for the very spirit of its neighbor.

It is, then, according to this introductory chapter, the Machine and that product of the Machine, the Mob, that are causing the inferiority of our literary product. Mechanism tends to create an "unfeeling order." The Mob enforces that principle of equalitarianism so necessarily dear to it; the result is a life of "a dreadful sameness of character." "With such a world, art in the older sense can no longer coexist. The creative effort, thus far, has never been mechanical; it has never lent itself to mass production. [It has been] reluctant to use the organs of groups or to live in the spirit of the masses."

Mechanism-Mob has, in short, created an order in which not only is the artist deprived of the proper emotional working conditions but in which, because it is an "unfeeling order," the very function of art is no longer valid. This encompasses Mr. Josephson's diagnosis of the cause of America's artistic insufficiency. It is a diagnosis unfortunately representative of the general run of thought about the problem.

One cannot avoid the impression that Mr. Josephson is content with so simple an explanation because of a rather too nice reverence for the whole profession of art. He must speak of it as "a lonely and personal labor." It is "sublimated play." It is the "making of uselessly exquisite or magnificent things." From the chasm which separates it from the other activities of the world it occasionally tosses certain fragments to mankind, which fragments are eventually useful to the human race.

With so vague and precious a conception of the function of art, it is scarcely surprising that Mr. Josephson is worried over the likelihood that eventually it will entirely disappear. It must be insisted, art—the literary art—is closer to life than the language of Mr. Josephson implies. It is not an aspect of life, but an instrument of life. Its function is ultimately the social and moral one of discovering and judging values. And as the social and moral problems of the modern world become more insistent, art is turning more explicitly to deal with them. The terms of this meeting are, properly, artistic terms, but the content is becoming increasingly philosophical. The works that mark the artistic heights of the modern world have consistently been those that have undertaken the philosophic issues and emotional confusions of that world.

In tones of rather irritating nostalgia, Mr. Josephson declares, "As one recalls the golden ages, the masters made their temples and cathedrals, their dramas and paintings while living in harmony, for the most part, with their contemporary world." To which one can only reply that there are other metals besides gold. It is, let us admit, impossible for us to have a literature of harmony—at least of the harmony of accord. It is not, however, too mystical an effort to imagine another harmony, a harmony of discord, the Heraclitean harmony of battle. This harmony our age has produced and in no small amount. Joyce, Mann, Lawrence, Eliot, Gide, and Proust have all written in the travail of opposition to their world.

Yet America has not made its contribution even to the harmony of battle. Mr. Josephson would have us accept the fact that American life is now no longer even a battle, but has become an all-inclusive machine. But this is patently not true. Never, for the true artist, can life become anything so static as a machine. For him America will present an even more intense battleground than Europe. We have a scene of injustice, decay, desperation, frightful confusion of soul. The probable eventual triumph of these things does not invalidate them for art.

But Mr. Josephson says that in America the artist has not the means to produce the ordered expression of this material. His energy is sapped by his constant "resistance to the milieu" as if the highest prerogative were the preservation of the individual type, the defense of the human self from dissolution in the horde. It is difficult to deny the necessity for this struggle. But we have the right to ask of the artist the ability to survive. In a certain sense his ability to survive the national emotional environment is as much a part of his artistic equipment as his talent.

It would be difficult to prove, after a close examination of contemporary American literature, that it suffers either from the failure of the artist to resist his milieu or from a diversion of artistic energy to the business of resistance. One will rather find that there is an astonishing number of fairly pretentious books, marked by a sort of half-intelligence and artistic aplomb that could not exist were not the writers fairly sure of their place in their environment and fairly comfortable in it. One will seldom find that these writers succumb to dangers of their milieu. Indeed, the whole inferiority of this considerable body of half-worthy literature lies in the fact that, in a different sense, it resists its milieu much too successfully—resists it by evading it or by looking at it with a careful half-an-eye.

We have been using the whipping-boy of this Mechanism-Mob a little too long. It has indeed many outrages to account for, but the inferiority of American art in the last fifteen years is not one of them. The fault for this must lie with the American artist himself. Whether he be a knave-artist, too lazy to acquire knowledge and to exert full intelligence, secretly distrusting the function of art, or a fool-artist, just unable to do any better, it is difficult to say. But just so long as books continue to be written and read, and just so long as writers convince themselves that they are dealing with realities, criticism can be valid only if it thinks in terms of the individual work and its accomplishment or failure of important meaning, and not in terms of social causes.

The Changing Myth
of the Jew

[Written for *The Menorah Journal* in 1930 or earlier, accepted and set in type by that magazine in 1931, but not published. First published in *Commentary*, August 1978. The editor of this volume wishes to express gratitude to Elinor Grumet, who discovered this essay in the American Jewish Archives, Cincinnati, in the course of her studies for a book on *The Menorah Journal*.]

THE subject of the Jew in fiction has been treated many times before, but the approach has always been much the same. It is typified—perhaps extravagantly—by Rabbi David Philipson's well-known book, *The Jew in English Fiction*. For Rabbi Philipson the problem resolves itself into this question: Is it permissible to deal with Jews in fiction at all and, if so, to what extent? And Rabbi Philipson comes to the conclusion that it is permissible to this extent: Jews may be written about if they are treated as Scott treated his Covenanters, George Eliot her Dissenters, or Hawthorne his Puritans. That is, Jews may be treated in fiction with some mention of their humorous foibles and vagaries but always with deep respect.

Though other writers have not always had Rabbi Philipson's professional cause for techiness, nevertheless they, too, have too often made their (sometimes very scholarly) works the vehicle of indignation against the misrepresentation of the Jew, of correction of slander, of contempt for the slanderous authors. Books so intelligent and thorough as Mr. M. J. Landa's *The Jew in Drama*, as Dr. Joshua Kunitz's *Russian Literature and the Jew*, Dr. Suzanne

Howe's "The Jew in 19th-Century English Fiction"[1] are all more or less engaged in vindicating the Jew. These writers have all worked on one fundamental assumption, unfortunately incorrect. They seem to suppose that it was the intention of those who wrote about the Jew to treat the Jew realistically, either as an individual or as a race, and that this attempt had failed because of ignorance and hatred. But it is very doubtful if, apart from such small touches of realism as were absolutely necessary for verisimilitude, there was any attempt made at "truth." The Jew was never treated in a way that demanded realism or truth—he was never treated as more than a type. The Jew in fiction was always an abstraction, a symbol, a racial stereotype created by men whose chief concern was obviously much less to tell the truth about the character of the Jew than it was to serve their own political and economic interests and their own emotional needs.

In short, the Jew in English fiction is a myth. A myth, not in the newspaper sense of a lie or fabrication, but in the scientific sense of a popular fable, a story "not exactly invented but combined and embellished at will, the actors of which cannot be submitted to the test of real history." And as with all myths, it tells more of the hopes and fears of the people that needed it and created it than of the Jews that figure in it.

The Jew in English fiction took many shapes, but fundamentally he remained the same. The Jew was a foreigner, the repository and embodiment of all that was outside the established order of good. He fulfilled the mystical social function of scapegoat, on which was bound the sins of the community.

When this is realized it becomes relatively unimportant to discuss the truth or untruth of the portraits of Jews in literature. As well discuss what particular breed of goat was used to carry the wool fillets into the wilderness. The important thing to understand is that, under whatever wool fillets, the goat is a goat—and why it is that men found it important to drive him into the wilderness.

[1] An unpublished essay for the Master of Arts degree, Columbia University Library. It has been of great help to me.

The Jew in fiction, then, fundamentally remains the same—a myth. But he takes many shapes; that is, the myth changes. It will be the purpose of this essay to describe the mutations of the Jewish myth in English literature. This myth is, of course, not gratuitous; almost always it serves some purpose of explanation or protection for its makers. And the particular shape it takes is not accidental. It is a political safety valve, as with the Hitlerites today. It is a bolster to social pride, as with Thackeray. It is a security of righteousness or piety, as in the myth of the Jew as radical or sensualist.

But this essay will not attempt to discover the political or social motive or use of each myth of the Jew. Often enough these will be apparent; to elucidate fully the cause and use of each myth requires another essay. All that will be undertaken here will be the statement of the myths themselves. And even within this restriction this essay will not be complete. *Daniel Deronda* has been made the farthest boundary of the essay, though certainly there have been plenty of new myths since. But it is believed that a description of the Jew in fiction from Chaucer to George Eliot should amply show how the myth-making faculty works.

I

The myth of the Jew is discovered in the beginning of English literature, introduced into one of the most charming of the *Canterbury Tales,* "The Prioresse's Tale." A little "clergeon," son of a poor widow, out of devotion to the Virgin, sets himself to learn the *Alma Redemptoris,* and this he sings on his way to school through the Jewish quarter. Satan, who has "in Jewes heart his waspes nest," eggs on the Jews to angry notice of the child; they hire "an homycide" who cuts the child's throat and casts him in a pit. But by the Virgin's power he sings the *Alma Redemptoris,* whereby he is discovered. The guilty Jews are torn to pieces by wild horses and hanged. The story ends with a prayer to St. Hugh of Lincoln

slayn also
With cursed Jewes as it is notable
For it is but a litel while ago.

That the story of Hugh of Lincoln was popular is testified by the existence of twenty-one versions of the ballad "The Jew's Daughter." In the ballad the story is substantially that of "The Prioresse's Tale" save that, although the dead boy speaks by supernatural agency, the religious note is lacking. By the strength of his kick, little Sir Hugh sends his football through the Jew's window. He walks about the Jew's "castell" (a reference to the stone houses which the Jews, especially of Lincoln, built for their defense and which at the time were rare among English dwellings) and sees the Jew's daughter at the window. She invites him in for the ball, but he replies:

> How will I come up? How can I come up,
> How can I come to thee,
> For as ye did to my auld father
> The same you'll do to me.

This reference to a past murder does not, however, occur in all versions. When once the child is enticed within (by the offer of an apple), the girl lays him on the meat-dressing table and (in most versions) sticks him "like a swine" with a penknife, the orthodox instrument of ballad child-murders. The murderess then wraps him in lead and drops him into a well. But the dead child calls to his distracted mother. In one of the versions, the Jewess takes staff and mantle and prays Heaven to be her guide "unto some uncouth land."

These two stories of child-murder give us the simplest and most enduring myth of the Jew—the Jew as active anti-Christ, singling out for his villainies the object of Christ's great solicitude. The ballad story owes its origin to an account in the *Annals of Waverly* for the year 1255, which tells us that a boy named Hugh was crucified by the Jews in parody of Christ. Matthew Paris, who wrote contemporaneously, also probably got his account from the *Annals of Waverly;* his version has it that all the Jews of England were invited to the crucifixion; that after the murder they disemboweled the body for magic uses and attempted to bury it, but the earth refused to keep it. They then threw it into a pit, where it was found by the child's mother. Paris recounts that a Jew named Copyn confessed, and that according to his confession the Jews tried every year to get a Christian child for the paschal lamb. Copyn and eighteen of the richest Jews, says Paris, were drawn to the gallows at the tails of mares and hanged; later the same punishment was visited on twenty-three other Jews. Other accounts accuse the Jew of practicing sacrilege on the Host. In short, the Jew is the active enemy of the Christian and of Christ, and his heart is the dwelling place of Satan.

Several things, however, lift both Chaucer's tale and the ballad above the simplicity of their sources. Chaucer, always a realistic psychologist, is careful to give his Jews a kind of credibility. For example, they do not act until Satan urges them on; again, they do not crudely commit the murder themselves but employ "an homycide." The details of the assemblage of the English Jews and of the crucifixion and disembowelment are omitted. And finally, Chaucer, though a topical writer interested in the local events and personalities of his time, goes out of his way to set the story in a foreign land—in "Asye."

But while the dark instinct of the race mind that lies behind the ballads rejects even more of the chronicle than Chaucer does, it hints at worse. The verse from Version A (quoted above), which refers to the death of Sir Hugh's father, implies a complication of events and motive of which the chronicles give no trace, a suggestion of more subtle and personal motives than that of crude religious hate. The crime is committed by the Jew's *daughter;* the Jew-and-daughter myth is one that develops very strongly, though generally the young Jewess abhors the practices of her father.[2]

---

[2] F. J. Child has one version (H) of the ballad which is particularly interesting. It was discovered in New York (where, it seems, vestiges of several ballads are to be found in children's game-chants). In this version, the Jew's daughter becomes the Duke's daughter; also Sir Hugh becomes "little Harry Hughes," and the lead in which the child is wrapped becomes tin. The causes of these changes are uncertain. Perhaps the change from Jew to Duke voices the feeling in Ireland against noble landlords; perhaps, together with the Sir Hugh–Harry Hughes change, it is the result of American democratic feeling.

II

For the writers of miracle plays of the fourteenth and fifteenth centuries there were two kinds of Jew—the Jews of the Old and of the New Testament. The former—especially the patriarchs and the kings—were treated with orthodox respect and admiration; the latter with hatred and contempt: Judas was the type of the Gospel Jew. Whether or not red hair was ever a common Hebraic feature, Judas's legendary red hair was early considered a racial characteristic. Perhaps it served to indicate the diabolic connection. As for the thirty pieces of silver, they became the symbol of the infamy of the medieval Jewish trade in money.

As the world passes from the theological universe of the Middle Ages to the commercial universe of Elizabeth's time, the myth of the Jew likewise changes from the theological to the commercial. No longer, as in Chaucer and the ballads, is he the anti-Christ acting from unfathomable motives of pure evil. Now he is the wily merchant and moneylender, acting for gain. Stephen Gosson, that dull and violent Puritan of the sixteenth century who called forth Sir Philip Sidney's *Defence of Poetry,* mentions the Jew in his *School of Abuse* with much violence against the bloody usurer. (The Puritans, of course, were the rising bourgeoisie.) Gerontus, the Jewish moneylender in Robert Wilson's *Three Ladies of London* (1584), proves the rule of Jewish depravity by his exceptional good temper. He is pointed out as a decent person among wicked Christians— "Jewes seek to excel in Christianity and Christians in Jewishness."

The Elizabethan interest in villainy was, however, not satisfied with Judas. The figure which perhaps interested the English Renaissance more than any other was Machiavelli. For the Elizabethans, the unscrupulous, diabolic energy of the Italian historian, as they conceived it (largely at second hand), both truly indicated the general temper of their own politicians and fulfilled a peculiar emotional need. Machiavelli becomes the archetype not only for the political schemer but for every plotting villain, the utmost of what a man might do in devilry; and his legend gives rise to a distinct type of drama which Professor Tucker-Brooke calls Machiavellian tragedy.

With this myth the two previous myths of the Jew amalgamated. The Jew had been Judas, functioning out of pure hate of Christianity, he had been Judas, functioning out of love for money. He remained both these things, but his methods changed. To the malevolence of Judas is added the *craft* of Machiavelli. He becomes a creature of plots and wits. Before him all virtuous Christian men are helpless, and he can be foiled only by accident or betrayal—or by the shrewdness of a woman.

Barabas, the protagonist of Marlowe's *Jew of Malta* (1590), is, of course, completely representative. Like all of Marlowe's characters, a person lusting for infinite supremacy, his desire for riches is tempered a little by his love for his daughter and much more by his passion for pure villainy. Having been deprived of the great part of his fortune, he engages on a career of revenge, using his daughter as a pawn. When her lover is killed by her father's machinations, she retires to a nunnery and the father, to punish her, poisons her and the whole convent. His lust for destruction grows madder and outweighs even his love of wealth; his craft grows with his madness into a maze of evasions, plots, and cross plots until he is betrayed to the awful death he had prepared for others.

Professor Tucker-Brooke conjectures that the figure of Barrabas was perhaps suggested by that of the sixteenth-century Portuguese Jew, Juan Miques (Michesius). Having been persecuted in Portugal, in Antwerp, and in Venice, Miques settled in Constantinople. Enormously wealthy, he gained great influence over the Sultan and was made Duke of Naxos and the Cyclades. It was he who instigated the attack on Cyprus in 1590. But the career of Miques was not isolated; there were enough rich and powerful Jews to foster a belief that they were concerting their power and energies into a plan for a Jewish world control. Barrabas says:

> They say we are a scatter'd nation!
> I cannot tell, but we have scrambled up
> More wealth by far than those that brag of faith.

> There's Kirriah Iairim, the great Jew of Greece,
> Obed in Bairseth, Nones in Portugall
> Myself in Malta, some in Italy,
> Many in France, and wealthy ever one:
> Ay, wealthier far than any Christian. . . .

The author can find no fitter person to speak the prologue to this representation of the Jew than Machiavelli himself who, after explaining his philosophy, begs grace for the Jew:

> And let him not be entertained the worse
> Because he favors me.

The prologue by Machiavelli contains the indication of a new element in the myth of the Jew—the element of knowledge.

The popular mind has always felt that knowledge and sin were closely related, if not identical. The fall from Eden and the destruction of the overwise Oedipus embody the feeling, and the medieval Church, with its condemnation of the pride of worldly intellect, expressed it. Machiavelli declares:

> I count religion but a childish toy
> And hold there is no sin but Ignorance

and Barabas, in his famous brag of all his past gratuitous wickedness, tells us that he has practiced two learned professions. As a physician, he "enrich'd the priests with burials," and as a military engineer, he slew friend and enemy with his stratagems. This suspicion of the learning of the Jew is one that grows to considerable proportions and still exists. In our own day, Mr. G. K. Chesterton and *The Commonweal* of New York feel that the works of Freud and Einstein are diabolic Judaic attacks on the good order of the universe.

The Merchant of Venice developed the Elizabethan myth of the Jew very little further. The Machiavellian superman disappears and the Jew becomes "more human." But the elements of the myth remain intact—the influence of Marlowe on Shakespeare is obvious. We have the father-daughter situation; the father's confusion of his daughter and his treasure (compare Barrabas's "Oh girle, oh gold,

oh beauty, oh my blisse!" with Shylock's rather vaudevillian paraphrase, "My daughter, oh my ducats"); the sexual desirability of
the daughter; and the betrayal of the father by the daughter. We
have the same racial arrogance and hatred of Christians. Shakespeare does, however, develop an apology and justification motif,
for it must be noted that however much the Jew is contemned and
whatever servile manners he assumes, he is endowed with the proud
position of aggressor ("Hath not a Jew eyes," etc.), which Marlowe
but crudely suggests.

In *The Merchant of Venice,* the identification of "Jew" with
"physician" (it is generally supposed that the play was suggested
by the execution of the Spanish Jew, Lopez, Elizabeth's physician,
for a plot to murder the Queen) reintroduces the flesh-and-blood
theme. This fear of vivisection had already been given expression in
Thomas Nashe's novel *The Unfortunate Traveler; or, Jack Wilton*
(1594), in which the hero lodges with a Jewish physician.

But the tendencies of the Elizabethan age toward fantasy and
extravagance, the high-flown writing of Spenser, Sidney, Marlowe,
were curbed by the rising power of Puritanism. The myth of the
Jew as malevolence incarnate wears out with other Elizabethan
myths. By the end of the sixteenth century, the Jew has disappeared
entirely as a major figure in literature. His appearance had never
been frequent, for he had, after all, been forbidden the country in
1290, not to return until the time of Cromwell, 1655, when his
numbers remained small and his lot hard. For many years now we
get him chiefly in reference, and there is even an attempt to treat
him "realistically." That is to say, if he is still vengeful and greedy
after the old myth, yet he is no longer heroic in size; now he is
become merely a petty usurer, a broker, a mercenary poisoner, a
pimp.

III

It is not until the romantic period that the Jew emerges again as a
definite myth. Romanticism is a word already so vague that no defi-

nition can save it, but we may accept the fact that there was a concerted change in European literature in the latter part of the eighteenth century and that the manifestations of the new literature were in some way related to each other and conseqent on much the same social and political changes. We are also safe in saying that romanticism usually involved, on the one hand, a return to a past supposedly dark and glamorous, an interest in the unusual and strange, in the supernatural and horrifying; on the other hand, an interest in the simple and the good. The myth of the Jew paralleled this dichotomy. The Jew was useful material for both tendencies. For the first, he was exotic and, even better, "Oriental"—that is, a person of strange rites and dark mysteries. He was anti-Christian and therefore demonic. He was learned in the Kabbalah, and his knowledge of the half-magic art of the physician was legendary. For the second tendency, he was appropriately miserable, wretched, and outcast.

The deep interest which the exotic tendency manifested in the demonic did not imply a love of the devil—though in Byron and in many other writers it went even to this length. But it did imply a certain frightened tolerance of him, and it was, on the whole, with much this attitude that the exotic romantic writers undertook the Jew, when, as was inevitable, they did take him up.

Horace Walpole's *The Castle of Otranto* (1764) started the interest in bleeding statues, talking portraits, clanking chains, and all the familiar mummery of terror-romanticism, and then the English romanticists came under the influence of the Germans, who, for their part, were turning more and more to folklore to get the materials of horror. Following their example, the English turned to their own past and "primitive" literature—to literature of the sixteenth and seventeenth centuries, the weird scenes of Shakespeare, the mortuary scenes of Webster, the devils and villainies of Marlowe, the demonic scenes of Milton. And with the return to the Elizabethans and to the ballads, they naturally rediscovered the possibilities of terror that lurked in the Jew. Terror-romanticism was not content with merely the materials of the old literature. It wanted also to recapture the tone. It sought to create figures as impressively huge as those of

Elizabethan literature. In this it had a certain success; indeed, its characters are huger than those of its models, but only as the Brockenspecter is huger than the traveler who casts it. With this desire for grandiosity, it is scarcely surprising that terror-romanticism, using the Jew, should use him in his most striking manifestation—his survival through all the centuries of Western history, his "eternality."

Thus it is that the Wandering Jew became for terror-romanticism the type of the mythical Jew, just as Machiavelli had been the Jewish type for the Elizabethans. The Machiavellian Jew and the Wandering Jew are at many points similar—in their power, their knowledge, their rhetoric—but they are different in this: that the Machiavellian Jew is purely a villain and the Wandering Jew, though he has committed a great and inexplicable crime, is repentant and even benevolent.

The figure of the Wandering Jew is a legendary one, dating back to the year 1228.[3] Roger of Wendover, in his universal history, *Flores Historiarum,* tells us that in that year there came to England a certain Armenian bishop who told that Cartaphilus, the guardian of Pilate's gate, was still alive and that he had had converse with him. The story that Cartaphilus related was that when Jesus was being brought back from judgment, he had struck him, saying, "Go faster, Jesus, go faster. Why dost thou linger?" Jesus had looked at him *severo oculo* and replied, "I am certainly going, but thou shalt tarry till I come." Doomed by this to live until the Second Coming, Cartaphilus goes every hundred years into a sickness and trance, from which he emerges again as a man of thirty. He is a most pious and grave person.

This legend, which has analogues in the mythology of many religions, is probably based on a literal and popular interpretation of Matthew 16:28: "Verily I say unto you, there be some of them that stand here which shall in no wise taste of death till they see the Son of man coming to his kingdom." The fate of eternal life

---

[3] For almost all my material on the Wandering Jew, I am indebted to Professor Eino Railo's book on terror-romanticism, *The Haunted Castle.*

in witness of his master was also accorded by some to St. John. (The confusion of Joseph with St. John, the beloved disciple, may be seen in the name Cartaphilus, which means "greatly beloved.") There are also elements in the legend of the story of Cain's punishment.

The legend of the Wandering Jew, flourishing chiefly in Spain and Italy, did not come to Germany until 1602 with the work *Kurtze Beschreibung und Erzehlung von Einem Juden mit Namen Ahasverus*. This book tells of a meeting between a certain bishop and a strange-looking man, who declared himself to be the shoemaker Ahasverus of Jerusalem who had forbidden Jesus, on his way to Golgotha, to rest before his house.

For a long time the legend remained merely a source of comedy. About 1770 Goethe contemplated, but did not write, a poem in which the eternal Ahasverus was to be the instrument of a history of religion and the Church. He imagined a meeting of Ahasverus and Spinoza which was to be the means of extolling Spinoza's philosophy. However, a German poet, Schubart, did write a poem (1787) in which he claims the Wandering Jew for romanticism, identifying him with every turmoil and wildness of nature, as he seeks his death by the angry elements. In Schiller's unfinished *Geisterseher* (1789), there is a person who has most of the eerie and imposing characteristics of the Wandering Jew as we know him. He also appears in a number of other works of the time.

The conception of the Wandering Jew as a serious character came into English literature with Matthew Gregory Lewis' *The Monk*, published in 1795. On a visit to Germany, Lewis had absorbed all the refinement of terror that romantic German medievalists had made on the crude shocks of *The Castle of Otranto*, and it was the greatly imitated success of his farrago of romance, anti-clericalism, faint obscenity, and horror that gave this new Jewish myth currency.

Lewis's Wandering Jew is an amalgam of all the legends about him. He is a man who speaks seldom and smiles never; he moves gravely and nobly. He is not permitted any personal belongings; nevertheless, he is generous and from a well-filled purse bestows many rich gifts. Dark, powerful, and majestic, his eyes flash black and somber from under heavy brows. Across his forehead, he wears a band of black velvet to hide the fiery cross set as a mark upon it. He has seen every country, he talks familiarly of races long dead. His knowledge is only less vast than his misery:

No one is adequate to comprehend the misery of my lot. . . . Fate obliges me to be constantly in movement; I am not permitted to pass more than a fortnight in the same place. I have no friend in the world and from the restlessness of my destiny I never can acquire one. Fain would I lay down my miserable life, for I envy those who enjoy the quiet of the grave; but death eludes me and flies from my embrace. In vain do I throw myself in the way of danger. I plunge into the ocean, the waves throw me back with abhorrence upon the shore; I rush into fire; the flames recoil at my approach; I oppose myself to the fury of the banditti; their swords become blunted and break upon my breast. The hungry tiger shudders at my approach, and the alligator flies from a monster more horrible than itself. God has set his seal upon me and all His creatures respect this fatal mark.

And so terrible is the power of his glance, that even the supernatural creatures quail before it; one look is sufficient to scare off the specter of the Bleeding Nun when it attempts to prevent the elopement of the lovers, Raymond and Agnes.

C. R. Maturin's *Melmoth the Wanderer* (1820) uses the high terror of *The Monk,* but more effectively, creating a mad, fanatic, half-lit world of great impressiveness. Melmoth, though a Gentile, is a combined Wandering Jew and Faust. He has sold his soul for eternal youth that he may acquire infinite learning. In time he becomes also a kind of Mephistopheles, tempting others to change places with him and elect his fate, for only if he succeeds in doing this can he attain to his wished-for death. But this modification of the Wandering Jew is not so important for us as the novel's two portraits of Jews with whom Monçada, a young Gentile fleeing the Inquisition, comes in contact. Monçada stumbles into a house whose master he finds to be a secret Jew. By the threat of exposure he forces the Jew to hide him. The Jew, forced into defending his

Judaizing, expresses himself in these terms: "I am one of that unhappy race everywhere stigmatized and spoken against, yet on
whose industry and talent the ungrateful country that anathematizes
us depends for half the source of its national prosperity." Monçada,
however, reflects of him, "he was a Jew *innate,* an impostor, a
wretch who, drawing sustenance from the bosom of our Holy
Mother the Church, had turned her nutriment to poison and had
attempted to infuse that poison into the lips of his son."

A little later Monçada must take refuge with another Jew,
Adonijah, who hides him in a subterranean cavern. This Jew, a
cross between physician and magician, exemplifies again the learned-
villain type. He has made a pact with the devil and suffers for it;
but despite this wickedness, and despite his collection of skeletons
of his relatives, the young Monçada finds impressive "the hoary
majesty of his patriarchal figure" and his "stern simplicity." It is
shameful to Monçada to have to become "the amanuensis of a
Jew for hire," but affliction makes him more tolerant: ". . . at this
moment I half believed that a Jew might find entrance and adoption
amid the family and fold of the blessed."

The second quarter of the nineteenth century saw the decline of
the novel of horror and the ripening of the historical novel. Into
this form the Wandering Jew—or modifications of him—fitted with
entire ease. The dissident religious movements of the eighteenth and
nineteenth centuries—themselves part of the romantic movement—
had spread knowledge of the Bible, and the Wandering Jew is
treated in closer connection with his historical Judaic background.

Heroic and powerful, but stripped of the supernaturalism that
had hitherto characterized him, he appears as the hero of the Rev-
erend George Croly's *Salathiel the Immortal; or, Tarry Thou Till
I Come.* There is much that is ridiculous in this book, as there
always is when romanticism exploits biblical lore, but it is full of a
rather fine grandiose rhetoric. First published in 1827, it appeared
again in 1905 in an edition by Funk and Wagnalls—an edition of no
little interest to lovers of Jewish *curiosa,* for it is fitted out with an

appendix in which are tabulated the sullen or eager *responsa* of Jewish rabbis and scholars to the question: What do you think of Christ?

The plot of Croly's book is simple and its details reasonably terrifying. Salathiel, servant in the house of Pilate, strikes Christ as he passes with the Cross. Bidden "Tarry thou till I come," he assumes immortality and a career of heroism and bombast. The nineteenth century is well under way and this new Wanderer expresses his tragic fate in terms of Byronic nationalism—the passing of great kingdoms and the suppression of once proud races are his concern and sorrow:

The name of Jew is now but another title for humiliation. Who that sees that fallen thing with his countenance bent to the ground and his form withered of its comeliness tottering through the proud streets of Europe in some degrading occupation and clothed in the robes of the beggared and the despised could imagine the bold figures and gallant bearing of the lion-hunters with whom . . . I spurred my barb up the mountain paths of Galilee.

So similar to Croly's book in its mad adventures, piracies, escapes, and "wild" prophecies as to necessitate a delay in its publication, Horatio Smith's *Zillah: A Tale of the Holy City* (1828) substitutes for the dignified grandiosity of *Salathiel* a rather unsuccessful facetiousness. The book is chiefly interesting for its depiction of what has come to be thought of as an important Jewish trait—moral arrogance. The High Priest, father of the heroine, is the exponent of this quality. He is ambassador to Mark Anthony, a position which gives him the opportunity of being in a constant froth of anathema and fulmination against Roman luxury. Matthew Arnold, one feels sure, read the volume in his youth and constructed his definition of Hebraism with it in mind. How consistently this myth has maintained itself may be seen in Mr. Edgar Johnson's recent fantastic novel, *Unweave a Rainbow,* where the Jew, Mordecai, avowedly a formalized, even mythical, figure, continues the mystical puritanism of Smith's High Priest.

As an antidote to this arrogance and fanaticism, we have the converted Roman, Felix, lover of Zillah, who turns up with an Orthodox beard. This tempering of Jew with pagan (again see Matthew Arnold) gives us the author's ideal Judaic type, the Jew dedicated to the practice of an all-embracing philanthropy and the maintenance of a universal toleration. "Let me not imagine . . ." says the new-bearded Felix, "that I am adoring the Deity, when I am only falling prostrate before my own opinion, enshrined in pride, conceit, and obstinacy."

In Bulwer-Lytton's *Leila; or, The Siege of Granada* (1838), the myth develops into the Jewish villain-hero already foreshadowed by the Elizabethans, and one of the most persistent and curious myths of the Jew. This anomaly, in its simplest form, was implicit in the Wandering Jew myth: the sin of the Wanderer was heinous, but his punishment is so dreadful that he becomes by means of it a virtuous person. The existence of good and evil, of heroism and villainy, in the same person, was an easy concept in a time that made Satan the hero of *Paradise Lost,* a time that glorified Cain and declared the devil to be a gentleman. The conception was perhaps always implicit in the character of Shylock; certainly since the actor Macklin's new—i.e., pathetic, heroic-villainous—interpretation in 1741 (which Landa bewails because it gave a credibility that makes it effective slander), it had become the accepted one.

The Jew Alamen, father of the Leila of Bulwer-Lytton's novel, is counselor to Boabdil, the weak Moorish king who was forced out of Granada at the time of Torquemada. He is a sorcerer and a maker of phosphorescent skeletons. A "Machiavel" indeed, but like the real Machiavelli, a devoted patriot, he is deeply race-conscious and well aware of the debasement of his people. He seeks not merely to gain toleration for the race but to raise it and perfect it. He attacks a subordinate for the "leprosy of avarice that gnaws away from our whole race the heart, the soul—nay, the very form of man." "A Jew," he cries to one who has taunted him, "A despised and despising Jew! Ask you more? I am the son of a race of Kings!" Thus far the hero. But as he is treacherously Machiavellian, dickering with both Christian and Moor; as he opposes the course of true love between Leila and Muza, the Moorish prince; as he murders Muza and Leila, married after the girl's conversion (it is easy for her to become a Christian for her Judaism is not "of the mundane and material sort"); and finally, as he bursts into satanic laughter, he is definitely the villain.

However, even this development of the myth fostered by the school of romantic history does not alter its essential character. The Jew remains throughout an eternal wanderer, a menacing, grandiose figure, darkly impressive, heroic in stature, proud but an outcast.

IV

The forces that were disrupting Europe were beginning to push the Jew into the stream of common existence. Slowly he was being forced, or was forcing himself, into the social structure of England. With more and more actual Jews to be seen on the streets of London, the myth which gave to the Jew a sort of sublime villainy became more and more vulnerable. However useful the heroic myth might still be for historical fiction, for those professing to write in terms of the everyday present it simply would not do. It was necessary to create a new Jewish myth that would have at least some semblance of reality.

We find, not surprisingly, that this attempt to refurbish the Jewish myth is first made in comedy. The nature of the attempt can easily be understood from a few of the titles: *Jewish Courtship, Mordecai's Beard, The Contrast; or, The Jew and the Married Courtesan.* In these pastiches a curious jargon was used to indicate Judaized English; the jargon grew more and more specialized, less and less real, the longer it was used. And now the Jew becomes a very different person from what he had been before in English drama. He remained nasty enough but no longer was he Machiavellian or mysteriously heroic; rather he became the dupe. Richard Brinsley Sheridan's *The Duenna* (1775), a dull, stupid opera, has the character of Isaac Mendoz who, desiring the hand of the heroine, has the duenna palmed off on him. His person is comic, he is little, ugly, and monkey-like; and it was a palpable hit when the duenna, trying to persuade her charge to favor him, said that he looked "so little like a Jew and so much like a gentleman." It is notable that the girl's father wants her to marry the Jew. This circumstance together with the duenna's remark show how the emphasis is changing at this time; the opprobrium is no longer moral or religious, but social.

The new myth comes to be based on the fact that the Jew is not a gentleman, on the assertion of a natural antithesis between the concept Jew and the concept Gentleman. Here, perhaps for the first time, we are encountering what we have come to call anti-Semitism in its present-day sense. The point of the new myth is apparent: by reason of his nature, the Jew is held to be outside the pale of society. Which conception is used of his nature, whether that of a dark superiority or that of a degraded inferiority, depends largely upon whether he is considered as a historical character or as living in the immediate present.

In the nineteenth century, as today, the Jewish myth was a useful instrumentality in the hands of conservative, chauvinistic, anti-democratic powers. Under its cover, they could fight the forces of democracy, the forces working for extended franchise, emancipation of the lower orders, liberation of oppressed minorities, the middle-class liberals. In consequence, the democratic forces found it often necessary, as part of their own struggle, to beat down the Jewish myth. Motivated in some such way as this, rather than by an unselfish, altruistic impulse to help an oppressed, outcast race, there arose those new pictures of the Jew which Rabbi Philipson and his school of rabbinical critics gratefully hail as noble defenses of the Jew, as the emergence after centuries of slander of the "true" character of the Jew at last. As a matter of fact, of course, these new portraits of the Jew are hardly more "true" than earlier ones. Commonly characterized as humanitarian efforts to defend the Jew against his maligners, to place him in a realistic human light, they are actually no more than reinterpretations of the common Jewish myths to suit new social purposes. Symbolic counterfoils too calculatedly apologetic to be real, they are but new counter-myths to set up against the old traditional myths.

Naturally these new counter-myths largely paralleled the lines of the two most popular mythical conceptions of the Jew. To the myth of the Jew as a degraded inferior they answered with an assertion of his natural goodness—the natural goodness of the humble and the oppressed: the Jew more sinned against than sinning. To the other myth, the fantastic notion of the Jew as powerful and all-knowing, they answered with a denial of the evil use of this power and omniscience. Of course, not all the writing about Jews of the period can be made to fit within these molds. Often, in the works of a single writer, as in Sir Walter Scott and Maria Edgeworth, various and often contradictory myths appear, as the writer is torn between one conception of the Jew and another. Often enough, too, vestigial remnants of early myths, which the age had seemed to have discarded, reappear. Personal factors too—the personal isolation of the writer, his personal experiences with Jews—intrude.

The defense of the Jew as a good and humble creature appears in its purest and almost lachrymose form in the works of George Cumberland, greatly beloved of Reform-rabbinical *belles lettres.* Rabbi Louis I. Newman has written a volume on him and Rabbi Philipson has panegyrized him.

Born in 1732 and dying in 1811, Cumberland lived in the era when sentimentality, humanitarianism, and the *comédie larmoyante* were coming into their own. Evidently a Man of Feeling, Cumberland was perhaps attracted to the Jews by the notorious conversion of the mad Lord George ("No Popery") Gordon to Judaism. Though Cumberland had himself done a little conventional Jew-teasing in his play *The Fashionable Lover,* he created the character Abraham Abrahams who, in 1785, began to write in Cumberland's paper, the *Observer,* in defense of the Jews. Abraham Abrahams reprobated the custom of always representing the Jew as a rogue, usurer, and buffoon and suggested that some dramatist "give us poor Jews a kind of lift in a new comedy." In accordance with this suggestion to himself, Cumberland wrote and, in 1793, produced *The Jew*.

The play was undoubtedly influenced by Lessing's *Nathan der Weise*. It is entirely artless and crude, but it was successful enough, was frequently revived, and Sheva, the old Jewish hero, was, we are told, considered one of the "fat" parts of the time. The simple plot is constructed to show how Sheva, outwardly a miser and usurer, is at heart a person of generosity and gratitude. How different is this Jew from the Machiavellian Jew! Far from acting for the evil of anyone, he is the poor lost lamb of the world. He has been saved by the heroine's brother from a London mob and by the heroine's father from the Inquisition in Cadiz and he is very grateful. He does not rend the sky with cries against injustice; all he wants is his little crust of peace. "We have no abiding place on earth," he says,

—no country, no home. Everybody rails at us, everybody points us out for their May-game and their mockery. If your playwriters want a butt, or a buffoon, or a knave to make sport of, out comes a Jew to be baited and buffeted through five long acts, for the amusement of all good Christians. Cruel sport!—merciless amusement! Hard dealings for the poor stray sheep of the scattered flock of Abraham! How can you expect us to show kindness, when we receive none?

Oddly enough, the name of Sir Walter Scott is usually linked with Cumberland's, as one of the new order which, for altruistic reasons, was determined (or so the theory ran) that the Jew be dealt with justly in literature. The truth is that Scott belonged definitely to the historic-romantic school and accepted its traditional patterns. The common Jewish belief is that in *Ivanhoe,* Scott (influenced by Washington Irving's description of his fiancée's friend, Rebecca Gratz) created new characters which for the first time dealt truthfully and fairly with Jews. The obvious fact is that the Jewish characters, Rebecca and Isaac, show little development from the "father-daughter" pattern of the early myths. Isaac, for all the geniality with which he is treated, is closely akin to Shylock; nor is Rebecca remote from Jessica. In *Kenilworth,* the Jewish character,

Zacharias Yoglan, a fawning, cheating chemist, is merely an old stereotype. Scott's best claim to "defend the Jew" rests on his creation in *Surgeon's Daughter* of Middlemass, an obvious counter-myth to the no-gentleman social myth of the Jew. Middlemass is a young Jew, handsome, dashing, hot-headed, and elegant—in almost all things the romantic hero. (A sign perhaps of the penetration of wealthier Jews into English society.) But Scott was being pressed for money by his Jewish creditors, Abud and Company, and in consequence, perhaps, he makes Middlemass also avaricious and a villain and ends his wicked career in India, where he is stepped on by an elephant.

In Maria Edgeworth's novel *Harrington,* written in 1817 at the request of a young Jewess of Richmond, Virginia, may be found practically all of the myths and counter-myths of the period, artlessly confused. The story tells of the struggle of young Harrington to rid himself of his fear and hate of Jews. He had been frightened by an "ol' clo'" man, Simon, and all the stories his nurse told him about Jews were of wicked ones. But at school he makes friends with Jacob the Jew Boy, who is marked by the new Jewish traits of patience, gratitude, and humility. Jacob the Jew Boy (so called by the author), who refers to himself as Poor Jacob, in large part breaks down Harrington's Judeophobia. At Cambridge, Harrington meets Israel Lyons, Hebrew scholar, rabbi, and man of the world, purposely prodigal to counteract the reputation for meanness which his race had incurred. Harrington sees Macklin give his sympathetic and serious interpretation of Shylock and is much impressed. Finally, he meets the aristocratic Spanish Jew, Montenero, and his beautiful daughter, Berenice. Love and aristocracy complete his capitulation to the harmlessness and impressiveness of Judaism. Harrington's father is the conventional eighteenth-century parent; he hates Jews until Montenero's generosity saves his fortune. Then he relents, consents to the marriage, and is rewarded by learning that Berenice's mother was an English Protestant. The book did not sell well and Miss Edgeworth was a little disgruntled by her championship.

Dickens's contribution to the new counter-mythology of the Jew —Riah in *Our Mutual Friend*—is by no means his happiest creation. Curiously enough, it was an answer to an extremely popular revival of an old Jewish myth for which he himself was responsible—the character of Fagin in *Oliver Twist,* the ghetto thief and spawner of thieves. The 1830's and '40's had brought the Jew into politics and business and the universities, and it was not pleasant for the newly-emancipated to have themselves identified before the English public with the submerged Jewish population, economically and socially unassimilated. Their chagrin was not that such a class existed, wretchedly poor, subsisting by various servile and often illegal oc-cupations, but that Dickens, choosing his villain from this class, referred to him as "the Jew" and thereby stigmatized the whole race, including themselves. Dickens was, of course, innocent of such in-tent. His was a simple mind, and looking for a myth convenient to his simple purpose, which was to present a picture of unalloyed wickedness, he quite simply returned to the Jew of the ballad, an abstract and mythical villain. His use of the phrase "the Jew," obvi-ously suggested by usage of the ballad, had no slander in it. Indeed, when Eliza David took him to task for maligning her race, he was genuinely contrite and strove to make amends with the character of Riah, a creature as impossibly good as Fagin was impossibly bad, but, unfortunately, unable to cope with the myth of Fagin, which has persisted, to the annoyance of respectable Jews and for the help of their opponents, down to this day.

With Charles Reade's *It's Never Too Late to Mend* (1856), an-other myth, having slumbered for a while, awakens with nineteenth-century adaptations. Isaac Levi, the benevolent old moneylender, is a simple and prosaic enough character, but he is a true descendant of the Wandering Jew. Like his forebear, he appears when and where one least expects him—in the Berkshire village, in the Aus-tralian camp. Always he is agile, crafty, and on the watch to revenge his wrongs, to show gratitude for kindness. Reade keeps us aware of his fineness and exotic color; in contrast to the vulgar natives of the village, he was as though "a striped jaspar had crept in among the paving stones." He is definitely Oriental and he looks to return to the East to die.

The life and works of Disraeli set the problem in a slightly new form—for here for the first time we see the Jew himself working on the Jewish myth. Paul Valéry says somewhere that it is every man's right to create for himself whatever character he wants, consciously and deliberately. We all do so to a certain extent; and many of us still find formalized racial patterns useful. Certainly Disraeli did; for his purposes he created a new myth composed of all that was glamorous and astonishing in the old myths, a myth which he not only used in his fiction but which he himself often acted in his life, with what political success we all remember.

This amazing Jewish myth we see first in the fresh sharpness of its conception in *Coningsby* (1834). The titular hero of this novel was drawn from Lionel de Rothschild, chief of the English Rothschild bank and always Disraeli's good friend. The ideal and mentor of this youth (in the novel he is not Jewish) is Sidonia—Disraeli himself. This young man, strikingly handsome with flashing dark eyes, is the descendant of a noble Spanish line reconverted to Judaism. Like the Wandering Jew, he knows every land. He is learned in all the wisdoms including those of the East, nor is he unacquainted with the medical art. Machiavelli-like, he has his fingers on the pulse of nations, and he nourishes in himself a vaulting ambition. Alone and lonely, he is kindly to many and sought after by all. He appears suddenly and as suddenly leaves, very likely on an Arab courser. The nation depends on him to lend it the interest on the national debt, but he is denied the occupations of a citizen. Yet he is loyal to England, though he nourishes a deep pride in his race and finds in it all the finest Tory qualities. Ambition and benevolent heroism are for him the breath of life.

Tancred (1847) is the working out of the pride of race which in *Coningsby* Sidonia expresses so passionately. Beginning with the thesis that the Northern Gentiles are of inferior stock, sprung from barbaric Baltic pirates, and that regeneration must come from the East, Sidonia sends Tancred, a young English nobleman, to come into contact with Eastern spirituality and faith so that he may bring them back to Europe. In Tancred's romantic and extravagant adventures, all the Jews who cling to their Jewishness receive the author's sanction, all who Europeanize or who compromise their racial heritage are scorned.

For Thackeray, the conservative English clubman, all this is very naturally nonsense and he takes a fall out of Sidonia and his pan-Judaism in his parody *Codlingsby*. On the whole, the parody—with its jeweled jews-harps, its narghiles lit with banknotes of large denominations, its climax in Sidonia's remark, "Even the Pope at Rome is one of us"—is apt. Behind it, of course, was the simple-minded, confident class snobbery always characteristic of Thackeray. Jews were merely no gentlemen; indeed, they were the very essence of the No-gentleman, of the Anti-gentleman. Sometimes they are credited with a certain crude generosity, as in *The Newcomes,* but more often they are the comic foils of the gentlemanly tradition. If they are wealthy they are ridiculous, like little Miss Swartz in *Vanity Fair*. Contrast this with Bulwer-Lytton who, in *My Novel,* sees the newly-arrived Jew as a vicious and grasping being, and gives voice to the simple class hatred which comes to be the dominant feeling about the Jew of the modern Gentile monied classes, jealous of the aliens who sought to share in their power and their social prestige.

George Eliot's *Daniel Deronda,* the last though certainly not the best novel of a novelist who in some ways stands very close to our own time, enshrined the Jew in what has become the most satisfactory (to Jews) Jewish counter-myth. Deronda is the foster-child of Sir Hugo Mallinger. Of exceptional beauty—"seraphic" indeed—and of great intellectual aptness and considerable knowledge, he is something of a dilettante, uncertain of his life, searching for an ideal. But for all his dilettantism, he has great moral force and it is this perhaps, even more than his beauty and charm, that makes him attractive to women. Many adore him, and Gwendolen, the heroine of the other side of the book (which is composed of two intersecting stories), makes him her conscience. As the boy grows, he develops all the burning nostalgic passion which, in place of blood or money lust, now so often comes to characterize the Jew in fiction. He becomes, too, not quite a person of this world; the implication is that the prophetic touch is on him—"fancy finding that he had a tailor's bill and used boothooks like our brothers."

The career of Daniel toward the discovery and fulfillment of his Judaism leads him to confront many aspects of it. His old (and rather admirably drawn) mother, who had tried to keep him from knowledge of his heritage, sits bitterly in her darkened foreign apartment and cries out against the unfeeling restraint which Judaism puts upon its women. She had become famous as a singer, but only after a fierce and sorrowful struggle against Jewish mores. "How could I know," she cries,

that you would love what I hated,—love to be a Jew! . . . My father only thought of fettering me into obedience. . . . I was to feel awe for the bit of parchment in the *mezuzah* over the door; to dread lest a bit of butter should touch meat; to think it beautiful that men should bind *tephillin* on them and women not . . . to love the long prayers in the ugly synagogue, and the howling and the gabbling, and the dreadful fasts, and my father's endless discoursing about our People. . . . I cared for the wide world and all I could represent in it. I hated living under the shadow of my father's strictness. Teaching, teaching for everlasting —"this you must be"—"that you must be." . . . I wanted to live a large life, with freedom to do what everyone else did, and be carried along in the current, not obliged to care. . . .

Daniel meets the Cohens, vulgar, money-grubbing, but warm-hearted and unaffected; Mordecai, the consumptive watchmaker, Spinozistic in his sweet asceticism, learned in Jewish lore, burning with nationalistic zeal; and Mirah, the perfect Jewish woman, whom Daniel marries. These people are, it is clear, largely mythical. That is, they are, on the whole, embodied abstract traits rather than individuals; moreover, the traits are not pure but exaggerated. But chiefly they are mythical because they are made to represent the Jewish people, and the Jewish people, even in the England of Eliot's day, were more diverse and less unanimously noble than Eliot pictured them. But undeniably George Eliot's Jews have a certain credibility too; it does not too much strain the imagination to say, "Jews are like that," and Jews as well as Gentiles have found some reality in them. This is because they have at least this much truth, that there are certainly some Jews who have similar traits in some degree. Also it may be because for the first time in English literature Jews are visualized not merely in the aspects in which they come in contact with Gentiles and the Gentile world, but in terms of their own life and their own problems. There is a genuine, inner, intimate quality about much of *Daniel Deronda,* which almost as much as its flattery makes it acceptable to the Jews themselves, and a model for later Jewish writers.

Indeed, George Eliot hit on a pattern which seems almost inescapable in doctrinaire writing about Jews. She is the first to deal with the problem of assimilation, and she wrote about Zionism at a time when it was still scarcely thought of in England, even as a chimerical notion.

When Daniel dedicates his life to Zionism, one has almost exactly the plot and machinery of Ludwig Lewisohn's *The Island Within* or of Milton Waldman's *The Disinherited.* From these novels, one sees how decidedly George Eliot is the originator of the modern myths which the Jews have constructed to present themselves, best foot foremost, to the world; she gave them their direction, a direction which Amy Levy, in her *Reuben Sachs* (1888), was probably the first to follow.

It is, therefore, with *Daniel Deronda* that this essay will conclude. It must remain for the reader to trace the Jewish myths to their further developments, through Meredith's portrait, in *The Tragic Comedians,* of the romantic Jewish radical—Lasalle, model for the modern myth of the Jewish radical, but wrapped close in the mantle of Sidonia and Deronda—through James Joyce's Leopold Bloom or Marcel Proust's Swann, to see how in our own day the Jew remains a myth, changing with the changing times, persisting always as a type and a symbol, useful to Jew or to Gentile, to one social force or another.

The question may be asked: What importance has an account of

material which is confessedly merely mythological? The importance
to the historian, the psychologist, the sociologist, the political thinker
is obvious. But to one interested chiefly in literature, the answer is
not so plain. However, one answer may be found in almost any
modern Jewish novel by a Jew. When the Jew, at the Emancipation,
entered into the life of the Western world, he found the myths
awaiting him. Sometimes he fought them, sometimes he accepted
them to his own advantage, often he went off and contemplated
them in great confusion of mind. When he came to write of himself he was not able to free himself from them. Some one of them
had become a Doppelgänger of his, moving by the side of the real
person we suppose he must be. And the task which every Jewish
novel presents to the critical reader—and the serious writer—is that
of disentangling what is mythical from what is actual. And that
task is difficult, for in the mythical there is usually, of course, a little
of what is true.

Carlyle

[A review of *Carlyle* by Emery Neff. *The Modern Quarterly*, Summer 1932]

MR. NEFF'S *Carlyle* has all the intrinsic virtues of the best tradition of scholarly biography. He treats the confused and disputed incidents of Carlyle's life with cool and revealing insight, and he builds up the background of the intellectual and social forces which shaped Carlyle's thought with the same deep knowledge of the nineteenth century which distinguished his earlier study, *Carlyle and Mill*. But over and above these intrinsic virtues, Mr. Neff's book has the extrinsic virtue of being peculiarly relevant to our period.

Today, when so many of our middle-class intellectuals are swinging left, it is well to remember that the position of the bourgeois intellectual in any proletarian movement has always been an anomalous and precarious one. However sincere he may be, the mind of the intellectual is so apt to be overlaid with conflicting values that it is impossible for him to be sure of his position; having so many values, he is likely to betray one to defend others. In this dilemma the recognition of his own training and nature can be his only safeguard against confusion and eventual missteps.

It is, therefore, a particularly appropriate moment for an analysis, such as this of Mr. Neff's, of the career of a man, a bourgeois intellectual, who, having begun as a radical, moved to the position of apologist for the very order he had attacked. In 1845 Engels wrote of Carlyle: "He, more than any other British bourgeois, understands

the prevailing social anarchy and demands the organization of labour. I hope that Carlyle, once he has entered the right path, may
be able to follow it to the end." But in 1892 he wrote, retrospectively:
"The February revolution transformed Carlyle into a thoroughgoing
reactionary. His righteous indignation against the philistines was
converted into a sour and philistine peevishness against the historical
tidal wave which washed him ashore and left him marooned."[1]

In his *Protestant Ethic and the Spirit of Capitalism,* Max Weber
has classically explained the thesis that the Protestant ethic was the
basis for the capitalist spirit. And although this thesis has been
somewhat qualified since the appearance of Weber's work, it cannot
be qualified below the point that the Protestant ethic at least gave to
capitalism a required rationalization and bracing. And certainly in
Carlyle's metamorphosis from radical to capitalist apologist, the influence of Protestant ideology is clearly apparent.

As a young man Carlyle thought that he had broken with Protes-
tantism. Eighteenth-century historical skepticism and mechanistic
cosmology had given him the "grave prohibitive doubts" which kept
him from the ministry. Yet it was with great relief that he later
found he could assert the validity of Christian ethics without
Christian "evidences." By Christian ethics, of course, he meant
Protestant ethics and, more specifically, Calvinist ethics. The transcendental content of *Sartor Resartus* has perhaps been overestimated; it exists largely as a dialectical bridge to the firm old ground
of Calvinism.

Carlyle was fevered with doubt and loneliness. His doubt was
the counterpart of the orthodox Calvinist's struggle with the fear
of damnation; his loneliness was the old Calvinistic loneliness of the
individual with God which no human agency could relieve. If
Carlyle found surcease in the transcendental denial of time and
space and in the assertion of the existence of the universe in the
mind of God, he came to this knowledge by the Calvinist formula:
we know these things, he tells us, because without knowing them

[1] The quotations from Marx and Engels in this review are taken from Ryazanov's
notes to his edition of the *Communist Manifesto,* pp. 203–206.

we should fall into despair and be unable to live. Just so did Calvinism lay it as a command upon its communicants that, though
they cannot know beforehand whether they be saved or damned,
they must assume the gift of grace. Just as Calvinism condemned
the self-consciousness that led to despair, so Carlyle inveighed
against the self-conscious, cogitating man, finding the leaders of
the French Revolution dangerous and the Revolution itself de-
generate when they became "conscious." Just as Calvinism recommended silence and hard work as means of surcease from doubt
and fear, so did Carlyle recommend them. Between the self-denying
thrift of (the Calvinist-trained) Benjamin Franklin and the "Lower
your denominator" of Carlyle, there is the difference of a material
mind at its simplest and a mystical mind at its subtlest, but the basis
of thought is the same in each.

Carlyle's radicalism received philosophical justification from transcendentalism. Transcendentalism destroyed the world-as-machine
for him, destroyed the necessity of evil which had been part of the
world-as-machine, and conceived the world as organic, changeable,
a thing not even of matter but of thought. Of a machine one had to
say, *Laissez faire,* but one could nourish the organic tree of life. But
from Calvinism Carlyle drew that specific ideology which, applied
to his radicalism, brought it full circle to reaction. His "hero" is, of
course, the man who has been granted "grace"; obedience to him
is obedience to the will of God. Hobbes was no better apologist for
the divinity of kings and a much less moving one. Carlyle's sharp
division of men into "sheep and goats, rulers and ruled, aristocrats
and canaille, gentlemen and fools" is but the extension of the categories of the saved and the damned and is quite as irrevocable. And
from Calvinism comes the notion of strict and rigid social control
which that sect, for all its individualism in religion, had put into
practice.

No one can gainsay the justice of Carlyle's fierce and effective
attack upon the liberal Whiggism of his day. It was individualism
at its most anarchic, and all the fair face of Mill's *Liberty* cannot
make beautiful the ugly chaos. The ideology with which Carlyle

combated it is in large part the ideology with which we today combat it. The realization of the failure of democracy, the recognition of the need to organize labor, to organize industry—these are the concepts which made Engels and Marx for a time so lenient to Tory opposition to the industrial liberals and especially lenient to Carlyle. But it is, for the present-day student, a little surprising that they could not see whither he must inevitably be led. The furious onslaught of his *Latter-Day Pamphlets* is no longer the attempt to save the poor from the anarchy of industrialism. In these pamphlets, Carlyle, attacking democracy, lumps the masses with the industrialists in his denunciations, though the masses were not yet enfranchised. They are apes and dogs; there is no work for them, but he suspects that they do not want to work and he suggests flogging and shooting as the remedy for this possible refusal. His anger now is not at the existence of misery but of anomaly: that, while starvation stalks the whites of Ireland and England, there is concern for the Negroes; that while thousands live in the noisome dark, well-lighted prisons are being built. Now he turns for leadership to the once-hated landed aristocracy, chivalrous, beautiful, bold; to the monied aristocracy, still a little uncouth but already "aristos." Now he longs for a mighty king and no parliaments, and now, more arrogant than Kipling, asserts the white man's *right* and calls for a far-flung imperialism. Now the sophistications of "right" and "might" with which *Sartor* had subtly played simplify themselves.

One begins to understand the pertinence (unconscious perhaps to Carlyle) of the virtues he had preached, of self-denial, obedience, unconsciousness, labor for labor's sake; under the light of the doctrine of the morality of might, of imperialism, of the inferiority of subject races, they become very clearly the capitalistic virtues.

Engels, who admitted Carlyle's influence, who used Carlyle's comparison between the condition of the workers in 1845 and the condition of the serfs in 1145 and who almost certainly took from him the passage in the *Manifesto* which relates to the inhuman relation between worker and employer, saw the force which made of a great and humane genius one of the exponents of oppression. That force was a preoccupation with religious values which kept Carlyle from looking realistically at events; which kept him from understanding that democracy was a necessary transitional phase and that its alternative was not aristocratic dictatorship; which kept him from understanding that "mammonism" was the inevitable result of private property and could not be banished by sermons.

It is a far cry from Ecclefechan to Rome, but today, as Mr. Neff tells us, Carlyle is one of the gods of the Fascist pantheon.

The Coleridge Letters

[A review of *Unpublished Letters of Samuel Taylor Coleridge*, edited by Earl Leslie Griggs. *The Nation*, December 27, 1933]

THE present state of European politics makes any monument to Coleridge deeply relevant. "The name of Coleridge," wrote John Stuart Mill, "is . . . likely to become symbolical of more important things, in proportion as the inward workings of the age manifest themselves more and more in outward facts." In so far as the inward workings of the age have manifested themselves in fascism, Mill's prediction has come true. Not that all of fascism is Coleridge, nor that all of Coleridge's politics is fascism. But Coleridge was the chief transmitter to the English-speaking world of the idealistic, absolutistic, and anti-materialistic philosophy which fascism, both in Italy and Germany, is now using to rationalize its fight against socialism. Recent essays have reminded us of the close affinity between Carlyle and Hitler, and Carlyle's works, now very popular in Italy, have afforded Mussolini a source for his phrases of contempt for the "swinishness" of material comfort. But though Carlyle, by reason of his hero-melodrama, is closer than Coleridge to the actualities of fascism, he was, for all his sneers at his master, Coleridge's disciple.

However, few of the letters included in the present edition throw much light on Coleridge's political and philosophical thought. The twenty-two long letters in which Coleridge explained his system to C. A. Tulk have been unfortunately relegated by Professor Griggs to a future separate volume. Of the many letters printed almost all have a personal interest. They do not contain material which changes the outline of Coleridge's life as it has been known—many of them have been seen and quoted by biographers, some have been printed before but only in part, or in garbled versions, or in obscure periodicals—but they fill that outline with enlightening detail.

Coleridge has an almost legendary place as the genius who failed. The judgment of failure was, of course, first Coleridge's own. He passed that judgment at least as early as his twenty-ninth year and held it for the thirty-three remaining years of his life. His friends and his public took it, perhaps, too literally. They seem to have forgotten that the standard of success which Coleridge set up was one that few mortals could have measured up to. But Coleridge believed himself a failure, and these volumes of letters are his own record and explanation of his defeat.

Although sometimes he berates himself for moral weakness, Coleridge is most inclined to place his failure at the door of his unhappy marriage and of his ill-health. The letters in this edition throw new and sharp light on his relations with his wife. He seems to have been always tender of her welfare; in the earlier letters he tries with touching delicacy to point out her faults and have her mend them. But he had married Sara Fricker out of misconceived duty, and her dull virtues did not compensate for the loving comprehension which he needed and which her intellectual and emotional mediocrity could not give him. His eventual feelings about her are expressed to his friends with brutal frankness. As for his ill-health, his verbose preoccupation with it (he had memorized Blancard's Latin Medical Dictionary in his youth) does not make it any the less real. The record of the autopsy performed on him shows that he was no hypochondriac, and though neurosis seems to have aggravated his physical ailments and to have been more responsible than they for the opium habit, his physical suffering must have been nearly as terrible as he represented it.

But there is more to the story of Coleridge's self-declared failure than this. It would be cruel to set aside his explanations as mere rationalizing, but marriage and health do not tell everything. The manner in which people regarded Coleridge tends to obscure certain larger possibilities of explanation of his life. He was treated as something between a child and a holy man. Predatory society went out of its way for him; at least two landlords offered him free lodging. The paternal benefactions of his friends are well known. One biographer has written of him as being like Wordsworth's Lucy Gray, a little child, "not far from home, but she hath lost her way." But Coleridge was not merely a blessed incompetent. He was a reservoir of all the culture of past Europe and an assiduous observer of contemporary Europe; his fate was bound up in its fate. The turmoil of events, the new forces let loose by the Industrial Revolution, called him to bring his powers to bear on them. The world of his time demanded a comprehensive and philosophic grasp.

Coleridge often referred to philosophy as a last resort to which he could retreat when his afflictions had robbed him of his "shaping power of Imagination." But before he had thought in this way of philosophy he had written, "I hope Philosophy and Poetry will not neutralize each other, and leave me an inert mass." The crippling conflict of poetry and philosophy has become a commonplace in the discussion of Coleridge. But its implications are great. It is as though Coleridge were declaring that the modern world needed something else than poetry, that it needed a setting in order before poetry could flourish. He himself in some part sacrificed his poetic talent to the achievement of that order.

One may perhaps ascribe to his neurotic inability to order his own life those elements of religious authoritarianism in his own conception of society which, when developed, lead to fascism. Yet even Mill was able to pray that all enemies of liberalism would be as Coleridge, and to point out that the perfect state would be founded on a combination of the ideas of Bentham and Coleridge—democracy and the centralized state, material well-being and cultural development, individual freedom and corporate loyalty.

The Autonomy
of the Literary Work[1]

[A review of *Academic Illusions* by Martin
Schütze. *The Modern Monthly*, January 1934]

A FEW months ago, in the *The Saturday Review*, Mr. I. A.
Richards wrote: "The worst threat to the world's critical
standards comes just now from the universities." He
claimed, however, for a large academic minority the perception of
the evil situation. Of this group Professor Schütze is one of the
most militant, learned and, within limits, most cogent; were his
book not so ruthlessly jargonistic one might claim more for it as an
instrument toward university reform. The aim of the book is the
projection of a new type of graduate training for the teacher of
literature; it proceeds, by analysis of the intellectual currents which
have produced the present university attitudes to literature, to define
an attitude to which the reformed schools should conform.

Professor Schütze agrees with Mr. Richards' recent article that
the source of the university's failure with literature lies in its
denial of the autonomy and validity of the poetic function. Two
tendencies have expressed this denial: what Professor Schütze calls
"factualism" (the study of literature by the fact-accumulating sciences) and dialectic-absolutism (in this connection the translation of
literature into philosophic generalities or the subsumption of spe-

---

1 Title supplied by the editor of this volume.

cific works of literature under categories that are made to appear absolute).

We must admit the justice of Professor Schütze's strictures on the general results of these two approaches to art. Art is, of course, more than the exemplification of a cosmic "principle," of a cultural or national "idea." It is more than the attractive statement of a general truth. That literary unperception to which Mr. Richards has reared a monument in *Practical Criticism* was in large created by a philosophy of literary teaching which made everything about a poem important save the poem itself.

But in stating the pre-eminent importance of the study of the formal relations of a work of literature, the success of its "structural idea" as against the general validity of whatever "conceptual idea" it may be forced to contain, Professor Schütze goes too far in reaction. In order to defend the self-sufficient validity of literature, he makes a sharp dichotomy between its function and process and the function and process of philosophy and science. Philosophy and science make general truths, "constants"—i.e. "entities of generalization which persist in the main unchanged in all their essential relation to their environment, no matter what combinations they enter." Literature, on the other hand, makes "integral variables"—responses to environment of a single "total personality"; the validity of these depends not on their absolute truth, but on the successful relation of the parts of the formulation of the response to the whole of the response. To attempt to generalize from the response of a personality to an event or complex of events is to betray the work of response. For the artist to attempt to respond with a concept and not with his personality is fatal to his work.

Now there is no doubt that if a critic says of a poem—say, Hopkins' beautiful "Spring and Fall: to a young child"—that its importance lies in its "idea" and that this idea is that "dissolution awaits every human life and that this is a very saddening thing," he is obviously talking about a thousand poems and betraying this particular one. If it is the essential fact about a hundred proletarian novels that they show the misery of the working class, their growing consciousness, their militant struggle and finally their victory, there are then ninety-nine novels too many. The fact is, of course, that the novels, if they have any validity, show much more than this, and in the *more* lies what makes each novel important. That *more* is the response of the "total personalities" of the author and of the character of each novel. So much of Professor Schütze's thesis is true.

But in denying that literature may validly use concepts because of its nature, Professor Schütze makes several confusions. First, he does not see that, though literature does not *discover* concepts or truths, it may *use* them. He forgets that in addition to the components of the "total personality" which he gives (will, memory, imagination, intuition, etc.) a concept may also be an integral part of total personality. Again, he forgets that concepts may be facts of the environment to which the artist responds, as, for example, social and economic concepts are inescapable facts of environment for the modern novelist. He forgets too that in ethical situations—which are the inevitable material of novels and plays if not poems—there is a close interaction of personality and concept. The final appeal is indeed, as Dewey says, to the ethical agent himself—that is, to his personality. "What does *he* really think the desirable end? What makes the supreme appeal to him? What sort of an agent, of a person, shall he be? This is the question finally at stake in any genuine moral situation."[2] But the person establishes his kind or quality by choosing among concepts.

In a passage in which he defends Thomas Mann's *Buddenbrooks* against the charge that it is a deficient book because it lacks an "idea" to make "necessary" the decay of the family, Professor Schütze exposes what is probably the root of his confusion. He says that the novel does not need "an a priori, absolute, ideological necessity." The words "a priori" and "absolute" are the fatal words of exposure. Mann indeed might well have explained the decay of the Buddenbrooks family by a concept; such an explanation would, of course, be no substitute for the brilliance of the book's insight but it might have given it an even greater trenchancy and it would

---

[2] Dewey and Tufts, *Ethics*, p. 210.

not of necessity have harmed it. But that explanation would not necessarily have been an *a priori* or *absolute* one. Perhaps it would have been the observation of the artist that the contradictions of bourgeois culture tend to attack the psychical health of its members. This would be neither a priori nor absolute. It would seem that Professor Schütze in attacking the bases of dialectical absolutism comes to believe that all generalizations are inevitably a priori and absolute. Mann, the artist, is clearer than Professor Schütze. Mann, as a matter of fact, does use a concept to explain familial and cultural decay, one that I believe inadequate—an analogical, biological theory. But at least Mann recognizes what Professor Schütze does not—that "total personality" responds within the iron limits of laws and necessities, that these are formulable and that the artist must often use these formulations to achieve the completeness of his response to the environment.

Politics and the Liberal

[A review of *Goldsworthy Lowes Dickinson* by
E. M. Forster. *The Nation*, July 4, 1934]

IN the epilogue to his life of his friend, Mr. Forster allows
Mephistophcles to question whether Dickinson merits the dignity of a biography. And when Mr. Forster has conceded that
perhaps Dickinson was neither a pre-eminent writer nor a practically effective man, he proposes to justify his book by demonstrating the admirable quality of Dickinson's personality. The refinement and charm of that personality no one will deny; but the
justification of Mr. Forster's book rests on something firmer and
broader—on Dickinson's being representative of a temper of the
human mind and the impasse which that temper has reached.

What that temper and its impasse are may best be stated by quoting from a letter which Dickinson wrote about his *A Modern Symposium*. Today that polite series of speeches by upper-class political
leaders and theorists of all beliefs from Tory to Anarchist is, with its
disregard of classes and interests, a scene from another world. But
even in 1905 it seemed remote from reality and Dickinson felt
called upon to explain his purpose:

. . . practical politics involves fighting, and the object of such a book
as mine, as it was Plato's long ago, is to raise the mind above the fighting attitude. There lies here obscurely the great problem of the relation
of ideals to passion and interests which I do not seem able clearly to
formulate.

This confusion never, apparently, left Dickinson. In terms of his
personal life it is easy enough to see how it arose. At Cambridge

he was attracted to mysticism and studied Plotinus. The high-minded, Ruskinian "social view" of the 1880's penetrated the mysticism; he turned to Plato, who, with Shelley and Goethe, formed his youthful views and influenced him throughout life. The three poets fostered in him a finely humanistic political attitude, but one whose overtones of mysticism provided him with his belief in "ideals"—as divorced from "passion and interests." Throughout his life he seems to have maintained a half-belief that truth was absolute and could be apprehended whole.

The essentially religious culture of unorthodox mysticism which was so strong in England, and America, in the nineteenth century, and of which Plato, Shelley, and Goethe were so integral a part, the culture which Matthew Arnold well exemplifies with his "disinterestedness," his "best self," his turning from economic reality, was eventually Dickinson's intellectual undoing. Not his alone, however, for he represented the fate of a large section of the intellectual class. The whole basis of the liberal-humanitarianism of the intellectuals of his generation was the divorce it made between "ideals" and "passion and interests." But since no such divorce exists in politics, "to raise the mind above the fighting attitude" was not to give the minds of this generation a higher function but to betray these minds into becoming the tools of the interests they truly hated.

Politically, Dickinson began as a Carlylean Tory, but he moved left through the years to become a Socialist, apparently of the *Modern Symposium* variety. However, his only strong political feeling was for the League of Nations. Never a pacifist—he was almost jingo during the Boer War, and but for his age he would have enlisted in 1914—he was nevertheless moved by the spectacle of the World War to a consuming hatred of all war. Before he retired to the melancholy silence of a peaceful old age he completed his study of pre-war diplomacy, *International Anarchy*. "Anarchy"—so vague a concept—was to him the cause of the great slaughter, and the only hope was "organization." The economic causes of the diplomatic anarchy he did not see or did not stress; the League of Nations—which he had been urging and whose name he is said to have coined—he conceived to be the only bulwark of the world against a recurrence of war.

The League was an "ideal" set against passions and interests. But history moved his "ideal" aside—disclosing the ugly passions and interests which it hid. The inevitable failure of the League ideal was the defeat of Dickinson and of the whole attitude that was merely liberal-humanitarian. Dickinson and the other men who held it were men of good-will whose remoteness from reality, interests, and forces allowed them to serve unwittingly the predatory and the evil-willed.

Mr. Forster has so understandingly portrayed this attitude and the temper of the middle-class mind that embraces it because they are largely his own. As a novelist, however, he has had the advantage of his political colleagues. Although the future does not belong to his kind of novel, ethically based on individual "understanding" and "tolerance," in personal life these virtues are still real. In political life, however, history has proved them to be catchwords that becloud reality in the service of the worst "passion and interests."

Willa Cather

[*The New Republic*, February 10, 1937]

IN 1922 Willa Cather wrote an essay called "The Novel Démeublé" in which she pleaded for a movement to throw the
"furniture" out of the novel—to get rid, that is, of all the
social fact that Balzac and other realists had felt to be so necessary
for the understanding of modern character. "Are the banking system and the Stock Exchange worth being written about at all?"
Miss Cather asked, and she replied that they were not. Among
the things which had no "proper place in imaginative art"—because
they cluttered the scene and prevented the free play of the emotions
—Miss Cather spoke of the factory and the whole realm of "physical
sensations." Obviously, this essay was the rationale of a method
which Miss Cather had partly anticipated in her early novels and
which she fully developed a decade later in *Shadows on the Rock*.
And it is no less obvious that this technical method is not merely a
literary manner but the expression of a point of view toward which
Miss Cather had always been moving—with results that, to many
of her readers, can only indicate the subtle failure of her admirable
talent.

If we say that Miss Cather has gone down to defeat before the
actualities of American life we put her in such interesting company
that the indictment is no very terrible one. For a history of American literature must be, in Whitman's phrase, a series of "vivas for
those who have failed." In our literature there are perhaps fewer

completely satisfying books and certainly fewer integrated careers than there are interesting canons of work and significant life stories. Something in American life seems to prevent the perfection of success while it produces a fascinating kind of search or struggle, usually unavailing, which we may observe again and again in the collected works and in the biographies of our writers.

In this recurrent but heroic defeat, the life of the American writer parallels the life of the American pioneer. The historian of frontier literature, Professor Hazard, has pointed out that Cooper's very first presentation of Deerslayer, the type of all pioneers, shows him a nearly broken old man threatened with jail for shooting a deer, a pitiful figure overwhelmed by the tides of commerce and speculation. In short, to a keen observer, the pioneer's defeat was apparent even in 1823. The subsequent decades that opened fresh frontiers did not change the outcome of the struggle. Ahead of the pioneer there are always the fields of new promise, with him are the years of heartbreaking effort, behind him are the men who profit by his toil and his hope. Miss Cather's whole body of work is the attempt to accommodate and assimilate her perception of the pioneer's failure. Reared on a Nebraska farm, she saw the personal and cultural defeat at first hand. Her forebears had marched westward to the new horizons; her own work is a march back toward the spiritual East—toward all that is the very antithesis of the pioneer individualism and innovation, toward authority and permanence, toward Rome itself.

The pioneer, as seen by a sophisticated intelligence like Miss Cather's, stands in double jeopardy: he faces both the danger of failure and the danger of success. "A pioneer . . . should be able to enjoy the idea of things more than the things themselves," Miss Cather says; disaster comes when an idea becomes an actuality. From *O Pioneers!* to *The Professor's House,* Miss Cather's novels portray the results of the pioneer's defeat, both in the thwarted pettiness to which he is condemned by his material failures and in the callous insensitivity produced by his material success. "The world is little, people are little, human life is little," says Thea

Kronborg's derelict music teacher in *The Song of the Lark*. "There is only one big thing—desire." When there is no longer the opportunity for effective desire, the pioneer is doomed. But already in Miss Cather's Nebraska youth the opportunities for effective desire had largely been removed: the frontier had been closed.

A Lost Lady, Miss Cather's most explicit treatment of the passing of the old order, is the central work of her career. Far from being the delicate minor work it is so often called, it is probably her most muscular book, for it derives power from the grandeur of its theme. Miss Cather shares the American belief in the tonic moral quality of the pioneer's life; with the passing of the frontier she conceives that a great source of fortitude has been lost. Depending on a very exact manipulation of symbols, the point of *A Lost Lady* (reminiscent of Henry James's *The Sacred Fount*) is that the delicacy and charm of Marian Forrester spring not from herself but from the moral strength of her pioneer husband. Heavy, slow, not intelligent, Forrester is one of those men who, in his own words, "dreamed the railroads across the mountains." He shares the knightly virtues which Miss Cather unquestioningly ascribes to the early settlers; "impractical to the point of magnificence," he is one of those who could "conquer but not hold." He is defeated by the men of the new money interests who "never risked anything"—and the perdition of the lost lady proceeds in the degree that she withdraws from her husband in favor of one of the sordid new men, until she finds her final degradation in the arms of an upstart vulgarian.

But though the best of the pioneer ideal is defeated by alien forces, the ideal itself, Miss Cather sees, is really an insufficient one. In her first considerable novel, *O Pioneers!* she already wrote in an elegiac mood and with the sense that the old ideal was not enough. Alexandra Bergson, with her warm simplicity, her resourcefulness and shrewd courage, is the essence of the pioneering virtues, but she is distinguished above her neighbors because she feels that, if she is to work at all, she must believe that the world is wider than her cornfields. Her pride is not that she has triumphed over the soil but that she has made her youngest brother "a personality apart from the soil." The pioneer, having reached his goal at the horizons of the earth, must look to the horizons of the spirit.

The disappearance of the old frontier left Miss Cather with a heritage of the virtues in which she had been bred but with the necessity of finding a new object for them. Looking for the new frontier, she found it in the mind. From the world of failure which she portrayed so savagely in *A Wagner Matinee* and *The Sculptor's Funeral*, and from the world of fat prosperity of *One of Ours*, she could flee to the world of art. For in art one may desire illimitably. And if, conceivably, one may fail—Miss Cather's artists never do— it is still only as an artist that one may be the eternal pioneer, concerned always with "the idea of things." Thea Kronborg, of the breed of Alexandra Bergson, turns all the old energy, bogged down in mediocrity, toward music. Miss Cather rhapsodizes for her: "O eagle of eagles! Endeavor, achievement, desire, glorious striving of human art."

But art is not the only, or a sufficient, salvation from the débâcle of pioneer culture. For some vestige of the old striving after new worlds which cannot be gratified seems to spread a poison through the American soul, making it thin and unsubstantial, unable to find peace and solidity. A foreigner says to Claude Wheeler of *One of Ours*, "You Americans are always looking for something outside yourselves to warm you up, and it is no way to do. In old countries, where not very much can happen to us, we know that, and we learn to make the most of things." And with the artists, Miss Cather puts those gentle spirits who have learned to make the most of things—Neighbor Rosicky, Augusta and, pre-eminently, My Antonia. Momentarily betrayed by the later developments of the frontier, Antonia at last fulfills herself in child-bearing and a busy household, expressing her "relish for life, not over-delicate but invigorating."

Indeed, "making the most of things" becomes even more important to Miss Cather than the eternal striving of art. For, she implies, in our civilization even the best ideals are bound to corruption. *The Professor's House* is the novel in which she brings the failure of the pioneer spirit into the wider field of American life. Lame as it is, it epitomizes as well as any novel of our time the disgust with life which so many sensitive Americans feel, which makes them dream of their pre-adolescent integration and innocent community with nature, speculate on the "release from effort" and the "eternal solitude" of death, and eventually reconcile themselves to a life "without delight." Three stories of betrayal are interwoven in this novel: the success of Professor St. Peter's history of the Spanish explorers which tears him away from the frontier of his uncomfortable and ugly old study to set him up in an elegant but stifling new home; the sale to a foreign collector of the dead Tom Outland's Indian relics which had made his spiritual heritage; and the commercialization of Outland's scientific discovery with its subsequent corruption of the Professor's charming family. With all of life contaminated by the rotting of admirable desires, only Augusta, the unquesting and unquestioning German Catholic seamstress, stands secure and sound.

Not the pioneering philosophy alone, but the whole poetic romanticism of the nineteenth century had been suffused by the belief that the struggle rather than the prize was admirable, that a man's reach should exceed his grasp, or what's a heaven for? Having seen the insufficiency of this philosophy Miss Cather must find another in which the goal shall be more than the search. She finds it, expectably enough, in religion. The Catholicism to which she turns is a Catholicism of culture, not of doctrine. The ideal of unremitting search, it may be said, is essentially a Protestant notion; Catholic thought tends to repudiate the ineluctable and to seek the sharply refined. The quest for Moby Dick, that dangerous beast, is Protestant; the Catholic tradition selects what it can make immediate and tangible in symbol and Miss Cather turns to the way of life that "makes the most of things," to the old settled cultures. She attaches a mystical significance to the ritual of the ordered life, to the niceties of cookery, to the supernal virtues of *things* themselves—sherry, or lettuce, or "these coppers, big and little, these brooms and clouts and brushes" which are the tools for making life itself. And with a religious ideal one may safely be a pioneer. The two priests of *Death Comes for the Archbishop* are pioneers; they happen to be successful in their enterprise, but they could not have been frustrated, Miss Cather implies, because the worth of their goal is indisputable.

From the first of her novels the Church had occupied a special and gracious place in Willa Cather's mind. She now thinks with increasing eloquence of its permanence and certainty and of "the universal human yearning for something permanent, enduring, without shadow of change." The Rock becomes her often repeated symbol: "the rock, when one comes to think of it, was the utmost expression of human need." For the Church seems to offer the possibility of satisfying that appealing definition of human happiness which Miss Cather had made as far back as *My Antonia*—"to be dissolved in something complete and great," "to become a part of something entire, whether it is sun and air, goodness and knowledge. . . ."

It is toward that dissolvement that Miss Cather is always striving. She achieves it with the "sun and air"—and perhaps few modern writers have been so successful with landscape. She can find it in goodness and in society—but only if they have the feudal constriction of the old Quebec of *Shadows on the Rock*. Nothing in modern life, no possibility, no hope, offers it to her. She conceives, as she says in the prefatory note to her volume of essays, *Not Under Forty*, that the world "broke in two in 1922 or thereabouts" and she numbers herself among the "backward," unaware that even so self-conscious and defiant a rejection of her own time must make her talent increasingly irrelevant and tangential—for any time.

"The early pioneer was an individualist and a seeker after the undiscovered," says F. J. Turner, "but he did not understand the richness and complexity of life as a whole." Though Miss Cather in all her work has recognized this lack of understanding of complexity and wholeness, and has attempted to transcend it, she ends, ironically enough, in a fancier but no less restricted provincialism than the one she sought to escape. For the "spirituality" of Miss

Cather's latest books consists chiefly of an irritated exclusion of those elements of modern life with which she will not cope. The particular affirmation of the verities which Miss Cather makes requires that the "furniture" be thrown out, that the social and political facts be disregarded; the spiritual life cannot support the intrusion of all the facts the mind can supply. The unspeakable Joubert, the extreme type of the verity-seeker, says in one of his *pensées:* " 'I'm hungry, I'm cold, help me!' Here is material for a good deed but not for a good work of art." Miss Cather, too, is irked by the intrusion of "physical sensations" in the novel.

Miss Cather's later books are pervaded by the air of a brooding ancient wisdom, but if we examine her mystical concern with pots and pans, it does not seem much more than an oblique defense of gentility or very far from the gaudy domesticity of bourgeois accumulation glorified in *The Woman's Home Companion*. And with it goes a culture-snobbery and even a caste-snobbery. The Willa Cather of the older days shared the old racial democracy of the West. It is strange to find the Willa Cather of the present talking about "the adopted Americans," the young man of German, Jewish or Scandinavian descent who can never appreciate Sarah Orne Jewett and for whom American English can never be more than a means of communicating ideas: "It is surface speech: he clicks the words out as a bank clerk clicks out silver when you ask for change. For him the language has no emotional roots." This is indeed the gentility of Katherine Fullerton Gerould, and in large part the result, one suspects, of what Parrington calls "the inferiority complex of the frontier mind before the old and established."

Yet the place to look for the full implications of a writer's philosophy is in the aesthetic of his work. *Lucy Gayheart* shows to the full the effect of Miss Cather's point of view. It has always been a personal failure of her talent that prevented her from involving her people in truly dramatic relations with each other. (Her women, for example, always stand in the mother or daughter relation to men; they are never truly lovers.) But at least once upon a time her people were involved in a dramatic relation with themselves or with their environments, whereas now *Lucy Gayheart* has not even this involvement. Environment does not exist, fate springs from nothing save chance; the characters are unattached to anything save their dreams. The novel has been *démeublé* indeed; but life without its furniture is strangely bare.

Marxism in Limbo

[A review of *Europa in Limbo* by Robert Briffault.
Partisan Review, 1937]

ALTHOUGH *Europa,* Robert Briffault's first novel, was admired and even "hailed," there were relatively few illusions about its literary merit. Even its admirers conceded
that Mr. Briffault, considered purely as a novelist, was not gifted
—that neither his characters, his prose nor his invention exemplified
any of the traditional virtues of the novel. To this a few critics
(Mr. Forsythe,[1] Mr. Briffault) had an answer ready, for they had
previously demonstrated that the novel form was the product of
the "shabby bourgeois mind" and an "outworn and artificial" convention: so that in the circles which account Mr. Forsythe the Marxian
Swift, Mr. Briffault's lack of literary feeling was taken to show
that he had transcended the bourgeois shams. However, most critical
opinion resisted this refreshing notion and continued to maintain
that Mr. Briffault's lack of talent was a pity, not a virtue, but nevertheless felt that it was more than made up for by great gifts of
intelligence and anger. And now the same judgment is being passed
on *Europa's* sequel, *Europa in Limbo.* It proceeds, I believe, from
the familiar Angelic Fallacy which concludes that when a writer
is, generally speaking, on the side of the angels—Mr. Briffault is a
well-known hater of chaos and injustice—he must for some reason
be admirable and the expressed grounds for his partisanship sound.

[1] Pseudonym of Kyle Crichton, writer and editor. (D.T.)

In this case the fallacy, though naïvely generous, can only indicate that the angelic forces are in a state of desperation or irresponsibility: nothing else could make them accept Mr. Briffault's authoritarian nihilism as intelligence or his spleen as anger.

What are the objects of Mr. Briffault's mind and emotion? Capitalism, of course: but chiefly capitalism as it manifests itself in sex and culture. For many reasons sex is a most useful index and symbol of a society's moral tone; all that matters in its novelistic use is the insight and proportion with which it is employed. Well, as for insight, Mr. Briffault writes about sex rather more frankly than the exposé articles of the old Sunday *American* though with little more perspicuity and with about the same feeling tone. And as for proportion, sex comprises almost the whole of the purview of moral action in both novels.

Indeed, it is difficult not to conclude from Mr. Briffault's books that if we are rightly enlightened about the sadisms of the Russian aristocracy, the perverse indulgences of well-born ladies and the cold promiscuity of female intellectuals, we have a good half of the knowledge necessary for understanding the motives of the Revolution and the chaos of Europe. Of course, the license-and-rape theory of social upheaval—the belief, for example, that the French Revolution was the action of a populace tired of its rulers' adulteries and sick of having its women violated—is well established and cinematically very sound. But it isn't exactly serious. The sexual habits of powerful reactionaries are undoubtedly very bad (though perhaps not wholly of capitalistic growth: see the classics of satire *passim*) but somehow it isn't very serious of Mr. Briffault to give us European Chaos, the Revolution and the Civil War in terms of perversity or excess. We remember that he is trying to educate both his hero and ourselves to revolution. We cannot help wondering if we ought to go to that great trouble to put off the chains of other people's unchastity.

This, then, is Mr. Briffault in the realm of moral and political action; and in the realm of thought he is quite as seminal. His great enemies are defunct ideas. Under his lash every extinct notion of the nineteenth century lies perfectly still. Ruthlessly he banishes our last stubbornly-held illusions about the survival of the fittest, the immutability of human nature, liberal democracy, the idealistic philosophies of reaction, Fabian socialism, the aesthetics of Ruskin.

Supererogation, though dull, is not dangerous. However, as we follow Mr. Briffault leading his Julian Bern through the education of pre-war Europe and now, in the new novel, through Europe in conflict, the feeling forces itself upon us that it is not so much capitalism, as Mr. Briffault thinks, that is the object of his hatred, but rather the human spirit and its whole career. For Julian and his Zena are vocally contemptuous not so much of the clear oppressors and the patent obscurantists. They do hate these, we gather, but their most articulate contempt is rather for some of the more energetically humane and decent examples of humanity. D. H. Lawrence is a controversial figure, so we need not instance the slander of him, but a man's opinions on Mozart, Goethe and Spinoza are an excellent clue to his sensitivity; Mr. Briffault, through the hero and heroine of *Europa in Limbo,* passes on all three. Mozart? The very essence of stuffy bourgeois decadence—makes free people want to open windows. Goethe? An inflated reputation. Spinoza? Our hero does not scruple to borrow where he has cursed: "There is but one liberty," he says, "that is of vital worth: . . . the liberty to think honestly." But Spinoza? A coward and a cheap liberal whose home is now quite aptly a brothel.

All this is, of course, downright vulgarity and expectable from the man who, in his *Breakdown,* advocated a post-revolutionary period of fifty years in which the cultural tradition of Europe would be locked away from the new society. But Mr. Briffault, I take it, is supposed to be a Marxist and this makes the vulgarity doubly culpable. If there is one thing the dialectic of history teaches it is an attitude on cultural matters the very opposite of this splenetic one. But that attitude is difficult and complex, while the attitude of spleen and vulgariy is simple and easy. And dangerous: because it is indiscriminate, irresponsible and ignorant of the humanity it seeks to control; because, rejecting all history, it believes that all good was born with itself. It wants not so much a liberated humanity as a sterilized humanity and it would gladly make a wasteland if it could call the silence peace.

The America
of John Dos Passos

[A review of *U.S.A.* by John Dos Passos. *Partisan Review*, April 1938]

U.S.A. is far more impressive than even its three impressive parts—*The 42nd Parallel, 1919, The Big Money*—might have led one to expect. It stands as the important American novel of the decade, on the whole more satisfying than anything else we have. It lacks any touch of eccentricity; it is startlingly normal; at the risk of seeming paradoxical one might say that it is exciting because of its quality of cliché: here are comprised the judgments about modern American life that many of us have been living on for years.

Yet too much must not be claimed for this book. Today we are inclined to make literature too important, to estimate the writer's function at an impossibly high rate, to believe that he can encompass and resolve all the contradictions, and to demand that he should. We forget that, by reason of his human nature, he is likely to win the intense perception of a single truth at the cost of a relative blindness to other truths. We expect a single man to give us all the answers and produce the "synthesis." And then when the writer, hailed for giving us much, is discovered to have given us less than everything, we turn from him in a reaction of disappointment: he has given us nothing. A great deal has been claimed for Dos Passos and it is important, now that *U.S.A.* is completed, to mark off the boundaries of its enterprise and see what it does not do so that we may know what it does do.

One thing *U.S.A.* does not do is originate; it confirms but does not advance and it summarizes but does not suggest. There is no accent or tone of feeling that one is tempted to make one's own and carry further in one's own way. No writer, I think, will go to school to Dos Passos, and readers, however much they may admire him, will not stand in the relation to him in which they stand, say, to Stendhal or Henry James or even E. M. Forster. Dos Passos' plan is greater than its result in feeling; his book *tells* more than it *is*. Yet what it tells, and tells with accuracy, subtlety and skill, is enormously important and no one else has yet told it half so well.

Nor is *U.S.A.* as all-embracing as its admirers claim. True, Dos Passos not only represents a great national scene but he embodies, as I have said, the cultural tradition of the intellectual Left. But he does not encompass—does not pretend to encompass in this book— all of either. Despite his title, he is consciously selective of his America and he is, as I shall try to show, consciously corrective of the cultural tradition from which he stems.

Briefly and crudely, this cultural tradition may be said to consist of the following beliefs, which are not so much formulations of theory or principles of action as they are emotional tendencies: that the collective aspects of life may be distinguished from the individual aspects; that the collective aspects are basically important and are good; that the individual aspects are, or should be, of small interest and that they contain a destructive principle; that the fate of the individual is determined by social forces; that the social forces now dominant are evil; that there is a conflict between the dominant social forces and other, better, rising forces; that it is certain or very likely that the rising forces will overcome the now dominant ones. *U.S.A.* conforms to some but not to all of these assumptions. The lack of any protagonists in the trilogy, the equal attention given to many people, have generally been taken to represent Dos Passos' recognition of the importance of the collective idea. The book's historical apparatus indicates the author's belief in social determination. And there can be no slightest doubt of Dos Passos' attitude to the dominant forces of our time: he hates them.

But Dos Passos modifies the tradition in three important respects. Despite the collective elements of his trilogy, he puts a peculiar importance upon the individual. Again, he avoids propounding any sharp conflict between the dominant forces of evil and the rising forces of good; more specifically, he does not write of a class struggle, nor is he much concerned with the notion of class in the political sense. Finally, he is not at all assured of the eventual triumph of good; he pins no faith on any force or party—indeed he is almost alone of the novelists of the Left (Silone is the only other one that comes to mind) in saying that the creeds and idealisms of the Left may bring corruption quite as well as the greeds and cynicisms of the established order; he has refused to cry "Allons! the road lies before us," and, in short, his novel issues in despair.—And it is this despair of Dos Passos' book which has made his two ablest critics, Malcolm Cowley and T. K. Whipple, seriously temper their admiration. Mr. Cowley says: "They [the novels comprising *U.S.A.*] give us an extraordinarily diversified picture of contemporary life, but they fail to include at least one side of it—the will to struggle ahead, the comradeship in struggle, the consciousness of new men and new forces continually rising." And Mr. Whipple: "Dos Passos has reduced what ought to be a tale of full-bodied conflicts to an epic of disintegration."

These critics are saying that Dos Passos has not truly observed the political situation. Whether he has or not, whether his despair is objectively justifiable, cannot, with the best political will in the world, be settled on paper. We hope he has seen incorrectly; he himself must hope so. But there is also an implicit meaning in the objections which, if the writers themselves did not intend it, many readers will derive, and if not from Mr. Whipple and Mr. Cowley then from the book itself: that the emotion in which *U.S.A.* issues is negative to the point of being politically harmful.

But to discover a political negativism in the despair of *U.S.A.*

is to subscribe to a naïve conception of human emotion and of the literary experience. It is to assert that the despair of a literary work must inevitably engender despair in the reader. Actually, of course, it need do nothing of the sort. To rework the old Aristotelean insight, it may bring about a catharsis of an already existing despair. But more important: the word "despair" all by itself (or any other such general word or phrase) can never characterize the emotion the artist is dealing with. There are many kinds of despair and what is really important is what goes along with the general emotion denoted by the word. Despair with its wits about it is very different from despair that is stupid; despair that is an abandonment of illusion is very different from despair which generates tender new cynicisms. The "heartbreak" of *Heartbreak House,* for example, is the beginning of new courage and I can think of no more useful *political* job for the literary man today than, by the representation of despair, to cauterize the exposed soft tissue of too-easy hope.

Even more than the despair, what has disturbed the radical admirers of Dos Passos' work is his appearance of indifference to the idea of the class struggle. Mr. Whipple correctly points out that the characters of *U.S.A.* are all "midway people in somewhat ambiguous positions." Thus, there are no bankers or industrialists (except incidentally) but only J. Ward Morehouse, their servant; there are no factory workers (except, again, incidentally), no farmers, but only itinerant workers, individualistic mechanics, actresses, interior decorators.

This, surely, is a limitation in a book that has had claimed for it that it is a complete national picture. But when we say limitation we may mean just that or we may mean falsification, and I do not think that Dos Passos has falsified. The idea of class is not simple but complex. Socially it is extremely difficult to determine. It cannot be determined, for instance, by asking individuals to what class they belong; nor is it easy to convince them that they belong to one class or another. We may, to be sure, demonstrate the idea of class at income-extremes or function-extremes, but when we leave these we must fall back upon the criterion of "interest"—by which we must mean *real* interest ("real will" in the Rousseauian sense) and not what people say or think they want. Even the criterion of action will not determine completely the class to which people belong. Class, then, is a useful but often undetermined category of political and social thought. The political leader and the political theorist will make use of it in ways different from those of the novelist. For the former the important thing is people's perception that they are of one class or another and their resultant action. For the latter the interesting and suggestive things are likely to be the moral paradoxes that result from the conflict between real and apparent interest. And the "midway people" of Dos Passos represent this moral-paradoxical aspect of class. They are a great fact in American life. It is they who show the symptoms of cultural change. Their movement from social group to social group—from class to class, if you will—makes for the uncertainty of their moral codes, their confusion, their indecision. Almost more than the people of fixed class, they are at the mercy of the social stream because their interests cannot be clear to them and give them direction. If Dos Passos has omitted the class struggle, as Mr. Whipple and Mr. Cowley complain, it is only the external class struggle he has left out; within his characters the class struggle is going on constantly.

This, perhaps, is another way of saying that Dos Passos is primarily concerned with morality, with personal morality. The national, collective, social elements of his trilogy should be seen not as a bid for completeness but rather as a great setting, brilliantly delineated, for his moral interest. In his novels, as in actual life, "conditions" supply the opportunity for personal moral action. But if Dos Passos is a social historian, as he is so frequently said to be, he is that in order to be a more complete moralist. It is of the greatest significance that for him the barometer of social breakdown is not suffering through economic deprivation but always moral degeneration through moral choice.

This must be said in the face of Mr. Whipple's description of Dos Passos' people as "devoid of will or purpose, helplessly impelled hither and yon by the circumstances of the moment. They have no strength of resistance. They are weak at the very core of personality, the power to choose." These, it would seem, are scarcely the characters with which the moralist can best work. But here we must judge not only by the moral equipment of the characters (and it is not at all certain that Mr. Whipple's description is correct: choice of action is seldom made as the result of Socratic dialectic) but by the novelist's idea of morality—the nature of his judgments and his estimate of the power of circumstance.

Dos Passos' morality is concerned not so much with the utility of an action as with the quality of the person who performs it. *What* his people do is not so important as *how* they do it, or what they become by doing it. We despise J. Ward Morehouse not so much for his creation of the labor-relations board, his support of the war, his advertising of patent-medicines, though these are despicable enough; we despise him rather for the words he uses as he does these things, for his self-deception, the tone and style he generates. We despise G. H. Barrow, the labor-faker, not because he betrays labor; we despise him because he is mealy-mouthed and talks about "the art of living" when he means concupiscence. But we do not despise the palpable fraud, Doc Bingham, because, though he lies to everyone else, he does not lie to himself.

The moral assumption on which Dos Passos seems to work was expressed by John Dewey some thirty years ago; there are certain moral situations, Dewey says, where we cannot decide between the ends; we are forced to make our moral choice in terms of our preference for one kind of character or another: "What sort of an agent, of a person shall he be? This is the question finally at stake in any genuinely moral situation: What shall the agent *be*? What sort of character shall he assume? On its face, the question is what he shall *do*, shall he act for this or that end. But the incompatibility of the ends forces the issue back into the questions of the kind of selfhood, of agency, involved in the respective ends." One can imagine that this method of moral decision does not have meaning for all times and cultures. Although dilemmas exist in every age, we do not find Antigone settling her struggle between family and state by a reference to the kind of character she wants to be, nor Orestes settling his in that way; and so with the medieval dilemma of wife vs. friend, or the family oath of vengeance vs. the feudal oath of allegiance. But for our age with its intense self-consciousness and its uncertain moral codes, the reference to the quality of personality does have meaning, and the greater the social flux the more frequent will be the interest in qualities of character rather than in the rightness of the end.

The modern novel, with its devices for investigating the quality of character, is the aesthetic form almost specifically called forth to exercise this modern way of judgment. The novelist goes where the law cannot go; he tells the truth where the formulations of even the subtlest ethical theorist cannot. He turns the moral values inside out to question the worth of the deed by looking not at its actual outcome but at its tone and style. He is subversive of dominant morality and under his influence we learn to praise what dominant morality condemns; he reminds us that benevolence may be aggression, that the highest idealism may corrupt. Finally, he gives us the models or the examples by which, half-unconsciously, we make our own moral selves.

Dos Passos does not primarily concern himself with the burly sinners who inherit the earth. His people are those who sin against themselves and for him the wages of sin is death—of the spirit. The whole Dos Passos morality and the typical Dos Passos fate are expressed in Burns's quatrain:

> I waive the quantum o' the sin,
> The hazard of concealing;
> But, och! it hardens a' within
> And petrifies the feeling!

In the trilogy physical death sometimes follows upon this petrifaction of the feeling but only as its completion. Only two people die without petrifying, Joe Williams and Daughter, who kept in their inarticulate way a spark of innocence, generosity and protest. Idealism does not prevent the consequences of sinning against oneself, and Mary French with her devotion to the working class and the Communist Party, with her courage and "sacrifice" is quite as dead as Richard Savage who inherits Morehouse's mantle, and she is almost as much to blame.

It is this element of blame, of responsibility, that exempts Dos Passos from Malcolm Cowley's charge of being in some part committed to the morality of what Cowley calls the Art Novel—the story of the Poet and the World, the Poet always sensitive and right, the World always crass and wrong. An important element of Dos Passos' moral conception is that, although the World does sin against his characters, the characters themselves are very often as wrong as the world. There is no need to enter the theological purlieus to estimate how much responsibility Dos Passos puts upon them and whether this is the right amount. Clearly, however, he holds people like Savage, Fainy McCreary, and Eveline Hutchins accountable in some important part for their own fates and their own ignobility.

The morality of Dos Passos, then, is a romantic morality. Perhaps this is calling it a bad name; people say they have got tired of a morality concerned with individuals "saving" themselves and "realizing" themselves. Conceivably only Dos Passos' aggressive contemporaneity has kept them from seeing how very similar is his morality to, say, Browning's—the moment to be snatched, the crucial choice to be made, and if it is made on the wrong (the safe) side, the loss of human quality, so that instead of a man we have a Success and instead of two lovers a Statue and a Bust in the public square. But too insistent a cry against the importance of the individual quality is a sick cry—as sick as the cry of "Something to live for" as a motivation of political choice. Among members of a party the considerations of solidarity, discipline and expedience are claimed to replace all others and moral judgment is left to history; among liberals, the idea of social determination, on no good ground, appears tacitly to exclude the moral concern: witness the nearly complete conspiracy of silence or misinterpretation that greeted Silone's *Bread and Wine*, which said not a great deal more than that personal and moral—and eventually political—problems were not settled by membership in a revolutionary party. It is not at all certain that it is political wisdom to ignore what so much concerns the novelist. In the long run is not the political choice fundamentally a choice of personal quality?

Evangelical Criticism

[A review of *Towards the Twentieth Century* by
H. V. Routh. *The New Republic*, July 20, 1938]

M R. ROUTH'S scholarly and illuminating history of Victorian and Edwardian literature is concerned not so much with the past as with the future. It is a work of evangelical criticism, expounding the whole duty of literature—to provide the synthesis of intellect and emotion, of truth and desire, which man needs for happiness. "Without sacrificing intellectual truth," literature must "restore our zest in life, our confidence in our species and consequently in our intimate selves," and Mr. Routh's literary history is intended to point out the pitfalls which in the past have prevented this true consummation.

That letters should guide life is a belief which, in some form or other, most of us would defend. It is a salutary idea and certainly Mr. Routh's devotion to it makes his study much more urgent and interesting than the usual literary survey. Yet, salutary as it is, nothing can be more obstructive of critical insight than its excess; and, shrewd critic as Mr. Routh is, his over-indulgence in it leads him into basic critical errors.

It was the Victorians, deprived of so many of the comforts of religion, who put upon literature the conscious responsibility for man's spiritual guidance and fortification. Carlyle most dramatically propounded the new status of secular letters; Matthew Arnold, to whose thought Mr. Routh has considerable affinity, elaborated it most compellingly. In many ways Arnold's theory was sensible and sinewy; what he called "adequate" literature was that which gave the reader an emotional adjustment with which he might effectively meet the world. But Arnold, confused by his commitment to religion, was sometimes—not always—inclined to carry his theory too far, with the result that he gave only a doubtful second place to Chaucer, Rabelais and Molière because they seemed to him to lack "seriousness," by which he meant that they did not do the quasi-religious job of composing the human spirit: they merely explored it.

Yet clearly the helps literature may give are far more various and subtle than Arnold conceived or Mr. Routh will consider. E. M. Forster, for example, tells how, when stationed in Egypt during the War and sickened by the rubbishy idealism war breeds, he was revived and restored to sanity by a book; and of all the books that might succor a human soul, this book was *À Rebours!* "Was it decadent?" says Forster. "Yes, and thank God!": the spectacle of des Esseintes being "selfish and himself" was what rescued him from the war bilge.

It seems to me that if, like Arnold and Mr. Routh, you ask too much of literature you get far less than literature can give. If, like Mr. Routh, you examine George Gissing under the aspect of all the lacks of modern life, just what of Gissing is left for you? The excessive demand blunts the critical edge; the interest of Henry James, Mr. Routh tells us, "generally ends with the technics of the intellect"; but it need end there only if you expect James to be the Law and the Prophets. Mr. Routh finds that Hardy as a poet is a failure because "he cannot mix his best self with his material, however artistic the execution. The resilience, expansiveness and vitality of human nature find no outlet. What he writes about does not serve the highest emotional experiences which imply self-fulfilment." I do not quite know what this means, but remembering what Hardy does do for his reader, Mr. Routh's protest is, I think, what people call wanting egg in your beer. Certainly it seems to be asking a writer to do what only a whole culture can do.

Mr. Routh calls up before the bar of criticism the great names of the last century to find out whether or not they have solved the human dilemma and left a recipe for wholeness. We know the inevitable result of the examination: they failed; and Mr. Routh's exposition of the ways of their failure makes a book eminently worth reading. Yet there seems something basically maladroit in conceiving their history in terms of failure. After all, in a very real sense, every age has "failed," and every writer "fails." Perhaps our very notion of a literary "age" is of a group of men who failed in similar ways to solve the human problem.

The Situation in American Writing: Seven Questions

[Contribution to a symposium of this title in *Partisan Review*, Fall 1939]

[1. *Are you conscious, in your own writing, of the existence of a "usable past"? Is this mostly American? What figures would you designate as elements in it? Would you say, for example, that Henry James's work is more relevant to the present and future of American writing than Walt Whitman's?*

2. *Do you think of yourself as writing for a definite audience? If so, how would you describe this audience? Would you say that the audience for serious American writing has grown or contracted in the last ten years?*

3. *Do you place much value on the criticism your work has received? Would you agree that the corruption of the literary supplements by advertising—in the case of the newspapers—and political pressures—in the case of the liberal weeklies—has made serious literary criticism an isolated cult?*

4. *Have you found it possible to make a living by writing the sort of thing you want to, and without the aid of such crutches as teaching and editorial work? Do you think there is any place in our present economic system for literature as a profession?*

5. *Do you find, in retrospect, that your writing reveals any allegiance to any group, class, organization, region, religion, or*

system of thought, or do you conceive of it as mainly the ex-
pression of yourself as an individual?

6. *How would you describe the political tendency of American*
writing as a whole since 1930? How do you feel about it your-
self? Are you sympathetic to the current tendency toward what
may be called "literary nationalism—a renewed emphasis,
largely uncritical, on the specifically "American" elements in
our culture?

7. *Have you considered the question of your attitude toward the*
possible entry of the United States into the next world war?
What do you think the responsibilities of writers in general are
when and if war comes?]

REPLY:

7. I should like to answer the last question first because I find
that it is the only one that I "face." The other questions are interesting but this one is immediate and crucial. The possibility of war is
the great objective and subjective fact which confronts every writer.

Whether or not he is wholly conscious of it, the writer lives by his
faith in continuity. He must feel that he himself will go on indefinitely to practice his craft; he must suppose a connection between himself and the past; and he must assume, however modestly,
that he has some connection with the future. This sense of continuity is, of course, attenuated or destroyed by the possibility of
war. Perhaps tomorrow, the writer feels, he will cease to be a writer
—and immediately it becomes infinitely more difficult for him to be
a writer today. He knows what war will mean: for the war period,
at the very least, there will be a cessation of literary activity in any
true sense; and perhaps—indeed, most likely—the postwar political
situation will discontinue the culture of the past and prevent the
culture of the future: there is every likelihood that the writer will
be either silenced or enslaved. This possibility of war must be sitting
like a raven on many a literary desk. But it is not sitting on all the
desks and that, now, is almost a worse fact than that it is sitting on
some.

I conceive that in the event of war the writer's responsibilities are: to survive, to remain undeceived, to keep others from being deceived.

6. This last question may be followed most appropriately by the penultimate one, for the willingness—even the eagerness—of so many intellectuals to accept war seems to me to be the direct outgrowth of the political tendency which has dominated American literature since 1930. This tendency began as a furious romantic revolutionism and is continuing as an angry self-righteous reformism of which war is to be an instrument. The literature dominated by this tendency has been enormously influential; for a large and important part of the intellectual middle class it has provided what is nothing less than a culture and an ethics. It has given these people "something to live for," a point of view, an object for contempt, a direction for anger, a code of excited humanitarianism. Perhaps this literary movement, politically effective rather than artistically successful, cannot be wholly reprobated, for it has stimulated a kind of moral sensitivity. But this is a moral sensitivity which seems to me dangerous in its insufficiency. The subject is too complex and too delicate to be treated briefly but what I feel about this literature of social protest is that, however legitimate and laudable is its intention of arousing pity and anger, in actual fact, because of its artistic failures, it constitutes a form of "escapism," and offers a subtle flattery by which the progressive middle-class reader is cockered up with a sense of his own virtue and made to feel that he lives in a world of perfect certainties in which critical thought and self-critical feeling are the only dangers.

The literary nationalism we are at present experiencing is of course an intensification of the ideology I have just commented on. All nationalism, like all conscious virtue, stands on the edge of vulgarity, and by nationalism I do not mean the love of one's land, language, and literature; nor do I even mean patriotism; but I do mean these emotions employed to prove that there is an intrinsic and nearly exclusive rightness in one's land, literature, and language. No doubt there are some political situations—not so many as we suppose, however—where nationalism serves truly good ends. I think the present American leftist nationalism, so much of it the reaction to the cold contempt of American life which was current a few years ago, so much of it the calculated policy of a party line, cannot be anything but vulgar and, in the end, downright chauvinistic.

1. This leads, of course, to Question One, about the "usable past." I think it can no longer be said, as Henry James said in his biography of Hawthorne, that the American writer lacks the sense of a rich past. There is a superb "thickness" about the feel of American life; and in any such "thickness" there must be a strong, even though unformulated, sense of the past. And part of this is a sense of a *literary* past. I do not mean by this a special consciousness of the canonical American writers. In my own case, for example, though I have great admiration and affection for the American classics and an increasing interest, I know that they have been far less important to me than the traditional body of European writers. What I do mean is that I have a fortifying sense that there is, simply, a past of literature which makes a present all the more possible; and this is something that, at various times in our history, our writers have not felt. As for the traditional body of world literature, I find that it becomes, for me, more and more "usable" and seems less and less in the past at all.

If I answer the question about Henry James and Walt Whitman by saying that I think James likely to be the healthier influence upon American writing, I must disclaim meaning any derogation of Whitman himself. For Whitman is a very great poet and subtler and more beautifully modulated than most people care to discover. But his influence is likely to be that of a mood and a manner and likely to encourage the simplified social emotions and the nationalism I have just spoken of. On the other hand, any influence that Henry James may have will be through the suggestiveness of his method. James is essentially critical and moral and therefore more energetic than Whitman. He is concerned with upsetting preconceptions and clichés; he sees the difficulties and dangers of the moral and social life; he is interested in the shadings and contradictions—in drama in the old sense, which is what I feel lacking in contemporary American fiction—and he stands against the black and white, the *de haut en bas,* simplified morality now so common. Clearly the complexity of the kind of judgment he uses and suggests will not be attractive to the group that puts John Steinbeck among the American classics and that is preparing for the "action" of war.

5. In Question Five the disjunction is obviously not a valid one. I think of my work as the expression of myself as an individual *and* (not *or*) as revealing an allegiance to a group and to a system—or, rather, a tradition—of thought. It seems to me necessary to conceive one's work in this way. The vulgar—but not ineffective—attack on "individualism" a few years ago accounted for the dullness, the lack of distinction (the word is significant here) of so much of the creative and critical writing that was done when the idea of the collectively written novel was seriously discussed. I suppose that one does not have to explain that, *in a certain limited sense,* there is no such thing as an individual—that a mind or a talent, almost by definition, is a social thing. But once we illegitimately extend that certain limited sense we run into confusion in morality, in politics, in literature. As for literature, I am quite willing to say that it is absolutely essential for the writer to cultivate his individuality to the top of its bent, and to resist all attempts to thwart it. If his "social consciousness" requires him to give a social reason for this, he can say that it is only as he varies from the usual that he has any social usefulness. And exactly because there is such a thing as an "individual" there is such a thing as an "allegiance."

My own literary interest—and I suppose that in a writer this is an allegiance—is in the tradition of humanistic thought and in the intellectual middle class which believes that it continues this tradition. Nowadays this is perhaps not properly pious; but however much I may acknowledge the historic role of the working class and the validity of Marxism, it would be *only* piety for me to say that my chief literary interest lay in this class and this tradition. What for me is so interesting in the intellectual middle class is the dramatic contradiction of its living with the greatest possibility (call it illusion) of conscious choice, its believing itself the inheritor of the great humanist and rationalist tradition, and the badness and stupidity of its action.

2. By and large, it is for this intellectual class that I suppose I write. It is a class that has grown enormously in the last decade. And no doubt the market for serious writing has grown with it. Naturally, a great deal of this writing is serious only in the sense that its publishers consider it to be serious or only because moral earnestness and intellectual pretension pass for seriousness. But then real seriousness is at all times a very rare quality.

4. Perhaps I am not qualified to answer the first part of Question Four, because I have never tried to make a living out of writing. I have little doubt that it would be for me next to impossible. I should like to say, however, that I have found teaching something more than a "crutch." Perhaps I have been exceptionally lucky, but I have found it not only a pleasant but an exciting and instructive kind of work despite its bad reputation. For criticism, at any rate, it seems invaluable to have to deal, on the one hand, with freshmen who are relatively intelligent but either ignorant of literature, or naïve about it or even inimical to it, for it forcibly reminds the critic how small a part literature plays in our world and it makes him bring his assumptions out of their professional cave; then, on the other hand, it is very salutary to have to face talented seniors who will give one no quarter; and the subject matter, the most interesting work of the past, is always a refreshment.

The problems of literary economics are too complex to be written about briefly. When we remember how the best writers of an age are sometimes commercially the most successful, how, again, they are sometimes the most obscure, or think of themselves as hacks, or depend on inherited wealth or position, or do their best work when they are fashionably taken up by a "decadent" society, or when they are neglected—when we consider all these contradictions and many more, we can speak of the ideal situation for the writer only with the greatest diffidence. I find it hard to imagine a condition in which literature will not be (in one sense, in the sense that medicine, say, need not be) a most competitive profession and one always forced to face social resistance. This seems to me to be in the nature of the literary activity; any artist in the degree that he is notable must always be making minor revolutions or supporting them, revolutions in taste and feeling. He is therefore always going to be rejected and resisted both by *some* part of his profession and by *some* part of society. No doubt this entails a certain amount of social waste. And no doubt the present social system wastes far more literary talent than other conceivable systems might; it wastes everything. On the other hand, it must be confessed that it allows and even encourages a great deal too.

I think I should be more willing to attack the literary waste in our present system (I mean apart from the general waste of human life and its best possibilities) if I had a clearer notion of how I should like to see the economic life of the writer organized. But whenever an alternative to literary laissez faire is put forward which undertakes to be more rational and thoroughgoing than WPA, it contrives to theorize literature into being more important than it is and should be, to make it into a form of religion and to bring it into the service of the state and eventually under the control of a bureau. It is hard to imagine a condition in which, as someone said, the state will pay the piper and the piper will call his own tune.

Hemingway and His Critics

[A review of *The Fifth Column and The First Forty-Nine Stories* by Ernest Hemingway. *Partisan Review*, Winter 1939]

BETWEEN *The Fifth Column,* the play which makes the occasion for this large volume, and *The First Forty-Nine Stories,* which make its bulk and its virtue, there is a difference of essence. For the play is the work of Hemingway the "man" and the stories are by Hemingway the "artist." This is a distinction which seldom enough means anything in criticism, but now and then an author gives us, as Hemingway gives us, writing of two such different kinds that there is a certain amount of validity and at any rate a convenience in making it. Once made, the distinction can better be elaborated than defined or defended. Hemingway the "artist" is conscious, Hemingway the "man" is self-conscious; the artist" has a kind of innocence, the "man" a kind of naïvety; the "artist" is disinterested, the "man" has a dull personal ax to grind; the "artist" has a perfect medium and tells the truth even if it be only *his* truth, but the "man" fumbles at communication and falsifies. As Edmund Wilson said in his "Letter to the Russians about Hemingway," which is the best estimate of our author that I know:

. . . something frightful seems to happen to Hemingway as soon as he begins to write in the first person. In his fiction, the conflicting elements of his personality, the emotional situations which obsess him, are externalized and objectified; and the result is an art which is severe, intense, and deeply serious. But as soon as he talks in his own person, he seems to lose all his capacity for self-criticism and is likely to become fatuous or maudlin.

Mr. Wilson had in mind such specifically autobiographical and polemical works as *Green Hills of Africa* (and obviously he was not referring to the technical use of the first person in fictional narrative) but since the writing of the "Letter" in 1935, we may observe of Hemingway that the "man" has encroached upon the "artist" in his fiction. In *To Have and Have Not* and now in *The Fifth Column* the "first person" dominates and is the source of the failure of both works.

Of course it might be perfectly just to set down these failures simply to a lapse of Hemingway's talent. But there is, I think, something else to be said. For as one compares the high virtues of Hemingway's stories with the weakness of his latest novel and his first play, although one is perfectly aware of all that must be charged against the author himself, what forces itself into consideration is the cultural atmosphere which has helped to bring about the recent falling off. In so far as we can ever blame a critical tradition for a writer's failures, we must, I believe, blame American criticism for the illegitimate emergence of Hemingway the "man" and the resultant inferiority of his two recent major works.

It is certainly true that criticism of one kind or another has played an unusually important part in Hemingway's career. Perhaps no American talent has so publicly developed as Hemingway's: more than any writer of our time he has been under glass, watched, checked up on, predicted, suspected, warned. One part of his audience took from him new styles of writing, of love-making, of very being; this was the simpler part, but its infatuate imitation was of course a kind of criticism. But another section of his audience responded negatively, pointing out that the texture of Hemingway's work was made up of cruelty, religion, anti-intellectualism, even of basic fascism, and looked upon him as the active proponent of evil. Neither part of such an audience could fail to make its impression upon a writer. The knowledge

that he had set a fashion and become a legend may have been
gratifying but surely it was also burdensome and depressing, and
must have offered no small temptation. Yet perhaps more difficult for
Hemingway to support with equanimity, and, from our point of
view, much more important, was the constant accusation that he
had attacked good human values. For upon Hemingway were
turned all the fine social feelings of the now passing decade, all
the noble sentiments, all the desperate optimism, all the extreme
rationalism, all the contempt of irony and indirection—all the
attitudes which, in the full tide of the liberal-radical movement,
became dominant in our thought about literature. There was demanded of him earnestness and pity, social consciousness, as it
was called, something "positive" and "constructive" and literal.
For is not life a simple thing and is not the writer a villain or a
counterrevolutionary who does not see it so?

As if under the pressure of this critical tradition, which persisted
in mistaking the "artist" for the "man," Hemingway seems to
have undertaken to vindicate the "man" by showing that he, too,
could muster the required "social" feelings in the required social
way. At any rate, he now brought the "man" with all his contradictions and conflicts into his fiction. But "his ideas about life"—I
quote Edmund Wilson again—

or rather his sense of what happens and the way it happens, is in his
stories sunk deep below the surface and is not conveyed by argument
or preaching but by directly transmitted emotion: it is turned into
something as hard as crystal and as disturbing as a great lyric. When
he expounds this sense of life, however, in his own character of Ernest
Hemingway, the Old Master of Key West, he has a way of sounding
silly.

If, however, the failures of Hemingway "in his own character"
were apparent to the practitioners of this critical tradition, they
did not want Hemingway's virtues—the something "hard" and
"disturbing." Indeed, they were in a critical tradition that did not
want artists at all; it wanted "men," recruits, and its apologists

were delighted to enlist Hemingway in his own character, with all his confusions and naïvety, simply because Hemingway had now declared himself on the right side.

And so when *To Have and Have Not* appeared, one critic of the Left, grappling with the patent fact that the "artist" had failed, yet determined to defend the "man" who was his new ally, had no recourse save to explain that in this case failure was triumph because artistic fumbling was the mark of Hemingway's attempt to come to grips with the problems of modern life which were as yet too great for his art to encompass. Similarly, another critic of the Left, faced with the aesthetic inferiority of Hemingway's first play, takes refuge in praising the personal vindication which the "man" has made by "taking sides against fascism." In other words, the "man" has been a sad case and long in need of regeneration; the looseness of thought and emotion, the easy and uninteresting idealism of the social feelings to which Hemingway now gives such sudden and literal expression, are seen as the grateful signs of a personal reformation.

But the disinterested reader does not have to look very deep to see that Hemingway's social feelings, whatever they may yet become, are now the occasion for indulgence in the "man." His two recent failures are failures not only in form but in feeling; one looks at *To Have and Have Not* and *The Fifth Column,* one looks at their brag, and their disconcerting forcing of the emotions, at their downright priggishness, and then one looks at the criticism which, as I conceive it, made these failures possible by demanding them and which now accepts them so gladly, and one is tempted to reverse the whole liberal-radical assumption about literature. One almost wishes to say to an author like Hemingway, "You have no duty, no responsibility. Literature, in a political sense, is not in the least important. Wherever the sword is drawn it is mightier than the pen. Whatever you can do as a man, you can win no wars as an artist."

Very obviously this would not be the whole truth, yet saying it might counteract the crude and literal theory of art to which, in varying measure, we have all been training ourselves for a decade. We have conceived the artist to be a man perpetually on the spot, who must always report to us his precise moral and political latitude and longitude. Not that for a moment we would consider shaping our own political ideas by his; but we who of course turn for political guidance to newspapers, theorists, or historians, create the fiction that thousands—not, to be sure, ourselves—are waiting on the influence of the creative artist, and we stand by to see if he is leading us as he properly should. We consider then that we have exalted the importance of art, and perhaps we have. But in doing so we have quite forgotten how complex and subtle art is and, if it is to be "used," how very difficult it is to use it.

One feels that Hemingway would never have thrown himself into his new and inferior work if the necessity had not been put upon him to justify himself before this magisterial conception of literature. Devoted to literalness, the critical tradition of the Left took Hemingway's symbols for his intention, saw in his stories only cruelty or violence or a calculated indifference, and turned upon him a barrage of high-mindedness—that liberal-radical high-mindedness that is increasingly taking the place of thought among the "progressive professional and middle-class forces" and that now, under the name of "good will," shuts out half the world. Had it seen what was actually in Hemingway's work, it would not have forced him out of his idiom of the artist and into the idiom of the man which he speaks with difficulty and without truth.

For what should have been always obvious is that Hemingway is a writer who, when he writes as an "artist," is passionately and aggressively concerned with truth and even with social truth. And with this in mind, one might begin the consideration of his virtues with a glance at Woodrow Wilson. Hemingway has said that all genuine American writing comes from the prose of Huckleberry Finn's voyage down the Mississippi, and certainly his own starts there. But Huck's prose is a sort of moral symbol. It is the antithesis to the Widow Douglas—to the pious, the respectable, the morally plausible. It is the prose of the free man seeing the world as it really is. And Woodrow Wilson was, we might say, Hemingway's Widow Douglas. To the sensitive men who went to war it was not, perhaps, death and destruction that made the disorganizing shock. It was perhaps rather that death and destruction went on at the instance and to the accompaniment of the fine grave words, of which Woodrow Wilson's speeches were the finest and gravest. Here was the issue of liberal theory; here in the bloated or piecemeal corpse was the outcome of the words of humanitarianism and ideals; this was the work of presumably careful men of good will, learned men, polite men. The world was a newspaper world, a state-paper world, a memorial-speech world. Words were trundled smoothly o'er the tongue—Coleridge had said it long ago—

> Like mere abstractions, empty sounds to which
> We join no feeling and attach no form
> As if the soldier died without a wound . . .
> Passed off to Heaven, translated and not killed.

Everyone in that time had feelings, as they called them; just as everyone has "feelings" now. And it seems to me that what Hemingway wanted first to do was to get rid of the "feelings," the comfortable liberal humanitarian feelings, and to replace them with the truth.

Not cynicism, I think, not despair, as so often is said, but this admirable desire shaped his famous style and his notorious set of admirations and contempts. The trick of understatement or tangential statement sprang from this desire. Men had made so many utterances in such fine language that it had become time to shut up. Hemingway's people, as everyone knows, are afraid of words and ashamed of them and the line from his stories which has become famous is the one that begins "Won't you please," goes on through its innumerable "pleases," and ends, "stop talking." Not only slain men but slain words made up the mortality of the war.

Another manifestation of the same desire in Hemingway was his devotion to the ideal of technique as an end in itself. A great deal can go down in the tumble but one of the things that stands best is a cleanly done job. As John Peale Bishop says in his admirable essay on Hemingway (which yet, I feel, contributes to the general misapprehension by asserting the evanescence of Hemingway's "compassion"), professional pride is one of the last things to go. Hemingway became a devotee of his own skill and he exploited the ideal of skill in his characters. His admired men always do a good job; and the proper handling of a rod, a gun, an *espada,* or a pen is a thing, so Hemingway seems always to be saying, which can be understood when speech cannot.

This does not mean that Hemingway attacks mind itself, a charge which has often been brought against him. It is perhaps safe to say that whenever he seems to be making such an attack, it is not so much *reason* as it is *rationalization* that he resists; "mind" appears simply as the complex of false feelings. And against "mind" in this sense he sets up what he believes to be the primal emotions, among others pain and death, met not with the mind but with techniques and courage. "Mind" he sees as a kind of castrating knife, cutting off people's courage and proper self-love, making them "reasonable," which is to say dull and false. There is no need to point out how erroneous his view would have been were it really mind that was in question, but in the long romantic tradition of the attitude it never really *is* mind that is in question but rather a dull overlay of mechanical negative proper feeling, or a falseness of feeling which people believe to be reasonableness and reasonable virtue. And when we think how quickly "mind" capitulates in a crisis, how quickly, for example, it accommodated itself to the war and served it and glorified it, revulsion from it and a turning of the life of action—reduced, to be sure, to athleticism: but skillful physical effort is perhaps something intellectuals too quickly dismiss as a form of activity—can be the better understood. We can understand too the insistence on courage, even on courage deliberately observed in its purity: that is, when it is at the service of the most sordid desires, as in "Fifty Grand."

This, then, was Hemingway's vision of the world. Was it a complete vision? Of course it was not. Was it a useful vision? That depended. If it was true, it was useful—if we knew how to use it. But the use of literature is not easy. In our hearts most of us are Platonists in the matter of art and we feel that we become directly infected by what we read; or at any rate we want to be Platonists, and we carry on a certain conviction from our Tom Swift days that literature provides chiefly a means of identification and emulation. The Platonist view is not wholly to be dismissed; we *do* in a degree become directly infected by art; but the position is too simple. And we are further Platonistic in our feeling that literature must be religious: we want our attitudes formulated by the tribal bard. This, of course, gives to literature a very important function. But it forgets that literature has never "solved" anything, though it may perhaps provide part of the data for eventual solutions.

With this attitude we asked, Can Hemingway's people speak only with difficulty? and we answered, Then it surely means that he thinks people should not speak. Does he find in courage the first of virtues? Then it surely means that we should be nothing but courageous. Is he concerned with the idea of death and of violence? Then it must mean that to him these are good things.

In short, we looked for an emotional leader. We did not conceive Hemingway to be saying, Come, let us look at the world together. We supposed him to be saying, Come, it is your moral duty to be as my characters are. We took the easiest and simplest way of using the artist and decided that he was not the "man" for us. That he was a man and a Prophet we were certain; and equally certain that he was not the "man" we would want to be or the Prophet who could lead us. That, as artist, he was not concerned with being a "man" did not occur to us. We had, in other words, quite overlooked the whole process of art, overlooked style and tone, symbol and implication, overlooked the obliqueness and complication with which the artist may criticize life, and assumed that what Hemingway saw or what he put into his stories he wanted to have exist in the actual world.

In short, the criticism of Hemingway came down to a kind of

moral-political lecture, based on the assumption that art is—or should be—the exact equivalent of life. The writer would have to be strong indeed who could remain unmoved by the moral pressure that was exerted upon Hemingway. He put away the significant reticences of the artist, opened his heart like "a man," and the flat literalness, the fine, fruity social idealism, of the latest novel and the play are the result.

The Fifth Column is difficult to speak of. Summary is always likely to be a critical treachery, but after consulting the summaries of those who admire the work and regard it as a notable event, it seems fair to say that it is the story of a tender-tough American hero with the horrors, who does counter-espionage in Madrid, though everybody thinks he is just a playboy, who fears that he will no longer do his work well if he continues his liaison with an American girl chiefly remarkable for her legs and her obtuseness; and so sacrifices love and bourgeois pleasure for the sake of duty. Hemingway as a playwright gives up his tools of suggestion and tone and tells a literal story—an adventure story of the Spanish war, at best the story of the regeneration of an American Scarlet Pimpernel of not very good intelligence.

It is this work which has been received with the greatest satisfaction by a large and important cultural group as the fulfillment and vindication of Hemingway's career, as a fine document of the Spanish struggle, and as a political event of significance, "a sign of the times," as one reviewer called it. To me it seems none of these things. It does not vindicate Hemingway's career because that career in its essential parts needs no vindication; and it does not fulfill Hemingway's career because that career has been in the service of exact if limited emotional truth and this play is in the service of fine feelings. Nor can I believe that the Spanish war is represented in any good sense by a play whose symbols are so sentimentally personal[1] and whose dramatic tension is so weak;

---

[1] In fairness to Hemingway the disclaimer of an important intention which he makes in his Preface should be cited. Some people, he says, have objected that his play does not present "the nobility and dignity of the cause of the Spanish people. It does not attempt to. It will take many plays and novels to do that, and the best

and it seems to me that there is something even vulgar in making Spain serve as a kind of mental hospital for disorganized foreigners who, out of a kind of self-contempt, turn to the "ideal of the Spanish people." Nor, finally, can I think that Hemingway's statement of an anti-fascist position is of great political importance or of more than neutral virtue. It is hard to believe that the declaration of anti-fascism is nowadays any more a mark of sufficient grace in a writer than a declaration against disease would be in a physician or a declaration against accidents would be in a locomotive engineer. The admirable intention in itself is not enough and criticism begins and does not end when the intention is declared.

But I believe that judgments so simple as these will be accepted with more and more difficulty. The "progressive professional and middle-class forces" are framing a new culture, based on the old liberal-radical culture but designed now to hide the new anomaly by which they live their intellectual and emotional lives. For they must believe, it seems, that imperialist arms advance proletarian revolution, that oppression by the right people brings liberty. Like Hemingway's latest hero, they show one front to the world and another to themselves, know that within they are true proletarian men while they wrap themselves in Early American togas; they are enthralled by their own good will; they are people of fine feelings and they dare not think lest the therapeutic charm vanish. This is not a political essay and I am not here concerned with the political consequences of these things, bad though they be and worse though they will be, but only with the cultural consequences. For to prevent the anomaly from appearing in its genuine difficulty, emotion—of a very limited kind—has been apotheosized and thought has been made almost a kind of treach-

---

ones will be written after the war is over." And he goes on: "This is only a play about counter-espionage in Madrid. It has the defects of having been written in wartime, and if it has a moral it is that people who work for certain organizations have very little time for home life." I do not think that this exempts the play from severe judgment by those who dislike it, just as I think that those who admire it have a right to see in it, as they do, a "sign of the times."

ery; the reviewer of *The Fifth Column* to whom I have already referred cites as a virtue Hemingway's "unintellectual" partisanship of the Spanish cause. The piety of "good will" has become enough and Fascism is conceived not as a force which complicates the world but as a force which simplifies the world—and so it does for any number of people of good will (of a good will not to be doubted, I should say) for whom the existence of an absolute theological evil makes non-existent any other evil.

It is this group that has made Hemingway its cultural hero and for reasons that need not be canvassed very far. Now that Hemingway has become what this group would call "affirmative" he has become insufficient; but insufficiency is the very thing this group desires. When Hemingway was in "negation" his themes of courage, loyalty, tenderness, and silence, tangentially used, suggested much; but now that they are used literally and directly they say far less than the situation demands. His stories showed a great effort of comprehension and they demand a considerable effort from their readers, that effort in which lies whatever teaching powers there are in art; but now he is not making an effort to understand but to accept, which may indeed be the effort of the honest political man but not of the honest artist.

An attempt has been made to settle the problem of the artist's relation to politics by loudly making the requirement that he give up his base individuality and rescue humanity and his own soul by becoming the mouthpiece of a party, a movement, or a philosophy. That requirement has demonstrably failed as a solution of the problem; the problem, however, still remains. It may be, of course, that politics itself will settle the problem for us; it may be that in our tragic time art worthy of the name cannot be produced and that we must live with the banalities of *The Fifth Column* or even with less. However, if the problem will be allowed to exist at all, it will not be solved in theory and on paper but in practice. And we have, after all, the practice of the past to guide us, at least with a few tentative notions. We can learn to stop pressing the writer with the demand for contemporaneity when we remember the simple fact that writers have always written directly to and about the troubles of their own time and for and about their contemporaries, some in ways to us more obvious than others but all responding inevitably to what was happening around them. We can learn too that the relation of an artist to his culture, whether that culture be national or the culture of a relatively small recusant group, is a complex and even a contradictory relation: the artist must accept his culture and be accepted by it, but also—so it seems—he must be its critic, correcting and even rejecting it according to his personal insight; his strength seems to come from the tension of this ambivalent situation and we must learn to welcome the ambivalence. Finally, and simplest of all, we can learn not to expect a political, certainly not an immediately political, effect from a work of art; and in removing from art a burden of messianic responsibility which it never has discharged and cannot discharge we may leave it free to do whatever it actually can do.

The Victorians and Democracy

[A review of *Lord Macaulay, Victorian Liberal* by Richmond Croom Beatty, *The Age of Reform, 1815–1870* by E. L. Woodward, *Victorian Critics of Democracy* by Benjamin E. Lippincott. *The Southern Review*, Spring 1940]

TO mean anything at all, the study of a man's relation to his culture must usually proceed as much by inverse as by direct ratios. The great are nourished in strange ways, sometimes as often by stones as by bread. But not a trace of the common paradox appears in the nurture of Macaulay; his time, his class, and his party raised him on the fat of the land. He was Whiggery's pampered darling and he made generous return of the affection that was lavished on him.

It is, of course, this perfect accord between himself and his culture that now makes us pass Macaulay by. We reject Whiggery and we not unnaturally reject the temperament and the talent which so accurately expressed it. The perceptive liberal of today, even the perceptive radical, is far more likely to respect the politics of Burke or Dr. Johnson than those of the liberal exponent of the anomalous 1832 Reform Bill. For Macaulay, pleading for liberty meant only the liberty of the substantial classes; he believed that a Golden Age was arriving at the behest of a god in the machine; with the arrogance of the spokesman of a class just coming to full power and not yet put to the proof, he was certain that the welfare of his class was the welfare of the nation; he had no doubt but that national good came chiefly from the effort of every man to enrich himself; he was sure that his ancestors were less wise than his contemporaries; and he could confidently project a society which remained static in its inner relationships while everlastingly progressing in comfort and knowledge.

We dismiss all these beliefs and we find it easy nowadays to dismiss their proponent: but perhaps rather too easy. Richmond Croom Beatty's reservations in his new and efficient study of Macaulay, *Lord Macaulay, Victorian Liberal,* are modern and right, yet it is hard to see what they add to Trevelyan's *Life and Letters* that most modern readers would not add for themselves; and certainly they prevent in Mr. Beatty's book the qualities that make Trevelyan's so interesting. It is perhaps too much to expect of a modern writer that he deal with Macaulay *con amore;* still, it was exactly Trevelyan's affection for his uncle that allowed him to bring out the things we ought to know—Macaulay's gusto, his spectacular and representative traits, and above all the peculiar success of his life. For Macaulay's life *was* a success and neither our modern rejection of his ideas nor the depressed misery of his last days can deny his genuine achievement.

What the nature of that achievement was perhaps Matthew Arnold has described most accurately. Arnold, who did not accept a single one of Macaulay's judgments, who in effect devoted his life to the refutation of all that Macaulay stood for, remarked of him that he was a great *civilizer.* And commenting on the fact that the library of an Australian colonist was likely to consist of a Bible, Shakespeare, and some volume of Macaulay, Arnold said that this was not surprising, for the Bible and Shakespeare were imposed upon Englishmen as objects of admiration and the immense popularity of Macaulay was "due to his being pre-eminently fitted to give pleasure to all who are beginning to feel enjoyment in the things of the mind." No doubt Arnold's left hand had something to do with the bestowal of this praise, but Arnold was too much the pedagogue, and too good a one, to be an intellectual snob and he knew what a rare and difficult talent is required to give the beginner a pleasure which he will pass beyond but not turn against. True enough, Macaulay flattered the notions and prejudices of his readers but he did not do so merely by repeating them. His flattery was finer than that. For one thing, he cast the current common notions in an artistic form that was, in its limited way, quite perfect. But more, he took the notions and carried them to new heights. If the prejudices themselves were Philistine, it was still something to lift Philistinism into the high reaches where they were invested with the glow of greatness from Milton or Bacon or Dr. Johnson. If Macaulay flattered the old preconceptions—and he did not always, for he could destroy them too, as in his excellent essay on Machiavelli—he also involved them with the great events and the great ideas of all ages.

Despite his arrogance, Macaulay knew his limitations. To McVey Napier, editor of *The Edinburgh Review,* he wrote, in the flush of his fame, that he was "not successful in analyzing the effect of works of genius." "I have written several things on historical, political and moral questions, of which . . . I am not ashamed . . . but I have never written a page of criticism on poetry, or the fine arts, which I would not burn if I had the power. . . . I have a strong and acute enjoyment of works of the imagination; but I have never habituated myself to dissect them." And he went on, "Perhaps I enjoy them the more keenly for that reason." Probably not: but he did enjoy them passionately. For Macaulay was wholly devoted to the intellectual life; political success was as nothing to him beside intellectual eminence and even beside intellectual enjoyment. It is well known how enormous was his ingestion of literature of all ages and in many languages, even in the midst of his busiest official times. Quantity, of course, may mean nothing in these things, but here it indicates the gusto with which Macaulay lived the life of the intellect. And to thousands of people of inferior capacities but similar tastes he was able to comunicate his pleasure. Nowadays only literary minds are seriously concerned with literature and usually in a wholly literary way; but Macaulay was a non-literary mind (in the modern sense) seriously concerned with literature and able to make it serious for people like himself.

In estimating his literary achievement it is important to remember

that he was a superb administrator with the administrator's passion
for order and no nonsense. No one could better dismiss the flum-
mery and cant of a badly managed bureau or more neatly puncture
the absurdity of a badly framed law; his redaction of the Indian
legislative code is said to be masterly and certainly nothing could
be more cogently expressed. And he dealt with literature with the
high and efficient hand of the administrator; his general run of
judgments approximates Samuel Johnson's middle flights of criticism in which Johnson is being the literary procurator. From his
administrative bent come Macaulay's literary vices but no less his
literary virtues; and their origin is significant of his time. For in
the Age of Reform, the role of administration, even apart from the
principles of government, was greater than we are likely to remember. When E. L. Woodward in his admirable *The Age of Reform,
1815–1870*—a work that certainly rivals and in some ways outshines
that of Macaulay's grandnephew, G. M. Trevelyan—gives so much
attention to the circumstances of the charge of the Light Brigade, it
is not because he is sentimentally interested in a sentimentalized
incident but because the famous blunder is typical and symbolic.
Aside from the broader questions of social justice, the great problem
of the nineteenth century was, as Mr. Woodward shows again and
again, the introduction of simple efficiency and the habituation of a
people to the feel of the thing, as we are told Russians today need
habituation to the feel of machinery. If Macaulay was always being
superior and impatient about the ways things went and people acted,
he had justification: things went badly and people acted clumsily.
And it was out of his notion of efficiency that his best literary qualities came—his ideal of historical research, which on the whole was
very high, his passion for arrangement and construction, and above
all his style, which is always directed toward quick and unambigu-
ous comprehension.

Needless to say, the administrator's view is limited by its ideal of
smoothness; whatever introduces a difficulty or a new consideration
is nonsense and a lapse from nature. The limitations of understanding which baffled Macaulay in the presence of genius and which

made him deny value to certain kinds of genius—to Coleridge, Wordsworth, Kant, Dickens, Melville—closed him off from certain kinds of political ideas which seem to demand genius itself for their first apprehension. The creative notions of modern politics, the ideas of human dignity, equality and responsibility, were entrusted in nineteenth-century England to the kind of poetic temperament Macaulay could not understand, to Carlyle, Ruskin, Arnold. These men, as they appear in Benjamin E. Lippincott's useful if rather too formalized study, *Victorian Critics of Democracy*, far overshadow the men who, in the temperament of their work, are closest to Macaulay. Maine and Lecky, however impressive in their special researches, in the field of general political thought are below the other three; their "practical" and "realistic" arguments in defense of aristocracy and private property turn out to be not much more than prejudice cloaked in scientism. True enough, the men of the poetic temperament could be bizarre and faddy, Ruskin most often, Arnold least often. And true enough, in their justifiable attacks on the middle-class democracy which Macaulay advocated they all could move from laissez faire to authoritarianism, Arnold a little of the way, Carlyle the whole way. But all three had what Macaulay, with Maine and Lecky, lacked—the notion of the interdependence of men, the idea of human responsibility, the conception of the delicacy and intricacy of social life.

Between the poets on the one hand and the social scientists on the other stands a man who is today too little read; Fitzjames Stephens remains, of all the figures in Mr. Lippincott's book, the freshest and most relevant. Like Macaulay an Indian administrator, he did not lack the poetic insight: he combined the dark vision of Hobbes with the complex mind of Burke. One of the great pessimistic political teachers from whom liberals hate to learn, he made bitterly clear, as Hobbes had done, the wide discrepancy between personal morality and political procedure. With Hobbes, he knew what modern liberals never wish to know, that the State is always force, however disguised, that government is always coercion, however gentle, and that both are necessary. With none of Burke's mysticism, he had much of Burke's dramatic sense of the contradictions of society and, trained in Benthamism, he derived his own utilitarianism not only from Bentham's but from Burke's. With the method of Benthamism he attacked John Stuart Mill's *Liberty*, demonstrating its evasiveness and inconclusiveness. He exemplifies the critical temperament which Matthew Arnold called for, the disinterested effort to see the object as it really is, without regard to party; the contradictions in him which this effort produced are always suggestive. He called himself a liberal, yet he undertook to show the limitations of the liberal assumptions. He hated revolution, yet he could defend a revolution. He believed in authority, yet he hated autocracy. He believed in free speech, yet he thought that it might be limited for utilitarian considerations. The outcome of his argument, it is true, is a defense of the status quo; yet whoever reads his *Liberty, Equality, Fraternity* will know with how much difficulty the status quo recovers from his defense.

Beside a man like this, Macaulay as a political thinker seems indeed what Christopher North called him early in his career and predicted he would remain: "a bright lad." For the society that he saw simply did not exist: he saw without insight or creativity. But a talented Whig in the first half of the century had no need of either when he could ride the historical wave on apodictic eloquence.

The Unhappy Story of Sinclair Lewis[1]

[A review of *Bethel Merriday* by Sinclair Lewis. *Kenyon Review*, Summer 1940]

IN the unhappy story of Sinclair Lewis' later career, *Bethel Merriday* is another and a redundant episode. To call it a failure would be to imply that it is at least an effort, and it is not that. Like all of Mr. Lewis' books since *Dodsworth*—which was an effort and a failure—it is not so much a work of creation as an act of faith in the "romance of" something. Just as Mr. Lewis stood witness for idealistic hotel-keeping in *Work of Art*, for reform and independent womanhood in *Ann Vickers*, for democracy in *It Can't Happen Here*, for the virtues of middle age in *The Prodigal Parents*, so now, in this latest product of his left hand, he testifies for the charms of the stage and of stage-struck youth.

Like all the novels of the last fourteen years, *Bethel Merriday* is an indulgence of Mr. Lewis' dream life. The man who made his mark as a realist has put his talents wholly in the command of the spirit of Tom Sawyer; Mr. Lewis, one feels, is always coming to his own funeral, always thinking of virtue as a thing misunderstood and appreciated too late by a grieving Aunt Polly; if he shows us life as a difficult business, we cannot help suspecting that he admires the difficulty—and does not quite believe in it—because it makes the adventure more romantic; it is that much more exciting when, to

[1] Title supplied by the editor of this volume.

help Nigger Jim escape, you make your pen out of a candlestick and use your blood for ink. Luckier than his Mr. Babbitt, who could spare so little time for his phantasies, Mr. Lewis has been able to give up his serious business to amuse himself with the emotions of suffering and righteousness, triumph and revenge.

The entrance of Mr. Lewis upon the literary scene was so dramatic, and the stature which he attained in his six successful years was so great, that the public has not yet ceased being curious about what he has to say. But the very least critical part of the public knows that he has forsaken his promise and that the man who set out as the passionate observer of American life has now become one of its strangest phenomena; it knows that it has witnessed something dismaying when it sees a man who began with the knowledge that "it is a complex fate to be an American," acquire, with the increase of years, the belief that to be an American is a gay adventure.

It was not Mr. Lewis but Henry James who wrote the sentence about the complexity of the American fate. Perhaps there is something disproportionate and even priggish in the juxtaposition of the two names. Yet there is point in the comparison beyond setting an American achievement beside an American failure. For Mr. Lewis' phantasies have this grace of maturity, without which we could dismiss entirely all his later work, that they are so curious about the moral life. In all the romancing, in all the boyish posturing, there is always some sense of what it means to be a disinterested man; indeed, this is Mr. Lewis' haunting theme: he gives his greatest measure of honor to the love of craft and technique, to creation or discovery, which, for him, always imply the good life. He likes to see his favorite people forced to some new frontier to free themselves from the morality of the crass and the dull. Like Ernest Hemingway, he has a love for the thing well done for its own sake, and to show the charms of professional devotion he has created his Gottlieb and his Arrowsmith, his Dodsworth, Ora Weagle, Ann Vickers and now Bethel Merriday. And it is here that Henry James comes in so patly, because he is in literature so much the sort of hero that Mr. Lewis, with a certain fresh vulgarity, loves to celebrate. James received but little honor from his nation, he never represented American literature to the world, and toward the end of his career he was never quite clear, when he read his publisher's statement, whether it was he or the publisher who owed the small amounts that appeared. The nature of his thought was such that it is —now—not surprising to find him spoken of (by Ezra Pound) as a "revolutionary" in morals; yet he was not really articulate about matters of morality but thought wholly as a craftsman, knowing that if one is a novelist one does not "deal" with morals except through novelistic arrangements. And James reminds us of the cause of Mr. Lewis' failure: it is that Mr. Lewis has little love and no respect for his own art; he lacks what he so admires in others, the delight in craft and the pleasure in forcing it to cope with difficult matter.

In his lecture "The Lesson of Balzac," James remarked that "for the most part, these loose and easy producers, the great resounding improvisatori, have not, in general, ended by imposing themselves." Mr. Lewis, of course, is wholly the loose and easy producer, and the question might arise whether his now depressing inadequacy does not arise from the novelistic method he uses. But, historically speaking, it is not at all certain that James is correct in his judgment; the improvisatori have impressed themselves enormously, and speaking critically, it is not easy to discriminate between the amounts of pleasure given, on the one hand, by the tight and careful work James especially admired, and, on the other hand, by the loose and easy productions; the quality of pleasure in each kind may be another matter, though even here we cannot, *a priori*, declare wholly in favor of the tight and difficult forms. James speaks of Balzac as standing "almost alone as an extemporizer achieving closeness and weight, and whom closeness and weight have preserved." If I understand rightly what James means by closeness and weight, I think they may be found as well in a rich abundance of matter as in the nice arrangement of a more limited material; one might venture the paradox, in despite of Mr. Eliot, that in the novel the spirit giveth life.

This defense of the "extemporizer" needs to be made in speaking of Sinclair Lewis because literary notions have changed rather importantly in the twenty years since he flamed across the sky with *Main Street*. A new generation is likely to believe that the roots of Mr. Lewis' fourteen years of failure are to be found in his six years of success—to believe, that is, that the failure lies in the method of improvisation, and so to dismiss the early work with the late. For the generation to which I refer has a conception of literature almost diametrically opposed to that of the advance-guard of two decades ago. It has built into its theory the closest critical thought, literary scholarship, new ideals of elegance, allusiveness and complication of form. One can admire this generation and yet feel a regret that it has become for our time the chief repository of literary seriousness: one can regret that the greater reading public, cut off as it is from this movement by reason of training and circumstance, is left to the sincere emptiness of the social novelists or to the swash of the "good story-tellers," and it is hard not to feel that something better was happening to the public when it was being confronted, twenty years ago, with Sherwood Anderson, Dreiser and the Sinclair Lewis of *Main Street* and *Babbitt*. I think it would be a misfortune if, in the new preoccupation with the opposite of looseness and easiness, the improvisatorial style should be made to seem even less creditable than it has become in the hands of most of its practitioners.

For the improvisatorial style, from Defoe down, has always had its own function and its own poetry; in our own literature we can see its best success in Mark Twain; and to both Defoe and Mark Twain Mr. Lewis' own work has an affinity. We may grant that improvisation is not adequate to the complexity of some of the most interesting aspects of the American fate, and even grant, too, that when Mr. Lewis modifies the loose and easy chronicle of events with the devices of "construction," he gives us *Babbitt,* which is clearly his best book. Yet we can still see that between improvisation and improvisation there is a difference. In *Main Street,* in *Babbitt* (which, of course, is improvisatorial enough), in *Elmer*

Gantry (often called a failure but really a considerable success in the genre of the rogue-novel), in *Arrowsmith* (which is absorbing despite its adoration of the high austerity of science) and even in *Dodsworth* (though to a lesser degree), the prose is quick, nervous, efficient, the details are all alive, the total effect is simple and—to use the adjective which will bring the best of Lewis into the line of the realistic English novelists—manly. But in all the later works, and perhaps especially in this latest, *Bethel Merriday,* the dominant feeling is one of nothing better than archness.

To come critically into the presence of a career like Mr. Lewis' is embarrassing if only because one is tempted into the heavy solemnity of trying to "explain" it. One of the standard methods of explanation is now pretty dead—the one by which some large part of a writer's failure is made to devolve upon American culture; but even if one were not weary of that as an idea, it requires so many modulations and it implies so many contradictions that it cannot be very practicable. Yet one small aspect of American culture may do something to explain the failure of Mr. Lewis and of other writers of his and of later generations: I suggest what is certainly not without its cause in the structure of our economics, the absence of any real conception of literature as a profession. It is not that the writer is disregarded but rather that, as a social fact, he is misconceived. It is increasingly rare, I think, to find the slow growth of a solid and developing body of literary work, except, perhaps, among poets. The writer is conceived to be an "event," and if he is not an "event" he is nothing. And to be an "event," to live in the light of eventfulness, works upon the writer an impossible hardship. If it does nothing else—and it does do more—it leads him into the psychological error (it is psychological rather than moral) by which he mistakes the sense of power, which success brings, for the creative effort which won his success. This, perhaps, is what used to be called the sin of pride, the natural punishment of which was the inability to see and to move flexibly with the shifts of circumstance.

Literature and Power

[*Kenyon Review*, Autumn 1940]

SOMETIMES we of the English-teaching profession must wonder whether our social function is anything more than pious—whether we are expected to do more than perform levitical chores in the temple of the respected forgotten dead. We begin to suspect, a little neurotically, that all practical men regard us with contempt and tolerate us only because they believe we pick up certain secret magics in the course of our mortuary duties. We can make no claim to the certainties of the physical sciences, cannot share in the explanation of the universe or in the creation of material goods. Nor can we, on the other hand, claim the immediacy and utility of the social sciences and say that we teach the arts of social organization or what is becoming to the good citizen.

If we are proud and honest, we retire to an animal faith in our enterprise. But it is hard to keep silent when all around us we hear society requiring that, in its hour of crisis, all its elements justify themselves by their works. We want to respond as do our colleague-disciplines, to explain how wholly at one we are with society, how we deserve our place because we too teach an art of knowledge and control. It is natural that we should want to make this affirmation; but perhaps from our having made it spring all our errors, our indecisions and our false busy-ness.

Our confusions are not new but times of crisis make us unusually aware of them. It may therefore be salutary to recall that the time in which our profession got its start was itself one of crisis and that some of our most basic errors came from responding to its necessities. Sometimes it is said that Matthew Arnold shaped the academic opinions of our time, and the judgment is, I think, accurate, needing only the modification that it was the more vigorous and memorable of these opinions that Arnold shaped. He may even be said to have established the teaching of English as an academic profession—I have in mind, of course, his whole critical career, but especially the lecture in which he first struck its note, his inaugural address as the Oxford Professor of Poetry. The language, the title and the intention of that address are all worth remarking: it was the first lecture by an Oxford Professor of Poetry to be delivered in English; it was called "On the Modern Element in Literature"; and it advanced as a prime critical canon a quality it called *adequacy*.

In speaking of the adequacy—that is, the ability to cope with an age—and of the modernity of literary works, Arnold was doing no more than to make explicit and bring into the university what had in fact been the most remarkable characteristic of literature since the French Revolution. It had been the chief effort of the romantics of the right, the left and the center to create a literature of *function* and even of *conscious* function. Intensely aware of their time, they undertook to cope with it by formulating problems and even by solving them, by directing men's energies, organizing their emotions, correcting their mistakes. They put their private feelings at the disposal of a widely public weal. Of this tendency Wordsworth is example enough and we can understand why the young Arnold, brought up under Wordsworth's personal influence and soaked in the idiom of romantic poetry, felt that Shakespeare, man of a more private day, was a baffling puzzle.

Yet Arnold was himself too much of a poet to believe that adequacy could be gained through doctrine alone and, especially in his youth, he was devoted to the silent and formal aspects of art; whenever he wrote to Clough on a literary subject it was to try to persuade his earnest friend that style and form are important above all other things. Then, during his later years, he had too robust a sense of the way the world goes to believe that literature could be a finally determinative factor in society. But although Arnold's modifications are supremely important in his thought, he was always sure that literature was not merely a symptom of civilization but actually a civilizing agent.

It is not a new explanation of this more or less sudden sense of literature's function to say that it was, among other things, a response to the diminution of the power of religion. Spinoza had suggested to both Coleridge and Arnold that the Holy Spirit which inspired the Bible was the same power that continued to inspire true poets. Arnold's theory of poetry—that when it was truly poetry it was a religious utterance—was the very essence of romantic theory. Literature, we may say, came to be the medium and the repository of the ethical values and the feelings that had once been peculiar to religion. And literature became even more. Carlyle, under the influence of Goethe, formulated the notion of the Man of Letters as not only a priest but a hero and a seer and thus made him co-equal with the political leader and the rival of the scientist. In short, literature took upon itself the very greatest responsibilities and arrogated to itself the most effective powers.

Meanwhile the schools were ready for a new humanistic subject. The old training in the classics has never fallen wholly into disrepute in England; nevertheless it did suffer from the incursions of a more positivist and a more democratic training. A growth of national feeling bolstered the pride in the national literature. A new generation begrudged the time required for what was after all the merest acquaintance with the literature of the old languages. And so, in part replacing the classics and sanctified by social, religious and political considerations, doubly sanctified by the possibilities it offered for scientific understanding, literature entered the universities and the universities became the churches of the secular Word.

We can understand how all this should have seemed very natural.

In a culture increasingly preoccupied with the problems of control and of knowledge for power, it was scarcely possible that literature should *not* believe that its very survival depended upon its being equally capable with other disciplines to share in the management of the world. And we cannot withhold our moral admiration from the ready courage with which it met its new task.

With literature offering this new rationale for itself, it was to be expected that the professors of literature should follow suit. How better could they justify themselves and their subject than by proclaiming that the essence of literature is indeed power, moral, political or scientific, and that they themselves were moralists, politicians and scientists? They thus committed themselves to a difficult task, an impossible task. In so far as they tried to acquit themselves of it creditably, certain individuals did indeed achieve stature and distinction. But as a professional undertaking their program could not succeed—because literature itself could not but fail in its own intention of being religion, science and politics. We must note, however, that when literature fails as a religion, science and politics, it does not necessarily fail as literature. But when the academic profession of literature assumes for its subject and for itself an impossible task, it must in the end face its own negation.

The latest work of a distinguished professor shows how this can come about. H. V. Routh's *Toward the 20th Century* is in some ways the most satisfactory history of nineteenth-century literature I know of. Its scholarship is wide and sound; it is brilliantly aware of the difficulties to which the writers of the time responded; it is critically very sensitive. Yet, because of one assumption that it makes, Mr. Routh's book has an odd invalidity. Mr. Routh believes that literature has a spiritual function—namely, to respond effectively to the spiritual troubles of its age. It must, according to this view, make a synthesis of life, resolve the cultural contradictions which make the good life difficult. It is with this assumption that Mr. Routh judges the literature of the last century. He finds—could he find anything else?—that none of it does what it should have done. Some works do some things, some do others, but none does all or enough. In short, the literature of the nineteenth century was a noble failure. But how can it be otherwise when it is required to serve, if not as dogma, at least as a gospel?

The result is that Mr. Routh is committed to the teaching of a subject-matter which he considers inadequate and mistaken. And whoever proceeds on Mr. Routh's basically religious view of literature will, if he is equally honest and intelligent, come to this same unfortunate position. A man like V. L. Parrington, whose large and sympathetic figure has had so great an influence on ideas about American literature, was less concerned than Mr. Routh with spiritual matters; but Parrington's political preoccupation yielded very similar results. For him, two such commanding personages in American literature as Hawthorne and Henry James are not much more than interesting failures because they did not offer effective answers to the problems of their time.

In other words, as soon as we make it a prime requirement for literature that it be effective, as soon as we ask that it do, first of all, the work of the will and earn its living by constructive activity, we are left with a subject of confessed inadequacy on our hands.

It is in this way that the frankly religious-political attitude to literature works itself out. But there are two other attitudes which, like this one, express our culture's exclusive concern with knowledge for the purpose of control. One of these is the belief that literature is primarily a material for scientific investigation. The other is the belief that literature is primarily a material for the historical imagination.

Of the excesses of the "scientific" attitude toward literature we have all had our hard thoughts. Indeed, we might almost wonder if the time may not have come for us to let up in our criticism of it. For although its values are not so important as its partisans think, it has contributed more to our understanding than we are sometimes willing to admit and its excesses should not discredit its virtues. Yet it must be spoken of, if only for the sake of completeness, as another example of literature as a concern of the will, in this case of the will expressed not through literature itself but through the scientific understanding taking literature as its object. It is worth noting about this method of study that, except in its most interesting and difficult aspects, it can be competently handled, like routine work in the physical sciences, by people of normally mediocre intelligence; it is therefore an excellent subject for examination. And so, in an expanding educational system, in a culture not wholly sure of its values, it offered itself as the best available method of graduate study, especially as it had the prestige of its scientific assumptions.

But the scientific attitude reached the plateau of its influence some time back; the historical attitude, by reason of its inherent progressivism, is in the ascendant. It takes over where science leaves off, at philology, bibliography and the belief that the understanding of "influences" is the understanding of a work of art. For the historical attitude great educational claims are made—most recently by L. C. Knights in a persuasive essay in the *Southern Review* (Winter, 1939). These claims are not necessarily extravagant. The historical imagination is a wonderfully humanizing faculty which, when developed, as in most people it is not, has the power of irradiating a great deal of human life. Of its practical value in politics, which is so often spoken of, one may be skeptical enough; as a method for instructing the student in the *right* social attitudes, it seems to me to depend entirely on the rightness of the teacher's own social attitudes; but as an almost aesthetic experience it can have a great philosophical and ethical value. It is needless to point out that literature has always been aware of these advantages of the historical imagination and has not only served it but has been gladly served by it.

But the conjunction of the historical and literary imaginations is not what is usually meant when history and literature are joined. On the contrary, what is much too often meant is not even that literature is a part of history, like battles and elections, but that literature can help us to an understanding of history. That is, history is supposed to be the weather, of which literature is the recording barometer.[1]

Now, from the point of view of history itself, there is something mistaken in regarding an integral event as an instrument of indication. Still, from the point of view of literature, there is in principle nothing wrong with literature being a datum in the study of history. But from the point of view of literature, there is something wrong when, in its study, the historical attitude comes to transform the literary work from a living thing to a dead datum. And this the historical method of our time must do, for by its usual assumptions a literary work is a wholly conditioned thing, a nearly mechanical response to economic or social events.

The questioning of the literary validity of certain methods of literary study does not, I hope, imply the belief in such a thing as "purity" in art, or sacrosanctity. Any method which can bring enlightenment to literature is appropriate. Questions of philology, of biography, of social life, of literary tradition are all essential to the understanding of a literary work. And what is more, any single work of literature is no one thing, fixed and immutable, but changes as our interests in it change.

But on the other hand, there is always the danger that all the multifarious processes which necessarily go on about literature will substitute themselves for literature itself. Perhaps we are all so habituated to substituting the processes that elucidate the object for the object itself that when one says "literature itself" the dismal notion of "purity" comes up again. An analogy with music-teaching may set things right. In the teaching of music to non-technical students, most devices of instruction seem to have failed. The old method of "explaining the meaning," of ferocious epithets and biographical gossip, has succeeded only in being ludicrous; the more recent method, whereby a setting of *Kulturgeschichte* is supposed to prepare the way to the music, is more "advanced" but not much more to the point. Apparently the best that can be done

---

[1] I have mentioned Mr. Knights's essay and therefore I should say that it specifically warns against just this doubtful technique.

is that minimal method (of which B. H. Haggin is a well-known exponent) which limits itself to the elucidation of the form and the isolation of the various parts of the piece. More than this in the way of pedagogy music seems to sweep aside; it insists on being a self-explanatory experience even for its least learned lover. For him the music does not depend on its social relevance or on its place in history; it has validity in itself and listening to it is not an "investigation" or an "understanding" of the mistakes of a past culture. It is an experience, a contemplative experience, and its value lies in being just that.

Contemplative experience has dangerous connotations. We think at once of *active thought* and in our time we know which of the two is the better, for we have in mind purposive, constructive action which, in a time of crisis, seems the only possible way of survival. Well, crisis requires its sacrifices, but it is a good rule to sacrifice one's interests, if one must, by suspending them rather than by distorting them. For normal life, at any rate, contemplative experience is indispensable. Such, it seems, is the opinion of the great mass of people, for by *contemplative experience* I mean those pursuits in which the faculties, though engaged, are concerned with their own exercise chiefly; for the mass of people such experience takes the form of engaging in difficult sports or watching complicated games. Traditionally this interest is set in opposition to the culturally superior interest in the fine arts, but actually the two interests have a greater affinity than the intellectual chooses to believe. There are relatively few good records of what people feel in practicing or watching their sports but it is clear that, after certain social factors, such as competition, have been abstracted, there remains a deep absorption, an intuitive appreciation of style and an almost mystical interest in technique. And it is for these things as much as anything else that the mass of people cherish their sports; in the sense that I have used the phrase, they offer the opportunity for contemplative experience and thus, in a mute way, seem to justify life.

It will not hurt us to think of literature as having to compete with these interests. True, literature starts with a certain disadvantage, for it cannot avoid being concerned with purposive activity. The emotions of activity and the words men use in their business are its material. It even brings into its orbit the very documents of activity—of politics, for example—when they have certain qualities, and it calls these literature too. But however concerned it may be with purposive activity, literature in its essence is concerned primarily with *how* the act is done and how its own powers deal with the act. This interest in *how* and the intense pleasure it can afford are what literature has traditionally tried to create. More and more, however, literature, concerning itself with the effective validity of what is done in the world of practice and what it can itself bring about in that world, grows indifferent to its own questions of style and form, and almost in proportion to what it explicitly claims for itself in responsibility. If we try to prophesy from the available evidence, we can almost see for the future the development of two kinds of literature—a literature of duty and a literature of pleasure. To this unfortunate state of affairs, if it comes about, the academic profession of literature will have contributed.

And if we abandon the idea of literature as an independent, contemplative experience, as a pleasure, a "gay knowledge," if we continue to make it conform to philosophies of immediate ends—trying, that is, to bring it into line with physical science, ethical religion and prognosticative history—and do not keep clear its own particular nature, we shall be contributing to the loss of two things of the greatest social value. Of these one is the possibility which art offers of an experience that is justified in itself, of nearly unconditioned living. Upon such experience, or even the close approach to it, we have learned to turn hostile faces; that is one of the strategic errors of our culture, for in the long run the possibility of such experience is a social necessity.

The second thing we shall lose is the awareness—it is ultimately practical—which comes only from the single-minded contemplation of works that arise from the artist's own contemplation of events and objects; this is an awareness of the qualities of things. In the realm of art we call these qualities style, in the realm of morals we call them character, in the realm of politics we have no name for them but they are finally important. To these qualities, especially in times of crisis, society seems to be stolidly indifferent; actually they are, after survival, the great social concern.

Perhaps all this says no more than that literature is an art, but perhaps the tendency of our profession permits one now to say a thing so simple. Each of the methods of literary study has no doubt its good reason for existence in the republic of letters. But if literature and the teaching of it are to justify themselves *as themselves* and not as handmaids of other disciplines, and if they are to have their proper influence, those who study and those who teach must have as the common element of their various methods the knowledge of what literature is. In our time, this is not an especially easy knowledge.

T. S. Eliot's Politics[1]

[*Partisan Review*, September–October 1940]

IT IS a century ago this year that John Stuart Mill angered his Benthamite friends by his now famous essay on Coleridge in which, writing sympathetically of a religious and conservative philosopher, he avowed his intention to modify the rigid materialism of utilitarian thought. Mill did not speak out for Coleridge for what are sometimes called "romantic" reasons—that is, because he thought transcendentalism was warmer and more glowing than utilitarianism. He did think so, but the reason he urged attention to Coleridge was that he thought Coleridge's ability "to see further into the complexities of the human feelings and intellect" offered something practical to add to Bentham's too "short and easy" political analysis. And he told his radical friends that they should make their prayer this one: " 'Lord, enlighten thou our enemies' . . . sharpen their wits, give acuteness to their perceptions and consecutiveness and clearness to their reasoning powers: we are in danger from their folly, not from their wisdom."

The book of Coleridge's which Mill mentioned most often was the volume usually referred to as *Church and State;* its full title is *On the Constitution of the Church and State, According to the Idea of Each* and it is from this work that T. S. Eliot's newest

[1] This essay, originally called "Elements That Are Wanted," would appear to have been considered for inclusion in *The Liberal Imagination*, but for some reason was not used. During the consideration the title was changed to "T. S. Eliot's Politics," as it is called here. (D.T.)

essay, *The Idea of a Christian Society,* takes not only its special meaning of the word "idea" but also its whole inspiration. Mr. Eliot has always said that a connection with the past, more or less consciously maintained, is necessary for intellectual and artistic virtue. For reasons which scarcely need exploration he himself has found his own most useful affinity with the seventeenth century and the thirteenth. Yet for all his enmity to Romanticism, his own true place in politics and religion is in the Romantic line of the nineteenth century. He continues the tradition of Coleridge and, after Coleridge, of Newman, Carlyle, Ruskin and Matthew Arnold —the men who, in the days of Reform, stood out, on something better than reasons of interest, against the philosophical assumptions of materialistic Liberalism. Their very language, if we except Carlyle's, is commemorated in his prose, and to their thought this book is the tragic coda.

A century has not seen the establishment of this line of thought, but then neither has that same century seen the establishment, though it has surely seen the dominance, of the thought it opposed. What we see at the moment is the philosophy of materialism—of the Right, the Left and the Center—at war with itself. In that war many of our old notions have become inadequate and many of our old alliances inoperative. We all of us, from our own feelings, can understand Mr. Eliot when, in giving up *The Criterion* after his long editorship, he spoke of a "depression of spirits so different from any other experience of fifty years as to be a new emotion." But a really new emotion implies a modification of all other existing emotions and it requires a whole new world of intellect to accommodate it. Certainly the old world of those who read what I am now writing cannot give it room. Indeed, can we say that that old intellectual world of ours any longer exists? Disordered as it always was, it seems now almost to have vanished.

I am far from thinking that Mr. Eliot supplies a new world, yet in this troubled time when we are bound to think of eventual reconstructions, I should like to recommend to the attention of readers probably hostile to religion Mr. Eliot's religious politics. I say no more than *recommend to the attention:* I certainly do not recommend Mr. Eliot's ideas to the allegiance. But here we are, a very small group and quite obscure; our possibility of action is suspended by events; perhaps we have never been more than vocal and perhaps soon we can hope to be no more than thoughtful; our relations with the future are dark and dubious. There is, indeed, only one connection with the future of which we can be to any extent sure: our pledge to the critical intellect. Of the critical intellect a critic has said that "it must be patient and know how to wait; and flexible and know how to attach itself to things and how to withdraw from them." Perhaps Mr. Eliot's long if recalcitrant discipleship to Matthew Arnold gives me some justification for quoting Arnold once again: of criticism he said that "it must be apt to study and praise elements that for the fulness of spiritual perfection are wanted, even though they belong to a power which in the practical sphere may be maleficent." It is with this sentence in mind that I urge the importance of Mr. Eliot's book.

In the imagination of the Left Mr. Eliot has always figured with excessive simplicity. His story was supposed to be nothing more than this: that from the horrible realities of the Waste Land he escaped into the arms of Anglo-Catholic theology. This account may or may not be adequate; but as we review the ten years in which Marxism flourished among the intellectuals and then decayed, we can scarcely believe that this story, if true, is the worst that could be told of a man in our time. Whatever is censurable in it depends on the blind power of that weary word "escape" and on our attitude to theology. For theology I certainly do not make a stand, but when Mr. Eliot is accused of "faith," of the "surrender" of his intellect to "authority," it is hard to see, when the accusers are Marxist intellectuals, how their own action was always so very different. If we have the right to measure the personal and moral value of convictions by the disinterested intellectual effort through which they are arrived at, we might find that Mr. Eliot's conversion was notably more honorable than that of many who impugned his decision.

Mr. Eliot's book is a small one, it is not overtly dramatic and it does not have an air of "power." To readers of a different persuasion it cannot offer a solution that will seem more comprehensive or more practicable than their own; it can only serve them by questioning their assumptions. Its point of departure is simple, even obvious. Mr. Eliot, believing that a nation's political philosophy is not to be found in the conscious formulation of its ideal aims but, rather, in "the sub-stratum of collective temperament, ways of behaviour and unconscious values" which go to make up the formulation, is unable to find, what most people so easily find, a polar difference between the political philosophy of the Western democracies and that of the totalitarian states. He does not say they are the same; their forms differ and their qualities differ. Yet the difference seems to him not one of principle but of degree; and when he considers how democracy is forced to defend itself from totalitarianism by adopting the totalitarian forms, he cannot think that the differences are dependent on more than time. To be maintained, the differences must be more than temporal, they must be principled, and Mr. Eliot cannot believe that the principles to be put in opposition to the totalitarian principles can be those of liberalism and democracy. Liberalism is a necessary negative element in politics but no more than that; as for democracy, Mr. Eliot says that it is so praised by everyone that its mention makes him think of the Merovingian Emperors and look around for the Mayor of the Palace.

But because totalitarianism is what he calls "pagan," the only possible opposing principle Mr. Eliot can find is that of Christianity. He cannot yet account England—the England which responded as it did to the events of September 1938—a pagan state, though he cannot call it actually a Christian one; it has a culture "which is mainly negative, but which, so far as it is positive, is still Christian." But because the situation no longer permits a negative culture, the choice will have to be made "between the formation of a new Christian culture and the acceptance of a pagan one."

More than once in the brief course of his book we hear from

Mr. Eliot that he is not interested in Christianity as revivalism and he quotes a "distinguished theologian" to the effect that the great mistake made about Christianity is to suppose it primarily a religion and emotional when in truth it is primarily dogma and intellectual. We are not, then, to be concerned with Christianity as pietistic feeling but with Christianity as a precise view of man and the world, which implies a social form. But as we prepare to hear the Idea[2] of a Christian society we have surely the right to ask the proposer what, in his opinion, caused the failure of such previous Christian societies as may be said to have existed. We have, too, the right to ask him what it is in the nature of Christianity which brought it to the condition in which men and nations, trained in a wholly Christian culture, felt constrained to discover the inadequacy of the dogmas which are now expected to save the world. He might perhaps answer that Christianity is right but not all-powerful and that there are human impulses with which it cannot easily deal. Or if, like Mr. Eliot, he admits a dialectical-materialistic interpretation of the past but not of the future, he might find a material cause which explains the past failure without limiting the future hope. Well, we must not put inadequate answers into Mr. Eliot's mouth, but it is indeed hard to imagine the answer that will satisfy our historical skepticism, a skepticism which is aroused, too, by Mr. Eliot's unexpressed sense that there was once a past whose political virtues are worthy and possible of recapture.

So much for our premised objections. They are certainly not diminished by the particular recommendations which Mr. Eliot goes on to make. He projects a society which will exist in three aspects—what he calls the Christian State, the Christian Community and the Community of Christians. This more or less Platonic triad exists, as we cannot help observing, on a rather minimal Christianity. For of the heads of his Christian State Mr. Eliot demands no more than that they be educated to think in Christian categories; for the rest, the criterion of their value is to be the

---

[2] "By an idea I mean . . . that conception of a thing . . . which is given by the knowledge of its ultimate aim." —Coleridge.

same to which statesmen have always submitted—not devoutness but effectiveness. "They may," Mr. Eliot says, "frequently perform un-Christian acts; they must never attempt to defend their actions on un-Christian principles." The State, we are told, is Christian only negatively and is no more than the reflection of the Christian society which it governs. Yet this society itself is not permeated by a very intense Christianity. The mass of its citizens make up the Christian Community and their behavior is to be "largely unconscious"—for, because "their capacity for *thinking* about the objects of faith is small, their Christianity may be almost wholly realised in behaviour: both in their customary and periodic religious observances and in a traditional code of behaviour towards their neighbours."

What is left, then, to give the positive Christian tone to the Christian Society is what Mr. Eliot calls the Community of Christians, a group reminiscent of Coleridge's "clerisy" but more exclusively an elite, constituted of those clerics and laymen who consciously live the Christian life and who have notable intellectual or spiritual gifts. It is they who, by their "identity of belief and aspiration, their background of a common system of education and a common culture" will collectively form "the conscious mind and conscience of the nation." They are not to constitute a caste and so are to be loosely joined together rather than organized, and Mr. Eliot compares them in their possible wide effectiveness with the segregated intellectuals who now write only for each other.

Of the specifically and immediately practical, Mr. Eliot says little beyond submitting his Christian Society to judgment according to its success in carrying out the reforms projected by Christian sociologists. The natural end of such a society is man's "virtue and well-being in community"; this is "acknowledged for all" but "for those who have eyes to see it" there is also the supernatural end of beatitude. Culturally such a society is to be pluralistic—perhaps in a limited sense of that word, though we are told that the Community of Christians will include minds indifferent or even hostile to Christianity. There is a certain faith in the good effect of smaller units of social organization than we now have; production for use is spoken of as natural and moral; the abolition of classes is mentioned as not an impossibility.

This, it is clear, is not a social vision likely to heighten anyone's ardor, but perhaps this is not wholly a fault when we remember that neither is it likely to engender despair by raising unrealizable expectations. Of its obvious inadequacies, some may be said to arise from certain deficiencies of Mr. Eliot's temperament where it joins with certain aspects of strict and theological Anglicanism, giving us such things as the cold ignorance of what people are really like, or a confusion of morality with snobbery or conformity, or even with a rather fierce Puritanism. More important than these, however, are the inadequacies which come from an insufficient view —insufficient even when we consider the self-imposed limitations of the work—of the relation of social forms to power and of power to wealth. Without a specific consideration of this problem even a religious politics—and even the most theoretical treatment of such a politics—must seem evasive.

Yet when we have recognized all the inadequacies of Mr. Eliot's conception there still remains a theoretical interest which in the long run has, I think, its own practical value, and this lies in the assumption upon which Mr. Eliot's society is based. Mr. Eliot has not written his apologia and has not, so far as I know, made a systematic statement of belief; but I think a sentence in his essay on Pascal makes clear what the grounds of his belief are. Mr. Eliot is talking about the "unbeliever's" inability to understand the way the "intelligent believer" comes to his faith; the unbeliever, he says, "does not consider that if certain emotional states, certain developments of character and what in the highest sense can be called 'saintliness' are inherently and by inspection known to be good, then the satisfactory explanation of the world must be an explanation which will admit the 'reality' of these values." This sentence, which could not have been carelessly written, indicates that Mr. Eliot is perhaps closer than he would admit to the pragmatic theology of Matthew Arnold which he so much disdains.

But the exact nature of Mr. Eliot's theology is not for the moment important. What touches our problem of a whole new intellectual world and what I should like to take hold of, not only for itself but for what it indicates beyond itself, is the morality with which Mr. Eliot is concerned. "I am inclined," he said some time ago, "to approach public affairs from the point of view of the moralist," and over and over again he has insisted that to think of politics and economics as independent of morality is impossible: impossible in an ethical sense—the political and economic theorist *should not* so consider them; and impossible in a practical sense—the theorist *cannot* construct his theories except on the ground (often unexpressed) of moral assumptions. "I feel no confidence in any scheme for putting the world in order," Mr. Eliot said, "until the proposer has answered satisfactorily the question: What is the good life?"

Everybody, of course, approves of morality. Even Leon Trotsky, who was suspicious of the morality of all moralists, spoke well of it. But, like Trotsky, most people think of morality in a somewhat ambiguous fashion: it is something to be cultivated after the particular revolution they want is accomplished, but just now it is only in the way; or they think of it as whatever helps to bring the revolution about. But Mr. Eliot thinks of morality as absolute and not as a means but an end; and, what is more, he believes that it is at every moment a present end and not one indefinitely postponable. He does not mean merely social good and the doing of it (though this enters too) and he does not mean anything which is to be judged only from a utilitarian point of view. He means something which is personal in a way we have forgotten and which, in a way we have denied, connects personal action with the order of the universe. When he says that he is a moralist in politics he means most importantly that politics is to be judged by what it does for the moral perfection, rather than for the physical easement, of man. For the earthly good of man—the localizing adjective is important for Mr. Eliot—is moral perfection; what advances this is politically good, what hinders it is politically bad.

Now I do not think, with Mr. Eliot, that morality is absolute but I do believe that his way of considering morality has certain political advantages over Trotsky's way or the Marxist way in general. If one thing more than another marks the culture of radicalism in recent years it is that a consideration of means has taken a priority over the consideration of ends—or perhaps, to avoid the chances of a means-and-ends misunderstanding, we might rather say that immediate ends have become more important than ultimate ends. The radical intellectual of today differs from his political ancestor of even twenty-five years ago in the interest he finds in the immediate method as against the ultimate purpose. And if we take a longer period we find an even greater difference. The preparatory days of revolution—I mean the days from Montaigne to Rousseau and Diderot—were the days in which men projected a great character for man. The social imagination, when it was fresher, gave the worlds of the future a quality which our projected worlds can no longer have. The French Revolution was advanced on the warmest considerations of personality—one thinks of Montaigne's Montaigne, of Rousseau's Rousseau and his Émile, of Diderot's d'Alembert and his Rameau's nephew. And it is incidentally significant that, after this time, in every nation touched by the Revolution, the novel should have taken on its intense life. For what so animated the novel of the nineteenth century was the passionate—the "revolutionary"—interest in what man should be. It was, that is, a moral interest, and the world had the sense of a future moral revolution. Nowadays the novel, and especially in the hands of the radical intellectuals, has become enfeebled and mechanical: its decline coincides with the increasing indifference to the question, What should man become?

The heightened tempo of events will go far toward explaining the change—the speed with which calamity approached, our sense of the ship sinking and our no doubt natural giving to survival the precedence over the quality of the life that was to be preserved. Much of the change can be laid to the account of Marx, for it was Marx, with his claim to a science of society, with his concept of materialistic and dialectical causation, who, for his adherents, made the new emphasis seem unavoidable. Considerations of morality Marx largely scorned; he begins in morality, in the great historical and descriptive chapters of *Capital,* but he does not continue in it, perhaps because he is led to believe that the order of the world is going to establish morality. He speaks often of human dignity, but just what human dignity is he does not tell us, nor has any adequate Marxist philosopher or poet told us: it is not a subject which comes within the scope of their science.

Yet not merely upon the tempo of events nor upon Marx himself can we lay the indifference to morality and to aims. It must fall on something of which Marx was indeed a part and of which the tempo is of course a part but of which each of us is also a part: on the total imagination of our time. It is the characteristic of this imagination so to conceive the human quality that it diminishes with ever-increasing speed before the exigencies of means.

Lenin gave us the cue when, at the end of *The State and Revolution,* he told us that we might well postpone the problem of what man is to become until such time as he might become anything he chose. One understands how such a thing gets said; but one understands too that saying it does not make possible a suspension of choice: it is a choice already made and the making of it was what gave certain people the right to wonder whether the ethics and culture of Communism were anything else than the extension of the ethics and culture of the bourgeois business world. For many years the hero of our moral myth was the Worker-and-Peasant who smiled from the covers of *Soviet Russia Today,* simple, industrious, literate—and grateful. Whether or not people like him actually existed is hard to say; one suspects not and hopes not; but he was what his leaders and the radical intellectuals were glad to propagate as a moral ideal; that probably factitious Worker was the moral maximum which the preoccupation with immediate ends could accommodate.

The diminished ideal which was represented by that Worker is what Mr. Eliot would perhaps call, in his way, a heresy. But from another point of view it is also a practical, a political, error. It is the error which lies hidden in materialist and rationalist psychology. Against it a certain part of the nineteenth century was always protesting. Wordsworth was one of the first to make the protest when he discarded the Godwinian view of the mind, advanced a psychology of his own and from it derived a politics. No doubt his politics was, in the end, reactionary enough; but it became reactionary for this reason as much as any other: that it was in protest against the view of man shared alike by Liberal manufacturing Whig and radical philosopher, the view that man was very simple and individually of small worth in the cosmic or political scheme. It was because of this view that Wordsworth deserted the Revolution; and it was to supply what the Revolution lacked or, in some part, denied, that he wrote his best poetry.

What the philosophy of the Revolution lacked or denied it is difficult to find a name for. Sometimes it gets called mysticism, but it is not mysticism and Wordsworth is not a mystic. Sometimes, as if by a kind of compromise, it gets called "mystery," but that, though perhaps closer, is certainly not close enough. What is meant negatively is that man cannot be comprehended in a formula; what is meant positively is the sense of complication and possibility, of surprise, intensification, variety, unfoldment, worth. These are things whose more or less abstract expressions we recognize in the arts; in our inability to admit them in social matters lies a great significance. Our inability to give this quality a name, our embarrassment, even, when we speak of it, marks a failure in our thought. But Wordsworth was able to speak of this quality and he involved it integrally with morality and all the qualities of mind which morality suggests. Eventually he made morality absolute and admittedly he engaged it with all sorts of unsound and even dangerous notions. But, as he conceived the quality, it was a protection against the belief that man could be made into a means and it was an affirmation that every man was an end.

It is a tragic irony that the diminution of the moral possibility, with all that the moral possibility implies of free will and individual value, should spring, as it does, from the notion of the perfectibility of man.[3] The *ultimate man* has become the end for which all temporal men are the means. Such a notion is part of the notion of progress in general, a belief shared by the bourgeois and the Marxist, that the direction of the world is that of a never-ceasing improvement. So far as Marxism goes, this idea seems to have a discrepancy with the Marxist dialectic, for it depends on a standard of judgment which, if not an absolute, is so close to an absolute as to be indistinguishable from it—the judgment of direction, the certainty of what "higher" signifies and what "better" signifies. One has only to hear a Marxist defend (as many a Marxist will) the belief that through the ages even art shows a definable progress and improvement to understand how untenable the notion is in any of its usual statements. And the progress which is held to be observable in art is held to be no less observable in human relations.

And from the notion of progress has grown that contempt for the past and that worship of the future which so characteristically marks the radical thought of our time. The past is seen as a series of necessary failures which perhaps have their value as, in the dialectical way, they contribute to what comes after. The past has been a failure: the present—what can it matter in the light of the perfecting future? And from—or with—a sense of the past as failure, and of the present as nothing better than a willing tributary to the future, comes the sense of the wrongness of the human quality at any given moment. For, while they have always violently

[3] I leave it to some novelist to explore the more subtle results of the confused denial of the moral possibility as it appears in the personal lives of radical intellectuals. They have used the denial, of course, to explain the conduct of men less equipped than themselves for thought; they have declared that the mass of men are not to be held morally responsible for their own deeds and that only history and environment are accountable. I think no one can reject this generous assumption. But questions must arise concerning what method we are to use in the judgment of men who are our equals in moral and intellectual training. And the same question about a method of judgment must arise about oneself, for in actual practice we do not easily tolerate people who are content to ascribe their personal—I do not mean their practical—failures to circumstance alone. That novelists have not dealt with this problem seems to me to bear out what I said about the failure of the novel in the hands of the radical intellectual. Two exceptions must be noted: Malraux's *Man's Fate* and Silone's *Bread and Wine*.

reprobated any such notion as Original Sin and by and large have held the belief that, by nature, man is good, most radical philosophies have contradicted themselves by implying that man, in his quality, in his kind, will be wholly changed by socialism in fine ways that we cannot predict: man will be good not as some men have been, but good in new and unspecified fashions. At the bottom of at least popular Marxism there has always been a kind of disgust with humanity as it is and a perfect faith in humanity as it is to be.

Mr. Eliot, as I have said in passing, has his own disgust; his later criticism has shown his pained surprise at any manifestation of life that is not canonically correct. But at least Mr. Eliot's feelings are appropriate to the universe he assumes, and at least he is aware of them and makes provision for them. Of his universe Mr. Eliot predicates two things: a divine ordination and an absolute morality. From these two assumptions spring two practical conclusions which are worthy of note. The first is that the life of man involves a dual allegiance, one to the Universal Church which represents the divinely ordained universe and one to the nation and the National Church which represents temporal necessities; and the commitment of the National Church to an absolute morality makes, within the nation itself, a dualism, for the National Church, in its function, may be in disagreement with the national state. This dualism constitutes, Mr. Eliot believes, a barrier against monistic solutions of political problems such as statism or racism, and the tensions it creates are, for him, the distinguishing mark of a Christian society. The second thing implied by Mr. Eliot's assumptions is that there exists a moral goal never to be reached and a political ideal never to be realized. The world, we are told, will never be left wholly without glory, but all earthly societies are sordidly inadequate beside the ideal. This moral Platonism puts, of course, a check upon the hopes of man and restricts the possibility of "progress" yet its tragic presuppositions have this good result: that they bar any such notion as that of a *final* conflict and prevent us from envisaging any such ultimate moral victory as will permit the "withering away of the state"; they make us admit that the conflict is everlasting and in doing so they permit us to exercise a kind of charity by which we may value the humanity of the present equally with that of the future.

We say that our assumptions arise from our needs and must suit our intentions, and so they must; and perhaps in relatively recent times intelligent men of religion have been more honest in admitting the necessary assumptive elements in thought than have the radical philosophers with their tendency to hold all assumption illegitimate. Mr. Eliot shares this honesty and his thought benefits from it and our thought may benefit from the virtues his thought has. But if our assumptions spring from our needs, it is nevertheless still true that the validity of our needs and the relations between our intentions and our needs may be logically and empirically tested. So tested, Mr. Eliot's polity will not, I think, stand. If, for example, he believes that there is an historical instance or a practical likelihood of a church effectively providing the "tensions" he speaks of, he is, I think, deceiving himself. I think, indeed, that, whatever his intentions, the ecclesiastical instrument upon which he relies is, in "the practical sphere," bound to be maleficent. If I have tried to say that the assumptions of materialism have largely failed us, it was surely not to conclude that the assumptions of supernaturalism can aid us. Based as it is on supernatural assumptions, Mr. Eliot's politics is no doubt thoroughly vulnerable. But I have spoken of it with respect because it suggests elements which a rational and naturalistic philosophy, to be adequate, must encompass.

An American in Spain

[A review of *For Whom the Bell Tolls* by Ernest
Hemingway. *Partisan Review*, January-February
1941[1]]

T
O anyone at all interested in its author's career—and who is
not?—*For Whom the Bell Tolls* will first give a literary
emotion. For here, we feel at once, is a restored Hemingway
writing to the top of his bent. He does not, as in the period of *To
Have and Have Not* and *The Fifth Column,* warp or impede his
notable talent with the belief that art is to be used like the auto-
matic rifle. He does not substitute political will for literary insight
nor arrogantly pass off his personal rage as social responsibility.
Not that his present political attitude is coherent or illuminating;
indeed, it is so little of either that it acts as the anarchic element
in a work whose total effect is less impressive than many of its parts.
Yet at least it is flexible enough, or ambiguous enough, to allow
Hemingway a more varied notion of life than he has ever before
achieved.

With the themes that bring out his craft most happily Hemingway has never been so good—no one else can make so memorable the
events of physical experience, how things look and move and are related to each other. From the beginning of the novel to the end,
one has the happy sense of the author's unremitting and successful
poetic effort. So great is this effort, indeed, that one is inclined to
feel that it is at times even too great, that it becomes conscious of

<hr>

[1] This review was slightly revised for its publication in *The Partisan Reader,
1934–1944,* and it is this altered version which appears here. (D.T.)

itself almost to priggishness and quite to virtuosity. About some of the very good moments—they are by now famous—one has the uneasy sense that they are rather too obviously "performances": I mean moments so admirable as the account of the massacre of the fascists by the republicans, as well as moments so much less good because so frankly gaudy as the description of the "smell of death" —the really superlative passages, such as the episode of El Sordo on his hill or Andres making his way through the republican lines, which are equal to Tolstoy in his best battle-manner, are more modestly handled. And the sense of the writer doing his duty up to and beyond the point of supererogation is forced on us in the frequent occurrence of the kind of prose of which Hemingway has always allowed himself a small, perhaps forgivable, amount when he wishes to deal with emotions which he considers especially diffi- cult, delicate, or noble. This kind of writing, obtrusively "literary," oddly "feminine," is most frequently used for the emotions of love and it is always in as false and fancy taste as this:

Now as they lay all that before had been shielded was unshielded. Where there had been roughness of fabric all was smooth with a smoothness and firm rounded pressing and a long warm coolness, cool outside and warm within, long and light and closely holding, closely held, lonely, hollow-making with contours, happy-making, young and loving and now all warmly smooth with a hollowing, chest-aching, tight-held loneliness that was such that Robert Jordan felt he could stand it. . . .

Yet the virtuosity and the lapses of taste are but excesses of an effort which is, on the whole, remarkably successful. And if we cannot help thinking a little wryly about how much tragic defeat, how much limitation of political hope, was necessary before Hemingway could be weaned from the novel of arrogant political will, neither can we help being impressed by what he has accomplished in the change.

I speak first and at some length of the style of *For Whom the Bell Tolls* because it seems to me that the power and charm of the book arise almost entirely from the success of the style—from the success of many incidents handled to the full of their possible interest. The power and charm do not arise from the plan of the book as a whole; when the reading is behind us, what we remember is a series of brilliant scenes and a sense of having been almost constantly excited, but we do not remember a general significance. Yet Hemingway, we may be sure, intended that the star-crossed love and heroic death of Robert Jordan should be a real tragedy, a moral and political tragedy which would suggest and embody the tragedy of the Spanish war. In this intention he quite fails. The clue to the failure is the essential inner dullness of his hero. Robert Jordan does not have within himself what alone could have made tragedy out of this remarkable melodrama—he does not in himself embody the tensions which were in the historical events he lived through. His fate is determined by the moral and political contradictions of the historical situation, but he himself explicitly refuses to recognize these contradictions, he stands apart from them. And since it is Jordan's fate that must provide whatever intellectual architectonic the novel is to have, the novel itself fails, not absolutely but relatively to its possibility and to its implied intention.

This failure illustrates as well as anything could the point of Philip Rahv's essay, "The Cult of Experience in American Writing" (*Partisan Review,* November-December 1940). For here again we have the imbalance which Mr. Rahv speaks of as characteristic of the American novel—on the one hand the remarkable perception of sensory and emotional fact, on the other hand an inadequacy of intellectual vitality. Consider as an illuminating detail the relation which Hemingway establishes between Robert Jordan and the leaders he admires, Goltz the general and Karkov the journalist. Both are cynical and exceptionally competent men, wholly capable of understanding all the meanings of the revolutionary scene. But they are Europeans and Robert Jordan is not; like the hero of Henry James's *The American,* he knows that there are machinations going on around him, very wrong but very wonderful, which he will never be able to understand. Nor does he really want to understand as his friends do. He wants, he says, to keep his mind in suspension until the war is won. He wants only to feel emotions and ideals, or, as a technician and a brave man, to *do* what he is told. The thinking is for others. Yet, like a Henry James character again, he must penetrate the complex secret: but he has no wish to use it, only to *experience* it, for he likes, as he says, the feeling of being an "insider," which is what one becomes by losing one's American "chastity of mind," telling political lies with the Russians in Gaylord's Hotel.

Hemingway himself, it would seem, has a full awareness of the complex actuality of the situation. Again and again, and always pungently, he brings to our notice the tensions and contradictions of a revolutionary civil war—describes the cynicism and intrigue and shabby vice of the Russian politicos, pointedly questions the political virtue of La Pasionaria, paints André Marty, in a brilliant and terrifying scene, as a homicidal psychopath under the protection of the Comintern, speaks out about the sins of Loyalist leaders and has only a small and uncertain inclination to extenuate the special sins of the Communists. Indeed, there is scarcely a charge that anti-Stalinists might have made during the war whose truth Hemingway does not in one way or another avow. Yet by some failure of mind or of seriousness, he cannot permit these political facts to become integral with the book by entering importantly into the mind of the hero. Robert Jordan, to be sure, thinks a good deal about all these things, but almost always as if they were not much more than—to use the phrase of another anti-fascist—a matter of taste. He can, in Mr. Rahv's sense of the word, *experience* all the badness, but he cannot deal with it, he dare not judge it.

In the end it kills him. And Hemingway knows, of course, that it kills him and is at pains to make it clear that, of all the things that prevent Robert Jordan's dispatch from arriving in time to halt the ill-fated attack, it is the atmosphere of Gaylord's Hotel that is ultimately culpable; it is Marty's protected madness that seals Jordan's fate. Were this kept in focus we should have had a personal tragedy which would have truly represented the whole tragedy of the Spanish war—the tragedy, that is, which was not merely a defeat by a superior force but also a moral and political failure; for tragedy is not a matter of fact, it is a matter of value. To Robert Jordan his own death is bitter enough, but only as the ultimate incident of his experience. Of its inherent meaning, of its significance in relation to its cause, he has no awareness. Nor is his lack of awareness an intentional irony of which the reader is to be conscious. Hemingway lets the casual significance fade, and Jordan's death becomes very nearly a matter of accident. The book seems to wish to say that the loving and brave will be separated and killed unless men realize their unending community; but it is not only a lack of community that kills Robert Jordan, it is all that is implied by Gaylord's Hotel and André Marty.

It is almost terrifying to see where an author can be led in unintentional falsification by his devotion to naked "experience." Hemingway knows that his hero must die in *some* moral circumstance; he lamely and belatedly contrives for Robert Jordan a problem of—courage. And so we get what we all like, and rightly like, a good fighting death, but in the face of all that Jordan's death truly signifies, this is devastatingly meaningless. Courage, we are told in a last word, is all: and every nerve responds to the farewell, the flying hoofs, the pain and the pathos, but we have been shuffled quite away from tragedy, which is not of the nerves but of judgment and the mind.

The major movement of the novel is, then, a failure, and a failure the more to be regretted because it has so many of the elements of great success. There is another movement of the novel that cannot be judged by quite the same standards of political intelligence—I mean all that part which deals with the guerrilla bands of the mountains. To judge this, one has to understand its genre; one has to see this part of the story as a social romance. I should like to draw on Mr. Rahv again: he remarks in another of his essays ("Paleface and Redskin," *Kenyon Review,* Summer, 1939) that Hemingway may well be understood as a descendant of Natty Bumppo. Certainly in each of Hemingway's heroes there is a great deal of the Leatherstocking blood, though "crossed" (as Leatherstocking himself would say) with the gentler, more sensitive blood of Uncas. And as Leatherstocking-Uncas, the perfect scout, Robert Jordan is all decision, action, and good perception, far more interesting and attractive than in his character of looker-on at the political feasts of the Russians where he is a kind of Parsifal, the culpable innocent who will not ask the right questions. But more than the character of this hero takes its rise from Cooper—more, too, than Hemingway's "sense of terrain" which Edmund Wilson speaks of as being like Cooper's. For when we think of how clear a line there is between Uncas, Chingachgook and Tamenund, the noble Indians, and El Sordo and Anselmo and the rest of the guerrilla band, we see how very like Cooper's is Hemingway's romantic sense of the social and personal virtues.

With Cooper, however, the social idealization is more formal, more frankly "mythical"—he does not quite require that we really believe in his Indians, only learn from them. But Hemingway does want us to believe in his guerrillas with their strange, virtuous Indian-talk, and he wants us to love them. We cannot truly believe in them. And we cannot quite love them because we sense, as we usually do in a love affair between a writer and a virtuous nation or people or class—such as between Kipling and the sahibs or, to speak of a minor but socially interesting writer of today, between Angela Thirkell and the English upper middle class—that there is pretty sure to appear, sooner or later, a hatred of the outlander. If one cannot make an identification with Hemingway's guerrillas— and it is difficult—it is because they suggest their own unique and superior moral charm rather than the human community the novel undertakes to celebrate.

There is something pretty suspect, too, in the love-story of this novel, which has so stirred and charmed the reviewers. By now the relation between men and women in Hemingway's novels has fixed itself into a rather dull convention according to which the men are all dominance and knowledge, the women all essential innocence and responsive passion. These relationships reach their full development almost at the moment of the first meeting and are somehow completed as soon as begun. Most significant, one feels of love in the Hemingway novels that it can exist at all only because circumstances so surely doom it. We do not have to venture very deep into unexpressed meanings to find a connection between Hemingway's social myth and the pattern of his love stories—in both there is a desperation which makes a quick grab for simple perfection. This desperation makes understandable the compulsive turning to courage as the saving and solving virtue. The whole complex of attitudes is, we might say, a way of responding to the imminent idea of death.

I am by no means in agreement with the many critics who, in writing about Hemingway, have expressed their annoyance that anyone should deal with death except as a simple physical fact. I am far from sure that our liberal, positive, progressive attitudes have taught us to be emotionally more competent before the idea of death, but only more silent; and I certainly do not assume that anyone is committing a political misdemeanor when he breaks our habit of silence. Yet in Hemingway's response to the idea of death there is something indirect and thwarted, as though he had not wholly escaped our reticences to meditate freely upon the theme, as could, say, a death-haunted man like John Donne, from whom Hemingway takes the epigraph and title of his novel. For Donne, death is the appalling negation and therefore the teacher of the ego. For Hemingway, death is the ego's final expression and the perfect protector of the personality. It is a sentimental error from which Donne was saved by his great power of mind. And it was from Donne's truer response to death that he learned the true nature of the ego, how little it can exist by itself, how "no man is an *Ilande intire of itselfe.*" Hemingway, so much at the service of the cult of experience, debars himself from what Donne learned from his contemplation of death. As a consequence, it is the isolation of the individual ego in its search for experience that Hemingway celebrates in this novel that announces as its theme the community of men.

The Wordsworths

[A review of *The Journals of Dorothy Words-worth*, edited by Ernest de Selincourt. *The New Republic*, August 24, 1942]

ABOUT a year ago a little volume appeared called *The Poetry of Dorothy Wordsworth*. Of course, Dorothy Wordsworth wrote no poetry, although her brother and Coleridge lifted many of her observations for poems of their own. But many people have felt that Dorothy's journals show her to be "essentially" a poet, a poet *manqué,* and Mr. Hyman Eigerman, the editor of the little volume, felt this so strongly that he selected eighty-four passages from the journals and arranged them in the form of free verse. This ingenious manipulation of what Dorothy Wordsworth wrote made me uneasy when I first looked at it, and now as I read the journals in Mr. Ernest de Selincourt's admirable new edition I feel even more strongly that it is exactly as a writer of excellent prose and not as an unfulfilled poet that Dorothy Wordsworth shines.

The opposition in our language between the words "poetry" and "prose" has always made trouble. We say, "This is poetic," and mean praise, but we cannot praise by saying, "This is prosaic." Yet we ought to be able to use just that word in commendation of Dorothy Wordsworth's writing. It has the prose virtues; it is plain, direct and firm; it has the prose cadences, the prose *tone* which is delightful to many ears. And when the emphasis of verse arrangement is imposed upon it, the virtues and charm vanish. Take the most famous sentences from the Alfoxden journal: "Grasmere very solemn in the last glimpse of twilight. It calls home the heart to quietness." The charm lies precisely in the evenness of emphasis with which we read, and this disappears when the sentences are arranged:

> Grasmere very solemn
> In the last glimpse of twilight.
> It calls home the heart
> To quietness.

Or take another passage:

It was a mild afternoon—there was an unusual softness in the prospect as we went, a rich yellow upon the fields, and a soft grave purple on the waters. When we returned many stars were out, the clouds were moveless, in the sky soft purple, the lake of Rydale calm, Jupiter behind. Jupiter at least *we* call him, but William says we always call the largest star Jupiter.

This has its own small unity and a nice little humorousness at the end; but the structure weakens, the sturdiness of tone evaporates and the humor turns into mere archness when we read it this way:

> There was an unusual softness
> In the prospect, as we went,
> A rich yellow upon the fields,
> And a soft grave purple in the waters.
> When we returned many stars were out,
> The clouds were moveless,
> In the sky, soft purple,
> The lake of Rydale calm, Jupiter behind.
> Jupiter at least we call him, but William says
> We always call the brightest star Jupiter.

And one last example. Dorothy writes:

O, thought I! what a beautiful thing God has made winter to be by stripping the trees, and letting us to see their shapes and forms. What a freedom does it seem to give to the storms.

Here the conception is better than its expression, but how much better is the prose expression than the verse which, by emphasizing the unlucky rhyme, *storms-forms,* and by picking out a line of sound in *be, trees, see, seem,* makes the statement more excited and for that reason trivial.

Mr. Eigerman's selections from the journals were made with sure taste and his experiment was eminently worth making; my reading of it differs from his and I express my difference only because, as it seems to me, we have grown callous to the possible virtues of prose and to its claims in its own right. Then too, I think we do Dorothy Wordsworth an injustice if we expect her to be always incandescent as in the passages Mr. Eigerman selects. As her youth passes, the personal tone diminishes; the incandescent and "poetic" passages become far less frequent even in the first Scottish journal and are rare in the journals of the Continental and the second Scottish tours, and as she began to think of writing not only for herself and William, but for a large circle of friends. The intimacy of the Alfoxden and Grasmere journals is a loss indeed, but the firm, unequivocal prose, marked by the old precise rhetoric of the eighteenth century, was still at her command to express the observations of her clear, sensible intelligence.

As for the Grasmere journal, I find it as fascinating as ever but one of the most painful books I know. "Nature never did betray / The heart that loved her": so Wordsworth had promised his sister in the great year of 1798. He was twenty-eight then, Dorothy two years younger. In a few years William was to learn and say how little one could believe this promise; Dorothy, in her own way, had learned it earlier. The Grasmere journal is usually remembered for its exquisite observations of nature and its record of homely pleasures, but it is also the record of a woman terribly betrayed by Nature, though not quite the Nature Wordsworth had in mind. For one thing, there is so much illness—concern over Coleridge's health, and William was so frequently ailing, and Dorothy herself is always recording her headaches, her disorders of the bowels and teeth, as matters of simple accepted fact. But not always simple accepted fact: "My tooth broke today. They will soon be gone. Let that pass, I shall be beloved—I want no more." This is in May,

1802; she was not yet thirty-one but a large part of her life was coming to an end—what she was much later to call "the shapeless wishes of my youth, wishes without hope"—for in November of that year William was to marry Mary Hutchinson. As the wedding date approaches, Dorothy's illness increases noticeably. Her straining for control becomes pitiable; she is unable at last to attend the ceremony but lies prostrate on a bed to wait the return of the wedding party and to make a third with the bride and groom on the wedding journey back to Grasmere.

The longest period of her life was peaceful but the end of the "betrayal" was grim and throws light on the beginning. In 1848 the Duke of Argyle was touring the Lake Country with his young wife. He passionately admired Wordsworth and he stopped to visit the poet, now seventy-eight. As the young couple walked through the woods to Rydale, they stepped aside to make way for a wheel-chair in which sat an old lady with blank and vacant eyes. They were chilled by the encounter but they recovered their spirits as they went forward to the house and were received cordially by their host. After a pleasant chat, Wordsworth consented to read one of his poems for them. He chose "Tintern Abbey," that first of his great meditations on the theme of man's growth and development. When he came to the apostrophe to his sister which includes the promise that "Nature never did betray / The heart that loved her," and reached the lines

> . . . In thy voice I catch
> The language of my former heart and read
> My former pleasures in the shooting lights
> Of thy wild eyes . . .

he put a special emphasis on the last words. The visitors later learned that the old lady of the vacant stare was Dorothy of the wild eyes; they must also have learned that she was not only mad but that in her lucid moments her tongue was wittily spiteful and obscene.

The Progressive Psyche

[A review of *Self-Analysis* by Karen Horney. *The Nation*, September 12, 1942]

READERS of this review, like its writer, will be diffident of judging the technical grounds on which Dr. Karen Horney has forced a schism in the ranks of American psychoanalysis. But Dr. Horney is not only a clinical physician; one of the few psychoanalytical writers of recent years to capture the imagination of the general public, she has established a philosophy of human nature and society on the basis of her divergence from Freud and has become, not one of the seminal, but surely one of the symptomatic minds of our time. Her work, therefore, may be judged not merely in a professional but also in a cultural context.

In her latest book Dr. Horney carries her rejection of Freud's theories about as far as it can go short of an explicit denial of the unconscious mind; she propounds the belief that by adapting the techniques of regular analysis a neurotic person can effectually psychoanalyze himself. Judging by the criteria available to a layman, it seems to me that Dr. Horney makes but a weak case for her belief. The evidence she adduces is, in point of quantity, not adequate; in all propriety, so important an idea—important because it controverts one of Freud's fundamental concepts but important too because it is sure to raise hope in so many hearts—should be advanced on a wider and firmer ground of fact. Dr. Horney cites but four illustrative cases of "occasional self-analysis"—that is, of people who, equipped with some degree of psychoanalytical knowledge, were able by their own efforts to gain insight into and relief from some simply motivated psychic disturbance. Of systematic self-analysis she gives but a single example, and the case of Clare, a young woman who ventured into self-analysis after a year and a half of analysis with Dr. Horney, is possibly suggestive but not convincing. This patient no doubt advanced her understanding of her unconscious motives and thereby won a measure of emotional freedom; yet it is not entirely clear why her discoveries about herself—they are not remarkably deep—were not in large part her belated, developing realization of insights to which she had been helped by Dr. Horney in the course of her regular analysis.

In place of evidence Dr. Horney gives us argument and moral exhortation. The argument is dashing but verbalistic and prestidigitary; I shall touch on some of its assumptions below, but I cannot help feeling that, in a popular book like this, exhortation is even more important than argument and that the exhortation is a little irresponsible. When Dr. Horney suggests that one of the advantages of self-analysis is the pride that comes from getting out of neurotic difficulties all by oneself, she implies assent to the popular feeling that there is something "humiliating" about psychoanalysis; and it is hard not to contemplate the even greater pride we might get from bringing ourselves up. When she tells us that, after all, a neurotic lives with himself all the time and therefore knows himself better than anyone else can, I do not understand her. When she tells us that "life itself is the best therapist," I find her trivial.

Then, too, I am disturbed by Dr. Horney's inconsistency in her own statements of the scope and value of self-analysis; she insists on its feasibility, says that some self-analysts have "dealt with problems that are generally deemed inaccessible even with the help of an analyst" and that some have succeeded where analysts have failed, questions whether self-analysis may not be conducted even without the occasional help and supervision which, as a general rule, she feels to be necessary; but when she commits herself to a summation of the possible effectiveness of self-analysis, she is far from sanguine: "Therefore after a period of common work with an analyst even patients who started with severe neurotic difficulties may in some cases be able to continue on their own, if necessary." I feel that a conclusion so tentative on a matter so important should have been confined to a scientific paper, not communicated with enthusiasm and more than a hint of promise to a general public always avid for new ways of psychic self-help.

For psychoanalytical theory the crucial point of *Self-Analysis* is its substantial denial of Freud's theory of "resistance." According to Freud, the neurosis, however painful, serves a certain purpose; the very symptoms which are so painful cloak impulses which the patient fears and cannot cope with. Even when they are pointed out to him by the analyst, the patient is likely to deny their existence because they are repulsive to his morals and pride; indeed, for a long time he will not even perceive them, for, perverse as the idea may seem, there are powerful forces in the unconscious mind which desire the unhappy neurotic status quo. Dr. Horney does not, to be sure, explicitly reject the theory of resistance which is so basic to the theory of the unconscious, but she does everything possible to minimize the fierce stubbornness Freud attributes to it. She insists that with the right spirit and a sufficient will (knowledge is of far less importance), the patient will be able to bring to light the hidden elements which the unconscious is at such pains to hide. No doubt it is the easier for Dr. Horney to maintain this because in her present book there is no slightest mention of those unconscious drives which are so horrifying to our conscious minds, such as homosexuality, sadism, masochism, Oedipus feelings. (Of course, many educated persons nowadays are willing to admit finding these elements in themselves, but their perception is at most a "novelistic" one, far short in intensity of a psychoanalytical realization.) The effect of Dr. Horney's position is that, though she continues to affirm her belief in the unconscious, she actually denies it by making it an unconscious so easily accessible to an untrained person working on himself; she seems to be talking rather of an "unawareness" or of what, by popular habit, is so often and so significantly substituted for unconscious, a "subconscious."

I have spoken of Dr. Horney as one of the symptomatic minds of our time; she is symptomatic—and most notably in her latest book —of one of the great inadequacies of liberal thought, the need for optimism. It seems to me that her denial or attenuation of most of Freud's concepts is the response to the wishes of an intellectual class which has always found Freud's ideas cogent but too stringent and too dark. They have always wanted a less tragic and strenuous psychology, a more reasonable, decent, and cooperative psyche, and Dr. Horney, in all her three books, has given them what they want.

The basis of Dr. Horney's divergence from Freud is an emotional one; her protest is always that Freud sets gloomy bounds to man's nature, that he is negative, cynical, without "faith." In her present book she quotes with approval a passage from Max Otto: "The deepest source of man's philosophy, the one that shapes and nour- ishes it, is faith or lack of faith in mankind." But there is no such simple alternative and it is dangerous to suppose there is—as we see when we understand what "faith in mankind" means for Dr. Horney. It means the belief that man is "free" and "good"—she has revived those old, absolute simplicities of eighteenth-century liberal- ism. To assert man's "freedom" she attacks Freud for finding man's psyche biologically determined; she often speaks of Freud as an old-fashioned dualist (it is clear that he is quite the opposite), but actually her own passionate rejection of the biological determination of mind constitutes a dualism of the most sterile sort and puts the attributes of body in a "lower" place. Further, in attacking Freud for his biological orientation, she makes the tiresome old mistake of confusing mind with the determinants of mind. Then, in the place of Freud's biological determination she puts a determination by culture: there can be no doubt that Dr. Horney has done psycho- analysis a service by forcing the cultural issue; Freud's views of culture, though suggestive, are surely not adequate. But Dr. Horney's view of culture is both vague and formalistic. Sometimes culture is a norm by which we judge whether or not a certain way of action is neurotic, but then again a culture may itself be neurotic, though by what norm we judge the culture (possibly a biological one?) we are not told. In Dr. Horney's hands culture becomes as much an absolute as she claims biology is in Freud's; but Freud saw a complex and passionate interplay between biology and culture, whereas Dr. Horney sees the individual infant as a kind of box into which culture drops this trend or that. The Freudian man may not be as free as we should like, but at least he has insides.

Then, in order to affirm that man is "good," Dr. Horney, like Erich Fromm, attacks Freud's theory of morals for representing morals as arising from forces themselves not virtuous. This Dr. Horney calls a fallacy of genesis, which of course it is not. She represents Freud as implying that virtue is not virtue because it springs from destructive or anarchic origins, but this Freud never does imply—Dr. Horney, by the way, is not the most reliable expositor of Freud; indeed, if anyone has committed the genetic fallacy, Dr. Horney has done so by implying that virtue can only be virtue if it springs from innate (biological?) virtue.

If we are to talk of faith in man, in the realistic rather than the sentimental sense of that phrase, it seems to me that of the two psychologies it is Freud's that demonstrates faith by daring to present man with the terrible truth of his own nature. When Dr. Horney speaks of faith, she does not mean faith so much as optimism, that emptiest of words. The psyche she has described has won wide assent in liberal, progressive circles exactly because it is a progressive psyche, a kind of New Deal agency which truly intends to do good but cannot always cope with certain reactionary forces. It is a flattering view of the mind and Freud's is not, but Freud's has the advantage of suggesting the savage difficulties of life.

Artists and
the "Societal Function"

[A review of *Writers in Crisis* by Maxwell Geismar, *Directions in Contemporary Literature* by Philo Buck, *The Novel and Society* by N. Elizabeth Monroe. *Kenyon Review*, Autumn 1942]

POETS, Shelley said, are the unacknowledged legislators of the world. The truth of the statement depends partly on the delicacy with which Shelley develops it, but chiefly on that word "unacknowledged." However, for some years an important body of criticism has declared that poets are the fully acknowledged legislators of the world or at least ought to be judged as if they were. Of this school of criticism these three books are the latest exponents.

Mr. Geismar's is the most important of the three because it is the most thoroughgoing and the most urgent and also because it has been the most widely noticed and praised. It is devoted to the demonstration of how the financial collapse of 1929 and the social misery of the following years brought a new prophetic grace to certain of our novelists, what Mr. Geismar calls a "spiritual positive" and a "sense of . . . societal function," and it propounds the belief that the future not only of literature but of democracy depends on the increase of this "spiritual positive" and this sense of "societal function."

Criticism nowadays cannot possibly avoid being concerned with the relation of art and society. But criticism has not done its work by passionately declaring that the relation exists or should exist. Criticism must think clearly and modestly about this important and difficult matter; it must not think like Mr. Geismar—it must not deal in the solemn magics of such phrases as "spiritual positive" and "societal function"; it must work not with attitudes but with ideas: Mr. Geismar's prose, overwrought and badly wrought, jittery rather than nervous, is the very prose for attitude, the very prose to prevent ideas.

Oh marvelous era of the plush speakeasy, the rolled stocking, the bouncing bond, heyday of the athlete and the salesman, paradise of the expatriate and the racketeer, blessed time of Irene and the Black Bottom, we greet you. As we advance to grapple with Whitman's direst fate, we hail you, gorgeous moment of our youth, mystic hour of the transatlantic toot, hail and farewell. With what reverence shall we now gaze back and tenderly treat those fragile ashes of a day forever past. For now the era of the historian himself is slipping by. Now we shall make rather than record your history.

I think that with language like this we can trust Mr. Geismar neither to make nor to record our history.

Consider the chapter in which Mr. Geismar uses Ring Lardner "to summarize the values of the nineteen-twenties." We might ask in passing just whose values Mr. Geismar is talking about: Lardner certainly did not summarize the values of Mr. Geismar, nor of Edmund Wilson, nor of myself, nor of my teachers, nor of *The Dial, The Nation* and *The New Republic*. But what is more important than this simplification of an era is the ground on which Mr. Geismar discusses Lardner's inadequacies. Lardner was a small, very intense talent. His reputation has been somewhat inflated because he was so handy for the critics to use as a symbol for his time. He is interesting for the ferocity of his misanthropic humor; sometimes this misanthropy leads him into rather dull misrepresentation but usually it is very successful. Yet Mr. Geismar finds him, though admirable, a symbol of inadequacy because "his solution of the basic problems of '29 was also as much a part of our world as the Dust Bowl. For he had none." This is critical revelation indeed— Ring Lardner had no solution for the basic problems of '29. Let it make us lenient to his memory to recall that he was of the company of W. C. Fields, Jimmy Durante, John Dewey and Alfred North Whitehead, none of whom had a solution for the basic problems of '29. And let us wonder if there *was* a "solution."

Lardner had a limited, intense, interesting talent. But here are four comments that Mr. Geismar makes upon him:

Blind to the central significance of what he wrote on sex, Lardner was evasive in the mere use of an honest terminology.

For Lardner was as helpless on the deeper meanings of life as his people about their immediate needs.

But he has no purpose to his anger, he has no positive to his hatred and he has no destination beyond destruction.

He saw no way to help his characters; he could only despise them. He could find no way to help himself. He began to despise himself.

No doubt all these statements are true of Lardner and they help to define his limitations; they say respectively that he was not Freud, Goethe, Marx, Jesus, none of whom, by the way, had Lardner's aseptic humor. And one wonders what Mr. Geismar thinks life is that he can demonstrate the inadequacy of a writer's work by showing that he did not bring the saving word and that he died despairing.

I am sure that if we are all converted to Mr. Geismar's belief in the value of the spiritual positive and the societal function there will be no writing at all or only bad writing. Under the burden of societal responsibility surely no writer could do his job. The hardest thing a writer has to do in the adjustment of his internal life is to chase away the imaginary people who stand over his typewriter: he must learn to please himself and only himself. No doubt the old notion of the writer at war with society had its extravagances but we do not correct these by saying that the function of the writer is to provide the stipulated salvation of the moment. And in his concern with spiritual positives Mr. Geismar neglects to understand how astringent and refreshing a good spiritual negative can be. How sound, how precise, how fruitful were Ernest Hemingway's spiritual negatives, and how the little shabbinesses began to come in, how the attitudes began to compete with the insights when those critics with whom Mr. Geismar has such affinity began to convince Hemingway of his need for a societal function and a spiritual positive! Mr. Geismar himself sees—and it is one of the stimulating perceptions of his book—how fabricated Steinbeck's spiritual positives are. This is not because Steinbeck lacks talent or a right philosophy but because he misconceives his role; he thinks like a societal function, not like a novelist.

If we are to talk about literature in its relation with social good and the future of democracy we ought to be aware how harmful literature can be. A book like *The Grapes of Wrath* cockers-up the self-righteousness of the liberal middle class: it is so easy to feel virtuous in our love for such *good* poor people! The social emotions can provide a safe escape from our own lives and from the pressures of self-criticism and generously feed our little aggressions and grandiosities. Shelley says that it would have been a pity if the philosophers of the Enlightenment had never lived, but, he goes on, "it exceeds all imagination to conceive what would have been the moral condition of the world if neither Dante, Petrarch, Boccaccio, Chaucer, Shakespeare, Calderon . . . nor Milton had ever existed." Some of these men were proud, even arrogant, in the ways they conceived their poethood; others were simple, humble or casual; all made their effect by telling the truth about life as they saw it, positive or negative; and they made their effect by being the men they were, by the tone and style of their utterance, not by setting out to fulfill their societal function. It is conceivable that books like Steinbeck's have an immediate useful effect by rallying people to the right side. But ultimately they leave hollowness and confusion.

And how can we expect to get better novels when more and more we try to think of the artist as a messiah? How can we properly judge a book when we feel that a really good book encompasses the whole of life and solves it for us? There is something in thus conceiving the function of art that—extravagant as it may seem to say so—suggests a real danger to democracy. I cannot help seeing the society that Mr. Geismar envisages as a kind of great passive child who says to the artist, "You have a responsibility to me." The last great artist before whom a nation lay passive and adoring, who solved—or dissolved—all problems with his spiritual positive, was Wagner.

One of the elements of Mr. Geismar's thought which allows him to give the artist so fatally an important place in social life is the simplicity with which he sees society. He tells us several times of the great effect that Steinbeck's novel has had upon our national thought. He is of course right: *The Grapes of Wrath* has had great effect. But it did not have this effect unaided. Rather, it was a part of a great cultural trend which was manifest in sociology, economics, psychology, pedagogy, literary scholarship, journalism, the churches, the movies; an important part of the population, by no means all, was expressing a political desire. I do not make this obvious point to diminish the importance of literature but only to suggest that, in so complicated a structure of intellectual responsibilities, literature's responsibility is not quite so great as Mr. Geismar says it is.

Mr. Buck's *Directions in Contemporary Literature* is more academic than Mr. Geismar's book and much less urgent but it is based on substantially the same assumptions. "Is there hope," Mr. Buck asks, "in a world thus distraught, with its physicians apparently in as hopeless a confusion of tongues?" The metaphor is perhaps mixed but the judgment of the role of the writer is clear: he is physician to the rest of us, even if he fails to cure. I find it strange in Mr. Buck that he should ever have supposed that there was good medicine in such soggy medico-legislative spirits as Hauptmann, Pirandello, Tagore and Romains, and that he, a mature man capable of writing books himself, should be surprised and disappointed that Proust, Gide, Huxley, Eliot and Mann do not bring specifics for our world-pains but only emotions and ideas. And at the end of his book Mr. Buck seems to find this strange too: he comes out with a medicine to end all medicines—"A return to the tradition of disciplined individualism and the supreme value of the unique individual." This, I suspect, means little, but it leads Mr. Buck to Montaigne, who gives meaning to what Mr. Buck means and wonderfully illuminates Mr. Geismar's book: "On all occasions men are too ready to throw themselves into other peoples' arms, to save their own, which alone are reliable and powerful, if they can make use of them. Every man rushes elsewhere and into the future, because no man has turned to himself."

Miss Monroe, in *The Novel and Society,* writes out of the smug provincialism of neo-Thomism but she is just as eager as the liberal Mr. Geismar to establish the writer's responsibiltiy to "values" and society. With Miss Monroe, however, there is no fussing around to hunt for values, she has them all nicely in their places and she tells us about them in mim, prodding, didactic sentences. It is a little startling to discover that The Novel is really six women novelists, admirable in the degree that they approach Catholicism but all more admirable than men. The more masculine a writer, the less Miss Monroe admires him; Fielding is far surpassed by Thackeray, who borrowed only Fielding's defects, and Dickens has a hold on us out of all proportion to his merits as a novelist. Miss Monroe is a kind of Prioresse of criticism, and though surrounded by beastly Reeves, Millers and Carpenters in the form of Hemingway, Dos Passos and Huxley, she will have no farthing of grease on her cup of life, so clean does she wipe her lip. She has a gift for making the most startling pronouncements, some of which her publishers have emblazoned on the book jacket: "Sinclair Lewis must have made a fortune at the expense of the society he proposes to satirize"; Hemingway's "novels seem tied down to an unhealthy imagination which cannot escape from what disgusts it—or ought to disgust it." But her most monumental statement is remarkable for its precise summing up of all the pious confusion about the social role of the writer: "It is time now for the novelist to forget his individual concerns and see that if society is allowed to die from inner decay the novel will also die, because society is the very life-blood of fiction."

M., W., F. at 10

[*The Nation*, November 21, 1942]

PROBABLY few *Nation* readers will have heard of the book
I am writing about. It has never been advertised in the literary
sections; it may never have been reviewed. It is *A Survey-
History of English Literature* by William Bradley Otis and Mor-
riss H. Needleman. Its aim is modest: it undertakes to present all
the useful facts and necessary opinions about English literature.
Barnes and Noble first issued it as one of a series of review-outlines
but is seems to have had an unusual success and it is now being
advertised and adopted as a required textbook for college courses.
This utilitarian, rather grubby-looking volume is, I think, one of
the symptoms of our intellectual condition.

My own interest in it is first of all aesthetic. For me there is a
pawky charm in its mysterious critical statements. I like to read of
Thomas Carew:

Gentlemen of the privy chamber (1628). Taster-in-ordinary to the
King (1630). Friend of Suckling. Brilliant wit, lover of women and
rime. Skilfully polished verse, neat and tuneful phrase, mastery of the
overlapped heroic couplet. Second only to Herrick, lacking the latter's
warmth and love of nature, but possessing a sensuous fancy and a becoming virility. . . . Best of his longer poems is "A Rapture," auda-
ciously amatory and "marred" by unreticent passionate "impurity,"
emphasizing the physical (and to some the "perverted") side of love
much in the way of Aretino and Donne. In the latter poem his expressions, metaphysical either through volition or constraint, are not inap-

propriately imaginative; e.g. "And we will coyne young *Cupids,*" and taste "The warme firme Apple, tipt with corall berry." Two of his most common stanzaic structures are *ababcc* and *ababb*.

Of this it is perhaps appropriate to remark, in the cryptic words the authors use of John Webster's work, that its "pornography is endemic rather than deliberate."

Then it is fascinating to read that Bacon's "counsels for the practical life are nucleated by three staple subjects" and to wonder why the authors wrote this rather than "stapled by three nuclear subjects." And there are those mad masterpieces of cautiousness from which we learn of Gibbon that "not only may his anti-Christian arguments be antiquated but his method of historical research may be defective or obsolete," and that his history is "somewhat sneering in its ironical deference toward Christianity." But most engaging of all is the system of parallel opinions, the columns of Suggested Merits balanced by the columns of Suggested Defects. Of *Beowulf* a Suggested Merit is "Broad study of character"; a Suggested Defect is "No minute characterization." Two Suggested Merits of Dr. Johnson are "Teacher of moral wisdom" and "Sonorous words," but a glance to the right discovers that two Suggested Defects are "A moralist in everything he wrote" and "Copious use of Latinized vocabulary." With an apparatus like this it is impossible to go wrong.

For example, under Alexander Pope we find:

Suggested Merits	*Suggested Defects*
2. Heatless, faultless lucidity. Polished and brilliant diction. Unerring choice of right word, incisive.	2. Poor in largeness of imagination. Rhetoric, not poetry. Periphrastic constructions and pretentious expressions.

In every class of English B1 (M., W., F. at 10) some students will take their stand as Merit men or Defect men, but they will be strong-minded rather than well-rounded. Well-rounded students with a proper feeling for the nuances of criticism will know how to deal with the problem of Pope's style: "Pope, by his polished and brilliant diction, his periphrastic constructions and pretentious expressions, achieved a heatless, faultless lucidity. As a result of his unerring choice of the right word he produced rhetoric, not poetry."

But literature is not always easy and even the well-rounded student will be stumped by the Wordsworth situation. For no sooner has he absorbed Suggested Merit 1, "Spiritual love of nature, cosmic sympathy for peaceful things," than he has to square it with Suggested Defect 1, "In a strict sense is not always a descriptive poet, nor a great nature poet." The chances are that he will prefer Suggested Merit 2, "Found God in Nature—pantheistic philosophy," to Defect 2, "Philosophy unorthodox, or materialistic, or pantheistic, or mystical"; with Defects so irreconcilable any sensible student will hang on to Merits. But then he will have to deal with Merit 5, "Love poetry while small in quantity, is important for its personal quality, intensity and significance," as against Defect 5, "Lack of intensity and passion; note the mention but not the expression of sexual passion."

Mr. Otis and Mr. Needleman lack taste and prose, but they have not been lazy—they have accumulated the facts, they have consulted the treatises and learned journals and they cite their sources assiduously and indiscriminately, so that even graduate students use the *Survey-History* as a cram-book, finding it more efficient than the older discursive histories. Perhaps a moderately intelligent graduate student could make use of the facts and laugh at the opinions—although not all the facts are correct (we are told that Swift in *A Modest Proposal* "proposes revoltingly that the Irish should fatten and eat their children for food") and although, in the study of literature, it is often hard to separate fact and opinion. But not all graduate students are moderately intelligent and the *Survey-History* is primarily intended not for graduate students but for undergraduate "majors" in English and for those students who are taking a "required" or an "elective" course in literature, perhaps the only one they will ever have. A concise manual of facts is useful, even a cram-book can be recommended if its purpose is properly understood, but the *Survey-History,* as I have said, is making its way in some of our colleges as a textbook, a historical and critical account of literature, an approved source of attitudes and ideas.

When we have this in mind, the *Survey-History* begins to seem less funny than it is. Of the graduate students and the "majors" in English, a large number become teachers; and it is not at all funny to think of teachers instructing young people in literature out of the opinions and in the style of the *Survey-History*.

It is not essential to anybody's education to know anything at all about Chapman's *Caesar and Pompey,* but when the student reads of this play, "Ethical reflection. Cato, the protagonist, commits suicide," he has been led to suppose that this nugget of inconsequence is a literary fact or idea. When he has been taught that "not the pitter-patter of hearts is involved" in the novels of Scott, "who apparently has no major purpose of crying in the wilderness" and "is quite blind to the abstract intelligence"; or that Sir Thomas Browne wrote "tasseled" prose; or that *The Tempest* is "poetically emotional" although "its character-outlines [have] no particular merit"; or that Milton's *Epitaphium Damonis* is superior to *Lycidas* "in sincerity and purpose"; or that Blake has "intense, ecstatic sensitiveness to impressions" but is "unable to depict his sensibilities," he —who is to be a member of the literary public, possibly a teacher— has had thrust upon him every shabby, fusty, third-rate vulgarity of opinion—I have chosen at random—that has ever attached itself to a work of English literature. Education for democracy? Perhaps we ought to begin with education for democracy's first element, simple intellectual decency.

And perhaps that is the element students are looking for when they turn away from literature to science or even social science. The honest student who takes his one course in literature with the help of the *Survey-History* or with a teacher who can use the *Survey-History* will surely be impatient to get it over with and go on to a less cynical subject. Even the literary student, the "major" in English, will surely need to be fortified by a native sense of intellectual honor if he is not to suppose that the study of literature is the jolliest of the disciplines because in literature anything goes.

In academic circles we hear a great deal about the sad estate into which literary studies have fallen and a great deal about what the function of the teacher of literature should be. Well, let us consider that the authors of the *Survey-History* made their book in an apparently successful effort to meet what is presumably an academic need; let us consider too that they made their book, as their footnotes testify, out of the precious essence of academic literary opinion. They have accumulated all the academic ideas, taking the good with the bad, distilling both into silliness, making a negation of commonsense and meaning. I am not trying to absolve the *Survey-History* nor to indict a profession; but clearly the *Survey-History* could not have been written without the connivance of a large number of teachers of English. And what is important is not that a foolish and vulgar book has been produced but that the written word is being treated without seriousness and respect by the very people who are supposed to be its guardians.

So the *Survey-History* is not a funny book after all. It raises grave thoughts. At the moment, however, I can escape the serious reflections by contemplating Defoe's lack of modern conveniences: I have just discovered in the *Survey-History* that one of Defoe's Suggested Defects is "No plumbing of the soul."

Under Forty

[Contribution to a symposium, American Literature and the Younger Generation of American
Jews. *Contemporary Jewish Record,* February
1944]

[*The participation of writers of Jewish descent in the development
of American letters is a relatively late phenomenon. In the nineteenth century such writers were virtually unknown, and even as
late as the first decade of this century scarcely more than half a
dozen authors of reputation belonged to the Jewish faith. At that
time the majority of Jews living in the United States were new-
comers who for obvious reasons were not prepared to contribute
creatively to the artistic culture of their new homeland.*

*But in recent decades much has happened to change this situation.
With the coming of age of the children of the Jewish immigrants,
we find that quite a few of them are taking their place in the front
ranks of American literature. They function in every sphere of
literary creation—as poets, novelists, playwrights and critics. Their
work is part and parcel of the national literary product, and this is
clear evidence of the fact that the American Jews have reached the
stage of integration with the native environment. They are spec-
tators no longer but full participants in the cultural life of the
country.*

*When all this has been said, however, there are still some pertinent
questions that remain to be asked and certain experiences—sometimes of a transparent and sometimes of a subtle nature—that remain
to be defined. The Jewish heritage is historically of so remarkable a
character, and its effects are so significant on every level of existence,*

that the American writer of Jewish descent can hardly dismiss it as irrelevant to his problems. Specifically, has this writer formed a conscious attitude toward his heritage or does he merely "reflect" it in a passive, haphazard, and largely unconscious fashion? Is there any valid sense in which one can speak of differences between the work of Jews and non-Jews—differences possibly relating both to the choice of literary material and to the imaginative use made of it? Are there certain themes or ideas that are characteristic of modern literature as a whole but toward which the Jew is more responsive, or responsive in a somewhat different way, than his Christian colleagues? Lastly, to what extent, and in what manner, has his awareness of his position as artist and citizen been modified or changed by the revival of anti-Semitism as a powerful force in the political history of our time? To list even a few of such questions is to realize their complexity. Whatever answers might be given will surely hold a psychological no less than an objectively social and cultural meaning.

Our aim in this symposium is to illuminate the various facets of the subject. Accordingly we have invited a representative group of American authors, all under forty years of age, to record their views and experiences, however briefly, in the pages that follow.]

IT IS never possible for a Jew of my generation to "escape" his Jewish origin. In order to be sure of this I have only to remember how, when I was a child beginning to read for pleasure, certain words would leap magnetically to my eye from the page before I had reached them in the text. One such word was "snake"; others were words of such sexual explicitness as a child is likely to meet in his reading; and there was the word "Jew." These were words, that is, which struck straight to the unconscious, where fear, shame, attraction and repulsion are indistinguishable. Yet there was no dramatic or even specific reason why the word "Jew" should produce (as it still produces) so deep, so visceral, a reverberation. I was never a victim of prejudice or persecution. My family was fairly well established; although my parents were orthodox in the form of their religion they had a strong impulse to partake of the general life and to want it for me. My childhood was spent in a comfortable New York suburb where a Jewish group formed around the synagogue an active community large enough to be both interesting and protective; at the same time we Jewish children were perfectly at home in the pleasant public school. Those were days in which Jews lived with an ampler hope than now; yet even then the word "Jew" could have for a Jewish child an emotional charge as strong as I have described.

A childhood feeling so intense obviously does not disappear. It is clear to me that my existence as a Jew is one of the shaping conditions of my temperament, and therefore I suppose it must have its effect on my intellect. Yet I cannot discover anything in my professional intellectual life which I can specifically trace back to my Jewish birth and rearing. I do not think of myself as a "Jewish writer." I do not have it in mind to serve by my writing any Jewish purpose. I should resent it if a critic of my work were to discover in it either faults or virtues which he called Jewish.

In what I might call my life as a citizen my being Jewish exists as a point of honor. The phrase is grandiloquent although I do not mean it to be. I can have no pride in seeing a long tradition, often great and heroic, reduced to this small status in me, for I give only a limited respect to points of honor: they are usually mortuary and monumental, they have being without desire. For me the point of honor consists in feeling that I would not, even if I could, deny or escape being Jewish. Surely it is at once clear how minimal such a position is—how much it hangs upon only a resistance (and even only a passive one) to the stupidity and brutality which make the Jewish situation as bad as it is.

The position I have described as mine is perhaps the position of most American writers of Jewish birth. It creates no surprise and no resentment until it is formulated. And when it is formulated it has, I supoše, a certain gracelessness—if only because millions of Jews are suffering simply because they have the heritage that I so minimize in my own intellectual life. I do not want to "answer" this confrontation—to do so, except at great length and with many modulations, could only make the position appear more graceless than it must seem to some. I would say, however, that we are on all sides required to imagine the unimaginable sufferings of masses of men and that while the most common failure of the imagination will certainly be insensibility, there is also the failure of merely symbolic action, of mere guilty gesture.

But the position I have described brings with it no feeling of guilt toward the American Jewish community. I hope I have enough knowledge and sympathy to understand what has led this community to its impasse of sterility, but understanding does not mitigate the perception of the unhappy fact. If what I have called my "point of honor" is minimal and even negative, if, that is, it does not *want* enough and is nothing more than a resistance to an external force, it seems to me that the position of the American Jewish community is to be described in much the same way. There is, I know, much show and talk of affirmation, but only to the end that the negative, or neuter, elements may be made more acceptable. As I see it, the great fact for American Jews is their exclusion from certain parts of the general life and every activity of Jewish life seems to be a response to this fact.

Jewish religion is, I am sure, very liberal and intelligent and modern. Its function is to provide, chiefly for people of no strong religious impulse, a social and rational defense against the world's hostility. A laudable purpose surely, but not a sufficient basis for a religion; and one has only to have the experience of modern Judaism trying to deal with a death ritual to have the sense of its deep inner uncertainty, its lack of grasp of life which must eventually make even its rational social purpose quite abortive. Modern Jewish religion at its best may indeed be intelligent and soaked in university knowledge, but out of it there has not come a single voice with the note of authority—of philosophical, or poetic, or even of rhetorical, let alone of religious, authority.

Of Jewish cultural movements I know something at first hand, for I once served as a minor editor of a notable journal of Jewish culture. The effort this journal represented was, it even now seems to me, a generous one; but its results were sterile at best. I was deep in—and even contributed to—the literature of Jewish self-realization of which Ludwig Lewisohn was the best-known exponent. This was a literature which attacked the sin of "escaping" the Jewish heritage; its effect, it seems to me, was to make easier the sin of "adjustment" on a wholly neurotic basis. It fostered a willingness to accept exclusion and even to intensify it, a willingness to be provincial and parochial. It is in part accountable for the fact that the Jewish social group on its middle and wealthy levels—that is, where there is enough leisure to allow a conscious consideration of social and spiritual problems—is now one of the most self-indulgent and self-admiring groups it is possible to imagine.

To describe this situation is almost to account for it. And to account for it is, in one sense, to forgive it. But in one sense only: for history does not forgive the results of the unfortunate conditions it brings, and, contrary to the popular belief, suffering does not confer virtue. As the Jewish community now exists, it can give no sustenance to the American artist or intellectual who is born a Jew. And so far as I am aware, it has not done so in the past. I know of writers who have used their Jewish experience as the subject of excellent work; I know of no writer in English who has added a micromillimetre to his stature by "realizing his Jewishness," although I know of some who have curtailed their promise by trying to heighten their Jewish consciousness.

The Head and Heart
of Henry James

[A review of *Henry James: The Major Phase* by
F. O. Matthiessen. *The New York Times Book
Review*, November 26, 1944]

THE interest in Henry James steadily grows—it is one of the
more heartening events of our literary life at the moment.
A few years ago James books were a drug on the second-
hand market. Now they are so rare that it becomes a matter for
surprise and comment that James's American publishers have not
yet undertaken to give us a good cheap edition such as Macmillan
of London gave England. Yet the new demand is in some measure
being supplied. Philip Rahv has just published his admirable selection of the short novels; Clifton Fadiman is preparing a volume of
the short stories; New Directions has brought out *The Spoils of
Poynton* and a collection of the tales about artists and writers, the
latter edited by Professor Matthiessen, whose present critical study is,
as we would expect, a most valuable addition to our understanding
of James.

As we watch this notable new interest we can suppose that some
of the absurd critical myths about James are beginning to sink out
of sight. The basic myth, of course, is that James is not properly
American and not properly democratic. No less a person than
William James held that view of his brother; in our day Vernon
Parrington and Van Wyck Brooks have vehemently insisted on it as
an article of American faith. Yet Walt Whitman, laying down the

specifications for an American democratic literature, might himself have drawn up the list of qualities that Henry James proposed to his art—James covenanted with his genius to deal only "with the fine, the large, the human, the natural, the fundamental, the passionate things."

His detractors, however, if perhaps they allow him *fine* as suggesting *fine-drawn, over-fine,* deny him all his other adjectives. To them he is precisely not large, not human, not natural, not fundamental, not passionate—in short, not American, not democratic.

It is just this view of James that is no longer tenable. Indeed, if we want an explanation of the new interest in James fiction we can find it in the moral vision of James as described by Theodora Bosanquet, one of his gifted secretaries. Miss Bosanquet wrote twenty years ago; since that time the view of the world she attributes to James has forced itself upon all of us.

When he walked out of the refuge of his study into the world and looked around him he saw a place of torment where creatures of prey perpetually thrust their claws into the quivering flesh of the doomed defenseless children of light. . . . Wherever he looked Henry James saw fineness apparently sacrificed to grossness, beauty to avarice, truth to a bold front. He realized how constantly the tenderness of growing life is at the mercy of personal tyranny and he hated the tyranny of persons over each other. His novels are a repeated exposure of this wickedness, a reiterated and passionate plea for the fullest freedom of development, unimperiled by reckless and barbarous stupidity.

If this description is accurate—and I am sure it is—Henry James stands at the very heart of the American democratic ideal.

His error, his generous error, was to suppose that others could see as firmly as he how much difficulty such a vision entails. He could bear what most of us shrink from—the knowledge of how dangerous, subtle and complex the social world and the moral life are. We Americans, so quickly charmed by mechanical complexity, are likely to resent being told that the moral life is at least as complex as, say, the New York telephone system. When Parrington and Brooks denounce James as not democratic and not American, they are, I think, equating democracy and America with simplicity.

Mr. Matthiessen puts the reason for their error in another way. He says that they do not understand in art the relation of form to content. It is much the same thing—in art, complexity is carried by form; in form lie the modulations, nuances, resolutions. Parrington had a high-minded concern with ideas, but he was nearly anaesthetic to form; he would never have understood what Flaubert meant when he said, "The public hates style—style makes it work, style makes it *think*." Mr. Brooks, more largely endowed with sensibility than Parrington was, is really no less resistant to the kind of thought that is carried by style and form.

But Mr. Matthiessen knows—it is what distinguishes him among critics who deal in a large way with American literature—that form and style speak as importantly, if not so openly, as the content of a work. "The separation between form and content," he says in his preface, "simply does not exist as the mature artist contemplates his finished work. That separation is a short-cut taken by critics, and its disasters are written large over the history of James' reputation."

Mr. Matthiessen deals only with the work of James's last period; it is this that he calls the "major phase." He is thus at the very heart of the battle, for hostility to James concentrates here. Never has there been so wide a discrepancy of critical judgment as over *The Ambassadors, The Wings of the Dove, The Golden Bowl.* Those who agree with Parrington and Brooks tell us that here can be seen the full evidence of those faults of head and heart which marked James's career, here in these huge fusses over nothing. On the other hand, the critical tradition in which Mr. Matthiessen stands—it includes in recent years Eliot, Auden and Spender— holds that here can be seen the full fruit of James's fortitude and dedication, his insight and love—here in these bright moments of genius.

To this dispute Mr. Matthiessen's book attaches a new dramatic interest. Mr. Matthiessen has had the inestimable advantage of reading James's working notebooks. In them are to be found not only James's jottings and germs of ideas but also those passionate exhortations to himself, as, after his disastrous venture into the drama, he rededicated himself to the novel late in life and with the sense that now or never would his gifts be justified. Nothing could be more moving than the excerpts from this record which Mr. Matthiessen gives us. We feel that if the novels which received this high devotion are actually failures, then there has never been a more poignant tragedy of artistic dedication; but if they are successful, there has never been so fine a triumph of artistic fortitude, so vital a reward for an "act of life."

To many readers the novels offer resistance to any quick judgment of their success. Their prose is difficult because of the colloquial cadences and the many modifications which resulted from James's practice of dictating, and also because of that rich metaphoric texture of the author's mind which Mr. Matthiessen deals with so well. A more serious difficulty is James's precise adherence to his scenario which prevents the characters from existing except in essential dramatic relation to each other.

For Mr. Matthiessen, as I have said, the novels of the major phase are successful, although in varying degrees, and his exposition of the elements of their success is sure to be illuminating to old as well as to new readers of James. I wish, though, that he had gone farther in the expression of his own intimacy with them. Concerned as he is with their aesthetic, he seldom suggests the quality of the pleasure, at once bright and grave, that they can give; and in dealing with the problems they propound he shrinks from a familiar, easy handling of their brilliant plots: he never really does tell us why, in *The Ambassadors,* Strether came to Paris after Chad—it is as if he had taken too precisely T. S. Eliot's too strict remarks on those "imperfect critics" who re-create the works they deal with.

It seems to me that Mr. Matthiessen, too strict with himself in relation to the charms of the novels, is rather too strict with James. Not every one admires that interesting short story "The Great Good Place," but I think it is too censorious in Mr. Matthiessen to call "vulgar" its fantasy of perfect recuperative rest. Again, I think that Mr. Matthiessen might allow more than he does to James's unconscious judgments; if, in *The Golden Bowl,* James does give explicit approval to Maggie's relation to her father and her father's relation to his unfaithful young wife, he also supplies all the evidence that allows our judgment to go contrary to his, and, being the kind of novelist he is, he probably expects us to take this into account.

It is this same strictness that makes Mr. Matthiessen's concluding remarks about James and the future of society not quite adequate to his subject, or, really, to what Mr. Matthiessen has himself told us about James. "His gradation of characters according to their degree of consciousness may be validly translated into terms of social consciousness"—but ought we not know that "consciousness" and "social consciousness" are by no means two separate things and that no act of "translation" is needed from one to the other? "His intense spiritual awareness . . . has told others besides Eliot that if religion is to persist it must be based on coherent dogma." But if James suggests a modern possibility—and I am sure he does—it is in the fact that (Mr. Matthiessen quotes Eliot as remarking it) his life was distinguished by "an exceptional awareness of spiritual reality," together with "an indifference to religious dogma."

I cannot think that the kind of language with which Mr. Matthiessen concludes his fine book—and does something less than justice to it—is the right kind of language to use of James. Granted that James is, as Mr. Matthiessen everywhere shows, the great novelist of a society at the sad end of a phase, still it is not with words like "gradation" or "rigorousness" or "dogma" that one should describe his achievement, but rather with words expressive of his passionate sorrow, his tragic indignation and his loving kindness. But if Mr. Matthiessen's concluding words are in error one has been taught to see their mistake by almost everything that Mr. Matthiessen has previously said in his exposition of James.

Sermon on a Text
from Whitman

[*The Nation*, February 24, 1945]

DEMOCRATIC VISTAS is Walt Whitman's most important single work in prose, yet it has never been familiar to American readers. For this there is some reason. The large pamphlet is the rather awkward amalgamation of two earlier pamphlets; it is often eloquent, but it is all too often marked by that dull explosiveness of syntax which Whitman found appropriate to his prophetic moods in prose; it is full of half-educated words and phrases—we hear of "the ostent," of "orbic bards," of "literatuses," of "stores of cephalic knowledge," of the "vertebration of the manly and womanly personalism," jargon bad enough in itself, ridiculous in the man who made so much fuss about literary pretentiousness in others, but forgivable in the genius who was trying, outside the established intellectual order, to see the future and the truth. For all its faults of manner, the little book is great; and in any discussion of the relation of American literature to American life it is a central document.

As its name suggests, *Democratic Vistas* is about the future of democracy. The future of democracy is made to depend, in a sense, on literature. I say "in a sense" because in point of fact Whitman believes that democracy depends on a certain condition of mind or state of being which is not induced by literature alone, but here he is concerned to urge upon literature its duty of fostering this crucial emotion.

Published in 1871, the pamphlet is in part the expression of Whitman's disappointment after his nearly mystical experience of the Civil War. To Whitman, his nation had been justified by the war. The personal qualities of the young soldiers he had nursed in the Washington hospitals seemed to him to have proved what he called the "religious" value of democracy. In terms of human quality—and for Whitman this was the only criterion—the American experiment was a success. Yet the years after the war terribly denied that success. Whitman can admire the glow and bustle of national expansion, but he sees that behind the façade there is reason for dejection and despair. "Society in these states," he says, "is canker'd, crude, superstitious, rotten." He sees a lack of all "moral conscientious fiber." He sees hypocrisy, superciliousness, a false intellectuality; puny bodies; bad manners; tepid amours—"the men believe not in the women, nor the women in the men." The business classes are depraved, the class of civil servants no less so. It is in *Democratic Vistas* that Whitman makes the often-quoted remark about the grandeur of a well-contested American election, but now he feels that politics is no longer spontaneous and representative—"these savage, wolfish parties alarm me."

To find a way of national salvation he turns to literature. In part what he wants from literature is what every nationalist critic wants; it is what Goethe in his nationalist moments wanted—a national "myth," a moral identity for the country, what Whitman himself calls in a hideous but telling phrase, "an American stock personality."

But Whitman wants something more. He is in the great romantic tradition, and he shares as fully as possible the large romantic belief in the political mission of the "literatus." With affinities to Wordsworth, Shelley, Carlyle, and Arnold, his view of the relation of literature to politics is closest to Schiller's. I do not know whether he had read Schiller's *Aesthetic Letters*—and certainly his statement is far less philosophically elaborate than Schiller's and no doubt the better for that—but like Schiller he conceives of literature as the intermediary between the necessary authority of government and the ideal condition of human freedom.

We must remember that for Whitman authority was no bad thing. He says that democracy may be defined by its free diversity, but he is not so naïve as to think that free diversity can exist without authority. If *Democratic Vistas* begins with ideas derived from John Stuart Mill's *On Liberty*, it goes on to speak handsomely of Carlyle's "Shooting Niagara," that desperate prediction of the anarchy democracy may bring.

The whole pamphlet is a tissue of such contradictions, or, rather, modulations. Whitman is always showing himself as a more complex intelligence than perhaps he wanted to be, or than many of his readers want him to be. We often hear that Whitman's thought is anti-dualistic. In actual fact, he lived in a world of dualisms—body-soul, past-future, mass-individual, liberty-authority, life-death. His characteristic way of thought is to support one term of a dualism, then hasten to protect the other. For him the oppositions, although antagonistic to each other, are not negations of each other. In more senses than one Whitman's view of the world was dialectical: the world as he knew it was the dialogue of the disagreement between the great antagonistic principles. In *Democratic Vistas* what concerns him is the antagonism between authority, the representation of the mass, the average, and freedom or individualism, what he calls "personalism." Democracy can exist only if authority can organize diversity; but democracy dies if authority encroaches on personalism. It is here, at this moment of delicate balance, that the call goes out to the poet.

It is not possible in short space to suggest the full richness and complication of *Democratic Vistas* or even to paraphrase all that Whitman says in it about literature. It is important to remark, however, how subtle a view Whitman took of the relation of literature to politics. He believes that literature is more important than congresses or acts of state, for literature affects the depths of a nation's scarcely conscious soul. He thinks that literature must deal with "the people," yet he does not think that it does its proper work by dealing directly with politics or by exposing social conditions. Indeed, Whitman is very firm against what he calls "the growing excess and arrogance of realism." The true poet, he says, works by "analogies," by "curious removes, indirections." In the face of the common belief that Whitman is the ancestor of the social realists, these words suggest that Marianne Moore, much more than Carl Sandburg, is his true descendant.

I said that Whitman made democracy depend on a certain condition of mind or state of being for which literature had a responsibility. "There is, in sanest hours, a consciousness, a thought that rises, independent, lifted out from all else, calm, like the stars, shining eternal. This is the thought of identity—yours for you, whoever you are, as mine for me. Miracle of miracles, beyond statement, most spiritual of earth's dreams, yet hardest basic fact, and only entrance to all facts." This, for Whitman, is the emotion which guarantees democracy.

It is worth observing that Whitman talks about personal *identity,* not about personal *value.* The sense of personal value is something very different. It suggests the comparative, the competitive—all the horrors of the struggle for status into which democracy, as we know it, corrupts itself. What Whitman is talking about does not permit comparison—it is the single absolute in the democratic conception.

Elsewhere in the pamphlet Whitman speaks of this sense of identity as the "centripetal isolation of a human being in himself," and goes on: "Whatever the name, its acceptance and thorough infusion through the organization of political commonalty now shooting Aurora-like about the world, are of utmost importance, as the principle itself is needed for life's sake. It forms, in a sort, or is to form, the compensating balance wheel of the successful working machinery of aggregate America."

It lies, as he says, "beyond statement," but he knows what it is, and he knows what it does, and he knows how it can be generated. Literature can generate it. But not literature only. Whitman himself got it from Italian opera, or from crossing Brooklyn Ferry, or from certain aspects of the sea. Mark Twain got it from the Mississippi and from Lake Tahoe, Thoreau from the woods—in the American experience it is commonly given by a certain relation to nature. In the human experience generally it is given by the full awareness and valuation of the biological crises—birth, love, death. Whitman, the poet of vital affirmation, got it perhaps most intensely from contemplating death. He thought that the coming American poets must have a deep consciousness of death. Whitman's very best poems are personal in theme; of these the two most remarkable are about death; and of these two even the great lament for Lincoln. "When Lilacs Last in the Door-Yard Bloomed," is less fine than "Out of the Cradle Endlessly Rocking," of which an English critic has said that it is "the world's supreme song of separation."

If you pick up Samuel Sillen's recent selection from Whitman— it is called *Walt Whitman, Poet of American Democracy*—you will not find "Out of the Cradle Endlessly Rocking." Nor can this exclusion be accounted for by lack of space—not when Dr. Sillen gives us thirty-five pages of his own ideas about Whitman to one hundred and twenty-five pages of the poet himself. You will not find it because Dr. Sillen "aims to present Whitman as a living force in the war against fascist barbarism as well as in the peace which America and the other United Nations seek to achieve through unconditional victory." And Dr. Sillen goes on: "Only a volume that is politically partisan in this sense could be truly representative of Whitman." To demonstrate an explicit partisanship Dr. Sillen selects much of Whitman's work that is of merely indifferent quality. We conclude that what is "truly representative" of a poet need not be his best work.

It is in line with Dr. Sillen's own political partisanship that he emphasizes the interest of the Russians in Whitman and Whitman's own considerable interest in Russia. This reciprocal interest undoubtedly has its significance; still, a less partisan editor would have kept it in mind that the French and German feeling for Whitman has been as notable as the Russian; or, remembering that Whitman's interest in Russia was shared by other Americans (Henry Adams and Brooks Adams among them), remembering too that Whitman could say in his large loose way, "The Russians I look upon as overgrown boys and girls," a more critical editor would have used a tone a little less like that of a church father finding in Vergil's Fourth Eclogue the prophecy of Christ. But Dr. Sillen wants a Whitman who is not only the poet of American democracy but also the poet of Russian nationalism and internationalism. He wants a Whitman canon that coincides with the ideals of current Russian thought. Whitman on the size of the country, on national growth, national loyalty, devotion to a leader, sexual acceptance, responsibility for oppressed minorities, confidence in a bulking material future, Whitman patting his country on its broad back—this is the Whitman Dr. Sillen wants, even though it is not always the poetically best Whitman.

And this Whitman Dr. Sillen "arranges"—but only one hundred and twenty-five pages of him in a format that is most prodigal of space: the kind of arrangement Dr. Sillen wants requires a minimum of the poet. The arrangement is made "logically" in order to "help clarify [Whitman's] basic interests and attitudes." This language of a sociology major is perhaps odd when used of a poet who was concerned with the arrangement of his own works, although not much concerned with logic. But with such language Dr. Sillen cuts Whitman down to size. Thus, if Whitman says, "Do I contradict myself? / Very well then I contradict myself / (I am large, I contain multitudes)," Dr. Sillen, with a proper disgust at inconsistency, bustles to assure us that Whitman doesn't *really* contradict himself— this is Whitman for the peace table, at which, as we know, contradictions will be forbidden—and to comfort us with the thought that "the apparent contradictions may be united."

And "united" they are, just as if they were nations. For example, Dr. Sillen wishes Whitman to be as pious as himself in the matter of science and materialism. He quotes: "I accept Reality and dare not question it, / Materialism first and last imbuing. / Hurrah for positive science! long live exact demonstration!" Perfectly characteristic—but Whitman could also say, "To the cry, now victorious —the cry of sense, science, flesh, incomes, farms, merchandise, logic, intellectual demonstrations . . . fear not, my brethren, my sisters, to sound out with equally determined voice, that conviction brooding within the recesses of every envisioned soul—illusions, apparitions, figments all!" Dr. Sillen is not unaware that Whitman made statements like this second one. Indeed, his awareness constrains him to qualify his own remarks about Whitman's materialism. But he makes his qualifications in this way: "This is not to suggest that Whitman was a consistent philosophical materialist, for he never did cast off the idealistic elements of his thinking inherited from Emerson and Hegel."

Never did cast off—as if this aspect of Whitman's thought were a dead skin, as if everything that was characteristic of his mind, including the hurrah for positive science, did not arise from his idealistic metaphysics. Democracy certainly does not depend on philosophical idealism, but Whitman's own democratic impulse did spring from his iealistic philosophy. The "I" of Whitman—and this explains why it is often hard to identify ourselves with it as we read —is not always a person: it is often the personal image of the idealistic absolute. That is why Whitman contains multitudes—and contradictions. Walt Whitman, democracy, and the absolute are images of each other. They contain everything, even what Dr. Sillen with a quaint severity calls "devotees of a life relieved of social discipline"—a strange word, that "relieved": is social discipline then so burdensome?—and they contain both the moment when we love science and material things and the moment when we are not satisfied by them. They contain both our impulse of subordination to the interests of the mass of men and our impulse of personal identity, each giving health and value to the other.

> One's-self I sing, a simple separate person,
> Yet utter the word Democratic, the word En-Masse

These are the first lines of *Leaves of Grass* and they are the first lines of Dr. Sillen's selection. But Dr. Sillen's response is all to the second line: En-Masse delights him but not the simple separate person. As a consequence he omits from his selection Whitman's finest expression of identity, the great elegy "Out of the Cradle Endlessly Rocking."

I am certainly not trying to take Dr. Sillen to task simply for omitting a single poem, no matter how fine. Nor am I trying to say that Whitman is not political or has no political relevance now, for I think quite the contrary is true. All over the world people and peoples, where they have not lost their lives, have lost their sense of personal identity to an extent painful beyond imagination. If a poet can possibly help restore it to them, Whitman is that poet. And as peace seems to approach, we, who will have some part of their fates in our hands, might well refresh ourselves on the nature of the hardest basic fact and entrance to all facts. Further, if the Russians now read Whitman avidly, as Dr. Sillen says they do, what a good sign it is, not merely flattering that a great ally should read our national poet but reassuring to those people, and they are numerous, who have kept some reserve about the Russian polity on the ground of its insufficiency of "personalism." Yes, Whitman is indeed a political poet, and relevant now.

And so I could understand it very well if Dr. Sillen, making a selection of Whitman with reference not only to America but also to Russia, had pointed to "Out of the Cradle" and said, "We in our democracy have had many failures, as no doubt you in yours. But we have had our successes too, and this is one—this poet of democracy who can feel this way about life, with this intensity, this ecstasy of love and loss, affirming in the song of our American mocking-bird our highest feelings about human life."

Had Dr. Sillen done this he would have been truly a political man, as Whitman was. But he is only a "political" man; he is unable to suppose that the Whitman of contradictions, of deepest simple personal feeling, can have reference either to American or to Russian democracy.

Dr. Sillen is committed to a political tradition of culture, which has, indeed, never looked with favor on the emotion that Whitman thought came in sanest moments, the emotion on which, as he believed, democracy depended. And Dr. Sillen's tradition of culture has of course had a considerable success, especially lately, when it has become demure and non-agitational, adopting—as in Dr. Sillen's introduction—the educational tone of those old professors of ours who knew what they were doing when they put us to sleep so that they could speak to our dreams. The chief reason for the success of Dr. Sillen's tradition is that all of us, latently and unconsciously, fear in ourselves the sense of identity, and wish to lose it.

The signs of this fear may be variously found. What seems now to mark our ultimate political hope is a willingness to give up all concern with the internal *quality* of the simple separate person and an unwillingness to believe that the adventurous expressions of art have an intimate relation to the adventure of political freedom. For instance, J. Donald Adams, with an eye to democracy, tells us that books of the future will take a certain reassuring shape, specifications to be provided by what he calls "the many." Or the liberal *New York Post* assures its readers that they do right to sneer at James Joyce: he is hard to read and does not advocate social legislation for the people. Or *PM,* for many the palladium of progressive thought, gives but grudging space to written literature, on the theory that the people are not interested in it. I remember the fishy—not hostile but perplexed—stare with which a famous liberal editor received my remark that culture was integral with politics; the gist of his polite reply was that some day we would finish with politics and *then* we would have literature. Of my friends of political goodwill it might be said that their tolerant indifference to literature is in proportion to the personal salvation they hope to derive from their feelings of political goodwill.

Well, political and social contradictions being now what they are, it is understandable that we should begin to fear even those vital contradictions, incident upon being human, which literature expresses —and why, like Dr. Sillen, we should suppose that they must be brushed aside for something we no doubt call a constructive point of view. For none of us quite likes himself these days, and so we are worried when a poet speaks of the sense of identity as being the miracle of miracles and also the hardest basic fact. Yet it is we, who despise ourselves and who fear the very thing that our democratic poet called the product of "sanest moments"—it is we who feel the responsibility of spreading democracy throughout the world. If there was ever a "contradiction" to scare us, here indeed is one within ourselves.

In modern times insurgent poets from Wordsworth through Baudelaire through Joyce have dealt in "contradictions" which they have expressed by paradox, strangeness, and even "absurdity." Their purpose has always been ultimately a political one; they wanted to shock us out of the way of seeing forced upon us by the political past and the institutional present. They have appealed beyond the institutional barrier to the sense of identity, knowing it to be spunky, alive, resistant—the basic fact and the hardest, hard enough to be the touchstone of every idea. Whitman was such a poet. I have mentioned Marianne Moore as such another. E. E. Cummings, not now in general esteem with people of high political feeling, is such another. There are many more. If I had the job of instructing anybody in democracy, I would send him first to the generous pages of these poets and say, "There is the hardest basic political democratic fact." And then I would point to Dr. Sillen's volume—not because it is in itself important and decisive but because it represents much that is—and say, "Are there, as you will now quickly see, is its negation."

The Problem of Influence

[A review of *Freudianism and the Literary Mind*
by Frederick J. Hoffman. *The Nation*, September
8, 1945]

FOR some time, one of the self-imposed tasks of academic
research has been the investigation of the creative writer's
debt to the systematic thinker. And all too often this investigation has proceeded on assumptions which are much too simple. It
is usually believed that the creative writer *uses* in his work *the idea*
which the systematic thinker *thinks up,* quite as if an idea were a
baton that is passed from hand to hand in a relay race, remaining
the same in each hand. But Frederick Hoffman, even though he
writes as an academic research scholar, understands that the question of influence cannot be reduced to such simplicity. Dr. Hoffman's prose is perhaps not always so lucid as the intelligence which
conceived and organized his book—I found myself questioning the
formulation of certain statements which I nevertheless thought
right in their intention—but his study of the relation of Freud's
ideas to literary practice is a work that the student of modern
literature will need to know. And every historian of literature and
ideas will do well to ponder its theoretical chapter on The Problem
of Influence.

Dr. Hoffman knows that an idea is not the unitary, irrefrangible
thing that most historians take it to be. He knows that it is modified
in its transmission by the kind of cultural environment into which
it falls, by the response to the kind of technical or figurative language

in which it is expressed, by the power of understanding of those who receive it, and by their own purposes and intention.

Certainly nothing could better illustrate the precarious existence of an idea and the precarious position of the historian of ideas than Freud's psychology. For no system has had to endure more misunderstanding—willed or unconsciously willed—or more intellectual braggadocio from people of normally good and modest intelligence, often while they are themselves making use of Freud's doctrines. It did not lie within the purview of Dr. Hoffman's work to observe that while the investigation of Shakespearean metaphor proceeds along lines that are closely analogous with the Freudian method, so precise a Shakespearean scholar as J. Dover Wilson contemptuously cites a certain *Sigismund* Freud; nor to point to the spectacle of the admirable biographer of Rimbaud and Baudelaire, Enid Starkie, who ritualistically knocks down a Freudian man of straw while she accumulates evidence for the Freudian case. But Dr. Hoffman does deal at length with the kind of understanding of psychoanalysis that was current in Greenwich Village in the days when Floyd Dell was the Freudian authority and friend "psyched" friend—what depths of the past lie in that lost, banal slang word! Those were the days when Ludwig Lewisohn warped Freud to the interests of Zionism and Waldo Frank understood psychoanalysis only when he chose to, misrepresenting it when that suited his doctrinal purpose of the moment, being in this rather like Arthur Koestler, who is a perfect intellectual coquette in the matter.

Of the writers Dr. Hoffman deals with—he wisely limits their number—perhaps only Thomas Mann really understood Freud with the ordinary intelligence we might reasonably expect of a writer, and also used him creatively in a large way and to the good advantage of his art. In this country, Conrad Aiken is notable for the seriousness of his interest; Aiken's understanding of psychoanalysis —not always unexceptionable—did his novels little good but it wonderfully informed certain of his stories and poems.

The case of D. H. Lawrence is interesting not only for Lawrence's inability to understand Freud, but for the light it throws on the methods of critics who lightly use the idea of "influence." Almost from the beginning of his career, Lawrence thought in an essentially Freudian way. Yet he reached his insights without having read Freud and when at last he came to deal with Freudian theory he was shockingly obtuse. Much the same can be said of Sherwood Anderson, who became distressingly coy whenever he spoke of Freud. Yet it is one of the clichés of criticism that both Lawrence and Anderson are the notable examples of Freud's influence on literature.

Making Men More Human

[A review of *The Humanities at Work. The Saturday Review of Literature*, September 15, 1945]

THE Second Regional Conference on the Humanities met at Denver in December, 1944, and the present volume is the report of its proceedings. The members, for the most part, spoke the easy literate language of our best academic tradition, that of William James, and only occasionally did they frame their thoughts in gilded *frames of reference* and such-like jargon. What they said does great credit to their sense of professional responsibility, their warm hearts, and their devotion to democratic ideals.

And yet I think they did not know what they were talking about. I do not mean that they were ignorant or befuddled, but only that they talked about one thing and thought they were talking about another. Two quotations illustrate this confusion:

Professor Irving Goodman: . . . Let me read a brief statement of aims of a high school chemistry course as formulated by the Armed Forces Institute after an analysis of thousands of statements from high school teachers:

1. The development of effective habits of thinking
2. Cultivation of useful work habits and study skills
3. Inculcation of social attitudes
4. Acquisition of a wide range of significant interests
5. Development of increased appreciation of music, art, literature, and other esthetic experiences
6. Development of social sensitivity
7. Development of better social adjustment

8. Acquisition of important information
9. Improvement of physical health
    10. Development of a consistent philosophy of life.

These broad objectives formulated for the high school course in chemistry closely resemble those of the Carnegie Institute on the college level.

Professor Edward J. Allen: . . . I have had to place myself in the position of society and ask myself, "What does society expect of the university?" Three things, I think: (1) to win the war; (2) successful reconstruction and reconversion; (3) permanent peace.

That is, Professor Goodman assigns to a high-school course in chemistry all the functions of a whole ideal culture. Professor Allen, in the name of society, assigns to the university two duties of the national state and one duty of the as yet unrealized world state. The Conference as a whole was not quite so extravagant, but it made much the same assumptions. The Conference wanted to say that it was worried by a society that is dominated by acquisitive ideals, by possibilities of enormous scientific power, and by the tendency of government to be less immediate to its citizens. It passionately wanted to ameliorate these conditions. That is why we must respect it. But it made the error—professional groups in times of crisis often make it—of forgetting the natural limitations of the profession it represents; it put upon formal education a social responsibility disproportionate to the nature of formal education.

In this excessive estimate of education's power and responsibility there is a danger to education itself. For when Chemistry 3 turns out not to have provided the love of Bach, the Alka-Seltzer glow of health, the consistent philosophy of life at the age of sixteen, and all the other things it has promised, ought not a practical and social-minded school board drop it from the curriculum as a failure? And if we decide that the universities are to provide permanent peace, should we not close them down when the outbreak of hostilities indicates that they have failed?

There is also a great danger to the true notion of democracy in the inflation of education's function. Literature recently made the same error of inflation when Van Wyck Brooks and his colleagues told us that writers were "priests," that their function was to "give life," and that democracy was threatened when writers did not do their duty as thus extravagantly laid down. But in a democracy no profession or group may be made, or may make itself, the scapegoat for the rest of democratic society. And throughout the Conference one could discern a virtuous but very passive hero—"the people"; and there was also a potential traitor—the university. The dichotomy is false and so is the characterization. If our universities are now in a bad way, it is in part because the people have allowed and even wanted them to be that way. This may not be a comfortable view of the matter, but it is, I believe, the democratic view.

The Conference decided that the Humanities have idled long enough and must now be put to work. And it is for society that the Humanities must work—the Conference explicitly dismissed Mark Van Doren's book on education because it speaks of the Humanities chiefly in relation to the individual. (The Conference was a little confusing in this matter of the individual, for although the "individual" is said to be one of the "values" of democracy, he is generally spoken of in contradistinction to "society.") A group of deans representing medicine, law, engineering, agriculture, and business, opened the sessions by agreeing that mere professional studies are not sufficient for the workers in their fields. Professional studies must be supplemented by social studies. That is easily understood. But professional studies also must be supplemented by the Humanities. The reason for this is not so apparent. The deans, and they are right, think the Humanities help make better men and citizens. They do not know how or why. They are even very modest about just what should be taught in the humanistic way. They wait for the professors to tell them.

But the professors, I fear, tell them little. They make many negative statements—no traditionalism, no overdepartmentalization. Well and good. On the positive side—integration. But, to "liberate society," what shall we teach? Composition. Yes, but—. Not too much English literature, says one professor, one would think we were still an English colony. Colorado students should read the poetry of Thomas Hornsby Ferrill and a novel, *Sykes' Second Hoeing. John Brown's Body* goes well anywhere. Professor Ashton tells of a letter from a student in the service who writes that he wishes he had read Plato, to which Professor Burgum replies that Plato is an "escape from the reality of the situation" the soldier is in, not so efficacious as "a couple of shots of whiskey."

But what shall be taught and why? The Conference proceeds to "synthesis" and congratulates itself upon its synthetic success. The Humanities have been put to work, although nobody quite knows what they are. They would seem to have something to do with Integration. But really they are only a lot of great books, music, and pictures, extremely interesting for teachers to talk about, extremely interesting to students when they are required to turn their minds to them. They will not save society or reform it. Their only effect is the one they have been traditionally observed to have—they give a kind of pleasure which, as their name implies, makes men more human. And that, as the Conference would admit, is the one aim of society itself.

Neurosis and the Health
of the Artist

[A review of *Leonardo da Vinci: A Study in Psychosexuality* by Sigmund Freud, and of *Stavrogin's Confession* by F. M. Dostoevsky, with a psychoanalytical study of the author, also by Sigmund Freud. *The New Leader,* December 14, 1947]

THE question of the mental health of the artist has intensely preoccupied our culture since the beginning of the Romantic Movement. Before that time it used often to be said that the poet was "mad," but this was only a manner of speaking, seldom meant literally. But in the late eighteenth century, with the development of a more elaborate and systematic psychology and a narrowing view of mental and emotional normality, the statement was more literally intended. Early in the nineteenth century Charles Lamb—who knew something of real insanity at close quarters—felt the necessity of dealing seriously with the belief that poetic genius was akin to madness and he disposed of the idea in his brilliant essay "The Sanity of True Genius." At the end of the century Bernard Shaw with equal cogency examined and dismissed Max Nordau's thesis that art was a form of mental degeneration.

But in recent years the tendency of criticism has changed. If criticism still insists on the sanity of art, it specifies the *essential* sanity of art and has its eye on the truth that lies in madness. And it is likely to hold that the mental ill-health of the artist is a necessary condition for the creation of the art that expresses the truth.

Perhaps for Americans the best-known recent statement of this view is the one made by Edmund Wilson who has summarized it in his striking phrase, "the wound and the bow." Wilson figures the essential nature of the artist by the situation of Philoctetes, the Greek warrior who was forced to live in isolation because of the disgusting odor of a suppurating wound that would never heal and who yet had to be sought out by his comrades because they needed the use of the magically unerring bow which he possessed. That is, the poet is a poet by reason of his sickness as well as by reason of his power. The poet himself has been content to accept this etiology of his art, even to the point of finding that his power comes from his sickness. Thus, W. H. Auden addresses a "Letter to a Wound," in which he speaks to his own "wound" in the cherishing language of a lover to his beloved and acknowledges the debts of insight he owes it—"Knowing you," he says, "has made me understand."

This view of the nature of the artist—of the literary artist most particularly—comes easily enough in a culture in which, to the thoughtful mind, the "normal" and "healthy" ways of established society seem insane: avowed madness and illness appear as health, if only because they controvert the established values. And of course one of the most notable intellectual constructs of our time, the Freudian psychology, is generally taken to give sanction to the belief that mental sickness is a condition of true vision and artistic creation.

I myself do not think that the sanction is legitimately derived from the whole import of Freud, although it may be speciously drawn from certain of Freud's statements, and I tried to say why in an essay of a few years ago ("A Note on Art and Neurosis," *Partisan Review,* Winter 1945). My statement of objections there no longer quite satisfies me, although I think its direction is right, and some day I should like to amplify and modify what I said.

This isn't the occasion for that attempt, but the publication this year of two of Freud's most notable studies of artists gives me the occasion to raise certain questions which are relevant for that revision.

1. *The uniqueness of the artist as neurotic.* It was one of the points of my essay that we make a mistake in seeing the artist as uniquely neurotic. The mistake is a natural one, for the artist and particularly the writer—and more writers are said to be neurotic than the practitioners of any other art—is aware of his moods and makes voluminous records of them, not only in his work, directly or indirectly, but also in his letters, journals and autobiographies. I said that a writer becomes a writer for reasons which are no more neurotic than the reasons that make a man a logician or a scientist although they may be wholly different, and that the incidence of neurosis among all other professions would be quite as high as among writers did we but choose to look for it as eagerly in other fields as in the profession of writing. What distinguishes a writer from other men is that it is his function to deal directly with the matter of psychic disturbance. The men of other professions are called upon to repress their awareness in the interest of their functions; but this does not make them less neurotic than the writer, though their neurosis may be of a different sort. According to Freud, sexual impotence is involved in every male neurosis; yet we might guess and could probably show that there is no higher incidence of impotence among writers than among physicists or bankers.

This particular point was brought into question by William Barrett in the course of his very brilliant essay "Writers and Madness" (*Partisan Review,* January-February 1947). Mr. Barrett insists on a clear distinction to be made between the motives that impel the scientist and the artist to their respective activities. The difference, as I understand it, is a difference in the claims of the ego. The claims of the artist's ego upon the world are personal in a way that the claims of the scientist's are not, and the artist's commitment is personal and complete in a way that the scientist's is not. The scientist, Mr. Barrett says, does indeed want prestige, "but if in this claim for prestige he responds to one of the deepest urges of his ego, it is only that this prestige may come to attend his person through the public world of other men; and it is not in the end his own being that is exhibited or his own voice that is heard in the learned report to the Academy."

This may be true so far as consciousness and social usage go. But Freud's monograph on Leonardo da Vinci suggests that it is not necessarily true in the unconscious. One of the problems that Freud sets himself is to discover why an artist of the highest endowment should have, as the years passed, devoted himself more and more to scientific investigation, with the result that he was unable (neurotically unable, if you will) to complete his artistic enterprises. The particular reasons Freud assigns need not be gone into here—all that I wish to suggest is that Freud understands these reasons to be the working-out of an inner conflict, the attempt to deal with the difficulties that have their roots in the most primitive situations; Leonardo's investigations were as necessary and "compelled" and constituted as much a claim of the complete personality as anything the writer does; and so far from being for the sake of public prestige, they were largely private and personal and were thought to be a sign of something very like insanity.

2. *The nature of neurosis.* The literary conception of psychic ill-health tends to be a static one. Wilson and Auden use the word "wound" and both require that its condition be immutable. The wound of Philoctetes can never heal. "Nothing will ever part us," Auden says to his beloved. And Mr. Barrett says that he prefers the old-fashioned word "madness" to the modern word "neurosis." (One might say that it is not quite for him to choose on a mere impulse of taste, for the words do not differ in fashion but in meaning.) Both in the idea of the "wound" and in the idea of "madness" something static is implied; we have the old notion of a mode or state of the mind. But a neurosis, as Freud abundantly makes clear in his essay on Dostoevsky, is anything but static. It is precisely dynamic, an activity. It is, indeed, a conflict. "There are,"

says Freud in the Dostoevsky essay, "no neurotic complete maso-chists"—by which he means that the ego that gives way to maso-chism (or to any other pathological excess) has passed beyond neurosis; the conflict has ceased but at the cost of the defeat of the ego and now some name other than neurosis must be given to the condition of the person who thus takes himself beyond the pain of the neurotic conflict.

To understand this is to become aware of the complacency with which the literary theorists regard mental disease. The unconscious of the neurotic individual is not equally complacent—it regards with the greatest fear the chaotic, anarchic and destructive forces it con-tains and it struggles mightily to keep them at bay.

And even if it could indeed be shown that the artist is actually more neurotic than other persons, we would still not have the right to conclude that his neurosis is the *source* of his powers. It would be far more reasonable to conclude that his neurosis is the con-comitant of his powers. For, as Freud says in the essay on Dos-toevsky, "the neurosis . . . comes into being all the more readily the richer the complexity which has to be controlled by the ego."

3. *The question of terminology.* The literary critic, when he speaks of mental illness, is likely to confine himself to the neurosis. Perhaps one reason for this is that neurosis is the most benign of the mental ills. Another reason is, of course, that psychoanalytical literature deals chiefly with the neurosis; its symptomatology and therapy have become familiar. Further, the neurosis is very easily put into a causal connection with the social maladjustments of our time. The other forms of mental illness of a more severe or of a degenerative kind are not so widely recognized by the literary person and are often assimilated to neurosis with a resulting con-fusion.

Yet even where the word "neurosis" might reasonably be thought to apply in the explanation of character traits, it is used with more alacrity by laymen than by Freud. Here the practice of psycho-analytical writers is somewhat to blame, for the concept of emo-tional normality has not been defined in a way to make it easily available—perhaps it cannot be—and much behavior that is called "neurotic" by psychoanalysts is not held by them to constitute actual neurosis. Yet it is salutary to see with what circumspection Freud uses the word. Leonardo, according to Freud, was shaped by his unconscious conflicts; there is evidence, which Freud accepts, that he was both homosexual and sexually inactive. Yet Freud says, "Let us expressly emphasize that we have never considered Leonardo as a neurotic. . . . We no longer believe that health and disease, normal and nervous, are sharply distinguished from each other. We know today that neurotic symptoms are substitutive formations for certain repressive acts which must result in the course of our development from the child to the cultural man, that we all produce such substitutive formations, and that only the amount, intensity and distribution of these substitutive formations justify the practical conception of illness."

Which leads us to wonder whether those writers who cherish madness and the wounded personality are not unconsciously subscribing to the narrow notion of normality which the eighteenth century created and which we have accepted, whether they are not too much surprised by the variety of forms that human life takes.

These are but a few of the many considerations raised by these two essays of Freud's. Space prevents a further exploration of what they suggest. But I must take a last fraction of space to say a word of deprecation of the dreadful prose into which Dr. Brill has turned the Leonardo essay: it reminds us how sorely we need a good new translation of Freud's work.

Treason in the Modern World

[A review of *The Meaning of Treason* by Rebecca West. *The Nation*, January 10, 1948]

EVERY war breeds its traitors, for treason is bound up in the very idea of allegiance. But the recent war, with its fifth columns, collaborators, and quislings, was exceptional in the variety and extent of the treason it bred, and it brought the question of national allegiance to the forefront of our minds. When Rebecca West's reports of the English treason trials first appeared in *The New Yorker* they were avidly read, and now their appearance in a volume has been met with even greater interest. This response is not limited to the people who live with their hands upon their hearts and make patriotism their loud business. Miss West's book is in a sense addressed to liberals; and the very people who a decade ago would have dealt with the idea of the nation not quite as a superstition but as, at best, a primitive survival are ready to listen, if not yet to agree, as Miss West speaks of the nation as one of the primary facts of social life.

In part, but only in part, this inclination to take the national idea with a new seriousness is the result of a new enlightenment. From the developing social sciences we have learned to question the old basic liberal belief that the only "real" social facts are economic, all else in society being but "superstructure." The life of man, we are now willing to believe, is much more complex and more obscurely rooted than any merely economic investigation will disclose.

Miss West has always known this; the knowledge is surely what makes her *Black Lamb and Grey Falcon* so remarkable a book, possibly one of the great books of our time. She has had a special place in our intellectual life because she maintains a liberal democratic position together with a strong traditionalism. She is in full accord with the social ethics of progressive thought; yet she perceives that progressivism has no true awareness of the deep instinctual roots of man, that what awareness it does have is likely to be a hostile one, and that in this respect it is in full accord with the acquisitive, competitive society it wishes to revise. The thesis of her present work is that treason is the extreme result of the modern alienation which has been caused by industrial society in cooperation with the excesses or deficiencies of liberal thought. In this argument the nation figures as a primary instinctual fact under the metaphors of *hearth* and *parents:* the hearth has been allowed to grow cold; the natural struggle between parents and children has not been resolved or mitigated in the traditional and natural way.

This is admissible and even true. But it tells only part of the truth. The whole truth is considerably more drastic than Miss West admits. And Miss West's prose seems unconsciously to know what Miss West's conscious mind prefers not to recognize. The prose no doubt deserves all the praise it has received, for it is very brilliant. But for the intellectual occasion it is too brilliant. Its rhetoric has a hectic flush; its richness of metaphor and allusion and modification is too lavish. Where we might expect the calm acceptance of the idea of the nation, we find an almost incantatory glorification of it; and we wonder what necessity Miss West found herself under to make her prose play so very many rings around her traitors, so to try them to the bone, deploying all the power of her remarkable mind to circumvent their knavish tricks and confound their politics.

Miss West's prose, in short, is anxious prose. And if we look for the cause of its anxiety we can perhaps assign this one: that it unconsciously knows and is seeking to repress an important and disagreeable truth—that the nation is no longer what Edmund Burke said it was, an almost mystical entity of language, custom, history, and destiny, but that it has become what Burke feared it might become, a medium for ideology.

Like Burke, Miss West makes ideology the enemy of the national idea. And no doubt she is right, for a nation that is identified with a conscious and extrusive ideology is likely to be either totalitarian or torn by civil strife. But whether we like it or not, our contemporary concern with nationalities—Germany, Russia, Spain, Argentina, England—is a concern with ideologies; and conversely our concern with ideologies is now colored by our feelings about nations.

Miss West understands the importance of ideology in modern life, but she fails to grasp its extent. That is why, writing of the condemned traitors, she so often relies on the concepts of psychiatry and on the language of "understanding." In England the old national idea is still strong enough to permit her to see an active ideologue as a crackpot and a crank, vicious in intent and sometimes in effect, but still an oddity, an eccentric. But this is to minimize the present or potential power of ideology, an error that the extreme—aesthetically speaking, the excessive—urgency of Miss West's prose then tries to adjust.

Of the three categories of traitors which Miss West distinguishes, only one was not ideological. This is the group which appears under the rubric of "The Children." The men of this group were of low social status and small education; their treason was of a petty and passive kind, committed usually out of a simple desire for comfort or safety while in the enemy's power, and at the enemy's behest, and void of any ideological motivation. These men no doubt represent a failure of their national society, for they had been left incapable of any large social idea—loyalty, for example, or social cause and effect. But every war since society began has had such traitors, and the wonder is not that the national idea should fail with these few but rather that it should so magically succeed with so many who were, in point of status and education, in no better case.

The second category of traitors consists of men who, in another age, could have been considered as little responsible for their deeds as the "children"; perhaps less responsible—for although John Amery and Norman Baillie-Stewart were not certifiably insane, they were clearly afflicted by mental aberration. Both enjoyed considerable social status—Amery as the son of a very distinguished family, Baillie-Stewart as a man of the upper middle class, a very competent officer in a good regiment. But status and opportunity are not fully decisive in the moral life, and nothing could be easier than to make out an abstract case for these men not being held accountable for their deeds. We dare not make the case because our age finds an evil use for them, as it found use for Hess, Göring, and Hitler himself, all of whom have been professionally described in psychopathological terms. Amery and Baillie-Stewart were useful to the enemy because of the authority of their upper-class voices on the radio. They believed of themselves that they were men competent to deal with large ideas and that they went over to the enemy because of their ideas; and it is only one of several ways of speaking to say that these ideas were insane, for they were believed and acted on by millions.

The category to which Miss West gives the greatest attention is the one which she calls "revolutionary." It is possible, by a refinement of psychiatric ideas which would not be extreme, to find the men in this category to be only less aberrant than Amery and Baillie-Stewart. Society seems to have made a continually adverse judgment on the psychic character of William Joyce, the fascist demagogue; his colleagues of similar political stripe seem to have similarly excluded themselves; and Dr. Allan Nunn May, the Communist physicist, certainly behaved in an erratic way. But all these were men of excellent mental equipment, and all were intellectuals. Joyce was an honor student at the University of London; May was a physicist of note. It would be a sad stroke for the future of mankind to absolve such men of responsibility.

The figure of Joyce dominates the "revolutionary" group and, indeed, the whole book. It is understandable that he should bulk so large and draw Miss West on to an almost compulsive interest in him, for he had malignly established himself in the British imagination as the Lord Haw-Haw of the German radio, the voice that so plausibly and in such good English mocked the English in their suffering and sought to break their courage. Further, he had certain clear similarities to Hitler—he had Hitler's sentimental ideal-ism and love of authority, hierarchy, and "heroism"; he was an outlander among a people he admired; he was a *lumpen*-intellectual and he lacked the ability to be absorbed by any established group. And yet in a sense he is already archaic, and the figure of the future is very likely Dr. Allan Nunn May.

It is difficult in the atmosphere of the moment to discuss with objectivity the implications of Dr. May's case. The tone of the recent Congressional investigation deserves to make people of liberal views believe that Communists are men who are persecuted for their generous humanitarian views, the way Percy Bysshe Shelley was. *The New Yorker* represents it as the height of suburban simplicity to believe anything about Communists except their own declarations that they are devoted to defending democracy. And no doubt, from what Miss West tells us about him, it would have been difficult to believe anything of an extreme sort about Dr. May. There was noth-ing malign in him, as there was in Joyce; he seems to have been the sort of man who lives specifically to be thought harmless. He was idealistic and humane; when he understood the intention of the atomic project he was working on, he was deeply troubled. If he then turned against England in his heart and felt no loyalty to his native land, he was in no different case from those liberal Germans who repudiated Germany because Germany had repu-diated what they lived by. Moved by the humanitarian, supra-national ideals that the world has paid lip-service to for many generations, he decided to give the results of his project's researches to the world. He gave them to a Russian agent. He seems then to have regretted his action, for he failed to keep an appointment with the spy and he subsequently confessed to the British police, main-taining his pathetic double-mindedness by refusing to reveal the identity although he revealed the nationality of the spy. A touch of the sordid or the absurd is introduced into Dr. May's case by his having accepted $700 for his treachery; yet this does not really make him the less notable as an early and perhaps primitive example of the individual who embodies within himself the struggle between nationality and ideology, a struggle that is bound to be all the more terrible because the antagonists cannot any longer keep themselves pure of each other and clearly defined.

Family Album

[A review of *The Times of Melville and Whitman* by Van Wyck Brooks. *Partisan Review*, January 1948]

WITH the publication of this volume Mr. Brooks takes himself entirely beyond the reach of the opinion, usually uttered with a mournful acerbity, that his work has fallen away from the fine critical intelligence of his early days. For it is clear from *The Times of Melville and Whitman*, if it was ever left in doubt by the earlier volumes of his account of American literature, that Mr. Brooks is not writing literary criticism at all and does not want to. Nor does he want to write literary history as that is usually understood. As for intelligence, he is not concerned with it. One has the impulse to describe his enterprise as an act of piety—until one remembers that in some sense every literary act is an act of piety, a commemoration of saints and heroes and an alliance with them, and that acts of piety can also be acts of intelligence. One must say then that Mr. Brooks is engaged in an act of piety of a particular, of a very simple, sort: an act of family piety.

The very rhetoric proclaims the nature of the enterprise. Mr. Brooks has perfectly assumed the character of that member of the family who holds in proud and capacious memory every last fact of family existence; it is not that such a person has no ability to select but that he has no wish to select—the more anecdotes, portraits, letters, muniments, eccentricities, candlesticks, silver thimbles, hunting crops, and Malay krises he can collect the more he can make the family resemble a nation or a universe, the more he can be sure it is really there, for the family, considered as a long continuity, is always threatening to show itself as a mere figment. Hence Mr. Brooks's concern with simultaneity: "When General Lee died in 1870 with three of the older Southern writers . . ."—it is not a death-pact but a reassuring reticulation of event, the family web made that much finer. As happens with every family historian, in the degree that Mr. Brooks remembers his antecedents, his pronouns forget theirs:

> Major John Richardson, the author of *Wacousta,* the best of the Canadian novelists, was outside the circle, the disciple of Cooper who died in New York, a pauper, forgotten even at home, after selling his faithful dog for a morsel to live on. He was buried in an unknown grave in 1852, the year in which William North arrived from England, the journalist who had studied in Germany at one of the universities and whose style was full of German metaphysics. He had published a novel attacking Disraeli, entitled *Anti-Coningsby*. . . . At twenty-eight he killed himself with a draught of prussic acid, and a few years later Stephen Foster, whom all the writers might have known, was picked up dying in the slums where he had been living. While Henry Clapp and Ada Clare held their Bohemian court at Pfaff's, Foster had slept in Bowery lodging-houses. . . .

And indeed it does not much matter who is who. In the compost-democracy of the great American family, discrimination is not in place. The world holds Uncle Walt and Uncle Herman in special esteem and so they are talked about at greater length, yet within the judgment of the family it is not perfectly established that they are really more valuable than Cousin Bret—of the California branch, but originally he came from New York—or any of the many score of the connection. Uncle Walt had a very warm family feeling, much to his credit; as for Herman, was it quite kind of him to keep so much to himself in his later years and to take so gloomy a view of things?

It is impossible to take seriously Mr. Brooks's effort to show how very real and nice and established the family has always been, how many people of charm and sensibility it has numbered. Yet it would not be fair to dismiss his enterprise as being wholly without point.

For Mr. Brooks responds to a real fact. To most Americans, even literate and literary Americans, the American past is very little inhabited. Nothing in the world is sadder than the statue of an American hero, standing naked of memory or interest. The greatest of our literary figures have the greatness of isolation or distance rather than of community and intimacy: we make our voyages to them and are much refreshed, but they are likely to remain the object of our intelligent tourist's curiosity. When it comes to the easily usable social tradition of literature, it sometimes seems that a foreigner, Tocqueville, speaks more immediately than any American across the American decades. And quite apart from literature and greatness, the ordinary day-to-day human past seems to exist in the American mind as attenuated, alien, even hostile in its discontinuousness with the present.

If this is true, it is not new—Henry Adams remarked the Civil War generals, the men who had saved the Union, walking empty and bewildered, their deed having no significance to the people among whom they walked and scarcely to themselves. And if it is true, it is not a sentimentality to regret it, for a nation without a living sense of its past is as deficient as a person in the same deprived case. But Mr. Brooks's enterprise is to be harshly judged precisely because it sets out to fill so genuine a lack but fills it so badly, for with a high devotion and a really grandiose ideal of scholarship it supplies America with a literary past of the blandest and most genteel sort, calculated to give pleasure only to the Philistine and to draw the mind and heart of no one, not even of the Philistine.

The State of Our Culture: Expostulation and Reply

*[Contribution to a symposium, The State of
American Writing, 1948: Seven Questions. Partisan Review, August 1948]*

PARTISAN REVIEW sent a questionnaire to a group of
American writers and published the answers in its issue of
August 1948 under the title "The State of American Writing,
1948: Seven Questions." What I wrote in reply to the questions
turned out to be a kind of addendum to the essay I had written two
years before to serve as the introduction to *The Partisan Reader*[2]
and I include it, despite its informality and occasionalness, for what
support and modification it brings to the earlier statement.

These are the seven questions:

1. *What, in your opinion, are the new literary tendencies or figures,
if any, that have emerged in the forties? How does the literary
atmosphere of this decade compare with that of the thirties? In
what way, too, does the present period differ from the first postwar period? Can the differences between the two postwar periods
be defined in relation to the European situation?*

2. *Do you think that American middlebrow culture has grown
more powerful in this decade? In what relation does this middle-*

---

[1] This title and introductory statement are attached to a copy of Lionel Trilling's
contribution to this symposium found among his papers and indicate that at one
time it was very likely his intention to include his reply in a collection of his writings, probably *The Liberal Imagination*. (D.T.)
[2] Reprinted in *The Liberal Imagination* as "The Function of the Little Magazine." (D.T.)

brow tendency stand to serious writing—does it threaten or bolster it?

3. *What is the meaning of the literary revivals (James, Forster, Fitzgerald, etc.) that have taken place of late? Is this a publishing phenomenon or is it an organic literary interest in the sense that the rediscovered writers of the past are in some way truly expressive of current literary needs?*

4. *It is the general opinion that, unlike the twenties, this is not a period of experiment in language and form. If that is true, what significance can be attached to this fact? Does present writing base itself on the earlier experimentation, in the sense that it has creatively assimilated it, or can it be said that the earlier experimentation came to a dead end?*

5. *In the twenties most writers were free-lancers, whereas now many make their living by teaching in universities. Has this change affected the tone and mood of literature in our time? Can it with justice be said that American writing has grown more academic since the twenties?*

6. *In recent decades serious literary criticism has shown a special bent for the analysis and interpretation of poetry. What is the significance of this concentration at a time when poetry itself has had an ever-diminishing audience? Would literature benefit from a critical concern, equally intense, with other genres of writing? In our time, when the fate of culture as a whole is called into question, does the basic meaning of the literary effort stand in need of re-examination?*

7. *What is the effect on American writing of the growing tension between Soviet Communism and the democratic countries? How are cultural interests affected by this struggle and do you think a writer should involve himself in it (as writer? as person?) to the point of commitment?*

REPLY:

If I am to answer your questions at all, I had better begin by reporting my resistance to them: I have been reading them over and over during several days and my mind seems to refuse to take hold of them. This isn't a reflection on their sensibleness, and at one time or another I have surely raised the same questions myself and tried to answer them in conversation or in teaching or in writing. But when I come to answer them formally, and in a body, and to the end of making a coherent comment on the state of American literature in this particular year or decade, my mind jibs.

This, I suppose, is because I am not comfortable about the idea of literature as an institution, which is what your questions somehow suggest it is. I feel easy enough with the idea of literature as a trade, and as a necessity, and as an instrument. And of course I recognize that it is intellectually quite legitimate to consider literature as an institution, yet I find that whenever I have to consider it in this way my curiosity wilts and my spirits sink—for me the classic situation of claustrophobia has become the literary "conference" in which quite sensible people discuss the condition of literature and the social function of the writer.

I like and respect literature as a trade and wish it could nowadays be a trade more often and more easily. I believe that it is a great help to certain kinds of writers to work in relation to a paying audience, even though a small one. To please and to tempt, to stay in touch with established conventions in order to use, circumvent and transmute them—this has the effect of keeping the artist's will under pressure, of hiding some part of his intention even from himself, thus permitting him to strike deeper both into his own unconscious and into that of his audience. I don't believe that the ideal situation of the artist is the freedom to work *only* in relation to his own will and intention.

And then I can understand literature as a necessity, which I take it to have been with such writers as Baudelaire, Rimbaud, and Kafka, a continuous demonstrative act, the full summation of their lives. These aren't my favorite writers but I think I know what they are up to—and what they are up to doesn't allow them to take "conditions" into account. And I can understand literature as an instrument, the way it was thought of by Blake and Lawrence, who consciously undertook to change the consciousness of society and for whom society's resistance to what they were saying was the given and accepted circumstance of their work.

These categories are not, of course, exclusive of each other. And they have one thing in common, which is the open *demand* of the writer—for money, or for attention to his internal world, or for a change in the external world. They have nothing to do with the idea of the writer which establishes itself whenever literature is discussed as an institution: that is, the idea of the writer as ideally a kind of highly privileged priest who is subsidized by a corrupt society to do it some good. On such occasions the self-pity that suffuses every statement, the hidden desire to become a civil servant, an undersecretary in charge of spiritual hygiene, suggest an essential lack of realism about the present social situation and, indeed, about any possible social situation.

Nothing I have said is meant as derogation of the guild spirit among writers, which at the present time is probably inadequate. To take account of the conditions of literature in the way of shop-talk and with the expectable bitterness and malice—that seems quite right. But I think it is useless and even harmful to spend time in formulating a clear and distinct idea of the literary weather—either you're embarked or you're not embarked. If you are embarked, the weather report can only tell you you're a fool. But what good does that information do you? And would you be any better off on shore? In modern times what we respond to in a writer is not literary power alone but literary power in conjunction with the ability to overcome and outwit the worldly situation. It's perfectly possible, as you suggest in the course of your questions, that things may come to such a pass that the writer will not be able ever to win. But he isn't helped to do what still remains to him to do by thinking about the deplorable conditions of his work. If he is to vanish, it is appropriate that he vanish in maledictions rather than in a self-commiserative sociological analysis of the discrepancy between his function and his fate.

With this said, I feel rather more able to go on to answer some of your questions. I'll begin with Question 2, under which, I think, Question 1 is subsumed.

2. We will only deceive ourselves if we continue to talk about contemporary culture in terms of highbrow and middlebrow. These detestable words suggest a cultural situation in which a small group deals with ideas and artifacts whose integrity is bound up with their difficulty, while another and much larger group deals with the dilution of these ideas and the facile simulacra of these artifacts. In such a situation we see the operation of intellect-prestige and sensibility-prestige, which are quite consonant with the other prestige notions of our civilization, the belief that there is an absolute, high-priced cultural best which can be acquired in cheap imitation. The result of this is the diminution of the common fund of middling responses to life, the depletion of the general stock of ordinary good sense and direct feeling. It may thus be said that the idea of highbrow culture as held by the middlebrow abets commercialized culture in its corrupting influence.

But this is only a residual situation, not the developing one. To understand the developing situation we must see that, while of course there still are partisans of a high and exigent culture, the mass of educated people—of intellectuals indeed—are becoming increasingly suspicious of culture and even hostile toward it. They don't know this and certainly they wouldn't admit it, for culture still has honorific meanings for the middle class. Yet the fact is that in their hearts they more and more reject the traditional methods of art, the methods of imagination, of symbol and fantasy.

This is true of the members of my own generation, who, it seems to me, grow increasingly indifferent and even antagonistic to the cultural monuments and heroes and qualities that the literary reviews celebrate as a matter of course. It is also true of the young of about the same intellectual standing. I recently gave a course in certain modern classics to some fifty undergraduates, most of whom were to enter the practical professions. They were remarkably intelligent young men, and, what is more, remarkably warm-hearted and decent. They worked with good will and enjoyment, and they were more than tolerant of my own commitments and enthusiasms; but as for themselves they were profoundly suspicious of Blake and Melville and Henry James, of Proust and Joyce and Yeats, of William James and Freud. They found these men—I noted down the adjectives—too indefinite, too aristocratic, too paradoxical, too remote from reality, not sufficiently understanding and sympathetic.

It must be observed that the rejection of the *method* of art extends to the *qualities* of art when these appear, as they do, in abstract or practical thought. Hence the suspicion of William James and Freud, which exists in the degree that these men show in their work the qualities of art—in the degree that they are creative and spirited, and not *literal*.

It is no doubt very easy to say that what I have been describing is simply Philistinism. And it is the easier because certain Philistines have undertaken to speak for this cultural group and to attack highbrow culture as pretentious or irresponsible or corrupt or insane. It is also possible to call it Stalinism, for Stalinism becomes endemic in the American middle class as soon as that class begins to think; it is a cultural Stalinism, independent of any political belief: the cultural ideas of the ADA will not, I venture to say, be found materially different from those of the PAC[1]; Parrington is the essential arbiter of the literary views of our more-or-less intellectual middle class, Parrington who so well plows the ground for the negation of literature.

Yet I think it won't do to dismiss this group and its attitudes with epithets, however just they be. I even find that I can't be wholly or merely hostile to the culture I describe, although I fear it—one can't be only hostile if one knows the people who make it up and gets the sense of their seriousness and the legitimacy of many of their aspirations. In addition, I am forced to admit that it isn't my ideal of a really good culture that the mass of intelligent people should devote a large part of their lives to dealing with difficult ideas and artifacts, and to come to believe that such an activity is—as Matthew

[1] ADA stands for Americans for Democratic Action. PAC probably refers to the strongly Stalinist Political Action Committee of the CIO. (D.T.)

Arnold said of someone's notion of the place of Biblical exegesis in the life of man—as much a natural function as to eat and copulate.

I believe that the group I describe is paying less and less lip-service to contemporary highbrow culture, that it has little regard for any anterior culture, that it is contriving a culture which will not be middlebrow at all in the sense of having reference, at one remove, to highbrow culture: it will be an inadequate culture and a *stupid* one, but it will be, at least for a time, satisfying in its inadequacy and dullness to the people who want it; it will contrive its own prestige and make the high and exigent culture more irrelevant than it is now. If we can think of highbrow culture as a unitary thing, it is very doubtful that its response to the cultural group I have described is a useful one. Its error lies not in its lack of "responsibility," which is a word that masks the demand for its emasculation, but in its lack of an aggressive impulse of survival. Some of my other answers may suggest what I mean.

3. The revivals you mention don't need a great deal of explanation. They aren't quantitatively very great. Yet they truly express a need, even though the need of a small number. The need is for mind to be applied to human life in its social and personal factuality and with the particular joy and goodwill of creativeness. People of almost all cultural groups are agreed that we are living in an extreme, even in an ultimate, situation; and very likely they are right. They are agreed too that the best way for literature to deal with this situation is to confront the reader with it, and as directly and literally as possible; and they may be right in their strategy. But I am inclined to think that they are promoting the paralysis of fear and hopelessness. Opposed to this is a residual feeling that one of the ways of preserving oneself is to take a serious delight in the qualities that presumably justify preservation; the revivals you speak of contribute to this serious delight.

4. Nowadays we are inclined to equate experiment in literature with the complicated apparatus of scientific experiment, or of quasi-scientific experiment such as is done with rats and mazes: for us the pre-eminently experimental is the contrivance of mechanical devices

of form. These may succeed in themselves, but in literature—the other arts may be different—they are seldom usefully communicated; it is hard for the continuator of a device or a method not to become a mere imitator—I can't see that Joyce's inventions have been used to any very good effect and I can think of many examples in which their use has crushed and obscured the writer's real quality. And our preoccupation with this kind of experiment has made us less sensitive to the less spectacular experiment that goes on whenever a writer of any originality is at work, the innovations in *style* without which nothing of value is done. There is in English what might be called a permanent experiment, which is the effort to get the language of poetry back to a certain hard, immediate actuality, what we are likely to think of as the tone of good common speech. One sees this in Skelton, in Chaucer, in the later Shakespeare, in Donne, etc. It was what Pound was after in his early days; it is what Yeats was after and what he achieved. Dante's middle style—the simplicity of speech of women at the market—and Stendhal's prose formed on the Code Napoléon, were analogous experiments. I like to think that our cultural schism may come to be bridged with the aid of a literature which will develop the experiment of a highly charged plain speech.

5. If American literature has grown more academic since the twenties it isn't because of the entrance of the writer into the university. One branch of writing has grown academic, in a neutral sense of reward, but at the behest of the literature of the twenties, which required and got a highly informed criticism. It seems to me that the university is a perfectly appropriate base of operations for the critic, though less so for the poet and even less for the novelist. Its disadvantage for the latter two does not lie in any antagonism that exists between the intellectual life and the creative life but rather in the antagonism between the pedagogical life (good enough in itself) and both the intellectual and the creative life. Yet with no desire to defend the university, and granting that it easily gives shelter to many minds that are, in the pejorative sense, academic in the extreme, my sense of intellectual society outside the university

is that it is quite as timid and stodgy as it supposes declared academics to be, that its attitudes are just as fixed and horrified and inelastic, although possibly its manners are a little easier.

6 and 7. For me these questions have an integral relation with each other. The tension between Soviet Communism and the democratic countries can be understood as, among other things, an expression of a tension which exists in our culture between two radically opposed views of man. The newspapers and the State Department will of course pervert the nature of this tension by means of all the gross clichés of current democratism, but we must not let this limit and confuse our understanding of the reality of the opposition between a simple and negative materialism and some other more complex and more possibility-creating view which I won't undertake to give a name to. I understand the great cultural work of the present period to be the development and establishment of this latter view. It is impossible for a writer with any pretensions to seriousness not to be involved in it. I understand the critical movement you refer to as being one of the manifestations of resistance to the simple and negative materialism which is endemic in modern materialism. Its significance to me lies beyond any mere increase of understanding of particular literary texts; and the intensity of its effort at a time when there is, as you say, an ever diminishing audience for poetry is a paradigm of the cultural situation as it now exists, for I take the intensity of its analysis and interpretation to represent its estimate, in the face of massive resistance, of the complication, manifoldness and possibility of the mind in the universe.

When I choose it as an example of resistance to the malign materalism pervasive through the world and established in Soviet Russia, I don't mean to inflate the importance of this critical movement, and perhaps it will be clear that I don't in fact do so, when I say that as an element of resistance it has not nearly done its work. It has not made its way among the groups that might be expected to feel its influence. After nearly twenty years of activity, it is still the *new* criticism. The notion prevails that it is abstruse and special, but this is not so; it has simply preferred to act a little haughty, a little shy, a little sullen, and even now, when it has won its way at least in academic circles, quite scaring the old-line scholars into apologetic self-consciousness, it makes out that it is still misunderstood. It has mistaken method for ideology, and pretends that all it offers is method. It should long ago have realized and admitted its ideology and carried its ark into battle. That it did not do so was an act of provincialism—or is this what you mean by academicism? Whatever name you give it, this is the fault of serious culture in general; it isn't serious enough, it doesn't properly estimate the seriousness of the situation, for it is only a frivolity to say that the situation is hopeless.

Orwell on the Future

[A review of *Nineteen Eighty-four* by George Orwell. *The New Yorker*, June 18, 1949]

GEORGE ORWELL'S new novel, *Nineteen Eighty-four,* confirms its author in the special, honorable place he holds in our intellectual life. Orwell's native gifts are perhaps not of a transcendent kind; they have their roots in a quality of mind that ought to be as frequent as it is modest. This quality may be described as a sort of moral centrality, a directness of relation to moral—and political—fact, and it is so far from being frequent in our time that Orwell's possession of it seems nearly unique. Orwell is an intellectual to his fingertips, but he is far removed from both the Continental and the American type of intellectual. The turn of his mind is what used to be thought of as peculiarly "English." He is indifferent to the allurements of elaborate theory and of extreme sensibility. The medium of his thought is common sense, and his commitment to intellect is fortified by an old-fashioned faith that the truth can be got at, that we can, if we actually want to, see the object as it really is. This faith in the power of mind rests in part on Orwell's willingness, rare among contemporary intellectuals, to admit his connection with his own cultural past. He no longer identifies himself with the British upper middle class in which he was reared, yet it is interesting to see how often his sense of fact derives from some ideal of that class, how he finds his way through a problem by means of an unabashed certainty of the worth of some old, simple, belittled virtue. Fairness, decency, and responsibility do not make up a shining or comprehensive morality, but in a disordered world they serve Orwell as an invaluable base of intellectual operations.

Radical in his politics and in his artistic tastes, Orwell is wholly free of the cant of radicalism. His criticism of the old order is cogent, but he is chiefly notable for his flexible and modulated examination of the political and aesthetic ideas that oppose those of the old order. Two years of service in the Spanish Loyalist Army convinced him that he must reject the line of the Communist Party and, presumably, gave him a large portion of his knowledge of the nature of human freedom. He did not become—as Leftist opponents of Communism are so often and so comfortably said to become— "embittered" or "cynical"; his passion for freedom simply took account of yet another of freedom's enemies, and his intellectual verve was the more stimulated by what he had learned of the ambiguous nature of the newly identified foe, which so perplexingly uses the language and theory of light for ends that are not enlightened. His distinctive work as a radical intellectual became the criticism of liberal and radical thought wherever it deteriorated to shibboleth and dogma. No one knows better than he how willing is the intellectual Left to enter the prison of its own mass mind, nor does anyone believe more directly than he in the practical consequences of thought, or understand more clearly the enormous power, for good or bad, that ideology exerts in an unstable world.

Nineteen Eighty-four is a profound, terrifying, and wholly fascinating book. It is a fantasy of the political future, and, like any such fantasy, serves its author as a magnifying device for an examination of the present. Despite the impression it may give at first, it is not an attack on the Labour Government. The shabby London of the Super-State of the future, the bad food, the dull clothing, the fusty housing, the infinite ennui—all these certainly reflect the English life of today, but they are not meant to represent the outcome of the utopian pretensions of Labourism or of any socialism. Indeed, it is exactly one of the cruel essential points of the book that utopianism is no longer a living issue. For Orwell, the day has gone by when we could afford the luxury of making our flesh creep with the spiritual horrors of a successful hedonistic society; grim years have intervened since Aldous Huxley, in *Brave New World,* rigged out the welfare state of Ivan Karamazov's Grand Inquisitor in the knickknacks of modern science and amusement, and said what Dostoevsky and all the other critics of the utopian ideal had said before—that men might actually gain a life of security, adjustment, and fun, but only at the cost of their spiritual freedom, which is to say, of their humanity. Orwell agrees that the State of the future will establish its power by destroying souls. But he believes that men will be coerced, not cosseted, into soullessness. They will be dehumanized not by sex, massage, and private helicopters but by a marginal life of deprivation, dullness, and fear of pain.

This, in fact, is the very center of Orwell's vision of the future. In 1984, nationalism as we know it has at last been overcome, and the world is organized into three great political entities. All profess the same philosophy, yet despite their agreement, or because of it, the three Super-States are always at war with each other, two always allied against one, but all seeing to it that the balance of power is kept, by means of sudden, treacherous shifts of alliance. This arrangement is established as if by the understanding of all, for although it is the ultimate aim of each to dominate the world, the immediate aim is the perpetuation of war without victory and without defeat. It has at last been truly understood that war is the health of the State; as an official slogan has it, "War Is Peace." Perpetual war is the best assurance of perpetual absolute rule. It is also the most efficient method of consuming the production of the factories on which the economy of the State is based. The only alternative method is to distribute the goods among the population. But this has its clear danger. The life of pleasure is inimical to the health of the State. It stimulates the senses and thus encourages the illusion of individuality; it creates personal desires, thus potential personal thought and action.

But the life of pleasure has another, and even more significant, disadvantage in the political future that Orwell projects from his observation of certain developments of political practice in the last two decades. The rulers he envisages are men who, in seizing rule, have grasped the innermost principles of power. All other oligarchs have included some general good in their impulse to rule and have played at being philosopher-kings or priest-kings or scientist-kings, with an announced program of beneficence. The rulers of Orwell's State know that power in its pure form has for its true end nothing but itself, and they know that the nature of power is defined by the pain it can inflict on others. They know, too, that just as wealth exists only in relation to the poverty of others, so power in its pure aspect exists only in relation to the weakness of others, and that any power of the ruled, even the power to experience happiness, is by that much a diminution of the power of the rulers.

The exposition of the *mystique* of power is the heart and essence of Orwell's book. It is implicit throughout the narrative, explicit in excerpts from the remarkable *Theory and Practice of Oligarchical Collectivism;* a subversive work by one Emmanuel Goldstein, formerly the most gifted leader of the Party, now the legendary foe of the State. It is brought to a climax in the last section of the novel, in the terrible scenes in which Winston Smith, the sad hero of the story, having lost his hold on the reality decreed by the State, having come to believe that sexuality is a pleasure, that personal loyalty is a good, and that two plus two always and not merely under certain circumstances equals four, is brought back to health by torture and discourse in a hideous parody on psychotherapy and the Platonic dialogues.

Orwell's theory of power is developed brilliantly, at considerable length. And the social system that it postulates is described with magnificent circumstantiality: the three orders of the population—Inner Party, Outer Party, and proletarians; the complete surveillance of the citizenry by the Thought Police, the only really efficient arm of the government; the total negation of the personal life; the directed emotions of hatred and patriotism; the deified Leader, omnipresent but invisible, wonderfully named Big Brother; the children who spy on their parents; and the total destruction of culture. Orwell is particularly successful in his exposition of the official mode of thought, Doublethink, which gives one "the power of holding two contradictory beliefs in one's mind simultaneously, and accepting both of them." This intellectual safeguard of the State is reinforced by a language, Newspeak, the goal of which is to purge itself of all words in which a free thought might be formulated. The systematic obliteration of the past further protects the citizen from Crimethink, and nothing could be more touching, or more suggestive of what history means to the mind, than the efforts of poor Winston Smith to think about the condition of man without knowledge of what others have thought before him.

By now, it must be clear that *Nineteen Eighty-four* is, in large part, an attack on Soviet Communism. Yet to read it as this and as nothing else would be to misunderstand the book's aim. The settled and reasoned opposition to Communism that Orwell expresses is not to be minimized, but he is not undertaking to give us the delusive comfort of moral superiority to an antagonist. He does not separate Russia from the general tendency of the world today. He is saying, indeed, something no less comprehensive than this: that Russia, with its idealistic social revolution now developed into a police state, is but the image of the impending future and that the ultimate threat to human freedom may well come from a similar and even more massive development of the social idealism of our democratic culture. To many liberals, this idea will be incomprehensible, or, if it is understood at all, it will be condemned by them as both foolish and dangerous. We have dutifully learned to think that tyranny manifests itself chiefly, even solely, in the defense of private property and that the profit motive is the source of all evil. And certainly Orwell does not deny that property is powerful or that it may be ruthless in self-defense. But he sees that, as the tendency of recent history goes, property is no longer in anything like the strong position it once was, and that will and intellect are playing a greater and greater part in human history. To many, this can look only like a clear gain. We naturally identify ourselves with will and intellect; they are the very stuff of humanity, and we prefer not to think of their exercise in any except an ideal way. But Orwell tells us that the final oligarchical revolution of the future, which, once established, could never be escaped or countered, will be made not by men who have property to defend but by men of will and intellect, by "the new aristocracy . . . of bureaucrats, scientists, trade-union organizers, publicity experts, sociologists, teachers, journalists, and professional politicians."

These people [says the authoritative Goldstein, in his account of the revolution], whose origins lay in the salaried middle class and the upper grades of the working class, had been shaped and brought together by the barren world of monopoly industry and centralized government. As compared with their opposite numbers in past ages, they were less avaricious, less tempted by luxury, hungrier for pure power, and, above all, more conscious of what they were doing and more intent on crushing opposition. This last difference was cardinal.

The whole effort of the culture of the last hundred years has been directed toward teaching us to understand the economic motive as the irrational road to death, and to seek salvation in the rational and the planned. Orwell marks a turn in thought; he asks us to consider whether the triumph of certain forces of the mind, in their naked pride and excess, may not produce a state of things far worse than any we have ever known. He is not the first to raise the question, but he is the first to raise it on truly liberal or radical grounds, with no intention of abating the demand for a just society, and with an overwhelming intensity and passion. This priority makes his book a momentous one.

Fitzgerald Plain

[A review of *The Far Side of Paradise* by Arthur Mizener. *The New Yorker*, February 3, 1951]

THE posthumous fortunes of Scott Fitzgerald took their decisive turn for the better when, in 1941, Edmund Wilson edited the unfinished novel, *The Last Tycoon,* and then, in 1945, brought out *The Crack-Up,* a collection of Fitzgerald's letters and autobiographical essays. With these two volumes in hand, no one could fail to understand what Stephen Vincent Benét meant when he said, "This is not a legend, this is a reputation." Fitzgerald's literary powers had always been there to be seen, and even in the darkest days had not lacked admirers, some of whom carried their regard to the point of fanaticism and cult, yet in general the legend so obscured the reputation that when *Tender Is the Night,* Fitzgerald's last completed novel and one of the best American novels of the decade, appeared in 1934, it was received by the reviewers with almost universal hostility or indifference. And when Fitzgerald died, in 1940, the owlish piety of editorial comment could memorialize him only as the flaming youth, the Idle Apprentice who had flung away his chance in life, the symbol, perhaps the instigator, of the heedless Twenties. But with his death the obstructive force of the legend somewhat abated, and *The Last Tycoon,* fragment though it was, could make it plain that Fitzgerald was a novelist of superb and developing powers, while the autobiographical matter of *The Crack-Up* put it beyond question that he was an intelligence of the greatest seriousness.

Yet, when we have taken into account all that insures his reputation, we still have to see that Fitzgerald is necessarily and properly a legendary figure. We must be on guard against substituting his life for his work, but it would be merely a willful literary priggishness not to see that the life and the work are continuous with each other. Fitzgerald was his own best subject, and he belongs to the company of greater men than he, from Goethe and Byron to Yeats and Gide, whose work exists in the aura of their personal lives, which by genius they made much more than personal. He himself claimed his own legend, and took a grim comfort in it. "I am not a great man," he said in a letter, "but sometimes I think the personal and objective quality of my talent and the sacrifice of it, in pieces, to preserve its essential value has some sort of epic grandeur." The right elements of his legend were, as he knew, not only his charm, his recklessness, and his love of pleasure and prestige but also his unique talent, his violated conscience, and, above all, his actual achievement. It is the understanding of the legendary quality of the man in this true sense that is the measure of the success of Arthur Mizener's life of Fitzgerald, *The Far Side of Paradise*.

Mr. Mizener's biography appears at a moment when Budd Schulberg's *The Disenchanted* is in the full tide of its popularity. A comparison of the two books is no doubt technically unfair to Mr. Schulberg, who has pleaded the privileges of the novelist with an epigraph quoted from Henry James, but it is inevitable, because what Mr. Schulberg tells us about the hero of his novel can scarcely fail to become part of the public image of Fitzgerald. *The Disenchanted* is not a bad novel of its kind, and, so far as it can be said to have reference to Fitzgerald, it is affectionate and generous, but taking it only as a story, and leaving aside all question of literal accuracy and spiritual truth, it suffers by comparison with Mr. Mizener's book. Mr. Mizener's advantage comes from his having written as a scholar; by the sobriety of his prose and his reliance upon documents and attestation, he commits himself to fact, and scarcely anything that Mr. Schulberg has invented as analogues of the facts of Fitzgerald's life can equal for interest what Mr. Mizener gives us of the facts themselves—such things as, for example, his picture of Fitzgerald's boyhood and adolescence, his sketch of Fitzgerald's parents (the gentlemanly, unsuccessful father, the dominating, ill-dressed, eccentric mother), and his account of the marriage of Scott and Zelda Fitzgerald. Mr. Schulberg's Jere Halliday could never have written Zelda's heartbreaking letter of farewell quoted by Mr. Mizener on page 236, nor could Manley Halliday ever have said, as Fitzgerald did in the worst days of the marriage, "Our united front is less a romance than a categorical imperative." Mr. Mizener writes not only as a scholar but also as a critic, and he is therefore able to deal adequately with the most important fact of all, the nature and quality of Fitzgerald's genius. Because he knows how much there was to be destroyed, his account of Fitzgerald's long self-destruction is deeply tragic, where *The Disenchanted* is only sad and depressing, for Mr. Schulberg can attribute to his doomed novelist nothing more than a happy prose style and a knack of observing the manners of the upper middle class. Fitzgerald had these gifts pre-eminently, but he did not write *The Great Gatsby* and *Tender Is the Night* by means of style and observation alone; he wrote them, as Mr. Mizener knows, out of an unflagging moral energy, of which one aspect was his fatal submission to the sanctions of social prestige.

This submission is an essential part of the Fitzgerald legend and we have to come to terms with it. It is likely to have the appearance of snobbery, and in some large part it *is* snobbery; Fitzgerald, it is true, could never represent the rich and powerful without the bitterest reprobation, yet at the same time he needed to be at one with them. Taking it as snobbery, we can find reasons to forgive or extenuate it. We can say of it that by means of it Fitzgerald, more than anyone else of his time, realized the rigorousness of the systems of prestige that lie beneath the American social fluidity. Then, too, as snobbery, it had a kind of innocence, something of the solemnity of childhood, when systems of prestige have a magical importance, and this, for Fitzgerald, must have been much intensified by the social ambiguity of his parents. Yet in an important sense Fitzgerald's social submissiveness is not snobbery at all, for its reference is not to a real society but to an idea of society, ultimately to an ideal of himself. "I would be capable," he said in a letter to John O'Hara, "of going to Podunk on a visit and being absolutely booed and overawed by its social system, not from timidity but because of some inner necessity of starting my life and my self-justification over again at scratch in whatever environment I may be thrown." He exaggerated the idea of society and his dependence upon it in order, we may say, to provide a field for the activity of his conscience, for the trial of his self.

It is this moral use of the idea of society that suggests Fitzgerald's kinship with Henry James and Proust. But the way in which Fitzgerald conceives of the self that is to be tried on the field of society links him with an older tradition, that of the great Romantics. When he died, his body was laid out in a second-class Los Angeles funeral establishment, in the William Wordsworth Room. There is irony here that comes from the difference between the two lives, from the fact that Fitzgerald could manage so little of the Wordsworthian plain living, but there is appropriateness, too. What Fitzgerald said about his capacity for ecstatic happiness might have been said by Wordsworth; both men gave a peculiar value to their boyhood and youth as definitive of their whole lives, and perhaps Fitzgerald's theory of emotional bankruptcy, his belief that he had a fixed fund of feeling that he would exhaust, derives from a similar theory Wordsworth held. Most of Fitzgerald's literary references were to the Romantic writers, and Wordsworth was a clear figure in his mind. So was Keats, from whose poem about youth growing pale and spectre-thin and dying he takes the title *Tender Is the Night;* his dominant literary mood is that of "La Belle Dame Sans Merci" and "Lamia." Indeed, between Fitzgerald and the Keats of the great letters there is an affinity of temperament that is almost startling—there is the same greediness for pleasure, and the intelligences that work on the greediness are remarkably alike, and they yield a similar moral quality; the Fitzgerald who said that his marriage had become less a romance than a categorical imperative is not very far from the Keats who wrote the amazing letter about the world being "the vale of Soul-making."

Fitzgerald engages our attention so deeply because he realizes something actual and immediate in our contemporary life, but this kinship of his with the Romantics suggests that he interests us for another reason as well, because he begins to seem an anachronistic figure—he is legendary in the sense of being a figure of the past. He thought of himself in this way; his notion of America involved the idea of deterioration, of old virtues coming to an end. He set great store by the "belief in good manners and right instincts" he had learned from his father, but he spoke of his father as the debilitated representative of an old idealism, "of the generation of the colonies and the revolution," snubbed and put down by "the new young peasant stock coming up every ten years." It was not only the old virtues that he saw doomed but also the energy of will and imagination. Gatsby, for all that he represents the raw energies of the Twenties, is as anachronistic as his author, for Fitzgerald makes him the symbol of a desire that modern life must deny, the wish to come face to face with "something commensurate to his capacity for wonder." Without the help of that phrase, "the capacity for wonder," no college textbook could hope to deal with the Romantic poets. What they wondered at was, above all, the self, and as our epoch more and more denies the value and even the possibility of the self, Fitzgerald seems to have ended what they began, to be as far off as they, and to shine with their light.

An American View of English Literature

[*The Reporter*, November 13, 1951]

A N English literary magazine recently undertook to celebrate the Festival of Britain with a series of articles on "the British idea in literature," and invited me to contribute. *The* British idea in literature! My first response was to suppose that the subject was impossible. How could one attempt to say what was *the* idea of a literature which had been flourishing for more than half a millennium? How could one even conceive the subject without betraying that living multiplicity of manners and matters, of temperaments and wills, which makes the glory of English letters?

But then I read carefully the exact terms of my invitation and saw that the subject was not really impossible after all. For I was being asked to deal with it "from the American point of view," and it seemed to me that if one looks at British literature from the American point of view—if, that is, one considers it in comparison with American literature—one may see that between the two literatures there is an essential difference which actually does suggest what might indeed be thought of as the "idea" of each.

The difference lies in the way the two literatures regard society and the ordinary life of daily routine. As compared to American

---

[1] Title supplied by the editor of this volume. The original title was "Dreiser, Anderson, Lewis, and the Riddle of Society."

literature, British literature is defined by its tendency to take society for granted and then to go on to demonstrate its burdensome but interesting and valuable complexity. And American literature, in comparison with British, is defined by its tendency to transcend or circumvent the social fact and to concentrate upon the individual in relation to himself, to God, or to the cosmos, and, even when the individual stands in an inescapable relation to the social fact, to represent society and the ordinary life of daily routine not as things assumed and taken for granted, but as problems posed, as alien and hostile to the true spiritual and moral life.

And it occurred to me to suggest that this difference is strikingly exemplified by two very well-known books, the two best boys' books in the two literatures. *Kim* obviously derives something of its inspiration from *Huckleberry Finn*—Kipling greatly admired Mark Twain—and the two books are similar at so many points that their wide divergence in social attitude is the more significant. The two boy-heroes are alike in that they delight in their freedom from all familial and social ties. But they are different in this, that Kim carries in an amulet case the evidence of his father's identity, and, as with many legendary heroes, the discovery of his ancestry is his destiny, while Huck, when eventually he hears of his brutal father's death, feels scarcely any other emotion than relief at his greater safety in his isolate freedom.

Both boys adopt surrogate fathers, and Kim adopts no fewer than three, of whom one has the authority of religion, one the authority of worldly wisdom, and one the authority of the state. But Huck's single adopted father, the Negro slave Jim, has no other authority than that of natural goodness. Both boys see much of the seamy side of ordinary life; Kim accepts it as a fine, rich show, the expectable field of his activity, but Huck judges it, condemns it, and forgives it. Forgives it, but can never be part of it. Where Kim learns to consent to society and even to become the eager servant of the state (finding no conflict of loyalty between his attachment to his lama and his commitment to the Indian Secret Service), the climax of Huck's adventures is his great moral crisis over his loyalty to

Jim, which issues in what he believes to be a complete separation not only from society but from God. And the end of his adventures brings him to his resolve to "light out for the Territory."

In short, at every point the English book says that initiation into society is possible, fascinating, and desirable, while at every point the American book says that virtue lies in alienation from society. And over the century and a half during which there has been an American literature, this difference from British literature may be observed. The clue to the nature and power of British literature in the nineteenth century is contained in Burke's phrase, "the grand mystery of social life." The clue to the nature and power of American literature is contained in the titles of two American works of fiction which have established themselves in the American mind in a more than literary way—*The Last of the Mohicans* and "The Fall of the House of Usher"—the image of the solitary man who survives his social group, and the image of the decay and collapse of the social fabric itself. Wherever American literature is great and interesting, these themes, or that variation of them which is the lighting out for the Territory, will be found dominant.

The impulse to withdraw from society which American literature so consistently expresses does not arise from the contempt for what society is in comparison with what it might be. Such a feeling is characteristic of, say, the English Romantic poets, or of Dickens. What we deal with in the great American writers is a rejection of society in essence, a disenchantment or disgust with the very idea of society. Poe's disgust, his images of desolation, madness, and decay, are obviously representative of a profound social negation, but Poe never hints the causes of his disgust—for him to have done so would have been to mitigate the extremity of his revulsion. Cooper is almost always interesting as a social critic and satirist, yet Cooper was truly free and powerful in his imagination only when he dealt with man outside of society, self-sufficient, autonomous, and anti-social.

Thoreau's suspiciousness of organized society is naturally better remembered than the horror he expressed of the human condition in general. He loathed the necessities of ordinary life, thought it a desecration of the divinity of language that it must be uttered by the mouth which also serves the animal necessity of eating, and believed that the domesticities of the farm were as corrupting as the cold intellectuality of Harvard College.

Emerson spoke of the high value to be placed upon the homely actualities, but nothing is more characteristic of Emerson than his lighting out for the Territory of Nature, the Oversoul, and individual personality. Our greatest poet, Whitman, traditionally serves us as the very emblem of the social life of democracy, as the celebrator of the daily routine of plain and ordinary people. But in point of fact Whitman cannot be properly read unless it is understood that his expression of enthusiasm for man in community is but a way of speaking of his real interests, which are Death and the All. His representation of social life is but a figure or analogue of the universe, and in fact a denial of the actuality of society. He cannot conceive society; he cannot conceive social conflict; his people are not persons; the old humanistic categories of tragedy and comedy, which imply valuation and preference—which imply, precisely, society—have no meaning for him.

The academic historians of American literature do not wish to recognize this pervasive asociality of our greatest writers. V. L. Parrington was an exception. For all his limitations, Parrington was an honest man, and he saw what was there to see, which accounts for his detestation of Poe, his contempt for Hawthorne and James, his dealing with Cooper and Melville on so low a level of understanding. But for the most part the academic historians, finding that our best literature does not conform to the progressive clichés or to the blueprint of the American character which academic populism has agreed on, simply ignore the divergence and rest content with claiming the sheer undifferentiated genius of our authors as one more contribution to the general affirmativeness and vitality of American life.

But what the academic historians of American literature now shrink from recognizing was boldly seen—and feared—by more than one writer of our classic period. Hawthorne believed himself to be hopelessly alienated from the actualities of common life, and it was to avoid the fate of his master that Henry James sought his career away from his country. Hawthorne went so far as to say that he did not write novels at all—meaning novels as they were written in England, as Trollope wrote them, with full attention paid to manners and the material circumstances of existence; what he wrote, he said, was "romances"—fictions that dealt in an almost allegorical way with psychological and moral ideas of a certain abstractness. And Hawthorne's characteristic theme is the mental and moral pride which induces man to withdraw from his fellow creatures in all their ordinary imperfectness. This same pride was for Melville a tragic *hubris,* the sin by which Captain Ahab was enthralled and destroyed. But in Melville's *Bartleby the Scrivener,* the definitive statement of social negation beyond which no modern despair has gone, it is not pride that motivates the terrible "I prefer not to," nor even a disgust with the social process, but simply an ultimate, invincible fatigue.

What our literary historians do not wish to see was fully seen and brilliantly noted almost thirty years ago by D. H. Lawrence in his remarkable *Studies in Classical American Literature.* Lawrence maintained that the American writers were recording a momentous and terrible event in history, the end of the humanistic social personality, the personality of hearth and board—and of bed, for American literature's desocialization was concomitant with its desexualization. And Lawrence regarded our classic literature with so intense an ambivalence, with so high an admiration and so strong a dislike, because he believed it to be bitterly undeceived in its recording of the death of the old personality at the same time that it connived in the killing.

The 1920's saw a change in the idiom of American literature. The social fact had for some decades been intruding itself upon the American literary consciousness in an ever more explicit way, and writers now thought expressly "in terms of society," and found virtue in essaying to represent the actual conditions of social life.

Yet if we look at the 1920's with eyes unblinded by the established formulations about realism and naturalism, we see that the characteristic tendency of American literature to abstractness and asociality maintained itself as strongly as ever before.

Now, to be sure, the relation of the individual to social fact is as inescapable as it is obvious, but the relation is seen as a dichotomous one—the individual here, society there—and as a grim problem to be solved, the solution being the individual's escape from or triumph over the social conditions. The impulse to establish the individual in isolate autonomy is as strong as it ever was.

The truth of this is borne out by three recent books about the careers of three eminent writers of the period—I make but a single category because *World So Wide,* the posthumous last novel of Sinclair Lewis, seems so little *by* the Lewis we like to remember and is as much *about* him as F. O. Matthiessen's *Theodore Dreiser* and Irving Howe's *Sherwood Anderson* (both published by Sloane in its American Men of Letters Series) are about those two writers.

Of the three men, Lewis stands a little apart from the other two; Dreiser and Anderson may be felt to have a temperamental affinity with each other that rather excludes their rationalistic colleague. Yet the community of interest is firm among all three. All were consciously and specifically American; all addressed themselves to the problems—or, rather, the problem—of American society, which they agreed in understanding as the securing of freedom for the individual personality. And yet as one looks now at their careers, it seems that society is the last thing in the world they were really interested in, and that the traditional meaning of the word "personality" was the last thing they could conceive.

This is most vividly suggested by the way the three men dealt with sexuality. All of them, in the fashion of their time, made sex an issue, and Dreiser and Anderson suffered for what was held to be their sexual outspokenness. Yet each of them found it impossible to represent a credible sexual relationship. The rights of sex, the necessity of sex, the grim defeats of sex—these they could deal with, at length and abstractly and with widely varying degrees of accuracy and cogency. But when it came to the relations between the sexes, Dickens at the nadir of his preoccupation with female purity could tell us more than they.

Irving Howe is explicit on this point with respect to Anderson. He remarks on the "curiously sexless quality of those of Anderson's later novels which have been read as sex-centered"; he says that "sex in Anderson's novels was little more than a compulsive gesture," that it was "not sex but sexual anxiety. . . ." Matthiessen is no less explicit about Dreiser. "As far as his work was concerned, he never managed to make a fully affecting expression of the passion that consumed him." And of the passion itself—Dreiser spoke of himself as being more interested in women than any man he had ever known—Matthiessen says that it seems to have been "the product of basic insecurity, of an almost desperate need to keep on proving himself." It was, we may say, as abstract as the sexual passion can become.

As for the quality of Lewis' conception of sexuality, it is perhaps best suggested by the appearance in his last novel of virtually the same dream of the lovely dancing girl with which, thirty years ago, Babbitt began his memorable day. Sex in Lewis' novels is always more openly adolescent and more respectable than in Anderson's and Dreiser's, but in the work of all three men its essential reference is to the "dream," to "beauty," to the unattainable ideal, never to the present and to actuality, never to personality. Indeed, nothing like personality ever appears in any of the women of their imagination until after the once-loved woman is seen as having at least the human actuality of a bore or a shrew.

In the course of his remarkably fine study of Anderson, a work at once objective and committed to a generous sympathy with its subject, Howe institutes a comparison between the way D. H. Lawrence dealt with sex and the way Anderson dealt with it. "[Anderson] believed in sex," Howe says, "but where in his work was the struggle between lovers that Lawrence so marvelously showed in *The Rainbow?* Where was the patient representation of the social context in which man is to revitalize his sexual life?"

The question is as pertinent to Dreiser and Lewis as to Anderson. Lawrence was a man of doctrine, of abstract ideas more fully developed than Anderson and Dreiser could conceive possible or than Lewis could conceive at all, yet he had the ability which they lacked of representing the reciprocal actualities of society and personality. And if we look for the explanation of his success and their failure, we can of course find some measure of reason in personal endowment, but the full explanation is not personal but cultural—he was permitted, and they were not, the sense of "the grand mystery of social life."

I do not mean to imply, of course, that a novelist's dealing with sex is the only index of his sense of social actuality. But what Anderson, Dreiser, and Lewis do with sex they do with virtually every human activity. Anderson, like Whitman, makes an elaborate show of being involved with the real, the actual, the simple, the simply personal, and speaks as if he were committed to the social and even to the political, while his real concern, like Whitman's, is with isolate, abstract states of feeling which are on the verge of the mystical and before which all particularity of sense and thought vanish.

Dreiser finds his traditional analogue in Henry Adams, who was at once the last representative of our classic literature and the inaugurator of our immediate modernity of explicit despair. Like Adams', Dreiser's interest in society arises from his self-pity over his exclusion from power; and like Adams, Dreiser transcends his interest in social power, turning to put himself into relation first with cosmic and then with divine power. It is not persons that interest him but more or less differentiated instances of the operation of abstract forces.

Anderson and Dreiser, quite apart from what our taste and judgment may lead us to feel about them, must always be of great interest simply for what they *are*—that is, late and deteriorated modes of a continuous tendency in American writing, exemplars of the sensitive, demanding, self-justifying modern soul. But Sinclair Lewis makes no such claim upon our attention. If he is interesting, it is because of what he does, not because of what he is. And for something like a quarter of a century it has been an open secret which no one quite liked to voice—so much had what he had previously done delighted us—that what he was doing made less and less claim on our interest. At one moment he seemed close indeed to the mystery of social life; perhaps no American novel since *Babbitt* has told us anything new about the American social circumstance. But then with each succeeding attempt, Lewis seemed to move further and further from the heart of the mystery, until in his last book he asks us to believe that " 'Did they, big boy?' slashed Roxanne" is an example of the repartee of a lively American girl, and that Americans of mean sensibility say "Lissen," presumably as against the "Lis-ten" of those of finer grain.

The pathos of failure is extreme, and one does not want to dwell on it longer than to ask why it was necessary. *World So Wide* is about Americans in Florence, and the juxtaposition of characters and setting brings Mark Twain and Henry James to mind, but the emphasis on the comedy of manners makes us wonder whether, in his effort to get again into touch with the mystery of social life, Lewis had not consciously put himself to school to Jane Austen herself, so intent does he seem to represent the pride and prejudice, the sense and sensibility, the foolish fictions and the gross vulgarities through which a man, in the conception of the true social novelist, must pick his way to find a measure of rational happiness. He even gives us a bullying baronet whose very name, Sir Henry Belfont, must have been first thought of and regretfully rejected by Jane Austen, and whose traits make him not less than a cousin of her General Tilney. The pretensions of Sir Henry are exposed when, in a violent scene, it is shown by the heroine that he is really by birth a provincial American.

But it is of no avail—the old, standard paraphernalia cannot serve to bring Lewis any closer to the mystery. *World So Wide* is the story of a youngish Midwestern architect whose nagging wife is fortunately killed; he goes to find his soul in Italy, where, of course, he finds that he does not need culture and liberation but only marriage with a girl who is like his former wife except that she does not nag, a girl who seems to him not so much a woman as a "chunk of Home." This is the epitome of virtually all the life careers Lewis has ever fancied, and as we contemplate it we begin to perceive that Lewis was really no more interested in society than Anderson and Dreiser. What he was interested in was a single human situation whose intended outcome was the denial of society, and also of personality—the situation in which an individual undertakes to be free from and dominant over society, only to submit as fully as possible and to sink prostrated into an abstract anonymity.

The Formative Years[1]

[A review of *The Life and Work of Sigmund Freud*, Volume I, by Ernest Jones. *The New York Times Book Review*, October 11, 1953]

I T would be difficult to say too much in praise of this first of the three volumes of Ernest Jones's life of Sigmund Freud. The interest and importance of the subject are, of course, manifest— Freud is one of the very greatest figures of our epoch. And Dr. Jones is his ideal biographer not only by reason of his forty years of association with Freud as friend and coadjutor, and of his own great intellectual authority in the psychoanalytical movement—he is permanent president of the International Psychoanalytical Association—but also by reason of the excellence of his expository style and the scope of his scientific and humanistic learning. The present volume is not only the fullest possible account of Freud's life up through the years of the great psychoanalytic discoveries but also, in the range of its reference, an important contribution to cultural history.

Dr. Jones has relied upon his personal knowledge of Freud only so far as it was proper for him to do so. He has the scholar's instinct for fullness and precision of detail and wherever possible he finds authority for his statements in record and document; he checks oral reports with the most scrupulous care. His truly monumental research was aided by the Freud family's having put at his disposal an enormous number of letters, manuscripts and family papers.

The biography may therefore be called an "official" one, but

[1] This title is taken from the subtitle of the volume under review. (D.T.)

certainly not in the sense that it is constrained from dealing freely with its subject. That Dr. Jones should write with great admiration for Freud's mind and character we take for granted. But where Freud's conduct was of a kind to do less than credit to himself, where it was extreme or ambiguous or neurotic, Dr. Jones makes no bones about characterizing and analyzing it. And indeed it would have been but a sad compliment to Freud had Dr. Jones surrendered the objectivity and the insight of psychoanalysis in dealing with the personality of its discoverer.

Freud, I have said, is one of the very greatest figures of our epoch. His effect upon contemporary thought and assumption is incalculable. Yet Dr. Jones's biography bears out the impression that Freud was anything but a contemporary personality. In many respects, indeed, he is antipathetic to our contemporary taste in temperaments. He lived by the inner light, he saw life under the aspect of personal heroism and believed that virtue consisted in making truth prevail against the resistance of society. In short, he was the very type of what David Riesman has called the "inner-directed" personality which dominated the nineteenth century and constituted its genius.

Such a personality makes but a limited appeal to our increasingly "other-directed" society with its ideal of blandness and cooperation and its suspiciousness of personal pre-eminence and self-assertion. Some of the renewed resistance which Freudian ideas—or at least "orthodox" Freudian ideas—have met with in the last decade is probably to be ascribed to the contemporary uneasiness with the personal style of Freud himself. A few years ago a hostile biographer, or psychographer, Miss Helen Puner, made it a chief part of her indictment of Freud that he actually believed that his ideas were right, that he sought to make them prevail, that he did not gracefully compound his differences with the men who modified his theories. Our culture would seem to have changed since the days when school children were taught that for Columbus to say, "Sail on! Sail on!" was brave and fine, not ill-natured and undemocratic.

Freud, we may say, was destined from birth for the heroic role. He was born with a caul, which may in part explain why he took so much pleasure in the history of David Copperfield, who had the same natal sign of good fortune. The eldest of seven children, he was his mother's favorite, and the hopes of the family were centered in him. In the middle years of the last century the ideal of personal distinction was still very strong and it was especially cherished by the recently enfranchised Jews of Vienna.

He was thus a "dedicated spirit, singled out" long before he knew what he was singled out for. He was without religious emotions, but he identified himself with the Jewish people in the heroic incidents of their history. His response to his Jewishness made him a protestant and a puritan in Catholic Vienna and thus partly accounts for his passionate love of England. For a period of ten years he read nothing but English books. He was devoted to Shakespeare, but his special feeling was for the protestant and puritan manifestations of English culture—he named one of his sons after Oliver Cromwell and he had a deep personal affection for *Paradise Lost*.

The youthful commitment to austerity and intransigence stood him in good stead when he proposed to the medical profession the early theory of psychoanalysis. He was undertaking to tell men of considerable scientific accomplishment, whose zeal for physical science had led them to regard the concept of mind as virtually a superstition, that the causes of hysteria were to be sought not in the nerves and not in the brain but in the mind. And he meant by the mind the emotions, the imagination and the will. To bear the opprobrium of this position there was need for the dour Cromwellian stubbornness and the Miltonic pride which in his young manhood had supplemented the Maccabean ideal of his boyhood.

In 1900, when the basic discoveries in psychoanalysis had been made, Freud said of himself: "I am not really a man of science, not an observer, not an experimenter, and not a thinker. I am nothing but by temperament a *conquistador*—an adventurer, if you want to translate the word—with the curiosity, the boldness and the tenacity that belongs to that type of being." This self-appraisal,

Dr. Jones remarks, was only half serious, and it tells only part of the truth, yet it gives us the clue to an essential quality of Freud's mind. It is exemplified in one of the most moving moments of thought I know, the moment when Freud, believing that he had the explanation of hysteria in a sexual trauma suffered in childhood, realized that every one of the stories of rape and seduction that his hysterical patients were agreed in telling him was untrue. His theory was shattered—until with a bold thrust of the imagination he perceived that the fantasy was a fact: it was a mental fact, and its meaning lay in its intention. The perception is a commonplace now, but only a conquistadorial mind could first have made and used it.

Although Dr. Jones's biography confirms the impression that Freud is a personality alien to our time, it also serves to mitigate the possible extravagances which may arise from that impression. There are those, of course, for whom Freud's life-style is in itself attractive. They like the personal reserve, the strictness and elegance of his character, and are positively drawn to the asperity and pessimism which so strikingly mark his vital affirmation.

Yet even those who respond to Freud in this way will take pleasure in the "human" traits that an extensive biography discloses. There is naturally something engaging and endearing in a Freud who, as a mature man, indulges in fantasies of being endowed by a millionaire whose child he has rescued from a runaway horse; who is superstitious and takes half-serious heed of omens; who has great regard for his tailor's opinion of him; who has his beard trimmed daily; who as a lover makes his beloved the daily gift of a red rose and writes her innumerable letters of extraordinary length and remarkable eloquence; who frets because he cannot buy his wife the gold bangle that seems to have been *de rigueur* for the wives of docents.

A biography of Freud is like any other biography in that it has for its primary purpose the satisfying of our curiosity about an eminent and interesting man. Toward this end Dr. Jones has done everything that a biographer can do. Detail is of the essence of biographical truth and Dr. Jones has not only given us as much detail as we can reasonably hope for but he has arranged it with great skill. He has dealt fully and frankly with the most personal aspects of Freud's life, his relations with his family, his courtship of his future wife, his complex and eventually unhappy relations with Josef Breuer, his collaborator in the pioneering "Studies in Hysteria," his strange friendship with Wilhelm Fliess.

But in addition to satisfying our natural and proper curiosity a biography of Freud should serve the purpose of aiding our understanding of Freud's science. Psychoanalysis is best comprehended not as a fully formulated system but rather as a developing idea in the mind of its discoverer. It is hard to imagine a better history of the development of Freud's idea or of the mind that conceived it than that which Dr. Jones has given us.

The Years of Maturity[1]

[A review of *The Life and Work of Sigmund Freud*, Volume II, by Ernest Jones. *The New York Times Book Review*, September 18, 1955]

PERHAPS the best way to praise the second volume of Ernest Jones's biography of Freud is to say that it is as good as the first volume—*Years of Maturity* is as dramatic and instructive a book as its predecessor, *The Formative Years and the Great Discoveries*. The commanding interest of the new work is, of course, renewed testimony to Dr. Jones's skill and gusto as a biographer. It is also to be understood as the measure of his subject's genius.

Freud is one of the rare, fortunate men whose mature years are as charged with heroic energy as their formative years. He surrenders to time nothing of the romance of growth, of trial, of high demand upon himself which so deeply engages us in the account of his early career.

The present volume covers the period from 1901 to 1919, from Freud's forty-fifth year up to his sixty-fourth. As the years pass, Freud is more and more preoccupied by the thought of death, and he speaks often of diminished energies. Yet by the end of the volume he still has not reached the point in his life when he will make the radical revisions of his theory which are represented by *The Problem of Anxiety*. That brilliant and crucial work is not to appear until 1926, when Freud is seventy.

The same energy which was to drive Freud to revise an important part of his theory is manifest in all his human relationships. It appears most notably in that one relationship which many men of

---

[1] This title is taken from the subtitle of the volume under review. (D.T.)

advancing years find it difficult or impossible to maintain—his relationship to himself. When Sandor Ferenczi insisted on the similarity he saw between Freud and Goethe, Freud first jokingly and then rather sharply repudiated the comparison. But it is accurate in at least this one respect, that Freud, like Goethe, had the power to maintain his direct, healthy, creative pleasure in himself.

The interest of Freud's mature life derives primarily from his gifts of mind and temperament. But it is of course much heightened by the great cultural drama in which he was involved. Freud had conceived a new idea and created a new science, which had to make their way against bitter opposition. What was perhaps harder, they had to survive the impulse of some early adherents to modify and sophisticate their full force. Freud avoided polemics, but he had necessarily to be at the center of the intellectual storm he had loosed. Whatever help he might eventually receive, it had to be *his* faith, *his* pertinacity and *his* judgment that were decisive for the future of psychoanalysis.

He had to live a life of congresses, committees, journals, yearbooks, debates and dissensions, submitting to all the dismaying machinery which a great idea inevitably generates. At the same time, his first duty was to the development of the great idea itself. The indication of how fully he discharged this primary duty is contained in the seven chapters which Dr. Jones devotes to the voluminous publications of this period.

As late as 1902, Freud was still working in virtual solitude. But in that year he was able to invite four physicians—Max Kahane, Rudolf Reitler, Alfred Adler and Wilhelm Stekel—to meet with him in a discussion group which later took the engaging name of the Psychological Wednesday Society. From this point on there was a steady spread of interest in psychoanalysis, slow at first but increasing in tempo. In 1904 the famous Eugen Bleuler of Zurich wrote to tell Freud that he and his staff had been using the methods of psychoanalysis; Bleuler's interest had been aroused by his assistant, C. G. Jung. James J. Putnam of Harvard, an attractive personality for whom Freud had a special wondering affection as the most puritanical of his supporters, began to write about psycho-analysis in 1906. In 1909 Freud was invited by Stanley Hall to lecture at Clark University, and he made his famous trip to America, which Dr. Jones is in a position to describe in amusing detail, for he, with Jung, accompanied Freud. In 1910 the International Psycho-Analytical Association was founded in sufficient strength to survive World War I.

In the same degree that Freud's ideas made their way, they were, of course, met with hostility. Even now, when they are established as part of the paraphernalia of the modern mind, they are often viewed with an uneasy, habitual irony. When they were first advanced, they were resisted with the ferocity of panic, of which Dr. Jones gives us what is probably the first detailed account. It is easy enough to express our pious, shocked surprise at the violence of the early antagonism, but to do so is in effect to deny the novelty and force of Freud's theories. It was not merely their sexual content that made them a scandal—they constituted nothing less than a new mode of thought.

The hostility to psychoanalysis was neither unexpected by Freud nor essentially disturbing to him. His heroic sense of life almost required opposition. What did trouble and depress him was the defection of his early adherents. He had been willing enough to voyage on strange seas of thought alone. But when at last he found company, he was grieved and angry when he lost it.

It is a commonplace of the adverse criticism of Freud to represent him as fiercely intolerant of any opinion that did not conform to the "orthodoxy" he had established. It must be said that nothing of this is confirmed by Freud's letters on the subject of dissensions and differences. The differences, we must keep it in mind, were not small ones—the theories of Adler and Jung are not modifications but denials of the theories of Freud. Yet Freud seems always to have tried to keep the differences from developing into actual schism. With Jung he temporized even beyond the point of prudence, although in part for prudential reasons. In his personal or intellectual criticism of the schismatics he is outspoken but never vindictive. He remarks of Adler that his errors are of an "honor-able" kind and he notes the "consistency and significance" of Adler's views.

The necessity of dealing with the personalities of the early days of psychoanalysis makes for Dr. Jones a task of considerable deli-cacy which, it seems to me, he discharges with great credit to himself. If Dr. Jones is to tell the truth about the characters and motives of the early schismatics as he sees it, he inevitably stands in danger of having it said that he has confused personal with in-tellectual issues. I do not think he has committed this fault.

The adherents of one or another of the schismatic psychoanalysts will no doubt wish to dispute Dr. Jones's interpretations, and their denials must be heeded. But Dr. Jones must report what he has observed and say what he believes. It can scarcely be a satisfaction to him to set down the failings or tragedies of so many of the leg-endary figures of the science to which he has devoted a lifetime. He does not speak lightly of the psychopathy of the gifted Otto Cross, or the brilliant and beloved Ferenczi, whom Freud called his "son" and who was Dr. Jones's own analyst, or of the moral deficiencies of Stekel or Otto Rank, or, in a different category, of the intellectual slowness of Max Eitingon or the "apathy" into which Hanns Sachs often fell. Indeed, of the famous "Committee," formed to serve as the "Old Guard" of Freudian theory, it is only the redoubtable Karl Abraham who wins Ernest Jones's full admiration equally as a man and as a mind.

It is not as edifying a history as we might wish, this early history of the analytical profession. But we temper our disappointment by remembering Freud's repeated caution against expecting too much either of psychoanalysis or of its practitioners. And for edification we return to Freud himself, one of the few great Plutarchian char-acters of our time.

Social Actualities[1]

[Introduction to *Selected Short Stories of John O'Hara*, Modern Library edition, 1956]

THE thing that we all know about John O'Hara's fiction—whatever else we may know—is that it is pre-eminent for its social verisimilitude. The work of no other American writer tells us so precisely, and with such a sense of the importance of the communication, how people look and how they want to look, where they buy their clothes and where they wish they could buy their clothes, how they speak and how they think they ought to speak. It is thus that they protect themselves with irony; it is thus that they try to wound with sarcasm; thus they mispronounce the weighty word they have somewhere read, thus they retrieve or obscure the error when once they have become aware of it. This is how they talk to the waiter.

But of course it isn't "they" who talk to the waiter. It is a particular person from a particular state and a certain town in that state, who was brought up in a certain part of the town which had well-defined feelings about all the other parts of town; he went to a certain college which favored certain manners, tones, affectations, and virtues. It is all this, and ever so much more, that makes a particular man speak to a waiter in the way he does, and O'Hara is aware of every one of the determining circumstances.

In the man's mode of address to the waiter there is, to be sure, something that is generally or "typically" American. But O'Hara's

---

[1] Title supplied by the editor of this volume.

peculiar gift is his brilliant awareness of the differences within the national sameness. It is commonly said that American life is being smoothed out to a kind of factory uniformity, that easy and rapid communication and an omnipresent popular culture have erased our particularities of difference. Perhaps this process actually is in train, but it is not so far advanced as people like to say it is, and O'Hara directs his exacerbated social awareness upon what differences among us do still remain.

The passionate commitment to verisimilitude which is so salient a characteristic of O'Hara's work is a very important trait in a writer. It is a good deal more important than we sometimes remember. "In this book a number of dialects are used, to wit: the Missouri Negro dialect; the extremest form of the backwoods Southwestern dialect; the ordinary 'Pike County' dialect; and four modified varieties of this last. The shadings have not been done in a hap-hazard fashion, or by guesswork; but painstakingly, and with the trustworthy guidance and support of personal familiarity with the several forms of speech." Mark Twain's anxious pedantic pride in the accuracy of the dialects of *Huckleberry Finn*—what part can it possibly have played in creating the wonderfulness of the book? What can it possibly have to do with the *truth* of the book? The relation between accuracy of detail and the truth and beauty of any book would be difficult, and perhaps impossible, to demonstrate. Yet we know with all our feelings that the writer who deals with facts must be in a conscientious relation to them; he must know that things are *so* and not some other way; he must feel the necessity of showing them to be as they really are.

This commitment to fact—to mere fact, as we sometimes say—is not of equal importance for all writers. But for some writers it is of the very essence of their art, however far beyond the literal fact their art may reach. This may be said of writers of quite diverse kinds. Without his devotion to the literal fact, Kipling would be nothing; the same is true of Hemingway. It is no less true of Flaubert. Melville could not have ventured the sublimities of *Moby Dick* had he not based them on the hard facts of the whaling business; whatever the heights of meaning to which Proust and Joyce may soar, they take off from a preoccupation with literal reality.

I speak of the specifically literary importance of detail and verisimilitude because I detect a tendency of our critical theory to belittle it; and also because I detect a tendency in some of the judgments that have been made of O'Hara to suggest that his devotion to the detail of social life is gratuitous and excessive. I think that there are occasions when it can indeed be said of O'Hara that he is excessive in the accumulation of the minutiae of social observation. His novel *A Rage to Live* is an example of this. In this work (which certainly has much to recommend it to our interest) the passion for accuracy is out of control, and we feel that we miss the people for their gestures and intonations, and the enumeration of the elaborate gear of their lives, and the record of their snobberies, taboos, and rituals. But if O'Hara's use of detail can sometimes be excessive, it is never gratuitous. It is always at the service of O'Hara's sense of the startling anomaly of man's life in society, his consciousness of social life as an absurd and inescapable fate, as the degrading condition to which the human spirit submits if it is to exist at all.

O'Hara has no lack of responsiveness to the elemental in human nature. Quite the contrary indeed—there are few contemporary writers who undertake to tell us so much about the primal facts of existence. But his characteristic way of representing the elemental is through its modification by social circumstance. What, we might ask, have death and snobbery to do with each other? In "Summer's Day," one of O'Hara's most striking stories, they are brought together in a very brilliant way. The elemental datum of the story is bereavement: an aging man has lost his only child, a daughter; she has committed suicide. But the story proceeds on a series of small observations which include the protocol of an exclusive beach club and the question of who is sitting on whose bench; the social position of Catholics; the importance of election to a Yale senior society; the kind of epicene gossip that well-brought-up adolescents might take pleasure in. And the elemental fact which we confront when the story comes to its end is a good deal more elemental than what we blandly call bereavement, it yields an emotion much more terrible than grief—the father's knowledge that he has reached the end of manhood and that the nothingness of life has overtaken him.

I have alluded to the objection that is sometimes made to O'Hara's degree of preoccupation with the social distinctions among people and with the details of behavior and taste that spring from and indicate these differences. The principle behind the objection is, I suppose, that these differences do not really matter, or at any rate that they ought not to matter. And perhaps especially that they ought not to matter at a time when all decent people are concerned to wipe out distinctions that lead to privilege, or to lack of privilege, or to conflict. The implication is that the awareness of the differences, and the belief that they have an effect on personality and behavior, constitute an enforcement of their existence; if we didn't think they were significant, they wouldn't exist and make trouble. It is not hard to have sympathy with this attitude, and certainly it proposes the right rule for personal conduct and for political conduct. But the good writer has a more complicated time of it than the good man and the good citizen. He has to serve not only the ideal but also the reality. He will be happy to say—and no one is happier to say it than O'Hara—that a man's a man for a' that, and a' that. But then he will have to go on to say that a Catholic's a Catholic, and a Jew's a Jew, and a Protestant's a Protestant, for a' that, and a' that. Not to mention an Irish Catholic, an Italian Catholic, a German Catholic; not to mention a Lithuanian Jew and a German Jew; and an Episcopalian and a Methodist, and a New York Episcopalian and a Boston Episcopalian, and a Northern and a Southern Methodist. And none of these people, if they tell the truth, will say anything else than that being of one group or another has made some difference to them down to the very roots of their being. The difference is not equivalent to their total humanity, but it is never trivial. It cannot be trivial, for its determinants are not trivial—religion is not trivial, national or ethnic tradition is not trivial, class is not trivial, the family is not trivial.

The differences among us have mixed moral results, good ones as well as bad ones. At the moment we are rather more conscious of the bad results than of the good. We ought not be concerned with our particularity, we ought not be proud of it, we ought not be resentful when it does not gets its due share of consideration, we ought not "over-compensate," we ought not be self-protective, we ought not worry about prestige, we ought not think in competitive terms, we ought not fret about status. We ought not, but alas we do. This is the social fact and O'Hara is faithful to it.

When once we have conceived the idea of a general essential humanity, nothing can seem more irrational than the distinctions which people make among themselves. They are absurd, and the society which makes up the sum of the distinctions, and has the duty of controlling them and of adjusting them to each other, shares their absurdity. Like most writers who effectively represent society in the full detail of its irrational existence, O'Hara is half in love with the absurdity. The other half of his feeling is fear. I suppose there are no two writers who at first glance must seem more unlike and less likely to sustain comparison than O'Hara and Kafka. Yet there is a recurrent imagination in O'Hara that brings him very close to the author of *The Trial*. It is the imagination of society as some strange sentient organism which acts by laws of its own being which are not to be understood; one does not know what will set into motion its dull implacable hostility, some small thing, not very wrong, not wrong at all; once it begins to move, no one can stand against it. It is this terrible imagination of society which is the theme of O'Hara's first novel, the remarkable *Appointment in Samarra;* it recurs frequently in the short stories, in, for example, "Where's the Game?," "Do You Like It Here?," "Other Women's Households," "A Respectable Place." This element of almost metaphysical fear in O'Hara's view of society is indeed impressive, and it is important to take account of it in any general view of his achievement. But it must not be thought to be more of a warrant of his seriousness than is his love of the absurdity of society for its own sake, his wonder at the variety which human pretensions can take, and his delight in its comicality.

The Person of the Artist

[A review of *Letters of James Joyce*, edited by
Stuart Gilbert. *Encounter*, August 1957]

IT IS one of our strict modern feelings about literature that the
mind which makes the work of art ought to be defined only by
the work of art itself—that there is something illicit and low,
or at least un-literary, about inquiring into the personality of the
man whose name is signed to the work. This is quite wrong. No
curiosity is more legitimate than that which directs itself upon the
connection between the "impersonal" creative mind and the "actual"
and "human" person. No question is more justified, or more beautiful, than that which asks how the ordinary human being transcends
himself in art. Between Bergotte read by the young Marcel at
Combray and Bergotte met at luncheon at the Swanns' there
is a shocking difference which we do right to contemplate. And
we should fail in humanity if we didn't wonder how it came
about that the despicable Monsieur Biche of Madame Verdurin's
parties developed into the splendid Elstir.

Among the great modern literary personalities there is none
whom it has seemed harder to connect with his work than James
Joyce. It was Joyce, of course, who gave us one of the classic formulations of the idea of the artist's impersonality. Stephen Dedalus,
in his famous discourse on aesthetics in *A Portrait of the Artist as
a Young Man,* says that "the personality of the artist, at first a cry or
a cadence or a mood and then a fluent and lambent narrative, finally
refines itself out of existence, impersonalises itself, so to speak." But

it is worth noting that the impersonality is covertly transferred from the artist to the person-who-is-the-artist, for three sentences later Stephen says that "the artist, like the God of creation, remains within or behind or beyond or above his handiwork, invisible, refined out of existence, indifferent, paring his finger nails." The impersonality of the artist is described in quite personal terms—it becomes a personal trait, or a social attitude; it is at once translated, as it were, into "indifference," which the young Joyce expresses by the arrogantly rude gesture of paring the fingernails. And there can be no doubt that Joyce thought of impersonality as a personal trait of his own, and one by which he set great store. Stephen Dedalus cannot be said to *be* Joyce, and much less can the Richard Rowan of *Exiles;* the Joyce critics often remind us of this and they are right. But these two characters do indeed *stand for* Joyce, and they make it plain that "impersonality," expressed by aloofness, irony, and condescension, was an attribute which he cherished. Stephen and Richard have the manner of speaking not in their own persons but as if they were ambassadors representing their sovereign selves at the court of some unpolished nation.

And apparently this was pretty close to the personal manner which Joyce actually used, or aspired to use. The point is but a small one, yet it does stick in the mind that when Stuart Gilbert was writing his commentary on *Ulysses,* Joyce asked him to refer to him as often as he could as Mr. Joyce. It was not impossible for Joyce to "unbend," it was by no means hard for him, especially as he grew older, to be courteous, often in a very sweet way, but most accounts of him lead us to suppose that he never involved his personality easily and naturally and pleasurably with anyone else's. In the preface to his edition of Joyce's letters, Stuart Gilbert speaks of the authoritativeness of Herbert Gorman's biography, and this authoritativeness we cannot doubt, if only because Gorman wrote with Joyce's consent and help. But Gorman is not able to get very far along with the job of literary biographer—he can suggest very little of the connection between the person and the artist. His habit of referring to Joyce in such phrases as "the Irish writer," "the exiled writer," "the Dubliner"—in contexts where this depersonalization has no special rhetorical intention—suggests that he had great difficulty in thinking of Joyce as really a person. He can make plain the fierce integrity, the heroic dedication and pertinacity, the unremitting single-mindedness. And it is indeed not hard to understand how the man whose temperament is marked by these qualities should be the author of *A Portrait* and *Exiles* and even *Dubliners*. But the more we perceive Joyce's rigorousness, his cultivation of the virtues of defense and attack, the harder it is to see how he could have been the author of one of the most delightful and charming books of the age.

It is time, I think, to use these two suspect words about *Ulysses*. It is time to forget the hard elaborateness of the many devices by which the book proceeds and by which the impersonality of the author is protected, and the solemnity of the ambience in which it has long existed, and to keep chiefly in mind its brilliance, its humor, its warmth, its pathos, its rich sentimentality, its eroticism, its beautiful simplicity of right feeling. Disengage it from our recollection of the battles that were fought over it, from its high status as a cultural symbol, from all the critical ingenuities it asked for and received, and take it with some of the simplicity it deserves. It will then be seen to be one of the kindest books in the world, one of the most loving and most forgiving, and therefore one of the saddest.

So there is the mystery: that *Ulysses* is what it is and that it was James Joyce who wrote it. From Gorman's biography, as I say, we gain no clue, no sense of how the man is related to the artist. But Joyce's letters of forty years do make the connection for us, and in a rather dramatic way.

They are not great letters. They don't support a view I expressed some years ago when I said that "among the letters of great men those of the great creative artists are likely to be the most intimate, the liveliest, and the fullest of wisdom." I said this under the influence of my enthusiasm for Keat's letters, and it is surely an extravagant generalization. It doesn't hold, for example, for Yeats's letters. And it doesn't hold for Joyce's. They are not remarkable in themselves, or not often. Yet taken in their continuity, they make a biographical document of the highest interest.

They begin with a great flourish, with the famous letter to Ibsen. Joyce is nineteen; the occasion of the letter is Ibsen's seventy-third birthday. There had previously been a kind of communication between the old and the young man—Joyce had published in *The Fortnightly Review* an essay on *When We Dead Awaken* and Ibsen had told William Archer of his pleasure in it; Archer sent word of this to Joyce, who took license from the message to address his great hero and master. It is really a superb letter—it is meant to be just that, in the literal sense of the word: it was the young man's announcement that he was claiming his birthright, that he was taking his place in the tradition. He speaks of his defiant advocacy of Ibsen's work at his college, and we do not fail to note that what he says he had put forward as Ibsen's "highest excellence" is his "lofty, impersonal power." He is nothing if not pugnacious: "It may annoy you," he says, "to have your works at the mercy of striplings but I am sure you would prefer hot-headedness to nerveless and 'cultured' paradoxes"—it is surely Shaw whom he is challenging. He is quick to protect himself from condescension: "Do not think me a hero-worshipper," he says, "—I am not so. And when I spoke of you in debating societies and so forth, I enforced attention by no futile rantings." He concludes with conscious magnificence:

But we always keep the dearest things to ourselves. I did not tell them what bound me closest to you. I did not say how what I could discern dimly of your life was my pride to see, how your battles inspired me— not the obvious material battles but those that were fought and won behind your forehead, how your wilful resolution to wrest the secret from life gave me heart and how in your absolute indifference to public canons of art, friends, and shibboleths you walked in the light of your inward heroism. And this is what I write to you of now. Your work on earth draws to a close and you are near the silence. It is growing dark for you. Many write of such things, but they do not know. You have only opened the way—though you have gone as far as you could upon it—to the end of "John Gabriel Borkman" and its spiritual truth—your last play stands, I take it, apart. But I am sure that higher and holier enlightenment lies—onward.

As one of the younger generation for whom you have spoken, I give you greeting—not humbly, because I am obscure and you in the glare, not sadly because you are an old man and I am a young man, not presumptuously or sentimentally—but joyfully, with hope and with love, I give you greeting.

It is very moving, this hail-and-farewell from the young hero to the old hero. It has the right generosity and the right touch of the heroic and tragic cruelty. It has the legendary note that was strangely possible in many artists' conceptions of themselves in the first years of the twentieth century. We listen to it now, when we hear it in the distance of the past, with the curiosity of epigoni; and there are those who hear it with the relieved awareness that this grandiose idea of the life in literature is now done with and forever impossible.

But after the first letter the Siegfried call is not to be sounded again. The dedication to art once made, and ritually and grandiosely, the high promises can be fulfilled only by slogging hard work, by dirty details. Joyce was not alone, he demanded help and he got it in one measure or another. Pound and Yeats, Edward Marsh, and H. G. Wells were among the many who undertook to relieve his difficulties or to advance his reputation. By 1917 Harriet Shaw Weaver had begun her generous and tactful financial help. But all the way it was hard going and it needed more than courage —it needed obsession and pertinacity, and shrewdness and even shamelessness. No small peasant proprietor, no shopkeeper could have been more willing than Joyce to scheme and calculate and haggle and do the mean chores. (The famous "secrecy, silence, and cunning" are, we must know, the personal weapons not only of artists and revolutionaries, but also of diplomats, operators, peasants, and shopkeepers.) After reading the letters, it is impossible not to see how deeply involved in class feelings Joyce was—Wyndham Lewis' old accusation that Joyce was forever worried about his gentility or gentlemanliness is perfectly true—and he thought of his genius not only as a sacred spiritual trust but as a property, as an investment that had to be made to pay.

I suppose that it can be said that the record of the long bitter enterprise does not show Joyce in an attractive light. He had to fight for his rights with publishers, in long letters stiff with detailed argument and the sense of aggrievement. The story of the battle for the publication of *Dubliners* is well known; it lasted over nine years and Joyce waged it alone. And this, of course, is but the best known of the occasions given Joyce for angry pertinacity. We can say of Joyce, as Johnson said of Dryden, that "he knew how to complain"; and complaint is, I suppose, not ingratiating. (But he never really complains about the torture of his eyes.) When at last his reputation began to grow, he hovered over it like a hen with one chick—no mention of his name is too unimportant for him to take note of, no word of praise is too small for him to take pleasure in; he can never have enough clippings of reviews, for he likes to send them to correspondents.

And through it all he seems to have attached himself to no one (outside his family) in a personal way: in the early years there is no one to whom he writes in the light and teasing way of friendship, let alone of intimate serious communication. There seems to be no evidence that at this time he had a close friend, and it is hard to see, if we can draw conclusions from his tone, on what terms he would have maintained friendship. The belief which so decisively marks Stephen Dedalus' character, that he is being conspired against and betrayed, is an important part of his creator's character. And even when, as time passed, he did come to write in the way of friendship, his manner is uncertain. Mr. Gilbert, speaking of the letters in their relation to the literary style of *Ulysses,* remarks on "the writer's skill in adjusting their tone, not merely their content, to the personality of his correspondents . . . many of Joyce's letters are the masterpieces of epistolary psychology. . . ." Rather too much adjustment, I should say, rather too much psychology. At other times adjustment and psychology quite fail. When he writes to Frank Budgen or Robert MacAlmon with the intention of easy camaraderie, the manner just about comes off, but we can see it being brought off, with undue effort. A letter of condolence to the widow of a boyhood friend is truly kind but hopelessly awkward and embarrassed. What Mr. Gilbert calls "the informative, whimsical, slightly deferent letters to Miss Weaver" make us think that that lady would more than once need all the generosity of spirit she so clearly had, not to feel a little snubbed and condescended to.

Yet it is in a letter to Miss Weaver that there occurs what may be thought of as the beginning of a revision in Joyce's conception of himself, a rather striking expression of ruefulness and self-doubt. The letter was written in 1921, when Joyce was thirty-nine years old, and in it he takes note of the legends about his character that had grown up during his long years of struggle. He lists the extravagant and malicious stories in some detail. "I mention these views," he says, "not to speak about myself but to show you how conflicting they all are. The truth probably is that I am a quite commonplace person undeserving of so much imaginative painting. . . . There is a further opinion that I am a crafty, simulating, and dissimulating Ulysses-like type, a 'jejeune priest,' selfish and cynical. There is some truth in all this, I suppose: but it is by no means all of me (nor was it all of Ulysses) and it has been my habit to apply this alleged quality to safeguard my poor creations."

It is as if he had come to view with some misgivings the "secrecy, silence, and cunning" which his Stephen Hero had invoked. And when once the long enterprise has reached its culmination, when once *Ulysses* has neared the end of its progress, and was known by at least a few to be a great work, the secrecy, silence, and cunning seemed to be no longer necessary and Joyce seems almost consciously to be trying to escape from their habit. The letters from this point on become very much more relaxed, as if by an avowed desire for relaxation, intimacy, and friendliness. In this Joyce does not always succeed—for example, the note in which he thanks Constantine Curran for what would seem to be a magnificent present, an eighteenth-century painted woodcarving of the arms of the City of Dublin, is almost cold in its gratitude. But in general the personal letters become warm, frequently playful, and, in a degree, self-revealing. I shrink from saying it, it is so much what every newspaper interviewer always seeks to discover and to reassure himself by, but the fact is as it is—that the Joyce of these letters was the simplest of men, the most (save the mark!) "human," the most conventional. It was not easy for him to form associations in the world, but the strength of his family associations was enormous and touchingly open. This, I suppose, has long been known of Joyce, but it presents itself to us in the letters with a new force. He never mentions his wife save in a way that suggests his admiration and affection, and the only thing that can make him angry at his daughter is some untoward behavior to her mother. All references to his son are warm and proud, and when his son marries and has a son of his own, Joyce envelops the whole family in his affection and in his joy over their familial existence—there is no difficulty at all in connecting the person with the artist of *Finnegans Wake,* that hymn to all recurrences, especially those of the family. His daughter Lucia was stricken by extreme mental illness; it cannot be said that Joyce showed great wisdom in his handling of her case, but his tortured concern for her never abates, and nothing could be more touching than the way he continues to affirm his pride in her and to speak of her talents, and the way he tries in secret to support her fatal pride by gaining for her the public recognition she wanted, for this poor girl's trouble was that she could not possibly compete with her father for the distinction she craved. His aunt Mrs. Murray is a person of the greatest importance to Joyce—all his letters to her are full of interest, especially those in which he writes to her about *Ulysses,* instructing her in the monetary value of the copy he has sent her, adjuring her not to lend it, the book-borrowing habits of Dubliners being what they are, conjuring her to read the *Odyssey* before she begins his book, and if not the whole *Odyssey* then at least Lamb's Tales, and he frets and fusses because she doesn't do what she should.

The death of his father devastates him. It must come as a surprise, and a pleasant one, to anyone who remembers the rough handling

Simon Dedalus is given in *A Portrait* and *Ulysses* that Joyce at fifty should be able to write—to T. S. Eliot—of being "very broken down" by the loss of his father. "I . . . was always in correspondence with him," he says. It is interesting to see how the need for loyalty asserts itself even at this moment. It is not only that "[my father] had an intense love for me" but that "I feel that a poor heart which was true and faithful to me is no more." In a letter to Miss Weaver he writes:

My father had an extraordinary affection for me. He was the silliest man I ever knew and yet cruelly shrewd. He thought and talked of me up to his last breath. I was very fond of him always, being a sinner myself, and even liked his faults. Hundreds of pages and scores of characters in my books came from him. His dry (or rather wet) wit and his expression of face convulsed me often with laughter. When he got the copy I sent him of *Tales Told,* etc. (so they write me), he looked a long time at Brancusi's Portrait of J. J. [this was a quite non-representational design on the cover of the *Shem and Shaun* volume] and finally remarked: Jim has changed more than I thought. I got from him his portraits, a waistcoat, a good tenor voice, and an extravagant licentious disposition (out of which, however, the greater part of any talent I may have springs) but, apart from these, something else I cannot define. But if an observer thought of my father and myself and my son too physically, though we are all very different, he could perhaps define it. It is a great consolation to me to have such a good son. His grandfather was very fond of him and kept his photograph beside mine on the mantelpiece.

I leave it to better scholars than myself to say whether Joyce's antagonism to psychoanalysis kept him from observing that his name and Freud's mean the same. And although it may at first seem an odd comparison, the two men were in many respects very like each other. They share the avowedly heroic intention and the ability to wait long for achievement and fame. They share a fierce, isolate pride, and the need for loyalty. They are at one in point of family feeling, especially in the disillusioned attachment to the father. And they share the paradox of being revolutionary in their work and rigorously conventional in their lives, a corollary, no doubt, of their family feeling. Joyce's propriety was really monu-

mental—nothing could be more amusing than his reiterated grievance that the wreath he had ordered sent to George Moore's funeral
was not mentioned in the papers, and nothing could be more touching than his saying of Moore, ". . . I hope I behaved toward him
during the three or four visits I paid him with the respect due to
his age, personality, and achievements." Neither Joyce nor Freud
liked the modern in art—Joyce seems to have been quite indifferent
to what was being done around him. He apparently knew a large
part of *The Waste Land* by heart, but I have the impression that
this is the only modern work he honors even by implication. He
had no admiration for D. H. Lawrence, and he mentions Proust
only to object—not unpleasantly—to Proust's fame as a competitor
of his own. He speaks of Picasso only to say how much better than
his Picasso's situation is. He is rather put out by a design of Brancusi's used as a decoration for the cover of *Tales Told of Shem and
Shaun*. He speaks of Brancusi as being "something of a fogey like
myself"—"But I wish he or Antheil, say, could or would be as
explicit as I try to be when people ask me: And what's this here,
Guvnor?" His tastes all go backward. Stephen Dedalus' judgment
of Byron as the greatest English poet may well have been affirmed
to the very end by his creator; the older man does not revise the
judgment of the younger that Newman is the greatest writer of
English prose. He is delighted when he learns that the universities
are taking him seriously. He asks that a copy of *Ulysses* be sent to
Professor George Saintsbury—"I am old-fashioned enough to admire him though he may not return the compliment." He speaks
with high pleasure of having received from the poet-laureate Robert
Bridges a signed copy of *The Testament of Beauty* "with an in-
scription expressing his full sympathy with what I am doing." He
expresses his astonishment at this, yet after all it seems to him but
an example of something he has noted of himself: "The rapprochement between myself and very old men is very curious." Very
curious—and not so very hard to understand.

Last Years of a Titan[1]

[A review of *The Life and Work of Sigmund Freud*, Volume III, by Ernest Jones. *The New York Times Book Review*, October 18, 1957]

ERNEST JONES has now given us the third and final volume of his life of Sigmund Freud. *The Last Phase* covers the two decades after 1919, from Freud's sixty-fourth year to his death in London at the age of eighty-three, and goes on to an extensive summary account of Freud's achievement and influence. It is a work which does not abate the fullness of detail and the robust vivacity of the two earlier volumes. As much as any man of our time, and more than most, Freud deserves and can sustain a biography of the monumental kind. Dr. Jones has worked on the large scale that is appropriate to his intellectual master, and there can be no question but that the completed book is what the two earlier volumes promised it would be—one of the important documents in the cultural history of our time.

Two years ago, writing in these pages about Dr. Jones's second volume, *Years of Maturity,* I said of Freud that he was one of the rare fortunate men whose mature years are as charged with heroic energy as their formative years, whose middle age is as interesting to us as their youth. The judgment can now be carried further.

[1] Title given to this review when it was reprinted in *The Griffin*, December 1957. (D.T.)

Freud in old age, even in extreme old age, engages our interest as fully as at any time in his life.

It is an interest that is charged with suspense. Reading Dr. Jones's first volume, we asked, "This infant, this boy, this young man, this pampered pet of his family—will he really turn out be Sigmund Freud?" Reading this last volume we ask, and no less eagerly, no less curiously, "This aging man, this old man, this dying man—will he remain Sigmund Freud?"

He did. And the record of his endurance, not in mere life but in his own quality of life, makes one of the most moving personal histories I know.

From the point of view of Freud's career, the years following 1919 were a time of triumph. The attacks on psychoanalysis certainly did not cease, but they became of far less consequence in comparison with the growing acceptance of Freud's theories. By 1920 it was possible for the Austrian Government to invite Freud to serve on a commission to investigate the therapeutic methods used in the army mental hospitals. No one now doubted that he was a force to be reckoned with. His seventieth birthday was publicly celebrated in Vienna, and other honors followed. His prestige among intellectuals may have been ambiguous, but it was none the less awesome.

Yet these were not years of peace for Freud, rather of suffering and darkness. Despite the high demand he made upon life, despite the powers of enjoyment he did undoubtedly possess, he had long regarded the human condition with a wry irony. Now, by the events of his life, the cruel and irrational nature of human existence was borne in upon him with a new and terrible force.

The defections of Otto Rank and Sandor Ferenczi are typical of Freud's experience at this time. Freud had never taken defection lightly, and Jung's break in particular had hurt him in a personal way. Yet the earlier schisms, painful as they may have been, were occurrences normal to a communal intellectual enterprise, the natural result of differences of temperament, culture and intellectual disposition. The defections of Rank and Ferenczi made an event of a different kind. They were involved with mental pathology and issued in sordid tragedy. Both men had been very close to Freud for many years, especially Ferenczi, whom Freud spoke of as his "son." It was not only that these two valued coadjutors undertook to revise psychoanalytic theory in simplistic and extravagant ways—both men fell prey to extreme mental illness and they died insane.

The shadow of death is heavy over the early years of the last phase. Anton von Freund, who had undertaken to advance the cause of psychoanalysis by means of his considerable fortune and to whom Freud was greatly attached, died in 1920 after long and terrible suffering from cancer. A few days later Freud received the news of the death, at twenty-six, of his beautiful daughter Sophie, his "Sunday child." In 1923 Sophie's son Heinz died at the age of four. Freud had a special love for this little grandson—he said that Heinz stood to him for all children and grandchildren—and his death was a terrible blow.

He experienced each death as the loss of a part of himself. He said that Anton von Freund's death was an important factor in his aging. Of Sophie's death he said that it was a "deep narcissistic hurt that is not to be healed." He believed that the death of little Heinz marked the end of his affectional life.

In 1923 he learned that he had cancer of the jaw. Thirty-three operations were to be performed, all sufficiently harrowing, and for sixteen years he was to live in pain, often of an extreme kind. The prosthesis he had to wear was awkward and painful, distorting his face and speech, and he was, as we know, a man of some vanity. ("My prosthesis doesn't speak French," he said in touching apology on the occasion of a visit to Yvette Guilbert.)

He had, of course, no religious faith to help him confront the gratuitousness of suffering. Nor did he have any tincture of "philosophy." He is as stubborn as Job in refusing to take comfort from words—even more stubborn, for he will not permit himself the gratification of *accusing*. The fact is as it is. Human life is a grim, irrational, humiliating business—nothing softens this judgment. He makes it as simply as any ancient Greek, as the *Iliad* itself.

Yet nothing breaks him and nothing diminishes him. He often says that he is diminished, but he is not. He frequently speaks of his indifference. But the work goes on. At seventy he publishes *The Problem of Anxiety,* which constitutes a radical revision of his theory; *Civilization and Its Discontents* appears when he is seventy-three. At his death he is still working on his "Outline of Psychoanalysis." He continues with his clinical work up to a month before his death. And nothing abates the energy and precision of his personal relationships.

He may indeed have been, as he said, indifferent to his own life, to whether he lived or died. But so long as he lived, he was never indifferent to himself. And this, surely, is the secret of his moral being. He had the passionate egoism, the intense pride that we call Titanic. *"Mit welchem Recht?"* ("By what right?"), he cried, his eyes blazing, when Dr. Jones told him in London that at the time the diagnosis had first been made, there had been some thought of concealing from him the truth about his cancer. He is very old, the episode is now long in the past, yet he springs to instant anger at the mere thought that his autonomy might be limited.

His very love seems to spring from pride. He says as much when he speaks of the "deep narcissistic hurt" the death of his daughter inflicted on him. Perhaps he implies a criticism of this trait when he goes on to say, "My wife and Annerl are hurt in a more human way." Yet if his way of love was less "human" than other ways, it was remarkably quick and strong. His own egoism led him to recognize and respect the egoism of others. What else induced him, a fatigued and overburdened man, to believe that he ought to answer all letters from unknown correspondents, to write, for example, at such length and so movingly—and in English—to an unknown woman in America who had addressed him in grief over her son's homosexuality?

He could be very bitter in his pride. He refused to accept a visit from the famous French psychologist Janet, believing that Janet had wronged him, and he insisted that Janet be told the reason for the refusal. But more often his pride led him in the opposite direction. He had once been bitter enough about the way he had been treated by Vienna, yet when it was time to escape to London after the Nazi coup, he resisted the idea of leaving, saying that he would feel like a soldier deserting.

It is often said of him that he was jealous of his authority and would bear no one near the throne. This was not the way his pride worked. In point of fact, he takes every possible occasion to tell his younger colleagues that he is not indispensable to psychoanalysis, that they must learn to walk their own ways without him.

It is said that he would brook no contradiction. Actually, when once he had given his personal trust, he was tolerant to the point of credulousness, as with Rank. He wrote to Ferenczi, "As for your endeavor to remain completely in agreement with me, I treasure it as an expression of your friendship, but find this aim neither necessary nor easily attainable." And at a time when Ferenczi was at such a theoretical distance from Freud that he himself believed that he ought not serve as president of the International Psychoanalytical Association, Freud insisted on his serving. His pride seems always to have been at one with principle.

The last book he read was *The Wild Ass's Skin,* Balzac's grim fantastic novel about the inevitable diminution of the vital powers. He said wryly, "This is just the book for me." Through all his years of pain he took no analgesic drug and only at the end did he consent to take aspirin. He said he preferred to think in torment to not being able to think clearly.

Communism and
Intellectual Freedom[1]

[Introduction to *The Broken Mirror: A Collection
of Writings from Contemporary Poland*. January
1958]

T HIS book must be thought of as an event. I do not say
this as a manner of speaking, as critics sometimes do when
they wish to suggest the intellectual or artistic importance of
a work. This book is an event in the grosser and more usual
sense in which we speak of an event in military or political history,
such as a battle or an uprising. It comes to us laden with the past
—it is the compendium and crux of many precedent events, most
of them grim, all of them grave. And it is charged with the future,
massive with what it may portend, and somber with undisclosed
fate. For this is an event that has yet to reach its conclusion; its
issue, which is of an ultimate importance, has not yet been decided.

The writers whose work is brought together in this volume are
all Poles. Most of them are young or youngish. All of them are, or
have been, Communists, or in active sympathy with the Communist
Party. But what constitutes the most significant element of their
homogeneity is that, in a Communist state, their relation to Communism being what it is, they fulfill the function which we have
come to think of as virtually definitive of the ideal conception of
the intellectual: they assert an intense critical preoccupation with
the relationship that should properly exist between society and

---

[1] Title supplied by the editor of this volume.

intellect. They conceive this right relation to be one in which the intellect is free, in which the Reason of State does not provide the excuse for the State to limit and control the activity of mind. The terms in which they express this idea are not in the least recondite, but, on the contrary, very simple and easy to recognize—they are the terms of the long tradition of humanism which holds that freedom of thought is a necessary condition for the acquiring of knowledge and for seeking truth, and also a good in itself.

At this point we must deal with the fact that these intellectuals—and I should add, these remarkably gifted intellectuals—were able for a time to express their ideas about society, and their hopes for it, through the ideology of Communism. By 1944, when Poland became a Communist state, there can have been no doubt about the nature of Communism as it had been established in Russia. No intelligent person could have been ignorant of the conditions of life in the Soviet Union; no intellectual could have been under any illusion about the conditions of the cultural life. What is more, the Russian behavior to Poland before and during and after the war gave clear and overwhelming evidence of the nature of the Communist morality. Nothing could have been more calculatedly ruthless than the Soviet intentions toward Poland. They involved not only a large territorial depredation but the eventual control of the whole nation through the establishment of a Communist regime. The latter enterprise was carried out by the systematic destruction of those elements—that is to say, of those people—whose political views were not likely to lead them to cooperate with the Communist government that was being contrived in Moscow. It was politics by decimation, and certain episodes of its practice perhaps still stick in the ever-shortening memory of modern man: the deportation of 1,500,000 Poles to Russia; the massacre of the 10,000 Polish officers in the Katyn forest; the refusal of Russian airfields to the Allied flyers who stood ready to help the people of Warsaw in their desperate uprising against the Germans and the immobility of the Russian army outside the city until a sufficient number of the insurgents should have been killed.

There were the facts, all clear to the view, beyond any possibility of being unknown. Yet even the traditional strong, overt feeling for their nation which still marks Polish intellectuals did not deter many of them from embracing Communism, the ideology of their nation's traditional enemy.

There were the facts, all clear to the view. But it is characteristic of a well-developed ideology that it can diminish or destroy the primitive potency of fact. This is especially true when an ideology embodies, as Communism does, the idea of "history," of process and progress—the fact of today, let alone of yesterday, becomes of no account before the adjustment and recompense that the future will bring. Sometimes, as we know, it is possible for the Communist ideology to make this effect even on the minds of people who live in an established and secure society. How much more readily will it make this effect on the minds of people whose nation has been overrun, whose economy has been destroyed, whose society has been shattered. One could not have a more moving account of what it means to exist under circumstances of this kind than Tadeusz Rozewicz's story in this volume, "The New Philosophical School." All that is left to people thus situated is the hope of restored community with their fellow men. That, and some idea of the future. More often than not the idea of the future is supplied to them by Communism—all over the world the intellectuals of disadvantaged countries can find no other idea of the future to be of equal power. Democracy, contrary to the fond expectations which Americans for a time entertained, is not for them an available idea. Even if they accept at face value and with the best will in the world the virtues we claim for democracy, when they think of democracy as a system of social organization, they conceive it to be ineluctably bound up, if not with capitalism, which almost inevitably they reject, then with an economic development far beyond any they can envisage for themselves in the near future. To such people the very rigors of Communism may well appear to lend the color of truth to the ideology. The system is validated by the hardship it entails. Desperate people do not easily imagine felicity—they will feel that what is appropriate to their hope is not security or comfort but some way of bringing to an end the humiliation of being passive under deprivation and suffering. They seek some consistent principle of action and they are the more reassured if the consistency is systematic and rigorous.

Eventually, however, the Polish intellectuals understood that Communism entailed not only the hardship they may well have envisaged but also a moral corruption which they had not permitted themselves to foresee. The writers whose work we read in this volume make their affirmations of freedom of mind in indignation and bitterness at the restraints that were put upon their minds, but also in disgust at what they were willing to believe, in revulsion from what they consented to say.

The intellectual life of Poland under Communism never matched the monolithic conformity of the intellectual life of Russia. The best known representation of Communist Poland is Czeslaw Milosz's *The Captive Mind;* this is a work to be admired on several scores, but more than one trustworthy observer has said that it goes beyond the facts in representing the Polish intellectuals as having wholly and happily capitulated to the Communist *mystique.* There was, of course, quite a considerable adherence to Communism on the basis of genuine conviction. But opportunism would seem to explain the adherence of some people, as no doubt prudence explains the consent of many more. The Catholic Church was indeed hard pressed by the government and quite effectually limited and controlled. But with the population almost entirely Catholic and inclined to be devout, the Church could not be liquidated and it served as a countervailing force. In its cultural life Poland had always been of the West; the regime undertook to orient the nation toward Russia and fostered hostility to Western, and especially to American, culture. It was a policy that met with no permanent success; the art and ideas of the West continued to engage the Poles and served to support a growing antagonism to Russia, which eventually found expression in politics, even in the Party itself.

In short, the Polish situation was of a kind in which it was possible for the intellectual life to survive. It had at least enough loose-ness to allow individual thinkers and writers to imagine that move-ment and change were not beyond hope, that there might be some point in asking questions about the State and about themselves. We may say that it was a situation that at least licensed the aware-ness of boredom and disgust, from which springs much of the energy of the intellectual and artistic life.

But the correction of Milosz's picture must not lead us to minimize the harshness which did actually prevail in the intellectual life of Poland. How very bad were the conditions of that life is abundantly attested to in the present volume. Pawel Hertz calls his reminiscences of the "sad years" between 1949 and 1953 "Recollections from the House of the Dead." The House of the Dead is his name for the offices of the Writers' Union. I have been told that there were no executions in punishment of cultural deviations—the Dead to whom Hertz refers are only spiritually deceased. But they were brought to their condition by coercion, even if that fell short of the threat of the penalty of actual death. Hertz leaves us in no doubt about this: "The atmosphere of gloom, evoked by drilling writers ceaselessly, admonishing them, using open threats, constantly identifying any non-conformity in thinking with hostility, qualifying opposition in cultural and theoretical matters by paragraphs of the criminal code—all this to the accompaniment of an increasing number of political trials and a mounting wave of arrests, silenced the literary group. The paradoxical situation arose in which ardent speakers at rallies would inveigh against their own interpretations of the ideas of their silent opponents." Inevitably, as Hertz goes on to say, "literature lost its moral and intellectual prestige and the writer lost the confidence of his own society."

In his striking play about the death of Socrates, "The Philosophers' Den," Zbigniew Herbert speaks of men who "have mastered the art of acquiescence." This is not a silent art. It is the art of speaking out loud and clear in the way one is expected to speak. And in order to speak as one is expected to, it is not enough to say the right things in the most orthodox way possible; one must make whatever one says a negation of that critical, dialectical, ironic (I use the words in the senses appropriate to Socrates) movement of mind which is the very essence of the intellectual life. To the truly acquiescent man all things must be as obvious, and as meaningless, as Socrates himself is to the Keeper of the jail.

. . . It's a simple matter really. Socrates was of proletarian origin. His father tried to make a living from his workshop, but he didn't get on too well. Competition, huge factories, big manufacturers—you understand. Socrates had to go out on the streets and earn his living by talking —so he became a philosopher because of economic conditions.

—Who made a martyr of him?

He did himself—or to be more exact, it was the result of his inability to understand the mechanism of history. As a proletarian, he ought to have become a people's tribune, an agitator. His platform was prepared for him: to fight, on the one hand against the reactionary upper bourgeoisie, and on the other, to seek for close contact with the progressive lower bourgeoisie. Simple, eh? But he preferred aristocracy and its precious disputes—about what is good and what is evil, about abstract justice from the moon. So he fell from the moon straight into jail. Thus one pays for betraying one's class. Bye, bye. Fight mosquitoes and idealism.

The indignation and bitterness and the boredom and disgust eventually found their expression. The present volume exemplifies the intensity of the affirmations of intellectual liberty that were made by the Polish intellectuals after the early months of 1956. And to a reader with any imagination of the way in which a cultural tendency accelerates, it will suggest how numerous such affirmations are. Few events of our time are so stirring as this large and dramatic repudiation of the Stalinist hegemony in culture. As it is exemplified in this volume, it is virtually unequivocal. There is but one instance of a writer finding it in his heart to say a word in apology for the old order. This occurs in Kazimierz Brandys' *nouvelle,* "The Defense of Granada," a work which is as accomplished as it is informative. The occasion is the last speech of Doctor Faul, the all-powerful Stalinist pundit who has been the puppet-master and Gray Eminence of the life of art, a man—or a figure—hated and feared by all. When the great change has come, he is permitted to surround himself with an aura of high dialectical-materialistic pathos as he speaks of the historical inevitability of his role, of the pain it had cost him to discharge his duty to the Revolution. But no other writer than Brandys gives any sign of a desire to save the face of Stalinism and the past. Nor does any other writer make use of the mode of thought which Brandys employs in tribute, as it were, to a former self. One of the striking things about this volume is the frank directness of the writers as they deal with past events to which they had been committed, and the happiness with which they exercise their common sense and their plain human judgment; the air they breathe is the bright air of reason and intention, not the miasma of historical necessity.

It is scarcely possible that anyone will read this book without feeling the impulse to be heartened for the future. The human mind, we are impelled to say, cannot be prevented forever from asserting its own nature and its own best needs.

It is a true thing to say, but if we say it, we must also say that the needs of the human mind are still very much at odds with the needs of most powerful forces.

If we speak of the future, we must speak with circumspection. We must take into account the fact that the assertion of freedom in Poland was not wholly autonomous. In saying this, I do not mean to question the autonomy of the intellectuals' desire for freedom. And certainly I do not mean to question the autonomy of their thought as they developed it under adverse conditions and as they now express it. But the freedom which they now claim for themselves was, up to a point, *permitted*. It was one of the consequences of the "thaw," as it is called, that took place in Russia after the death of Stalin. I am aware that there were notable demonstrations of Polish intellectual independence before the thaw, but the full outburst was subsequent to it. Granted that the behavior of the Poles went beyond the point of permission, that the waters flowed more freely than had perhaps been anticipated by those who decreed that the ice should melt, that even the Communist Party of Poland asserted an independence that had not been bargained for by the Russian Party—it is still true that the situation in Poland followed upon a decision of the Russian Party.

Only one writer in the present volume observes this. In his "Notes for a Biography," Wiktor Woroszylski remarks that a colleague had expressed himself as being outraged because the thaw had not been initiated by the artists themselves. To this Woroszylski replies: "I personally do not feel humiliated that, thanks to the decisive moves of the leadership of the Communist Party of the Soviet Union, and of our own Party, I acquired the vision I had lacked before, so essential for resolving my doubts and unrest."

Taken out of its context, this has an ominous sound, which does not, however, do justice to its author. For Woroszylski goes on to qualify his acceptance of Party direction—he speaks of being gratified by the fact that the artists and intellectuals had entered the new era "not as docile agents and barometer-watchers, but as deeply committed participants." I understand him to be saying by this that he finds it possible to receive his "vision" from the Party because the Party decision was made in response to the desires of the artists and intellectuals, that he believes the thaw to be indicative of the Party's intention to democratize itself.

So far as Poland goes, this may be a reasonable belief. Even though I have in memory the disturbing suppression of *Po Prostu,* I should not want to close my mind to the possibility that the Communist Party of Poland is, or will become, a Communist Party of a different kind from that of Russia, and that it is responsive to the actual wishes of the Polish people. I cannot presume to say what the political wishes of the Polish people are, but I think there is little doubt about what the intellectuals want—a humane and humanistic socialism. In his essay in the present volume, Leszek Kolakowski moves gently and circumspectly as he undertakes to distinguish the permanent from the transitory aspects of Marxism, but the results of his discrimination are radical: by the transitory aspects of Marxism he means Stalinism, which he quite rejects; by the permanent aspects of Marxism he means a kind of pragmatism or instrumentalism. Jan Strzelecki in his "Notes: 1950–1953" goes somewhat further than Kolakowski. Basing himself on assumptions that are flagrantly humanistic, he questions in an ironic and most cogent way the very psychology of the revolutionary and dismisses the creed upon which the revolutionary culture has existed for some three decades. If this is to be the direction of Polish thought, and if the ideas of Polish writers are going to make their way into politics and find eventual expression in the policies of a democratized Party, then indeed it will be possible for a considerable measure of freedom to be established in Poland under national Communism.

But is the question of Polish freedom to be answered in Poland? I think not—I think it is to be answered in Russia. Woroszylski, in proposing the idea that the thaw is an aspect of the democratization of the Party, means the Russian as well as the Polish Party. There will be not a few in the West to share his belief. Of these I am not one. I am sure that in the Soviet Union there are many people who are as eager for intellectual freedom as were the intellectuals of Poland. I am sure that the Party will not grant it to them. Even a little freedom is a dangerous thing—those who have a little never fail to want a great deal more. And intellectual freedom can produce nothing that the Soviet Union, at this moment of its history, can be supposed to find use for—unless it can also be supposed that the Soviet Union intends now to bring to an end its efforts to extend its power. A class of free Russian intellectuals would in all likelihood deal with Marxism in a way not very different from the way in which Polish intellectuals are dealing with it. That is to say, they would demonstrate the emptiness and inhumanity of Stalinist Marxism. Russia may not at the moment wish to cherish anything that bears Stalin's name—although who can tell what will be cherished a few months hence?—but Stalinist Marxism, under whatever name, is essential to Russia. You do not undertake to convert or subvert or conquer the world with a program of pragmatism or instrumentalism. Humanism does not encourage the iron single-mindedness that is needed for domination. For this only Stalinist Marxism will serve.

No, I cannot imagine that freedom will come to the Russian intellectuals in the near future. And if it does not, and if it does remain to the Polish intellectuals, and if the tenor of their thought continues to be as I have described it, and if their ideas actually do have a decisive influence in the political life of the nation, then Poland will not be what the Soviet Party intended it should be, an instrument of the Soviet Union, and indeed scarcely even an appropriate ally. If the Soviet Union consents to be balked of its purpose, Polish freedom may survive and develop; if not, not.

Does it need to be said that the danger in which the Polish intellectuals stand makes their affirmation of freedom the more splendid?

Proust as Critic
and the Critic as Novelist

[A review of *Contre Sainte-Beuve* in *Proust on Art and Literature*. *The Griffin*, July 1958]

O F the 398 pages of *Proust on Art and Literature*, 119 pages are devoted to brief miscellaneous essays and notes written by Proust between 1896 and 1919. The rest of the volume is given over to the posthumous work called *Contre Sainte-Beuve*, of which it can be said that it is one of the most remarkable pieces of critical writing in existence. I do not offer this as a judgment of its value, about which I shall speak presently, but rather as a comment on the singularity of its form.

Contre Sainte-Beuve comes to us in a translation—a good one, I think—by Sylvia Townsend Warner, and in her preface Miss Warner gives an account of the genesis of the strange work. In 1908, in a period of illness and indecision following the death of his mother, Proust wrote to two of his friends, Georges de Lauris and Madame de Noailles, that, bad as his health was, he yet wanted to undertake an essay on Sainte-Beuve. But he cannot make up his mind, he says, whether to write it straight off as an orthodox essay in literary criticism, or in another way which he has conceived, in which he would "begin with an account of a morning. Mamma would come to my bedside and I would tell her about the article on Sainte-Beuve I want to write and enlarge on it." It was the latter course that he chose, with the result that we have not only an extensive and cogent polemic against Sainte-Beuve but also what amounts to a sketch for *Remembrance of Things Past*. For Mamma does indeed come to Marcel's bedside and he does indeed tell her about the article on Sainte-Beuve that he wants to write, but this does not happen until the last of seven chapters devoted to child-hood and youth in which many of the most important episodes and themes of *Remembrance of Things Past* are presented, although of course with far less elaborateness than they were destined even-tually to achieve. And when at last Sainte-Beuve's hash has been settled, Proust returns, by ways that are more or less devious, to the reminiscences and meditations that are to engage him for the rest of his life.

What is perhaps the most striking aspect of *Contre Sainte-Beuve* considered in its relation to *Remembrance of Things Past* is that in the opening pages of the essay there appear the alpha and omega of the novel, the two decisive moments of reminiscence by which the novel may be said to be bounded. The essay, if that is what it is to be called, is introduced by a prologue, the second paragraph of which sets forth, quite briefly, the happy sensations of the author when, on a cold winter day, a cup of tea was brought to him by his old cook (not by his mother), together with a rusk (not a madeleine), which he ate after dipping it in the tea. Close upon this there follows an account of the sensations that result from the author's stepping on two uneven paving stones and nearly losing his footing.

The first occurrence in its developed and altered form is now one of the best known incidents in literature—it must sometimes seem to the reader of Proust that the eating of the Apple in the Garden was not so very much more momentous than the tasting of the madeleine on the sofa. The uneven paving stones are less well known than the madeleine because they play their part at the very end of a novel which is more often begun than finished. They make for Marcel an experience which is homologous to his experience of the madeleine. After the end of the war, Marcel returns to Paris from a stay at a sanatorium. He is greatly depressed, for he has come

312 SPEAKING OF LITERATURE AND SOCIETY

to the realization that he can now never hope for health, and he despairs of ever becoming a creative artist. He attends the great afternoon party of the Princess de Guermantes, that new Princess who had once been Madame Verdurin. As he enters the courtyard of the Guermantes home, he steps back to avoid an automobile and almost losses his balance on two ill-matched flagstones. At this he is (in Wordsworth's lovely phrase) surprised by joy—a great happiness floods his being. His depression quite vanishes; he loses his anxiety; intellectual doubts seem no longer possible. The experience of the uneven flagstones had served, as that of the madeleine had done years before, to awaken him to a true and happy sense of his life. The experience is on this occasion twice repeated, once by the sound of a spoon struck against a plate by a clumsy waiter, once by the touch upon Marcel's lips of a starched napkin. Seeking to discover the reason for his joy, Marcel finds it in the power of memory, but not of the habitual institutionalized memory, the memory of the mind, but the memory that is truly personal. He reflects that it is our reliance upon the former that convinces us that life is dull and drab; could we but learn to trust the other memory, the personal, the unintellectual—the essential—memory, we would be certain of life's beauty. And this experience of true reminiscence, thrice undergone on one occasion and therefore portentous, convinces him of his vocation as an artist.

Marcel's sense of vocation, of his having been called to a fate, must inevitably bring to mind Wordworth's great moment in the summer dawn in the fourth book of *The Prelude*. Marcel's experience, however, is different from Wordsworth's in that it is not as Wordsworth's was, a general commitment to the creative life. Wordsworth's actual aesthetic decisions were all to come; at the moment when he knew himself to be a dedicated spirit, he had no idea what sort of poetry he would write. But Proust's aesthetic decisions were of the essence of his moment of dedication—it is a particular kind of work that he is called to do; and his—understanding of what he must do involves his rejection of certain forms of literary art—the hard, superficial art of the intellectualized consciousness—and his contempt for the practitioners of it. The aesthetic theory to which Marcel commits himself in *Time Recaptured* is an elaborated recapitulation of the aesthetic theory of *Contre Sainte-Beuve,* of which the first sentence is: "Every day I set less store by the intellect." It seems to me that Sainte-Beuve is not really a significant example of what is usually meant by intellect; and, in point of fact, Proust's case against him is ultimately not made on the basis of his intellectuality, rather on the basis of a deficiency of delicacy, of a downright vulgarity. Be that as it may, Proust undertakes, as he says, to call upon the intellect to establish the inferiority of the intellect by demonstrating the falsity of Sainte-Beuve's critical theory and practice.

But the intellect is not to be called on for some time to come, and Sainte-Beuve, having been mentioned once in the Prologue, will not be spoken of again for seven chapters—before he launches his polemic, Proust devotes himself to the exercise of the faculty which he is undertaking to defend. The first chapter of *Contre Sainte-Beuve,* called In Slumbers, begins with a primitive version of the famous meditation on sleep with which *Remembrance of Things Past* opens, and there follow other childhood memories, including a scene of masturbation at the age of twelve which is notable for being perhaps the only recollection of this kind which is idyllic and poetic, not laden with guilt and terror. A second chapter, Bedrooms, continues the theme of bed and sleeplessness. A third, The Days, is a meditation on unknown girls and the dream of pleasures. A fourth, The Countess, is a reminiscence of an aristocratic lady who had occupied an apartment on the same court as the Prousts; Marcel represents himself as having become her lover many years after his first acquaintance with her and she serves as the occasion for a discourse on the fictionizing and idealizing aspect of love. With the fifth chapter, we begin to believe that we may yet have sight of Sainte-Beuve, for The Article in *Le Figaro* is about writing, or, rather, the thoughts of praise and fame that possess one young writer as he comes upon his essay on the front page of the morning paper; and it introduces Mamma, very charmingly, for the first thing we are told about her is that, if ever she knew that the morning mail brought Marcel a letter which would please him, or that *Le Figaro* that morning carried an essay of his, she would carefully compose her face into an air of detachment as she gave him the mail and the paper so as not to apprise him of the pleasure that was to come and thus diminish it. But from the article in *Le Figaro* the line of reminiscences turns off to the momentary encounter with a pretty young girl, who, at a wayside stop in a wild ravine in the Jura, came through the train selling *café au lait;* she is perhaps the prototype of the young peasant girl so memorably seen on the road in *Within a Budding Grove* and she makes the occasion for a disquisition on the nature of desire. Chapter Six, The Sunbeam on the Balcony, turns back momentarily to the article in *Le Figaro* but is soon occupied with other matters, most especially Marcel's relation with Gilberte Swann, although neither she nor her parents are named. Chapter Seven, Talking to Mamma, after an account of Mamma's tenderness and wit and literary preferences, brings us at last Sainte-Beuve:

"Listen! I want to ask your advice. Sit down."

"Wait till I've found the armchair. Its not very easy to see in here, I may say. Should I tell Félicie to bring the electric lamp?"

"No, don't. I might not be able to go to sleep again."

"Still Molière," she said laughing. *"Forbid the torches to approach, sweet lady."*

"You're settled? Good! Now this is what I want to tell you about. I've an idea for an article, and I want your opinion on it."

"But you know that I can't give you advice about such things. I'm not like you, I don't read great books."

"Now listen! The subject is: Objections to the method of Sainte-Beuve."

"Goodness! I thought it was everything it should be. In that article by Bourget you made me read, he said that it is such a marvelous method that there has been no one in the nineteenth century who could make use of it."

"Oh yes, that's what he said, but it was stupid. You know the principles of that method?"

"Go on as if I didn't."

And Marcel does as she asks, to this effect: "To have devised the Natural History of the Intellectual, to have elicited from the biography of the man, from his family history and from all his peculiarities, the sense of his work and the nature of his genius—this is what we all recognize as Sainte-Beuve's special achievement, he recognizes it as such himself, and was right about it besides."

It is a characterization that in the present day would in itself constitute virtually the whole of any condemnation of Sainte-Beuve that the writer wished to make—nothing more would be needed than the statement that Sainte-Beuve believed that from a man's personal life could be derived "the sense of his work and the nature of his genius." For the last twenty years a powerful criticism has lectured us on the necessity of focussing our attention upon the work of art itself and has deprecated the interest in the person who made the work. Criticism has gone, I think, rather too far in this direction, and out of its resistance to personality it has contrived a rather precious and affected attitude of literary purity. But at the time that Proust wrote, the "psychological" investigation of literature was still new enough to command an unquestioning interest, and it was still necessary, if one wished to deal adversely with it, to say at length, as Proust does, that the man and the artist are not the same person, that from his family history, and from all his peculiarities, we derive no sense whatever of his work and no knowledge whatever of the nature of his genius.

It is worth observing that Proust does not make his objection to Sainte-Beuve's method on the ground that the artist is being demeaned or that his privacy is being invaded. And despite his desire to depreciate the rational faculties, he exhibits none of the conventional squeamishness at the idea of the artist being subjected to an investigation of a "scientific" sort—I can detect in Proust no impulse to protect the idea of the creative mind as being "free" and unconditioned. (And indeed it would have been strange had Proust taken this ground, he who can tell us at precisely what moment in his childhood his will was destroyed by the indulgence of his parents!) What Proust's objection to Sainte-Beuve's method is based on is the perception that it is inaccurate in its scientific pretensions—Sainte-Beuve does not see the object as in itself it really is, he does not perceive the actual nature of the work of art or of the artistic process.

When I said that nowadays it would have been enough for Proust to describe Sainte-Beuve's method in order to discredit it, I did not mean to imply that literary scholarship has wholly rejected the method of biographical investigation. It of course has not done so. But the best of literary scholarship has learned not to pretend that it can demonstrate the nexus between the personality that biography discloses and the act of creation. Its best effect is to make palpable the mystery of the creative process, or to suggest the exigencies, both material and psychological, against which the creative process asserts itself. To take an example, a rather obvious and easy one: The poetry of Yeats makes very frequent reference to circumstances in the poet's own life. What is more, our judgment of Yeats's poetry is to a very considerable extent the judgment of a person, and not merely of a poet-person: it is one of Yeats's poetic devices to speak in his poetry as a man-person, and his career as a poet is used as a subject for his poetry. With this invitation from the poet-person himself, we should be less than human if we did not seek to acquire any information that was available about the man-person. And anyone who has done so is pretty sure to feel that, as a result, he stands in a more intimate relation to the poetry, that he understands it better. This is not an illusion. Nor is it entirely an illusion when he believes that he has acquired a fuller understanding of the creative process that made the work—not *entirely* an illusion, for what has happened is that he has become, as it were, habituated to the characteristic activity of this creative process, that he sees it in the homeliness of the circumstances that make its conditions: Yeats's genius, we may say, has come to seem more and more consonant with Yeats's life. But no knowledge of the poet's life serves to account for the particular operation of his genius, for its *effect* in any poem or any line or any phrase. The only thing that can be thought to account for an effect is the reader's knowledge of his own life in conjunction with his knowledge of the life of the race as that is expressed in literature.

But if literary scholarship has acquired a pretty thorough awareness of this limitation of the biographical method, psychoanalysis still lacks it, and it is in the psychoanalytical dealing with the creative process that the tradition of Sainte-Beuve is to be found.

When psychoanalysts encounter the resistance of literary people to their researches—as they so often do—they are likely to think that it is based on the idea which we might expect Proust to make in his polemic against Sainte-Beuve and which, as I said, he never actually does make—the idea that the artistic mind is unconditioned and that the pure delicacy of art must be protected from the prying eyes and the unclean paws of science. This idea does indeed now and then find expression, but I do not think it is the real ground for skepticism about the psychoanalytical dealings with art. As I watch psychoanalysis at work upon art, although I find that it can often be enlightening about one or another aspect of a particular work of art, or of a particular artist, it seems to me that it is wholly at a loss when it touches upon the question that really, and quite naturally, most engages it—the question of how the nexus between personality and creative power is made. Psychoanalysis hides its failure from itself, sometimes by directing its investigations upon mediocre works of art, sometimes by not stating openly just what it is that it seeks to discover. But that it does fail is made plain by the fact that it virtually never addresses itself to questions of language, of style, of dramatic form. It can deal, and sometimes very well, with the connection between biography and certain substantive matter in a work, but it never undertakes to say why a work, or a part of a work, has its power over us when another work, or passage, of similar sort does not; nor does it ever undertake to say where in the biographical facts about the creator of the work the explanation of this power is to be found.

Proust's insistence that we cannot assume that the poet-person is identical with the man-person constitutes the only theoretical ground of his case against Sainte-Beuve. The considerable remainder of his argument consists of the demonstration of the inadequacy of Sainte-Beuve's particular judgments. It is an inadequacy that frequently takes the form of a failure of generosity and of delicacy. This is expectable enough. Sainte-Beuve's identification of the man with the artist, his belief that he could discover the truth of the work of art by means of the scientific investigation of the artist's biography, is a Philistine error, and Proust's rage against Sainte-Beuve is the expression of the natural hostility of the artist toward the Philistine. "At no time does Sainte-Beuve seem to have understood that there is something special about creative writing and that this makes it different in kind from what busies other men and, at other times, busies artists. He drew no dividing line between the state of being engaged in a piece of writing and the state when in solitude, stopping our ears against those phrases which belong to others as much as to us, and which whenever we are not truly ourselves, even though we may be alone, we make use of in the consideration of things, we confront ourselves and try to catch the true voice of the heart, and write down that, and not small talk." I do not know just what name we ought to give to the quality of existence and perception which Proust thought the artist should achieve. An approving reference to Carlyle's conception of the artist as against Sainte-Beuve's suggests that words like *transcendence* and *natural supernaturalism* would not be inappropriate; and whatever we do call it, it has to do with Appearance and Reality, with the illusory appearance of the material and social world, with the reality of the Idea: indeed, the passage from Carlyle to which Proust refers speaks of the Divine Idea. Sainte-Beuve was capable of responding only to the world of appearance, and to the extent of not being able to distinguish the man-in-society from the author, or to conceive that, as Proust puts it, "a book is the product of a different *self* from the self we manifest in our habits, in our social life, in our vices." His personal acquaintance with the man Stendhal, whom he knew, stood in the way of his understanding of the novelist. The man Baudelaire, whom he knew and for whom he had considerable feeling of a kind, was a *nice fellow,* one who *improved on acquaintance* and had *perfectly correct manners;* the poet Baudelaire he understood scarcely at all. Nor was he able to do better by Balzac, whose work he grossly misjudged.

The chapter in which Proust defends Balzac from Sainte-Beuve's misapprehension and denigration is the most substantial and the most attractive flight of criticism in the whole *Contre Sainte-Beuve.* The affinities between Proust and Balzac are no doubt as manifest as the abysses between them, and it is not the affinities alone that make the ground of Proust's love of Balzac. "To love Balzac! Sainte-Beuve, who was so fond of defining what it meant to love someone, would have had his work cut out for him here. For with the other novelists, one loves them in submitting oneself to them; one receives the truth from a Tolstoi as from someone of greater scope and stature than oneself. With Balzac, we know all his vulgarities, and at first were often repelled by them; then we began to love him, then we smiled at all those sillinesses which are so typical of him; we love him, with a little dash of irony mixed in our affection; we know his aberrations, his shabby little tricks, and because they are so like him we love them." And nothing could be better in praise of Balzac than the concluding paragraph of the chapter:

About Balzac, Sainte-Beuve does as he always does. Instead of discussing Balzac's *Femme de trente ans,* he discusses women of thirty in general, and after a few words about Balthazar Claës (in *La Recherche de l'absolu*) he talks about a real-life Claës who actually left a book about his own searchings for the absolute, and gives long quotations from this production—of no literary value, needless to say. Looking down from the height of his false and baleful ideal of the gentleman of letters, he misjudges Balzac's harshness towards Steinbock (in *La Cousine Bette*), that mere amateur who conceives nothing, who produces nothing, who does not understand that to be an artist one must devote the whole of oneself to art. Here Sainte-Beuve rears up with ruffled dignity against the phrase that Balzac uses: "Homer . . . cohabited with his Muse." It is not, perhaps, very happily expressed. But really there can be no interpreting the masterpieces of the past unless one judges them from the standpoint of those who wrote them, and not from the outside, from a respectful distance, and with all academic deference. That the outward conditions of literary production should have changed during the course of the last century, that the calling of the man of letters should have become a more absorbing and excluding affair, is quite possible. But the inward, mental laws of that production cannot have changed. That a writer should be a genius occasionally, *so that* for the rest of his time he may lead the pleasant life of a cultured social dilettante, is as false and silly a notion as that of a saint pursuing a life of the austerest contemplation so that in Paradise he may lead a life of vulgar enjoyment. One is nearer to understanding the great writers of the ancient world if one understands them as Balzac did, than as Sainte-Beuve did. Dilettantism has never created anything. Even Horace was certainly closer to Balzac than to M. Daru or M. Molé.

The chapter on Balzac is followed by an account of Monsieur de Guermantes' relation to Balzac. In *The Guermantes Way* the Duke is said to have said that he "adored" Balzac. In its context the avowal seems insincere, a mere piece of social vivacity. But now we have evidence that it was quite genuine, that the Duke was truly addicted, reading the novels undiscriminatingly, unliterarily, making a very pleasant spectacle in his unenlightened devotion.

With Monsieur de Guermantes' Balzac Sainte-Beuve and criticism are for a time forgotten in favor of the concerns that are later to be central to *Remembrance of Things Past*—the manners of the Guermantes, the vices and sufferings of Charlus (under the name of Comte de Quercy), the famous disquisition on homosexuality; in the chapter called The Return we have, with Mamma as the deuteragonist, an early version of the scene in which Marcel reassures his grandmother about his ability to sustain her death. But the last chapter returns to literary discourse; we recognize it as matter that is to be part of Marcel's meditation in *Time Recaptured*. The concluding paragraph is memorable:

The fine things we shall write if we have talent enough, are within us, dimly, like the remembrance of a tune which charms us though we cannot recall its outline, or hum it, nor even sketch its metrical form, say if there are pauses in it, or runs of rapid notes. Those who are haunted by this confused remembrance of truths they have never known are the men who are gifted; but if they never go beyond saying that they can hear a ravishing tune, they convey nothing to others, they are without talent. Talent is like a kind of memory, which in the end enables them to call back this confused music, to hear it distinctly, to write it down, to reproduce it, to sing it. There comes a time in life when talent, like memory, fails, and the muscle in the mind which brings inward memories before one like memories of the outer world, loses its power. Sometimes, from lack of exercise or because of a too ready self-approval, this time of life extends over a whole lifetime; and no one, not your own self even, will ever know the tune that beset you with its intangible delightful rhythm.

The Last Lover

[A review of *Lolita* by Vladimir Nabokov. *The Griffin*, August 1958[1]]

I

VLADIMIR NABOKOV'S novel *Lolita* was first published in Paris in 1955. Its reputation was not slow to reach the country in which it had been written and in which, presumably, it could not be published. Reviews of the book appeared in some of the more advanced literary journals, and in 1956 *The Anchor Review* published a sizable portion of the novel, together with a thoughtful comment on the whole work by F. W. Dupee. Copies of the book in the Olympia Press edition were brought back to the United States by returning travelers and were passed from hand to hand in a manner somewhat reminiscent of the early circulation of *Ulysses* in the Twenties and *Lady Chatterley's Lover* in the Thirties.

I use the qualifying *somewhat* because the borrowing and lending of *Lolita* did not proceed in the aura of righteous indignation which had attended the private circulation of the two earlier books. The bland acceptance of what would once have been called censorship and denounced as such—actually there never was an American legal ruling on *Lolita*, only a caginess on the part of the American publishers—was perhaps the result of a general cultural change from the Twenties and Thirties, an aspect of the diminished capacity for indignation that has often been noted of the Fifties. Or it

---

[1] The text used here includes some minor revisions made by the author on his copy of the published version of this essay in *Encounter*, October 1958. (D.T.)

may imply the recognition that Mr. Nabokov's book, in tune with the temper of the times, is very much less weighty and solemn than Joyce's or Lawrence's, that it does not proclaim itself to be, and is not, a work of genius. Or, again, it may suggest that readers have discovered that *Lolita* really is, as the conditions of its first publication would lead us to suppose, a shocking and scandalous book.

Certainly its scandalous reputation was affirmed by the action of the French government in suppressing it. When I was in Paris not long after its publication I tried to buy a copy, and as I stood at that foremost counter in Galignani's on which are piled the standard dirty books for English and American tourists, I was told by the clerk that the sale of *Lolita* had been made illegal just the day before. This was at a time when the French were going in for suppressing books on a rather large scale. I heard it said that they were doing so in response to representations made by the English government, which was concerned to stop the flow of indecent or questionable literature across the Channel. Perhaps this was true, although it is really not necessary to account in any special and elaborate way for the displays of literary squeamishness that the French make every now and then. But this time their heart was not in it, and shortly after my visit *Lolita* became again available.

So much for the pre-history of *Lolita*. Now [1958] the book has been brought out by an American publishing firm of entire respectability and everyone may buy it and read it and judge it for himself.

The legitimizing of *Lolita* must not mislead us about its nature. It must not tempt us into taking the correct enlightened attitude— "Well, now, what was all the fuss about? Here is the book brought into the full light of day, and of course we can very plainly see that there is nothing shocking about it." The fact is that *Lolita* is indeed a shocking book. It means to be shocking and it succeeds in its intention.

But it is not shocking in the way that books which circulate in secret are usually said to be shocking. I shall presently try to say in what ways—there are several—the book does, or should, shock us. Now I shall simply report that *Lolita* is not pornographic as that word would be used in any legal complaint that might conceivably be made against it.

I specify the legal use of the word in order to distinguish that from my own use of it. As I used the word, its meaning is neutrally descriptive, not pejorative.[2] I take it to mean the explicit representation in literature (or the graphic arts—or music, for that matter) of the actual sexual conduct of human beings. (I suppose I should include anthropomorphic gods, demons, etc.) It seems to me that this representation is a perfectly acceptable artistic enterprise. I expect that, if it is carried out with some skill, it will raise lustful thoughts in the reader, and I believe that this in itself provides no ground for objection.

I should like to be entirely clear on this point. I am not taking the position of liberal and progressive lawyers and judges. I am not saying that literature should be permitted its moments of pornography because such moments are essential to the moral truth which a particular work of literature is aiming at; or because they are essential to its objective truth; or because, when taken in context, they cannot really arouse the normal mature reader to thoughts of lust. I am saying that I see no reason in morality (or in aesthetic theory) why literature should not have as one of its intentions the arousing of thoughts of lust. It is one of the effects, perhaps one of the functions, of literature to arouse desire, and I can discover no ground for saying that sexual pleasure should not be among the objects of desire which literature presents to us, along with heroism, virtue, peace, death, food, wisdom, God, etc.

This, as I say, is not the position taken by the liberal lawyers and judges. And having read a good many of the American legal opinions in matters of literary censorship, I have come to think that the liberal line of argument, although it comes out on the right side in some ways, is shallow and evasive. I have been told by lawyers that

---

[2] I am aware that a pejorative meaning, is, as it were, built into the word, that it derives from *porne*, the Greek word for prostitute. But we have no other word to express the idea; and the attempt to invent a prettier one is bound to compromise the position I wish to maintain.

there is no other way for them to go about things, that they must defend indicted books by taking a hypocritical view of their sexual passages, owlishly arguing that these passages when "read in context" have no special significance or effect, that they are "essential" to the "total artistic effect of the work." No doubt the forensic necessity is what the lawyers say it is, but their submission to it does not advance the cause of honesty.

My position in this matter does not lead me to argue that censorship is always indefensible. My use of the word pornographic follows, of course, that of D. H. Lawrence in his famous essay, "Pornography and Obscenity," and I go along with Lawrence in distinguishing the pornographic from the obscene. It seems to me that if we are going to be frank in our demand that sexuality be accepted as an element of human life which should be available to literature like any other, we must be no less frank in recognizing its unique nature as a literary subject. For most people it is the very most interesting subject, the subject that is most sought for, even though with shame and embarrassment. It is, if we look at it truthfully, a uniquely influential subject—no part of the individual life is so susceptible to literature as the sexual expectations and emotions. As Lawrence said in effect, there are discriminations to be made among kinds of lust, of which some tend to humanize, others to dehumanize us. This gives society an unusually high stake in sexuality as a literary subject, and although I have no great confidence in the ability of society, through the agency of the courts of law, to make the discrimination accurately, it seems to me natural that the effort at discrimination should be made, and appropriate that it should be made through the courts.

The purpose of my digression on censorship is simply to make plain the grounds for my saying that in the sense in which the courts use the word, it is not possible to call *Lolita* a pornographic book. It is, to be sure, the story of an erotic episode, and the story is told in such a way that erotic emotions and sensations are always before the reader. By my own definition of pornography, there is one scene to which the word can be applied—other readers may perhaps find more—but it is unlikely that any court, working under the standards of acceptation that have been established over the last few years, would apply the word in the legal sense even to that scene. And, indeed, *Lolita* takes very little of the wide latitude in the representation of sexual behavior that is nowadays permitted to fiction, in point either of language or of explicitness of description.

That is what I mean when I say that if *Lolita* is, as I have called it, a shocking book, it is not for the reason that books are commonly thought to be shocking.

II

Lolita is the story of the love of a man in his forties for a girl of twelve. The narrative is in the first person, the memoir or confession of the lover, written by him while awaiting trial for murder. Upon his sudden death before the trial begins, his manuscript is edited by John Ray, Jr., Ph.D., presumably a professor of psychology.

Humbert Humbert is the fictitious name under which the narrator presents himself. It is, as the "editor" remarks in his solemn preface, a bizarre name, and Humbert himself says that of the possible pseudonyms that had occurred to him, this one "expresses the nastiness best." It is in some way indicative of his nature that he takes a kind of pleasure in its being misheard and misremembered; he adopts the distortions and represents himself variously as Humbug, Humbird, Humburger, Hamburg, Homberg. He is, as the editor says, "a mixture of ferocity and jocularity that betrays supreme misery perhaps, but is not conducive to attractiveness." He is indeed anything but attractive. The jocularity can sometimes rise to wit, sometimes to wildness, but it can also sink to facetiousness and reach the brink of silliness. Humbert is a man without friends, and he desires none. His characteristic mode of thought is contemptuous and satirical, but we do not know what makes his standard of judgment, for it is never clear what, besides female beauty of a certain kind, has ever won his admiration. His ferocity takes the form of open brutality to women. He is the less attractive by reason of the style in which he chiefly writes about himself—whoever has tried to keep a journal and has been abashed at reading it by the apologetic, self-referring, self-exculpating whine of the prose, and by the very irony which is used to modify this deplorable tone, will recognize the manner of most of *Lolita*. Humbert himself recognizes it and asks forgiveness for it—he is nothing if not self-conscious and he is as self-contemptuous as he is self-defensive.

By no means attractive, then. Yet he does not fail to effect an intimacy with us. His unrelenting self-reference, his impious greediness, seduce us into kinship with him. He is in every way a non-hero, an anti-hero; but his lack of all admirable qualities leaves perfectly clear—was no doubt devised to leave perfectly clear—the force of the obsessive passion of which he is capable.

Humbert is the son of a generally European (Swiss, French, Austrian, Danubian) father, who owned a luxury hotel on the Riviera, and of an English mother. His European birth and rearing are of considerable importance, for if the narrative is primarily the history of his love-affair with an American girl-child, it is incidentally the history of his love-affair with America. It is a relationship sufficiently ambivalent, charged with as much scorn and dislike as tenderness and affection, but perhaps for that reason the more interesting, and yielding a first-rate account of the life of the American road, of hotels and motels, of dead towns and flashy resorts, of skating-rinks and tourist caves, of Coke machines and juke boxes, of all that pertains to mobility and transience, to youth and uninvolvement.

By the time he has reached maturity H.H. (as he sometimes calls himself) has come to the realization of the most important fact about his nature. Grown women repel him, not in the degree that he cannot have sexual relations with them, but in the degree that they can give him no pleasure. His sexual desire can be aroused and truly gratified only by girls between the ages of nine and fourteen. The social sanctions against the indulgence of this taste being of the most extreme sort, H.H. lives a deprived life. On several occasions he has had to take refuge in mental hospitals. He makes no great claims for his sanity, all he insists on is the madness of psychiatrists, and it is a chief dogma of his view of his erotic idiosyncrasy that no explanation of it can possibly be made. He tells us that his "very photogenic mother died in a freak accident (picnic, lightning)" when he was three, and nothing seems to him more absurd than the idea that his passional life might have been influenced by this event. It is probable that the author does not intend an irony here, that he quite agrees with Humbert in thinking the idea comical.

But Humbert does trace the strict condition imposed upon his love to a childhood episode, to his first passionate attachment, experienced as a boy one summer on the Riviera. The object of his passion, who reciprocated it, was a little girl named Annabel, who soon after died of typhus. Her name and her fate are significant, intended to recall the Annabel Lee of Poe's poem. The marriage of Poe to the fourteen-year-old Virginia Clemm is touched upon several times in the course of the story, and can, I think, be made to throw light on what the novel is up to.

The image of the lost Annabel fixes itself upon H.H.'s mind. To girls of her kind, having her beauty, charm, and sexual responsiveness, he gives the name *nymphets.* "Between the age limits of nine and fourteen there occur maidens who, to certain bewitched travellers, twice or many times older than they, reveal their true nature which is not human, but nymphic (that is, demoniac); and those chosen creatures I propose to designate as 'nymphets.' " [The accent should probably come on the first syllable, otherwise we get, as someone pointed out to me when I put it on the second, the heavy sound and eventually the ugly appearance of *nymphette,* which must inevitably suggest the very opposite of a nymphet, a drum-majorette.] The further description of the nymphet emphasizes the demoniac quality—"the fey grace, the elusive, shifty, soul-shattering, insidious charm"—upon which the Greeks based their idea of the disease of nympholepsy and later peoples their conceptions of Undines, Belles Dames Sans Merci, and White Goddesses.

In middle age, in a New England town, Humbert discovers Dolores Haze, called Lolita, a middle-class schoolgirl of twelve, and conceives for her an irresistible desire. In order to be near Lolita and to make opportunity to possess her, Humbert marries her mother. It cannot be said that he exactly murders his new wife—it is only that, having read his diary in which he had set forth his reasons for marrying her and the details of his dislike of her, she runs distractedly out of the house and is providentially hit by a passing car. The way is now quite clear for the stepfather. Believing that Lolita's innocence must not be offended, he has for some time made elaborate plans to drug the child, but in the end it is Lolita who ravishes Humbert; a month at a summer camp had served to induct her into the mysteries of sex, which to her are no mysteries at all, and she considers that H.H. is rather lacking in address.

The relation that is now established between Humbert and Lolita is of a double kind. His sexual obsession, so far from abating, grows by what it feeds on. Lolita accepts his sensuality with cool acquiescence, and even responds to it physically, but she is not moved by desire, and she is frequently bored and has to be bribed into compliance. Sensuality, however, does not comprise the whole of Humbert's feeling. He is *in loco parentis*—I have forgotten whether or not he makes a joke on this—and his emotions are in some part paternal. Lolita passes for his daughter, and his brooding concern for her, his jealousy of her interest in other males, his nervous desire to please or to placate her, constitute a mode of behavior not very different from that of any American father to his adolescent daughter. Nor is Lolita's response to Humbert very different from that which American girls of her age make to their fathers. She maintains toward him the common alternation of remote indifference and easy acceptance, and finds his restriction of her freedom a burden which is not much lightened by his indulgence.

Inevitably, of course, she undertakes to "get away," and inevitably she makes another man the instrument of an escape from a tyranny which for her is less that of a lover than of a father. All Humbert's jealous fantasies come true; Lolita takes up with a perverse middle-aged playwright—who is as much concerned to torture Humbert as to win Lolita—and after a period of very skillful deception, runs off with her lover. Her desertion of Humbert brings his life to an end and he exists only to dream of regaining her love and of destroying her seducer. After the passage of some years, he does at last find Lolita; she is married, not to the perverse lover but to a deaf and worthy young technician, by whom she is pregnant. At seventeen, her status as a nymphet has quite gone, yet for Humbert her charm is unabated, still absolute. It is so even though he observes "how womanish and somehow never seen that way before was the shadowy division between her pale breasts." He begs her to return to him. She refuses—it is to her a surprising idea that he loves her or had ever loved her: she is as unrecognizing of his feeling for her as if she were indeed his daughter—and Humbert goes off to murder the playwright. We learn from the editor's preface that Lolita dies in childbed. Humbert dies of heart disease.

III

This, then, is the story of *Lolita* and it is indeed shocking. In a tone which is calculatedly not serious, it makes a prolonged assault on one of our unquestioned and unquestionable sexual prohibitions, the sexual inviolability of girls of a certain age (and compounds the impiousness with what amounts to incest).

It is all very well for us to remember that Juliet was fourteen when she was betrothed to Paris, and gave herself, with our full approval, to Romeo. It is all very well for us to find a wry idyllic charm in the story of the aged David and the little maid Abishag. And to gravely receive Dante's account of being struck to the heart by an eight-year-old Beatrice. And to say that distant cultures—H.H. gives a list of them to put his idiosyncrasy in some moral perspective—and hot climates make a difference in ideas of the right age for female sexuality to begin. All very well for us to have long ago got over our first horror at what Freud told us about the sexuality of children; and to receive blandly what he has told us about the "family romance" and its part in the dynamics of the psyche. All very well for the family and society to take approving note of the little girl's developing sexual charms, to find a sweet comedy in her growing awareness of them and her learning to use them, and for her mother to be open and frank and delighted and ironic over the teacups about the clear signs of the explosive force of her sexual impulse. We have all become so nicely clear-eyed, so sensibly Coming-of-Age-in-Samoa. But let an adult male seriously think about the girl as a sexual object and all our sensibility is revolted.

The response is not reasoned but visceral. Within the range of possible heterosexual conduct, this is one of the few prohibitions which still seem to us to be confirmed by nature itself. Virginity once seemed so confirmed, as did the marital fidelity of women, but they do so no longer. No novelist would expect us to respond with any moral intensity to his representing an unmarried girl having a sexual experience, whether in love or curiosity; the infidelity of a wife may perhaps be a little more interesting, but not much. The most serious response the novelist would expect from us is that we should "understand," which he would count on us to do automatically.

But our response to the situation that Mr. Nabokov presents to us is that of shock. And we find ourselves the more shocked when we realize that, in the course of reading the novel, we have come virtually to condone the violation it presents. Charles Dickens, by no means a naïve man, was once required to meet a young woman who had lived for some years with a man out of wedlock; he was dreadfully agitated at the prospect, and when he met the girl he was appalled to discover that he was not confronting a piece of depravity but a principled, attractive young person, virtually a lady. It was a terrible blow to the certitude of his moral feelings. That we may experience the same loss of certitude about the sexual behavior that *Lolita* describes is perhaps suggested by the tone of my summary of the story—I was plainly not able to muster up the note of moral outrage. And it is likely that any reader of *Lolita* will discover that he comes to see the situation as less and less abstract and moral and horrible, and more and more as human and "understandable." Less and less, indeed, do we see a *situation;* what we become aware of is people. Humbert is perfectly willing to say that he is a monster; no doubt he is, but we find ourselves less and less eager to say so. Perhaps his depravity is the easier to accept when we learn that he deals with a Lolita who is not innocent, and who seems to have very few emotions to be violated; and I suppose we naturally incline to be lenient toward a rapist—legally and by intention H.H. is that—who eventually feels a deathless devotion to his victim!

But we have only to let the immediate influence of the book diminish a little with time, we have only to free ourselves from the rationalizing effect of H.H.'s obsessive passion, we have only to move back into the real world where twelve-year-olds are being bored by Social Studies and plagued by orthodonture, to feel again the outrage at the violation of the sexual prohibition. And to feel this the more because we have been seduced into conniving in the violation, because we have permitted our fantasies to accept what we know to be revolting.

What, we must ask, is Mr. Nabokov's purpose in making this occasion for outrage?

I have indicated that his purpose cannot be explained by any interest in the "psychological" aspects of the story; he has none whatever. His novel is as far as possible from being a "study of" the emotions it presents. The malice which H.H. bears to psychiatry is quite Mr. Nabokov's own; for author, as for character, psychiatric concepts are merely occasions for naughty irreverence. Psychiatry and the world may join in giving scientific or ugly names to Humbert's sexual idiosyncrasy; the novel treats of it as a condition of love like another.

And we can be sure that Mr. Nabokov has not committed himself to moral subversion. He is not concerned to bring about a sexual revolution which will make paedophilia a rational and respectable form of heterosexuality. Humbert's "ferocity and jocularity," what we might call his moral facetiousness reaching the point of anarchic silliness, make the pervasive tone of the narrative, and that tone does have its curious influence upon us, as does the absoluteness of Humbert's passional obsession. Yet any anarchic power to which we may respond in the novel is quite negated when, near the end of the history, H.H. reflects, in a tone never used before, on the havoc he has made of Lolita's life.

It is of course possible that Mr. Nabokov wanted to shock us merely for shocking's sake, that he had in mind the intention of what might be called general satire, the purpose of which is to make us uneasy with ourselves, less sure of our moral simplicity than we have been: this he brings about by contriving the effect I have described, of leading us to become quite at ease with a sexual situation that should outrage us and then facing us with our facilely given acquiescence.

And then of course Mr. Nabokov may be intending a more particular satire, upon the peculiar sexual hypocrisy of American life. I have in mind the perpetual publicity we give to sexuality, the unending invitation made by our popular art and advertising to sexual awareness, competence, and competition. To what end is a girl-child taught from her earliest years to consider the brightness and fragrance of her hair, and the shape of her body, and her look of readiness for adventure? Why, what other end than that she shall some day be a really capable airline hostess? Or that she shall have the shining self-respect which, as we know, underlies all true virtue and efficiency? Or that her husband and her children shall not be ashamed of her, but, on the contrary, proud to claim her as their own? So say the headmistresses, the principals, the deans of women, the parents. But in every other culture that Mr. Nabokov is aware of, which is a good many, the arts of the boudoir were understood to point to the bed, and if they were taught early, they were understood to point to the bed early.

But I think that the real reason why Mr. Nabokov chose his

outrageous subject matter is that he wanted to write a story about love.

IV

Lolita is about love. Perhaps I shall be better understood if I put the statement in this form: *Lolita* is not about sex, but about love. Almost every page sets forth some explicit erotic emotion or some overt erotic action and still it is not about sex. It is about love.

This makes it unique in my experience of contemporary novels. If our fiction gives accurate testimony, love has disappeared from the Western world, just as Denis de Rougemont said it should. The contemporary novel can tell us about sex, and about sexual communion, and about mutuality, and about the strong fine relationships that grow up between men and women; and it can tell us about marriage. But about love, which was once one of its chief preoccupations, it can tell us nothing at all.

My having mentioned Denis de Rougemont and his curious, belated, supererogatory onslaught on love will indicate that I have in mind what I seem to remember he calls passion-love, a kind of love with which European literature has dealt since time immemorial but with especial intensity since the Arthurian romances and the code of courtly love. Passion-love was a mode of feeling not available to everyone—the authorities on the subject restricted it to the aristocracy—but it was always of the greatest interest to almost everyone who was at all interested in the feelings, and it had a continuing influence on other kinds of love and on the literary conventions through which love was represented.

The essential condition of this kind of love was that it had nothing to do with marriage and could not possibly exist in marriage. Alanus Capellanus in his manual on courtly love set it down as perfectly obvious doctrine that a husband and wife cannot be lovers. The reason was that theirs was a practical and contractual relationship, having reference to estates and progeny. It was not a relation of the heart and the inclination, and the situation of the lady made it impossible for her to give herself in free-will because it was expected that she give herself in obedience. That the possibility of love could exist only apart from and more or less in opposition to marriage has been, by and large, the traditional supposition of the European upper classes, which have placed most of their expectations of erotic pleasure outside of marriage.

It was surely one of the most interesting and important of cultural revisions when the middle classes, which had been quite specifically excluded from the pleasure and dignity of love (one cannot be both busy and a lover), began to appropriate the prestige of this mode of feeling and to change it in the process of adopting it. For they assimilated it to marriage itself, and required of married love that it have the high brilliance and significance of passion-love. Something of that expectation still persists—it is still the love-poetry and the love-music and the love-dramas of passion-love in its later forms that shape our notions of what the erotic experience can be in intensity, in variety, in grace.

But inevitably the sexual revolution of our time brought the relationship between marriage and passion-love to a virtual end. Perhaps all that the two now have in common is the belief that the lovers must freely choose each other and that their choice has the highest sanctions and must not be interfered with. Apart from this, every aspect of the new relationship is a denial of the old ideal of love. If one can rely on the evidence of fiction to discover the modern idea of the right relation between a man and a woman, it would probably begin with a sexual meeting, more or less tentative or experimental, and go on to sexual communion, after which marriage would take place. There would follow a period in which husband and wife would each make an effort to get rid of their *merely symbolic* feelings for the other *partner* in the marriage and to learn to see each other *without illusion* and as they are *in reality*. To do this is the sign of *maturity*. It enables husband and wife to *build a life together*. In the *mutuality* and *warmth* of their *together-*

ness their children are included. Toward each other, as toward their children, they show *tolerance* and *understanding*, which they find it easier to do if they have a *good sexual relationship*.

The condition toward which such a marriage aspires is *health* —a marriage is praised by being called a *healthy* marriage. This will suggest how far the modern ideal of love is from passion-love. The literal meaning of the word *passion* will indicate the distance. Nowadays we use the word chiefly to mean an intense feeling, forgetting the old distinction between a passion and an emotion, the former being an emotion before which we are helpless, which we have to *suffer,* in whose grip we are *passive*. The passion-lover was a sick man, a *patient*. It was the convention for him to say that he was sick and to make a show of his physical and mental derangement. And indeed by any modern standard of emotional health what he was expected to display in the way of obsessional conduct and masochism would make his condition deserve some sort of pretty grave name. His passion filled his whole mind to the exclusion of everything else; he submitted himself to his *mistress* as her *servant,* even her *slave,* he gloried in her *power* over him and expected that she would make him suffer, that she would be *cruel*.

Obviously I am dealing with a convention of literature, not describing the actual relationship between men and women. But it was a convention of a peculiar explicitness and force and it exerted an influence upon the management of the emotions down through the nineteenth century. At that time, it may be observed, the creative genius took over some of the characteristics of the lover: his obsessiveness, his masochism, his noble subservience to an ideal, and his antagonism to the social conventions, his propensity for making a scandal.

For scandal was of the essence of passion-love, which not only inverted the marital relationship of men and women but subverted marriage itself. It could also subvert a man's social responsibility, his honor. In either case, a scandal resulted, the extent of which measured the force of the love. Typically it led to disaster for the lovers, to death. For one aspect of the pathology of love was that it made of no account certain established judgments, denying the reality and the good of much in the world that is indeed real and good. In this respect lovers were conceived of much as we conceive of the artist—that is, as captivated by a reality and a good that are not of the ordinary world.

Now it may well be that all this is absurd, and really and truly a kind of pathology, and that we are much the better for being quite done with it, and that our contemporary love-ideal of a firm, tolerant, humorous, wry, happy marriage is a great advance from it. The world seems to be agreed that this is so—the evidence is to be found in a wide range of testimony from the most elementary fiction and the simplest handbook of marriage up to psychoanalysis and the works of D. H. Lawrence, for whom "love" was anathema. But the old ideal, as I have said, still has its charm for us—we still understand it in some degree; it still speaks to us of an intensity and grace of erotic emotion and behavior that we do not want to admit is entirely beyond our reach.

If a novelist wanted, for whatever strange reason, to write a novel about the old kind of love, how would he go about it? How would he find or contrive the elements that make love possible?

For example, if love requires scandal, what could the novelist count on to constitute a scandal? Surely not—as I have already suggested—adultery. The very word is archaic; we recognize the possibility of its use only in law or in the past. Marital infidelity is not thought of as necessarily destructive of marriage, and, indeed, the word *unfaithful*, which once had so terrible a charge of meaning, begins to sound quaint, seeming to be inappropriate to our modern code. A few years ago William Barrett asked, *à propos* the effect of *Othello* on a modern audience, whether anyone nowadays could really comprehend and be interested in the spectacle of Othello's jealousy. I think that both comprehension and interest are possible. There are more than enough of the old feelings still left—nothing is ever thrown out of the attic of the mind—to permit us to understand perfectly well what Othello feels. Here we must be aware of the difference between life and literature. It is of course not true that people do not feel sexual jealousy; it is still one of the most intense of emotions. But they find it ever harder to believe that they are justified in feeling it, that they do right to give this emotion any authority. A contemporary writer would not be able to interest us in a situation like Othello's because, even if he had proof in his own experience of the actuality of jealousy, he could not give intellectual credence, or expect his readers to give it, to an emotion which in Shakespeare was visceral, unquestionable, of absolute authority.

But the breaking of the taboo about the sexual unavailability of very young girls has for us something of the force that a wife's infidelity had for Shakespeare. H.H.'s relation with Lolita defies society as scandalously as did Tristan's relation with Iseult, or Vronsky's with Anna. It puts the lovers, as lovers in literature must be put, beyond the pale of society.

Then the novelist, if he is to maintain the right conditions for a story of passion-love, must see to it that his lovers do not approach the condition of marriage. That is, their behavior to each other must not be touched by practicality, their virtues must not be of a kind that acknowledges the claims of the world. As soon as mutuality comes in, and common interests, and cooperation, and tolerance, and a concern for each other's welfare or prestige in the world, the ethos of the family, of marriage, has asserted itself and they lose their status of lovers. Their behavior to each other must be precisely not what we call "mature"—they must see each other and the world with the imperious absolutism of children. So that a man in the grip of an obsessional lust and a girl of twelve make the ideal couple for a story about love written in our time. At least at the beginning of his love for Lolita there are no practical moral considerations, no practical personal considerations, that qualify H.H.'s behavior. As for Lolita, there is no possibility of her bringing the relation close to the condition of marriage because she cannot even imagine the female role in marriage. She remains perpetually the cruel mistress; even after her lover has won physical possession of her, she withholds the favor of her feeling, for she has none to give, by reason of her age, possibly by reason of her temperament.

Then the novelist must pay due attention to making the lover's obsession believable and not ridiculous. Nowadays we find it difficult to give credence to the idea that a man might feel that his reason and his very life depended on the response to him of a particular woman. Recently I read *Liber Amoris* with some graduate students and found that they had no understanding whatever of Hazlitt's obsessive commitment to Sarah Walker. They could see no reason why a man could not break the chains of a passion so unrewarding, so humiliating. I later regretted having been cross at their stupidity when I found myself doubting the verisimilitude of Proust's account of the relation of Swann to Odette. But our doubts are allayed if the obsession can be accounted for by the known fact of a sexual peculiarity, an avowed aberration. Pathology naturalizes the strange particularity of the lover's preference.

I may seem to have been talking about *Lolita* as if in writing it Mr. Nabokov had undertaken a job of emotional archaeology. This may not be quite fair to Mr. Nabokov's whole intention, but it does suggest how regressive a book *Lolita* is, how, although it strikes all the most approved modern postures and attitudes, it is concerned to restore a foredone mode of feeling. And in nothing is *Lolita* so archaic as in its way of imaging the beloved. We with our modern latitude in these matters are likely to be amused by the minor details of his mistress's person that caught the lover's fancy in the novels of the nineteenth century—the expressiveness of the eyes, a certain kind of glance, a foot, an ankle, a wrist, an ear, a ringlet; with our modern reader's knowledge of the size and shape of the heroine's breasts, thighs, belly, and buttocks, these seem trifling and beside the point. Yet the interest in the not immediately erotic details of the female person was not forced on the lover or the novelist by narrow conventions; rather, it was an aspect of the fetishism which seems to attend passion-love, a sort of synecdoche of desire, in which the part stands for the whole, and even the glove or the scarf of the beloved has an erotic value. This is the mode of H.H.'s adoration of Lolita, and against the background of his sexual greed, which he calls "ape-like," it comes over us as another reason for being shocked, that in recent fiction no lover has thought of his beloved with so much tenderness, that no woman has been so charmingly evoked, in such grace and delicacy, as Lolita; the description of her tennis game, in which even her racket has an erotic charm, is one of the few examples of rapture in modern writing.

It seems to me that it is impossible to miss the *parti pris* in Mr. Nabokov's archaeological undertaking, the impulse to mock and discredit all forms of progressive rationalism not only because they are stupid in themselves but because they have brought the madness of love to an end. But Mr. Nabokov is not partisan to the point of being dishonest about the true nature of love. It is H.H., that mixture of ferocity and jocularity, who reminds us that "Love seeketh only self to please. . . . And builds a Hell in Heaven's despite." The passages in which Humbert gives voice to this judgment are not as well done as one might wish; they stand in an awkward relation to the tone and device of the book. Yet perhaps for that very reason they are the more startling and impressive (if we do not read them in a mood which makes them seem to verge upon the maudlin).

And in the end H.H. succumbs, and happily, to the dialectic of the history of love. I have represented passion-love as being the antithesis of marriage and as coming to an end when the conditions characteristic of marriage impose themselves, by whatever means, upon the lovers. Yet it is always to marriage that passion-love aspires, unique marriage, ideal marriage, marriage available to no other pair, but marriage nonetheless, with all the cramping vows and habitualness of marriage. And it is just this that H.H. eventually desires. Mr. Nabokov is, among his other accomplishments, an eminent entomologist and I shall leave it to some really rigorous close-reader of fiction to tell us what an entomological novelist wants us to do with the fact that *nymph* is the name for the young of an insect without complete metamorphosis. Probably nothing. But he is also a scholar of languages and he knows that *nymph* is the Greek word for *bride*. He does not impart this information to us, yet he is at pains, as I have remarked, to put us in mind of the rapturous, tortured marriage of Poe and Virginia, and one of his last meditations on Lolita is of the constancy she evokes from him despite the ravages of time having destroyed the old incitements to lust:

. . . There she was with her ruined looks and her adult, rope-veined narrow hands and her goose-flesh white arms, and her shallow ears, and her unkempt armpits, there she was (my Lolita), hopelessly worn at seventeen, with that baby, dreaming already in her of becoming a big shot and retiring around 2020 A.D.—and I looked and looked at her, and knew as clearly as I know I am to die, that I loved her more than anything I had ever seen or imagined on earth, or hoped for anywhere else. She was only the faint violet whiff and dead leaf echo of the nymphet I had rolled myself upon with such cries in the past; an echo on the brink of a russet ravine, with a far wood under a white sky, and brown leaves choking the brook and one last cricket in the crisp weeds . . . but thank God it was not that echo alone that I worshipped. What I used to pamper among the tangled vines of my heart, *mon grand péché radieux,* had dwindled in its essence: sterile and selfish vice, all that I cancelled and cursed. You may jeer at me, and threaten to clear the court, but until I am gagged and half-throttled, I will shout my poor truth. I insist the world know how much I loved my Lolita, *this* Lolita, pale and polluted, and big with another's child, but still grey-eyed, still sooty-lashed, still auburn and almond. . . .

I am not sure just how I respond to the moral implication of this passage—I am not sure that with it, as with other passages in which H.H. speaks of the depth and wild solemnity of his love and re-morse, Mr. Nabokov has not laid an emotional trap for the reader, that perhaps H.H.'s last intensities ought not to be received with considerably more irony than at first they call for. I don't say this with the least certitude. It may be that Mr. Nabokov really wants us to believe with entire seriousness that we are witnessing the cul-mination of H.H.'s moral evolution. Perhaps he even wants us to believe that his ascent from "ape-like" lust to a love which chal-lenges the devils below and the angels up over the sea to ever dissever his soul from the soul of the lovely Annabel Lee constitutes the life-cycle of the erotic instinct. I can, I think, manage to take seriously a tragic Humbert, but I find myself easier with Humbert the anti-hero, with Humbert as cousin-german to Rameau's nephew.

I don't want to put my uneasiness with the tragic Humbert as an objection. Indeed, for me one of the attractions of *Lolita* is its ambiguity of tone—which is pretty well exemplified in the passage I have quoted—and its ambiguity of intention, its ability to arouse uneasiness, to throw the reader off balance, to require him to change his stance and shift his position and move on. *Lolita* gives us no chance to settle and sink roots. Perhaps it is the curious moral mobility it urges on us that accounts for its remarkable ability to represent certain aspects of American life.

Reflections on a Lost Cause: English Literature and American Education

[*Encounter*, September 1958[1]]

I

I MUST begin with an apology, especially to the members of the faculty who may be among my audience. For I mean to talk about a matter of the curriculum.

This is a subject which is not, I believe, intrinsically sordid. And I have no doubt that in that Platonic university to which, some day, all of us will be called, we will all go glad and singing to our ideal faculty meeting about the ideal curriculum. But here on earth things are different—here on earth the broaching of the subject of the college curriculum must inevitably bring to the faculty mind the image of multiplying committees and endless debate, of the willfulness of colleagues, of weary failures of communication, of special interests valiantly defended, of fatigued compromises that can give satisfaction to no person, to no department, to no principle.

But in addition to apology, I can offer some degree of reassurance. The matter of the curriculum that I mean to talk about is not likely to be a topic of either lively or dreary debate. It is, I think, a lost

[1] Delivered as a lecture at the University of the South (Sewanee, Tennessee) and originally published in the *Sewanee Review*, Summer, 1958. (D.T.)

cause. With each year the desperateness of its situation becomes more manifest.

Are you so very much surprised, are you so deeply shocked, when I say that I am referring to the study of English literature?

Perhaps you will meet my statement with incredulity. You will point to the enrollment in the English departments of our graduate schools, and you will point to the catalogues of our colleges, to the large offering (as it is called) that the English departments make to undergraduates, and you will say that never before has the study of literature been so lively as now.

I quite agree—never before has the study of literature been so lively as now. I cannot speak of all colleges and universities, but undoubtedly in the Eastern states there is an unprecedented interest in literature. It is my impression that this new, strong interest prevails in other sections of the country as well. And the interest which we find in the colleges and universities is reflected in the culture of the nation at large. The situation of literature, or of any of the arts, is never good enough, is never really good, and I do not want to seem to represent America as a nation in which literature is held in appropriate esteem, or as a nation of a peculiar fineness of taste. Yet if I look back over my own experience of our life in literature, I cannot help feeling that there is nowadays a responsiveness to literature, an easiness with it, which did not exist thirty years ago and which constitute an important change in our culture.

Yet at the same time it can be said that the study of English literature is in decline—I mean the study of the literature of England. When I was an undergraduate in the Twenties, the study of the literature of England was the very essence, or at least the very core, of an education in the arts. It was the most important element of what used to be called the cultural part of education: that was before the word "culture" came to be used chiefly in the anthropological and sociological sense, when Matthew Arnold's meaning of the word still prevailed.

Some of you will remember that the beginning of this part of education was likely to be the so-called survey course. We began with *Beowulf* and for two semesters we loped through the centuries until we came to a dead stop with Stevenson or Kipling or Thomas Hardy. (Yeats was then a minor poet.) The medieval lyric, the Tribe of Ben, the Metaphysical poets, the Cavalier poets; the mystery plays, the Tudor drama, the Elizabethan drama, the Jacobean drama, the Restoration drama; Sir Thomas Browne, Burton, Addison and Steele, the familiar essayists of the Romantic period, the prophets of the Victorian age; the Romantic poets and the Victorian poets—this was the matter of our study. The anthologies which contained this matter proliferated and their pages grew in size and beauty. They burst the bounds of a single volume and appeared with ponderous authority in two. After the survey course, the student with some appetite for culture would go on to take more advanced and specialized courses, usually in some particular period of English literature. Those to whom the appetite was lacking were presumed to have been given their chance for a well-rounded education by the survey of English literature. (Well-rounded was the word used in praise of education in those days, rather as if education were a dumpling.)

But nowadays the survey course in English literature, once universally believed to be a necessity in any curriculum, becomes increasingly rare and seems increasingly old-fashioned. In general the study of the literature of England is no longer what it once was, the very heart of the humanistic part of a college education. And in the high schools English texts are scarcely used at all—even Shakespeare barely holds a place.

There are, to be sure, exceptions among the colleges. And it is certainly true that in our graduate schools the courses in English literature are still at the center of literary study. Yet no one who has dealings with graduate students can fail to know that, however strong their commitment to literature may be, the status of English literature is lower with them than it was with the students of twenty-five years ago. Their relation to their subject is different. They are less at ease with it. Their devotion to it is less.

To me it seems that this condition of affairs has certain consequences that are not good, and before I conclude I shall say what these consequences are. But my purpose in doing this will not be an instrumental one. I shall speak of these bad consequences only in the interest of awareness-in-general and not with any idea of trying to reverse the trend. For one thing, I believe that there is much that is good in this trend and much that is necessary. If I speak of bad consequences at all, it is with the sense that in any cultural decision you have to take the bad with the good—you have to pay something for what you get. For another thing, the trend *cannot* be reversed. The forces that make it are at the moment too powerful.

Let me say what these forces are.

Certainly the political influences on our literary education should be mentioned first. Culture and politics are always intimately related and never more than today, when culture has been overtly politicalized, when UNESCO undertakes to serve the pride and contentment of all national cultures, when no embassy is without its cultural attaché, and when primacy in cultural matters is felt to be— or was felt to be until a few months ago—nearly as much a national advantage as primacy in science. The radical intellectuals of the Thirties used to say that ideas are weapons, and nowadays the most respectable government officials understand, or try to understand, that *belles lettres* are weapons.

If we talk politically, we must talk brutally: we must say that a chief reason for the decline of the study of the literature of England is the decline of England. For certainly the bulking power of England was one of the reasons for the study of English literature in America. I don't, of course, mean to imply anything like subservience in our old strong interest in English literature. It is inevitable and expectable that the culture of a powerful nation should have a special interest. It is entirely natural that, when it is considered as an entity, it should engage the mind more than the culture of a nation that is not a dominant and decisive force in the world. The reasons may be intrinsic or they may be extrinsic: the energy, the sense of destiny, of a fate in process of unfolding, may actually find expression in a national literature to make it more interesting, or they may merely associate themselves with the national literature, creating an aura of interest around it. However the case may be, what a challenging clangor there was for us years ago in that word *Elizabethan!* It engaged the imagination with ideas of courage and vigor—not to love Elizabethan literature was not to love life. That feeling no longer exists. In my own college Shakespeare holds his pre-eminence, but undergraduates no longer have their old enthusiasm for his contemporaries. We used to jib and jibe at the Victorians, but we learned to submit our minds to Carlyle and Ruskin and Matthew Arnold, feeling that their problems were our problems; to the undergraduates of today they are quite alien. For us the literature of the Restoration was interesting not only in itself and not only because it was frank or lewd, but also because it was the expression of England at an important moment in its history. We said *"the* Restoration" as naturally as if it had been a monarchy of our own that had been restored. But when, a year or two ago, a course in Restoration drama was offered by a gifted and admired professor in Columbia College, it was received by the undergraduates with a stony reserve—that is, they did not register for the course—which indicated that they had no idea of who or what was being restored to what or whom, let alone how much bawdy talk had passed in the transaction.

The image of England that is now likely to exist in the American mind is not powerful enough to support a lively imagination of the literary periods that to us were so vivid. It is no longer true, as it once was, that any educated man's intellectual equipment includes a knowledge of the history of England in some considerable detail. In law and politics the connection between England and America was thought to be very close—the development of English liberties, for example, was thought to be our concern, for to these liberties we traced our own. A course in English history was part of the high-school curriculum, as it no longer is. Now, even with my gifted students, I can with each year count less and less upon a knowledge of English events or an understanding of the English social system.

The literary imagination, as Hazlitt said, allies itself with power, and tends to withdraw its attachment when power declines. At the present time it is the history and literature of their own country which most engages the minds of Americans. Nothing is more remarkable in the intellectual history of the last decades than the development of American studies in our universities. One might say that the fact ought not to be remarkable at all, that nothing could be more natural and expectable than that the history and literature of one's own country should take precedence over the history and literature of any other nation, no matter how close and relevant its culture may be to one's own culture. But thirty years ago this could be said only in a hortatory way, as calling Americans to their patriotic intellectual duty. In 1930 the late Carl Van Doren gave up his Columbia University lectures on American literature since the Civil War; it was not until fourteen years later that the University thought it necessary to institute a new course on the same subject. That is to say, three decades ago we were all very conscious of America, conscious of ourselves as Americans, conscious of the implications of American power, yet our consciousness was not of a kind to produce the enormous concentration on American subjects which we now witness. That had to wait upon the new sense of American destiny which came with the decline of English power.

Only then, it seems, could we really begin to think of American literature as being a separate entity, with its own special qualities which existed of and by themselves, with its own history peculiar to itself, with its own kind of development. When Matthew Arnold visited this country in 1883 he expressed astonishment, and horror, at hearing reference made to "American literature." There could be, he said, *no such thing*—there was only English literature, whether written by Englishmen or by Americans. And he expressed the hope that never would we be so provincial, so parochial, so small-minded in our national feeling, as to countenance the idea of a specifically American literature. We smile at this now. All the world recognizes a particular quality in our literature which is American or nothing, and perhaps the English recognize it most of all, they see how different this quality is from the quality of their own literature. What this difference is in poetry has been very skillfully described by W. H. Auden and David Daiches in a pair of articles published last year in *The Anchor Review*. What the difference is in prose fiction has been discussed by Richard Chase in his brilliant *The American Novel and Its Tradition*. I don't mean to say that the uniqueness of American literature was not perceived and asserted until now, but it was not perceived and asserted so boldly, it was not made the informing idea of a critical and scholarly activity such as we now witness. One of the first writers to insist on this uniqueness in a significant and striking way, to say that the American mind was a new kind of mind and had done a new kind of thing, was D. H. Lawrence. His *Studies in Classic American Literature* is now universally admired and understood, but I can remember the time when it was admired and understood by a shy minority and when by most of its readers it was thought eccentric and absurd. The acceptance of its doctrine had to wait upon our present sense of American destiny, and upon the energy of self-assurance and self-examination that this permits and requires.

The new interest in American studies, I need scarcely say, has grown at the expense of the interest in English studies.

Then we can take note of a competitor with English studies of a very different kind. Even in England the study of English literature in schools and universities is a discipline of relatively recent growth. The Honours School in English was not established at Oxford until 1893. The first chair in English literature was not established at Cambridge until 1910. The usual explanation of the development of English studies was that something in the humanistic line was needed to take the place of classical studies, which were falling into disfavor. This is much too simple a summary of the facts of the case, but for our simple purpose it will serve. The spread of democratic education in England put Greek and Latin at a disadvantage and the literature of the vernacular at an advantage. In the English universities, and in the American universities too, the disciplinary nature of English studies was insisted on: in part for the sake of the academic prestige of the new study, the systematic, the philological, the *tough* aspects of the subject were emphasized. Yet at the same time, and especially in American collegiate education, there was the desire to make use of the study of literature not merely for intellectual but for spiritual ends. Half a century ago people did not talk so unashamedly as they do now about "the whole man," or about the social usefulness of cultivating sensitivity and sympathy by means of the arts. Certainly the deans of engineering and medical schools and sociologists and the heads of industrial corporations did not conceive, as they do now, that humanistic subjects have some good effect upon the general intelligence and the general moral tone of a person. But in that former time they still talked about "the education of a gentleman," even if as a thing of the past, and they believed that something had come to the gentleman from the study of the literature of Greece and Rome. There were no more gentlemen, there was no more Greek and Latin, but it was thought —or it was shyly hoped—that what had come to the gentleman from his old studies might perhaps be given to the democratic man in the process of his new kind of education. This was the chief rationale of the required course in English literature in American colleges.

Behind this idea there was surely Matthew Arnold's "The Study of Poetry" and all that Arnold had said about culture—Arnold's influence on American collegiate education cannot be overestimated. But if you are going to set intellectual and spiritual store by the influence of "the best that has been thought and said in the world," it eventually becomes a question whether you are exerting a very great influence by asking a student to consider the charm of Waller's "Go, lovely rose," or, not to prejudice the case, the perfection and power of Marvell's "To His Coy Mistress." That is to say, it became a question whether a great deal of the most delightful and cherished part of English literature had any bearing on intellectual and spiritual training as it can be conceived by makers of curriculums.

This question and the answer given to it, and similar questions and answers, led eventually to a most important event in our col-

legiate education. In 1937 Columbia College instituted the required
course for Freshmen that was called Humanities A. The rationale
of this course was very simple and quite right. It held that it was
absurd to suppose that a man was educated at all if he had not
had the experience of certain very great books in all literatures. This
view of education had been introduced to the College by John
Erskine just after the first World War and had been partly realized
in the General Honors course for selected juniors and seniors.
Erskine's idea had to make its way against formidable opposition,
but it did make its way and it eventually established itself in the
freshman Humanities course.

Now, when you come to make a list of the very great names in
literature from Homer to Goethe—Goethe was at first the outer
limit of the list, although now it is Dostoevsky—and you feel that, in
the nature of the case, you *must* include two Greek historians, two
Greek and several later philosophers, and four Greek dramatists,
there are only a very few English writers who can advance an
unquestionable claim to a place on the list. Shakespeare does, of
course. So does Milton. But Chaucer's claim comes to seem questionable. The list is not a wholly fixed canon, it changes a little
from year to year, and Chaucer was once included. But coming as
he did after St. Augustine and Dante, he was thought by the
teachers of the course to be rather local, even insular. Fielding was
for some years on the list—there was still some force to the opinion
which prevailed when I was in college that *Tom Jones* is one of the
very greatest of novels. But this opinion has lost what force it had
twenty years ago—at the moment it isn't a very lively opinion in
many people's minds that Fielding is a great novelist at all: in our
age of criticism I can think of but a single critical essay that has
been devoted to *Tom Jones*.[1] Indeed, nothing could indicate better
the tendency of feeling about English literature than the decline of
the reputation of Fielding, whose charm for many readers had
surely been that he was so very *English* an English writer. Even-

[1] I had in mind Ronald Crane's essay. But now comes William Empson with his
own essay on *Tom Jones* and with mention of Middleton Murry's.

tually *he* vanished from the list. Swift, with *Gulliver's Travels,* was on it from the first and he has held his place through thick and thin.

So there is our list of the most important writers of the West, and it includes of English writers only Shakespeare, Milton, and Swift. I was a member of the first instructorial staff of the Humanities course and I can recall my feelings about the smallness of the English representation: I was glad of it. I was delighted by the range and sweep of what was before me. It made all of English literature seem rather confined, rather local. If one *had* to teach freshmen, what a relief it was to discuss the great resounding ideas of the ages, the nature and origin of evil, the nature of fate, the relation of the individual to the state, the nature of sovereignty, the wonderful sin of *hubris,* without which, apparently, there would be no literature at all and no history. For it is inevitably ideas that are discussed in the Humanities A classroom, great, bold, primitive, basic ideas. And this makes, I believe, a very good subject matter for young men of eighteen—I thought then, and still think, that it makes the best subject matter.

The Humanities course of Columbia College has had, as you know, a very considerable influence. Using it as a model, but departing from it in small ways and in large ways, many colleges have devised courses which undertake to acquaint the student with the range of world literature. With that phrase, "world literature," which is now part of the argot of our collegiate education, there enters yet another rival of English literature. The Columbia College Humanities course was not conceived of as a course in world literature. Rather, it was a course in the literary and intellectual tradition of the West, what is called the Judaic-Hellenic-Christian tradition. But surely, a good many teachers asked, this is a questionable, an *artificial* limitation? Events, they said, are forcing upon us a larger view of culture than this, a global view of culture. Events are bringing into question the preponderating importance of the Judaic-Hellenic-Christian tradition. For a time, we of the West have dominated the world. But we know that we can no longer dominate it, ought no longer dominate it, should never have dominated it. We thought we could teach and lead others: we have sinned the sin of pride. Now we must listen to new voices too long unheard. There is the voice of China, there is the voice of India, and very likely a good many others when we come to look for them. If we listen to these voices, then the voices of the Judaic-Hellenic-Christian tradition become but one in a great chorus. And of course any one national, temporal part of that voice comes to seem small and thin indeed, let alone any personal part of it. Can we spend our students' time on Keats when all the Upanishads wait?

One more circumstance, the last I shall mention, helps to explain the decline of the study of English literature. This is the nature of *modern* literature, its very engaging and formidable nature.

First as to its engagingness. I have but to mention the names of the writers who have dominated the literary scene during the last quarter of a century to lead you to accept my statement, extreme as it is, that there has never been a literary constellation which has received so intense, so passionate, so concentrated, and so intellectual an attention. Yeats, Eliot, Joyce, Lawrence, Proust, Mann, Gide, Kafka, Faulkner: this is to select only those who make the most obvious display of power. Each one of them evokes from his admirers a passionate intensity which has in it an element of theological fervor. This is understandable and even appropriate—for it is impossible to comprehend these writers without perceiving that they all express a sense of crisis, a belief that man is at some turning point of his fate. No other constellation of writers that I can think of has ever so fully involved the moral life of their readers. The idea expressed in 1925 by Ortega y Gasset that modern literature was taking a direction away from the "human" is perfectly absurd: what earlier group of writers has ever been so extreme and so overt in its concern with the human situation or has had so human, so personal, a response?

Can we be surprised if students—especially those of the kind we like most, those with sensitivities tuned to the world around them, with the impulse to see some connection between their formal education and their spiritual fate—should find the study of these writers of special importance to them? Can we even be surprised if these students should be incredulous and a little impatient when we tell them that the poets of the English Romantic movement have much of the apocalyptic quality of the modern writers that so engage them, and that at least they are remarkably relevant to the modern writers? Or if these students, having time to take a course either in the modern writers or in the Romantic poets, but not in both, should choose the former?

So much for the engagingness of the modern writers which works to draw off our students' interest from the old tradition of English literature. A word now about what I have called their formidableness—their difficulty. This we all recognize, and the effect of our recognition has been to suggest to us the difficulty of all literature and to bring about the great proliferation of critical theory and practice in the interests of interpretation. At the present moment there is a reaction against the large critical movement of the last two decades, especially against that kind of criticism which assumes that every literary work presents a difficulty: in its extreme forms it is said to assume that every literary work is a *problem* or a *puzzle,* or, as T. S. Eliot has put it, a lemon to be squeezed until the juice of meaning runs. I have no wish to get involved in the issue of this reaction. I am aware that modern critical practice has sometimes gone to extravagant lengths in interpretation, yet I find that there really is a good deal of difficulty to be encountered in literature, often where it is least suspected, and it seems to me to be profitable and interesting to press harder upon a work of literature than my temperament naturally inclines me to. In short, I am concerned neither to attack nor to defend the modern criticism, but only to remark that it is a literary discipline which inevitably engages a considerable part of a student's or teacher's time and curiosity, and that it is in effect yet another competitor with English studies as they used to be understood.

And this is not to mention that the more or less newly developed concern with criticism and *method* has been institutionalized in elementary courses which undertake to teach the college student how to read and understand literature—and of course not English literature only, or chiefly, but any literature that might come his way, and of course, since a method is involved, with an emphasis upon the method and the single isolated work rather than upon the breadth and catholicity of reading which once was assumed to be the goal of the study of English literature.

II

I have given what I think are the chief reasons why the literature of England no longer holds its old pre-eminence in our minds and our curriculums, and why, as time goes on, it will probably be assigned an even smaller place. To take note of this phenomenon is to commemorate a significant moment in the history of the American imagination. It is the moment when Americans conceive of themselves to be living in a fully developed culture, which is to be described in its own positive terms, not merely by negative comparison with other cultures, which has its own history, its own laws of development, its own tone and quality, its own destiny.

But, as I said at the beginning, we lose something when English literature retires from its central place in our humanistic study. What is it that we lose?

It seems to me that it is exactly at the moment when we conceive American culture to be fully developed that we most need the awareness of what, on another occasion, I spoke of as *the other culture*. The occasion was an address on Sigmund Freud, and in trying to account for Freud's courage, for his personal integrity and his ability to withstand the disadvantages of his early circumstances in Vienna, I cited, among other things that helped him, a certain element of his education. It was an old-fashioned classical education and it enforced upon the boy, as I said, "the image of *the other culture,* that wonderful imagined culture of the ancient world which no one but schoolboys, schoolmasters, scholars, and poets believed in." And I went on to speak of Freud's mastery of English and of

English literature and his early love of England: he loved England for the same reason that generous spirits have loved Greece—that is, for moral reasons: England was for him the land that licensed the wonderful multiplicity of Shakespeare, the land of Milton (who was Freud's favorite English poet) and of Cromwell, the land that would not brook tyranny.

Now I do not think that in our modern situation the culture of Greece can have for us the high moral sanction it once had for Europe. Nor can the culture of England mean to a student in America in the twentieth century what it meant to Freud in Vienna in the nineteenth. Yet the lively and informed awareness of another culture is still of very great importance in education.

This importance is in the first instance intellectual. Nothing is of greater value in the training of the mind than the exercise of the ability to imagine life as it was lived in distant times and distant places. How it was done in *that other place,* how it was said in *that other time,* how it was felt *there* and *then*—this is not merely the historical imagination, it is one of the faculties of developed mind in general. When we undertake to judge the accelerated movement of graduate students away from English literature toward American literature, chiefly American literature of the late period, we may indeed be witnessing an admirable preoccupation with the native tradition and with present circumstances, but we may also be witnessing a failure of the imagination which is fatal to the student of literature. Having myself for some years given the graduate course at Columbia in the later period of American literature, I cannot help seeing a continuity between most students' interest in American literature and those theories of secondary education which insist that the student cannot possibly understand a work of literature that does not relate to his own experience, that to ask him to reach beyond that experience is to offer him an affront that cannot be tolerated in a democracy. If we consider it as it manifests itself in the secondary schools, the trend away from English literature—it is almost completed—is a form of anti-intellectualism. There is no doubt much to be charged against the old curriculum—in its conception and in its teaching there was probably a considerable infusion of mere gentility. And I suppose it has the political disadvantage, in a nation whose ethnic origins are so various, of seeming to suggest that one ethnic group, by reason of our special interest in the culture associated with it, is superior to all others. And of course the secondary school situation is far more complex and difficult than it used to be. Yet the New York high school I attended drew its students chiefly from the sons of immigrant families, and to these boys those genteel teachers of ours taught Burke's Speech on Conciliation, and Hazlitt, Lamb, De Quincey, and Macaulay, and *As You Like It, The Merchant of Venice, Macbeth, Hamlet, A Tale of Two Cities,* and a good deal more. They taught with authority—Mr. Walter Johnson's lessons in Milton's minor poems are the basis of everything I may now know about poetry—and they would have said that exactly *because* the texts were beyond the experience of the boys it was necessary for the boys to master them. I look back at the experience as being of the very essence of democracy.

At this point the proponents of the Humanities and of World Literature will ask whether their programs do not make occasion for just that exercise of the imagination beyond immediate experience that I have spoken of. Yes, in some degree they do. But, as I have said, the Humanities course deals chiefly with ideas; it cannot do otherwise. This is a good beginning but it can only be a beginning in the process of developing the historical or cultural imagination. As for the World Literature courses, in their implied rejection of the special value of the cultures that lie nearest to us and that are traditional with us, in their affirmation of the equal value of *all* cultures, there is an implied denial of the actuality, of the force and value, of *any* culture.

Then too we must be aware of the deficiencies of literary study that is carried on chiefly through translation. I should be the last person in the world to take a high or a pure position about reading in translation. And yet it is true that literary study, if it is to fulfill its implied promises, must sooner or later be the study of language. It is true even though we who teach have not yet devised ways of talking about language that will seem substantive and not trivial to students who are not, or not yet, adepts in literature. And if it is true, then the study of literature in translation only, or chiefly, must always be incomplete or inadequate. Since there is but little hope that the literature of any foreign language can be widely studied in America in its own language, then the literature of our own language must always have the first place in our course of literary study.

At this point the members of the American Civilization courses abate their antagonism to my discourse. The literature of our own language!—how right I have suddenly become. And how bright in their demonstration shine the broad new fields of American Studies!

They do indeed, they shine very bright. But I am by no means sure that they are the pastures to which our steps should tend in undergraduate education.

In some ways the study of American literature does indeed recommend itself as an educative subject as compared with the study of World Literature. For American literature can be studied systematically, as World Literature, being so very big, cannot. It offers us the opportunity to look at a whole literature seen as an entity, with its history, its development, the complete interrelation of its parts. Maybe you will say that this is not a virtue—I know, of course, that there is a strong body of opinion that stands against the systematic and historical study of literature, representing it as non-literary, a mere contrivance of the academy. But we must not let ourselves be hustled into a condemnation of the systematic and historical study of literature. It is not a mere modern academic invention. The arts have always been known systematically and, in so far as possible, historically—this is the way the painter knows painting, the musician music, the poet poetry.

But, you will ask, why not the systematic study of American literature? The answer can be quite simple: because American literature is not sufficiently extensive in its history. Thus, when we consider the study of language, we must see it as a clear disadvantage that American literature has no Chaucer. When we consider the study of prosody, it is a clear disadvantage that we have no Wyatt, that the study of American prosody begins with Walt Whitman. A deficiency appears again when we come to study the relation of literature to institutions and the general culture—America, alas, has no seventeenth century, and for the systematic study of literature a seventeenth century is indispensable. And when we come to the study of the relation of literature to ideas we are in a similar plight. Consider what may be done with the relation of English literature to that great general European event which we call the French Revolution—there is scarcely a work of literature for sixty and more years after it that cannot be shown to be in one way or another a response to this event. Compare this with the relation of our literature to the most dramatic event of our history, the Civil War, by which, as you will suppose, I mean not only the physical event but the ideas which the event expressed. It is a striking fact of our culture that the involvement of our literature with the Civil War is slight indeed.[2]

I believe that I have a very clear sense of how difficult and complex American literature is. And difficulty and complexity constitute an invitation to systematic study. But the difficulty and complexity of American literature are, I believe, of a special kind, and this specialness cannot be understood without reference to a more fully developed national literature. Another way of saying this is that the nature of American literature cannot be understood without reference to English literature.

I am sure that I need not be at pains to protest that nothing I have said is to be taken as in the least a derogation of the quality of American literature, or to imply that the great classics of American literature should not be studied in college. What I am saying is that American literature systematically considered is not the matter that

2 I ventured to say this before I had read the summary of the lecture "The Civil War and American Literature" which Daniel Aaron gave at the celebration of the centenary of Gettysburg College. Professor Aaron substantiates my statement in considerable detail. I, of course, don't mean—nor does Professor Aaron—that the Civil War has not presented itself to the American literary mind as a dramatic and picturesque event.

should be the central matter of instruction in literature in our colleges.

I began by saying that in raising the question of what we lose with the diminishing importance, perhaps the disappearance, of English studies I had no practical intention, and I hoped to imply that I had no polemical intention. I have been a *little* polemical but I really could not possibly presume to be practical. Our educational situation is much too thick to permit anyone to be easily prescriptive—there are just too many things of high importance that need to be learned for any educational plan to encompass them. I shall be quite content if in raising my question I have helped to make somewhat clearer the complex actualities of our general cultural situation at the present time.

Paradise Reached For

[A review of *Life Against Death* by Norman O.
Brown. *The Mid-Century*, Fall 1959]

I AM writing about a book that I haven't yet finished reading.
Which is not to say that I have not gone through Norman O.
Brown's *Life Against Death* from cover to cover—I have, and
my pencil has marked passages on virtually every page. Nor do I
mean that the book presents special difficulties to my comprehension.
The psychoanalytical concepts with which the author deals are not
exactly simple, but his prose is lucid even where it is intense, and
he has it in mind to address himself not to some arcane professional
group but to the educated lay reader. I am in no uncertainty about
what Mr. Brown is saying; his theory of the radical change that
must be brought about in human nature seems quite clear to me.
But I know that I shall not have done with the book until time
and habituation have brought me into a more intimate relation
than I yet have with the arguments that Mr. Brown makes for the
necessity, the possibility, and the desirability of the change he ad-
vocates.

This will suggest something of the importance I attach to *Life
Against Death*. I believe it to be one of the most interesting and
valuable works of our time.

In his Introduction, Mr. Brown speaks of his book as taking the
same direction as Herbert Marcuse's *Eros and Civilization* (1955).
The two books together make a contribution to moral—and, by
implication, political—thought which cannot be overestimated. Like

Professor Marcuse's book, which deserves to be far more widely known than it is, *Life Against Death* is based on Freud. Both books controvert Freud's pessimistic view of the possibility of human happiness, but they derive from Freud himself the intellectual sanction for the speculations which contradict his conclusions. In their effort to find an ultimate ground of hope, they look for the hidden implications and tendencies of Freud's system of ideas, and they reject, with impatience and contempt (deserved, I believe), the optimism of the neo-Freudians, which is achieved only at the cost of jettisoning the essentials of psychoanalysis. Neither book yields to the other in point of courage, but of the two Mr. Brown's is the more far-ranging and thoroughgoing, the more extreme, the more shocking. The author presses upon us its extremity and shockingness. He tells us that it demands of the reader, as it demanded of him, "a willing suspension of common sense." He speaks of it as an "eccentric" book, which does not try to be "right" but merely to "introduce some new possibilities and some new problems into the public consciousness." And he goes on: "Hence the style of the book: paradox is not diluted with the rhetoric of sober qualification. I have not hesitated to pursue new ideas to their ultimate 'mad' consequences, knowing that Freud too seemed mad."

It is of some interest to know that the author of this avowed extravagance is a professor of classics (at Wesleyan University). He tells us that in 1953 he felt "the need to re-appraise the nature and destiny of man," and in consequence "turned to a deep study of Freud." It is of course not a scholarly brag when Mr. Brown calls his study "deep"—it is a simple description of the way he read Freud: that is to say, not glancingly, with an eye to "insights," but as a whole, systematically, pressing hard upon such internal contradictions or inadequacies as appeared, and with the conviction that he was dealing with a system of ideas that, in its radicalism and paradox, was true. The result is that whatever else *Life Against Death* may be judged to do, it gives us the best interpretation of Freud that I know. It represents psychoanalysis not as it is blandly conceived by the progressive wing of the American middle class, but in all its bitter complexity, in all its uncompromising tragic force.

Mr. Brown's originality as a moralist lies in his intellectual method rather than in his intention. In his introduction he speaks of the signs which suggest that the direction of his thought "may not be quite as eccentric as it seemed when it was being thought out (1953–1956)." But the only "sign" to which he specifically refers is *Eros and Civilization,* "the first book, after Wilhelm Reich's ill-fated adventures, to reopen the possibility of the abolition of repression." The concept of repression as used here is specifically Freudian and it refers not merely to the mechanisms at work in the individual person to control or seemingly extirpate his instinctual drives, but also to the whole structure of culture, which is at once the instrument of repression and its fine fruit. And the culture that Mr. Brown has in mind is Western culture—when he gives his book the secondary title, "The Psychoanalytical Meaning of History," he refers to the history of the development of Western culture at the behest of repression, of our culture as it is Aristotelian and Cartesian, as it is intellectualized and highly moralized, as it is scientific and instrumental, as it sets more store by the aggressive than by the erotic impulses. But if we speak of directions of thought, it is surely true that one of the most traveled mental roads of our time is that which arrives at the rejection of the repressions which have created, and are perpetuated by, our Western culture. For more than half a century one of the chief characteristics of our culture has been its revolt against itself. For English-reading people the great ambiguous charter of that revolt—if we leave Blake out of account—is Conrad's *Heart of Darkness* (1898), which promulgated, although no doubt unconsciously, the Dionysian doctrine of Nietzsche's *Birth of Tragedy,* a work which is central to Mr. Brown's thought. This is not the place to trace the line of passionate discontent with the established Western morality which found its most notable expression in André Gide, or the impulse to return to a primitive mode which permits a recent writer on Joyce (Herbert Howarth in *The Irish Writers*) to explain the appeal of Molly

Bloom by her being so thoroughly in accord with the "twentieth century desire to de-mechanize, renew contact with the earth and the rhythms of nature." Whether it be under the influence of a dream of a primitive sexual immediacy as proposed by Reich, or of Zen, or Yoga, or Existentialism, or simply of unformulated impulse, a large and important part of our society is learning to reject the constraints—the repressions and sublimations—which were once taken for granted as being the immutable and inescapable essence of our culture.

The peculiar force of Mr. Brown's book does not lie, then, in his diagnosis of the disease or in the particular quality of his vision of health. The tyranny of the intellect, the hegemony of science, the excess of aggression, the insufficiency of erotic freedom—when he describes our culture in these terms he says nothing very new. Nor is his originality to be found in his representation of the values of immediate, various, and unrestrained feeling, or in his praise of the heuristic powers of art as against those of science. His force and his originality lie rather in the complexity he is willing to ascribe to the etiology of the human illness, and the inherent difficulty of cure that he implies even as he says that a cure must be found or we perish.

For he does not allow himself the dialectical comfort—which the neo-Freudians, among others, are so quick to take—of a villainous culture or society which imposes repression upon us, against, as it were, our naturally better nature. Mr. Brown follows Freud in his later rather than his earlier formulation of the theory of repression, and he understands that repression is not imposed from without but from within. The child generates his own repression of his infantile sexual impulses, and although the culture, as represented by the parents, does indeed enforce the repressive activities of the child's psyche, it does not initiate them. Which is to say that neurosis is the natural condition of man as we know him.

As we know him—but is it the natural condition of man as he must continue to be? What I have called Mr. Brown's courage lies in his acceptance of the grounds for the Freudian pessimism—

Freud's belief in the neurotic constitution of the human psyche as being ultimately a given condition of biology—and *then* challenging the pessimism. An example of the extent of his daring is the dead set he makes upon what he calls the "tyranny of genitality." He does not accept the idea, held universally by Freudian analysts, that a crucial test of a successful individual development is the absorption of all the impulses of infantile sexuality into mature genital sexuality. This means, negatively, that he is not in accord with all those (D. H. Lawrence, for example) who conceive of the opportunity for freedom of genital sexuality as a therapeutic condition for the individual and as the test of a culture. For Mr. Brown the repression of genital sexuality is not the real issue, which he finds to be the repression, or sublimation, of the "polymorphous-perverse" impulses of the infantile state, at the behest of, among other agencies, the "tyranny" of adult sexuality.

What, then, does Mr. Brown want? Is it what Baudelaire calls *"le vert paradis des amours enfantins. . . . L'innocent paradis, plein de plaisirs furtifs"*? Well, yes: something of the sort; at any rate, something green, Edenic, innocent, taking full account of the child that is father to the man. He asks for the resurrection of the body, for an end to sublimation, for human relationships that are based on "erotic exuberance" and not only on that but on the free expression of narcissism, on these rather than on aggression. Mr. Brown, unlike most psychoanalysts, accepts the validity of Freud's conception of the death-instinct, as I think he is right to do. Following upon this acceptance, his argument runs thus: If we bring about the resurrection of the body in its joy, we shall learn to accept death as a part of life, and thus cease to strengthen and pervert the death-instinct, which, in its strengthened and perverted form, manifests itself in the dominance over our minds of the category of time, in fear, in rigorousness, in aggression, in repression, in sterility.

Mr. Brown is nothing if not a devotee of eschatology, which he defines not as the knowledge of last things but as "the substance of things hoped for." He is nothing if not Utopian. At some other time I hope to write about his book at much greater length, and then—I am sure with no abatement of admiration—I shall put to it the questions that rise in my thoroughly anti-Utopian mind. For the present, however, I should like to agree with him on the intellectual value of Utopian thought—for the present I am content to read him as I read William Blake, with all practical objections suppressed before the pleasure of hearing a man who says that he will not cease from mental fight till he has built Jerusalem in England's green and pleasant land.

There are so many brilliant things in *Life Against Death* which I haven't had space to notice that I cannot hope to repair my omissions in a concluding sentence; but I should like to single out the chapters on Jonathan Swift (XIII: The Excremental Vision) and on Martin Luther (XIV: The Protestant Era) as remarkable examples of the psychoanalytical interpretation of literature.

The Assassination of
Leon Trotsky[1]

[A review of *The Mind of an Assassin* by Isaac
Don Levine. *The Mid-Century*, January 1960]

O N August 20th of the coming year a man named Ramón
Mercader will leave a jail in Mexico City, having served
a sentence of twenty years. His full name is Jaime Ramón
Mercader del Rio Hernandez. He does not admit to this name. To
his friends in Paris in the Thirties he was known as Jacques
Mornard, and on all occasions of interrogation he has insisted that
he is Jacques Mornard Vandendreschd, the son of a Belgian diplo-
mat. In Mexico he was known as Frank Jacson, the odd spelling
of the common name being an error of the Soviet agency that provided him with his false passport. It was as Frank Jacson that he
was introduced into the household of Leon Trotsky, whom he
murdered with a blow of a *piolet,* an ice-axe such as mountain-
climbers use.

Isaac Don Levine's *The Mind of an Assassin* is the account of the
life and character of this man. Mr. Levine adduces the evidence,
accumulated over twenty years, which leaves no doubt of Mercader's identity, and he summarizes the voluminous record of the
investigations of Mercader's psychic life which Mexican penal
psychologists made during his imprisonment. As a "personality"
Mercader is of no interest whatever. A Rorschach test reveals him

[1] Title supplied by the editor of this volume.

to be "an intelligent and sensitive person, who has withdrawn emotionally from intense relationships. There is an element of laziness and passivity about him, due to his detached attitude. He gives the external impression of a rather well-adjusted banal person who is ready to do the accepted thing at the risk of overcommitting himself. He is shown to be fearful and self-destructive in his inner self. But to conceal from the world that self . . ."—and so on. One has met hundreds of Mercader's kind and has endured, without being quite aware of one's suffering, the curious boredom they generate. But Mercader's lack of interest as a person is exactly what makes him of surpassing interest as a human fact. He is one of the Nothings that civilizations have no doubt always produced but which modern civilization produces in a striking mutation— that is, with consciousness and aspiration, with the awareness and dread of their Nothingness, with the desire to be Something. He became Something, he became an agent and instrument, a creature of the Communist ideology and ethos. He is entitled to wear the Order of Hero of the Soviet Union, although the regalia of the Order has not yet reached him; it is still in the possession of his mother.

His story being a truly modern one, we are asked to think of Mercader in his connection with his parents, especially his mother. Caridad Mercader was born in Cuba of an upper-class family. She was schooled at a French convent and in her adolescence seems to have experienced a brief and hysterical religious vocation. Her family settled in Barcelona and in that city, at the age of nineteen, she married, her husband being a conventional, dull man. At the age of thirty-three, having borne three children, Caridad's ennui was intense and she turned to artistic and intellectual pursuits and to the free society these implied. She was very spirited and sexually very attractive. She came to Communism by way of a love affair and is said to have had sexual relations with a great many of the Communist notables of France and to have been most amusing in her accounts of their erotic behavior. When the Civil War broke out in Barcelona, she displayed great personal courage and remarkable powers of leadership and became one of the leading personalities of the Loyalist forces. The great love of her life seems to have been for Leonid Eitingon, a leader of the Soviet undercover forces in France which concerned themselves with the liquidation of defectors. Caridad Mercader was her lover's colleague in this work and she is said to have been an effective operator—she is credited with having carried out some twenty "executions." It was this skillful apparatus that liquidated Leon Sedov, Trotsky's son, in 1938. The chief agent of this murder was a man whom Sedov thought of as his close and trusted friend, Mark Zborowski, who for some years lived and worked in this country as a respected ethnologist and who was indeed very gifted in his secondary profession. Zborowski had long been involved in the general campaign against the Trotskys and he was implicated in Trotsky's assassination, which was, however, chiefly in the charge of Eitingon; Caridad Mercader was his close coadjutor in the operation.

Between this fierce mother and her eldest son there was an unusually close physical resemblance. To the young man she was heroic and glamorous and lovable, and he modeled himself upon her—the curious deadness in his temperament, the toneless quality of his courage, the neutrality of his determination, the lack of joy of his narcissism suggest a deficiency in his conception of an actually masculine ideal. Ramón, like Caridad, undertook to live the political life in the Communist dispensation. In the Civil War he was a political commissar of the 27th Division on the Aragon front, holding the rank of lieutenant. After the war he was recruited to the Soviet underground in Paris. In 1938 he was assigned to the operation to liquidate Trotsky.

No one, I suppose, could be more unlike this assassin than his designated victim. It is, no doubt, all too easy to regard the character of Leon Trotsky in a sentimental way, led to do so by his defeat and exile, and by the drama and pathos of his death. He was surely a ruthless man, as the terrible Kronstadt episode shows, and had he remained in power in Russia, and grown in power, it might well have come to pass that he would have become a repellent figure, even though he would never have shown the vulgar brutality of Stalin. As things turned out, however, there can be no question of his charismatic charm. He was a man of great intellectual force and he was a confirmed "intellectual" in every good sense of that abused word. I can still remember, so many years later, what a relief it was, after all the Communist rubbish about literature, to come on his *Literature and Revolution,* with its high disdain for the run-of-the-mill "proletarian" critical theory, with its feeling for the necessary autonomy of literature. His mind was certainly not safe from the falsities of dialectical materialism and when he once ventured to engage in debate with an intellect both shrewder and more innocent than his own, he suffered entire defeat—one of the most brilliant pieces of argument I know is John Dewey's answer to Trotsky on the relation of moral ends to means. Yet the fact is that Trotsky was concerned with such questions and wished to debate them. He had the pride of the intellectual, to which was added the pride of the soldier, justifiably, for he had created the Soviet armies and had commanded them in their eventual victory. And his pride is, I think, his chief claim upon our sympathy. It manifested itself in his style of conduct which was large-minded and graced by the sense of *noblesse oblige,* in his grave dignity, in the high valuation which he put upon personal manners—nothing in Mr. Levine's book is so moving as the account of the courtesy Trotsky showed to the man who was to kill him and the remarks he made to his wife after the private interview he gave to Mercader to discuss a political essay the young man had written: he was disconcerted by the impoliteness of his visitor. "Yesterday he did not resemble a Frenchman at all. Suddenly he sat down on my desk and kept his hat on all the while."

It was Trotsky's magnanimity—one might almost say his courtesy —that doomed him. Trotsky lived in Mexico City in a state of siege, surrounded by armed guards, for he knew that he was under sentence of death, that Stalin would not rest until his great adversary was silenced: some day the attempt would be made, and one attempt or another must be successful. He know, too, that the assassin would enter his home as a friend, as a member of the household. Yet even after the bold night attack led by the famous Mexican artist Sequeiros, in which the house was entered, machine-gunned and bombed and his little grandson wounded, Trotsky refused to accept the rule which his guards proposed to him as necessary, that all his visitors be searched; he could not endure the idea that his friends be subjected to such treatment.

The acceptance of Mercader as a member of the household was not difficult. It was effected through the innocent agency of Sylvia Ageloff, "a 28-year-old social worker who lacked glamor," daughter of a respectable Brooklyn family, a member of the Trotskyist party. Just what was her relation to Trotsky and his wife is not made sufficiently clear by Mr. Levine. He says that she was the "confidante of Trotsky and his entourage" and rather vaguely describes her as having perhaps served as a "courier" for Trotsky. It would seem that a good many people were in and out of the house in relationships that were partly social, partly political, and likely to have a domestic tone, for Trotsky was nothing if not patriarchal, and Sylvia appears to have been regarded as a valued intimate of the family. During a visit which she made to Paris in 1938, the Soviet underground apparatus arranged that she should meet "Jacques Mornard," who promptly became her lover. He accompanied Sylvia when she returned to Mexico and her intimacy with the Trotskys; she introduced him as her husband and he was readily accepted as such. No one seems ever to have questioned his reliability; his relationship with Sylvia vouched for him. (One has the impression that the Trotskys were parentally glad that Sylvia had married at last and wanted to be nice to her husband.) In all probability it was Mercader who asked for and was granted admission when Sequeiros and his gang made their attempt. He had struck up a friendship with one of Trotsky's bodyguards, a feckless youth from New York, Sheldon Harte, who was on duty when the attack was made; Harte, who opened the door to the invaders, probably did so because he recognized a friend; and the probable reason for the abduction and murder of Harte was to prevent his disclosing Mercader's complicity in the attack.

It was not until four days after the shattering Sequeiros episode that Trotsky and his assassin actually met. This was on May 28, early in the morning, while Trotsky was working in his chicken yard. They shook hands, and Trotsky invited the guest to join the family at breakfast. Neither Trotsky nor his wife Natalia quite liked the man, but he was Sylvia's husband and they were polite to him. On August 17, Trotsky granted him a private interview to discuss an article he was planning. It was then that he conceived a distaste for his visitor on account of his bad manners, and spoke of this to Natalia. On August 20 Mercader called in the afternoon to go over his manuscript with Trotsky. He looked wretched and complained of his health. Trotsky said, "Your health is poor again. You look ill. . . . That is not good." Then Trotsky tore himself away from the feeding of his rabbits and they went into the study.

When once the blow had been struck, the assassin lost some of his nerve. Trotsky's scream—"very long, infinitely long and it still seems to me as if that scream were piercing my brain"—and his rush at his assailant, whose hand he bit fiercely, seem to have immobilized Mercader. His mother and Eitingon were waiting, in separate cars, to help him make good his escape, but he was easily taken by Trotsky's guards. When, after a period of great inner turbulence, he regained his composure, he addressed himself wholeheartedly to his next great concern, which was to maintain his pseudonymous identity, or at least to conceal his real identity, the disclosure of which would make it plain at whose behest he had committed his act.

For me the interest of Mr. Levine's admirable book was foregone, being assured by its subject. So it must be for anyone who ever responded in any degree to Trotsky as a contemporary mind and personality. But its interest goes far beyond Trotsky himself, extending to one of the most important facts in the world today, the Soviet ethic in its single-minded ruthlessness. Nothing is easier than to recognize its nature in an abstract way. But when it is seen abstractly, it is seen inadequately; it acquires the bland neutrality of an Historical Fact, and as such it comes to be "accepted"—known but not reckoned with. If it is to be seen truly—existentially, as we say nowadays—it must be seen in connection with the personalities it creates to serve it. And for the American reader I cannot imagine a better account of this connection than that which Mr. Levine's book provides.

An American Classic

[A review of *Let Us Now Praise Famous Men* by James Agee and Walker Evans. *The Mid-Century*, September 1960]

I T is only a single year less than two decades since James Agee and Walter Evans published *Let Us Now Praise Famous Men*. It is only a year less than a quarter-century since the two young men made their trip to Alabama to gather the material about American rural poverty upon which their remarkable book was based. Some of us will not want to believe that that much time has passed that quickly, but to the scared astonishment which we feel at yesterday morning turning out to be nothing less massive than The Past, one thing does come as relief—the clear knowledge that all the years have given us no reason to alter our opinion of the beautiful book. Houghton Mifflin has just brought it out in a new edition, with an exquisite memoir of Agee by Evans and with the number of Evans' photographs augmented from thirty-one to sixty-four, and to those who admired it when it was first published, it will be apparent that they are required to yield to envious time none of their admiration at all.

The thought is sustaining.

My own admiration for the book was expressed in the review which I wrote for *The Kenyon Review* (the Winter issue of 1942).[1] Here, in its entirety, is what I said:

I feel sure that this is a great book. To its greatness both its parts contribute equally, the thirty-one photographs by Walker Evans,

[1] This review was titled "Greatness with One Fault in It." (D.T.)

the long text by James Agee. The photographs are wholly successful; the text fails in an important way but it is nonetheless great.

The subject of the book is the lives of three Alabama tenant
families. But in dealing with this subject, the book creates another
which gives it its great moral importance. It poses this question:
How may we—"we" being the relatively fortunate middle class that
reads books and experiences emotions—how may we feel about the
—and the word itself proclaims the difficulty—underprivileged?

Evans and Agee made their trip to Alabama on assignment from
Fortune Magazine; they were to prepare an informative article on
tenant farming. *Fortune* turned down their finished job: the attitude
of clear, cool investigation had been manifestly impossible. You
cannot be cool about misery so intense, nor clear about people with
whom you have lived. What attitude, then, can serve? Christian
pity is not enough. Liberal concern and good will are hopeless; lack
of passion is here an insult. The "social consciousness" of the
Thirties which flowered in Hemingway and Steinbeck, in Odets
and Irwin Shaw, which millions found so right, proper and noble,
did indeed have a kind of passion, and perhaps it had the virtue of
being better than nothing. But how abstract and without fibre of
resistance and contradiction it was, how much too apt it was for
the drawing-room, how essentially it was a pity which wonderfully
served the needs of the pitier.

This, though he puts it far more fiercely, was the problem that
presented itself to Agee. He had lived with these Alabama people
and found that he loved them. How was he to write about them
without betraying them to the facile emotions?

For Evans, or at least for Evans with his camera, the problem
did not exist; or if it did exist, Evans and the camera solved it. It
has always seemed to me that Evans' work is of quite a different
order of things from the usual examples of "the art of the camera."
For it seems to me that photography, when it tries to do serious
things, is the most imprecise of all the arts. Whether because of inherent limitations or because of its uncertain place in the artistic
hierarchy, it promises seriousness and produces *Kitsch*. It is false in

its emphasis, shallow in its distortions, bathetical in its sentiments (see, for example, the much admired Mexican picture of Paul Strand) and sentimental in its simplicities, which are in the tiresome manner of the official-regional school of straight-edge painting led by Benton and Grant Wood. The superiority of Evans to all this could no doubt be described in technical and aesthetic terms, but what always immediately strikes me about his work is its perfect *taste,* taking that word in its largest possible sense to mean tact, delicacy, justness of feeling, complete awareness and perfect respect. It is a tremendously impressive moral quality.

Evans' pictures are photographic in the sense that people mean when they say "merely photographic," they are very direct, they even appear to be literal, and how the moral quality gets into them I do not exactly know; I suppose it is because Evans wants it to be there. Perhaps the most remarkable picture in this book (I think it is one of the finest objects of any art of our time) is the third, the picture of Mrs. Gudger. It shows a woman with a beautifully bony face, thinning black hair, sunken or perhaps bitten-in mouth and sun-narrowed eyes. The face is a single concentrated phrase of suffering; you are bound to have an immediate outgoing impulse toward it, but this is at once hemmed in, at once made careful and respectful, by what the camera does. It is significant that, like all the pictures in the book, this is a portrait; it was "sat for" and "posed" and not only does the pose tell more than could be told by unconsciousness of the camera but the sitter gains in dignity when allowed to defend herself against the lens. The gaze of the woman returning our gaze checks our pity; and it is further checked by the camera's observance of the strands of jetty hair, of the sharp horizontals of eyebrows, eyes and mouth which are repeated in the three parallel shadows of the clapboard wall behind, and by the camera's light emphasis on the early wrinkles and the puckered forehead, which are delicately repeated in the grain of the wood. In this picture, Mrs. Gudger, with all her misery and perhaps with her touch of pity for herself, simply refuses to be an object of your "social consciousness"; she refuses to be an object at all—everything in the picture proclaims her to be all subject. And this is true of all of Evans' pictures of the Gudger, Woods, and Ricketts families.

It is with the perfect taste of Evans' photographs that Agee must compete. He knows the peculiar trap of each attitude. He conceives art to be as hopeless a means of expression as journalism. "Above all else: in God's name don't think of it as Art. Every fury on earth has been absorbed in time as art, or as religion, or as authority in one form or another. The deadliest blow the enemy of the human soul can strike is to do fury honor. Swift, Blake, Beethoven, Christ, Joyce, Kafka, name me one who has not been thus castrated." And again: "If I could do it, I'd do no writing at all here. It would be photographs; the rest would be fragments of cloth, bits of cotton, lumps of earth, records of speech, pieces of wood and iron, phials of odors, plates of food and excrement. . . . A piece of the body torn out by the roots might be more to the point." He cannot use these people as "material" for Art and supply the intelligent reader with the proper social emotions. He himself is not sure how to order his own feelings about what he has seen. He must conceive his part of the book as a series of false starts and inadequate attempts—as an inevitable failure, for failure alone can express the inexpressibleness of his matter.

I began by saying that Agee's text fails in an important way; I of course did not mean this inevitable and intended failure, which is part of Agee's conscious method and attitude. And certainly I did not mean that Agee fails as a writer to execute what he undertakes. On the contrary, nine out of every ten pages are superb. Agee has a sensibility so precise, so unremitting, that it is sometimes appalling; and though nothing can be more tiresome than protracted sensibility, Agee's never wearies us: I think this is because it is brilliantly normal and because it is a moral rather than a physical sensibility. To be sure, his judgment fails him now and again and some of the introspective and meditative passages turn furiously purple. But against this we can set the scores of astounding scenes he has created: the Negro singers, the three people on the hopeless farm, the two young Negroes overtaken on the road, the departure of Emma; and with these many of the meditations, such as the one on the paradox of the beauty which he cannot help seeing in the poverty; and the precise descriptions of the method of work, of financial arrangements, of house-gear, of clothes (especially the disquisition on overalls), of the graveyard. The book is full of marvelous writing which gives a kind of hot pleasure that words can do so much.

The failure I referred to is certainly not literary; it is a failure of moral realism. It lies in Agee's inability to see these people as anything but good. Not that he falsifies what is apparent: for example he can note with perfect directness their hatred of Negroes; and not that he is ever pious or sentimental, like Steinbeck and Hemingway. But he writes of his people as if there were no human unregenerateness in them, no flicker of malice or meanness, no darkness or wildness of feeling, only a sure and simple virtue, the growth, we must suppose, of their hard, unlovely poverty. He shuts out, that is, what it is a part of the moral job to take in. What creates this falsification is guilt—the observer's guilt at his own relative freedom. Agee is perfectly conscious of this guilt and it is in order to take it into account that he gives us so many passages of autobiography and self-examination; he wants the reader to be aware of what is peculiar and distorting in the recording instrument, himself. But his device, intended in the interest of objectivity, does not succeed. For one thing, too much of our attention is taken with subtracting Agee from his record, even though we respect both the invitation to subtract and the personality we are asked to deduct. And then, despite Agee's clear consciousness of his guilt, he cannot control it. It overflows and carries away the truth that poverty and suffering are not in themselves virtue.

And yet, even when this failure has been noted, Agee's text still is, it seems to me, the most realistic and the most important moral effort of our American generation.

There is nothing here that I want to change except, in some passages, the mode of expression. I remember that I felt some embarrassment about using the word *great*. It is likely to be a suspect word when one uses it of one's contemporaries. It has the look of advertising about it, and perhaps I was encouraged to use it for advertising reasons, wanting to counteract the relative indifference with which the book was being received. Now I am glad that I did use it—it turns out to be the just and accurate word. With the passing years, Evans' photographs seem even nobler than they did at first, Agee's text strikes me as being even more finely passionate than I remember its being.

The objection I made in the penultimate paragraph I would still make, but I would make it now in a somewhat different way. I think I have pointed to what is indeed a fault in Agee's moral vision, but I should now want to speak of it not as a "failure" but as an example of what Gregory Bateson once called The Essential Error. Bateson was noting the fact that in the work of every literary critic who has ever influenced our thought and taste there could be found some systematic error, some persistently or obsessively skewed part of his perception, which was, Bateson said, ineluctably bound up with his power of seeing what truth he did see. So it was with Agee and his resistance to admitting that the bad mixed in with the good. This, I think, was not so much an inability to see the fact as the passionate will to deny it—I think it was in my last conversation with him that he spoke with disgust of Freud's conception of "ambivalence," the idea that love may, and usually does, coexist with hatred of the same person; it seemed to me then that his brilliant intensities of perception and his superb rhetoric required him to affirm, if not actually to believe, that the human soul could exist in a state of radical innocence which was untouched by any contrary.

But perhaps my later and gentler formulation does the book no service—maybe in treating it "understandingly," in not confronting it polemically, as it were, I am aiding the process by which a work is perverted from the terrible actuality it intended for itself into "art." I did not, of course, begin the process—by now the book is in a fair way to becoming an American classic. Shortly after its publication, it went to the remainder shops; it used to seem to me that outside of a very few people, mostly friends of Agee and Evans, the book was unheard of, and even that it was met with a kind of willed apathy: I think I never heard it praised in "intellectual" circles. But then it began to appear in those bargain lists which more or less special bookstores advertise in more or less special magazines. Then, not long after, if one wanted to buy a copy for a friend, it could be had only at a premium, for it acquired an underground reputation which grew yearly, and to this the new edition is the response. There is nothing, I fear, to be done to stop the book's being admired as a work of art and as a classic. And after all, this in itself is not harmful, being at least generous; and there will always be some young person turning up to recognize that these pictures and this text constitute not merely an aesthetic object but a moral act.

He will not find that the passage of nearly two decades has diminished the importance of that act. The particular situation that engaged Agee and Evans will not engage him, and there is even the likelihood that he will not quite know what a sharecropper is. But he will be under no illusion that *Let Us Now Praise Famous Men* deals merely with a particular situation. He will understand that it confronts with grace and courage the complexity and dangers of the peculiarly modern necessity to make ourselves aware of the misery of disadvantaged people and to declare ourselves in some way answerable for it.

Yeats as Critic

[A review of *Essays and Introductions* by William Butler Yeats. *The Mid-Century*, Summer 1961]

IN 1935 Yeats received proposals for what he speaks of in one of his letters as "an expensive American collected edition of my works." The plan seemed practicable enough to induce him to write a general introduction and also prefaces to the volumes which were to contain his plays and his critical essays, but in 1937 the project was given up. Some day it will have to be revived, although without the stipulation of expensiveness—how fine a thing it would be if American and British publishers were to collaborate in a series of editions of the modern masters which would have the completeness, and the handiness, and the handsomeness, and the scholarship of the *Pléiade* editions in France! In the meantime, however, it cannot be said that Yeats suffers from unavailability. What must amount to his complete works has been brought out over the last decade, although in a piecemeal fashion. In addition to the collected poems, we have volumes which comprise the plays, and the autobiographies, and the "mythologies." And now in a large and well-printed book, Macmillan has given us the collection of the criticism. It includes the essays written between 1896 and 1915, which made up the volumes called *Ideas of Good and Evil* and *The Cutting of an Agate,* and twelve later essays and introductions brought together for the first time.

No one, I suppose, will assert that Yeats's criticism has the place in the canon of his work that everyone assigns to Eliot's criticism in *his* canon. It is of course Eliot's poetry which makes the first claim on our attention, as it will make the first claim on the attention of posterity, but there can be no doubt that Eliot's critical work, although at the moment it has fallen off in prestige and influence, will always be regarded, quite apart from the poetry, as being of great importance in itself. It is certainly connected with the poetry in intimate ways, but it asserts its own autonomous life—when we read Eliot the critic, we are sufficiently aware that his judgments all go to support the practice of Eliot the poet, yet we do not doubt that the critic has addressed himself to literature for its own sake and to literary problems which are his not alone in his character of poet. The same cannot be said of Yeats as a critic. Whatever his subject may be, his essential reference is only to his own work as a poet. Indeed, it can be said of Yeats that he never saw himself as really a critic at all; he never had, what Eliot obviously does have, an "image" of himself in the critic's role, and took no pleasure in the critical act, not even when he wrote explicitly about himself. In a letter to Ethel Mannin in which he refers to the expensive American collected edition, he speaks of the irritation and distaste he has for the work on the introduction and prefaces—"I hate writing prose," he says. "The only kind of prose I write is a great trial."

But if we cannot say that Yeats's criticism stands in the great tradition, it is equally impossible to deny that it has its own high interest. This interest derives exactly from the circumstance that the scope of the essays is restricted by the writer's special concerns as a poet and from the fact that the writing of them went so much against the grain of his inclination. Yeats was a critic not by free intention but perforce, and he himself has accurately described the conditions that required him to undertake an activity he neither liked nor approved. In his essay on Rabindranath Tagore, written in 1912, he tells of putting the following question to a Bengali friend: "In your country is there much propagandistic writing, much criticism? We have to do so much, especially in my own country, that our minds cease to be creative, and yet we cannot help it. If our life was not a continual warfare, we would not have taste, we would not know what is good, we would not find hearers and readers. Four-fifths of our energy is spent in the quarrel with bad taste, whether in our own minds or in the minds of others."

Yeats's complaint against the imposed necessity of criticism serves to identify the one element of modern literature which, more than any other, defines its differences from all earlier literatures—the writer's intense consciousness of the circumstances in which he exists and carries on his work, his unremitting and troubled and bitter awareness of his culture.

At this date it need scarcely be said that the word "culture" in this context does not have the meaning which Matthew Arnold gave it—most of us have almost forgotten the old honorific sense of the word which denotes a body of great and good ideas and utterances, "the best that has been thought and said in the world"; we have become habituated to using the word in its neutral anthropological or sociological sense, which refers to some social entity in its thought and conduct, in its assumptions and ideals, in its manner and style. And although Arnold would have been startled and dismayed by his talismanic word being used in this way, he himself was deeply involved—no one more—in all the considerations that our meaning implies. Arnold's great subject, whether in poetry or criticism, was the public circumstances in which poetry comes into being, in which the private and spiritual life is lived. Hence his preoccupation with matters of social class, of which his characterization of the middle class, the Philistines, is best remembered. Hence, too, his elaborate play with ethnic qualities seen as determinants of culture: the moral intensity of Hebraism, the intellectual vivacity of Hellenism, the German vulgarity and coarseness, the French lucidity (and salaciousness), the Norman administrative talent, the Celtic impracticality, magic, and charm—qualities which, though ethnic, he did not conceive as fixed and immutable but as being susceptible of enhancement or diminution at the behest of reason.

Arnold was certainly not the first literary man to deal with his national culture as an object of the critical intelligence and with a view to changing and improving it. He would have said that he had learned this mode of thought from Goethe. Nor was Arnold unique in his time—we cannot mention a great Victorian writer who did not deal directly with the deficiencies of his culture, although not with the bitter desperateness, the sense of separateness, of "alienation" [we are tired enough of the word to suggest that I ought to put it between ironic quotation-marks, yet the word still refers to an actuality] of the great moderns. But Arnold, as I have observed elsewhere, has a special relevance to Yeats. Like Arnold, Yeats cherished the memory of that gypsified Oxford scholar of the seventeenth century of whom Glanvill had written, and, like Arnold, wrote of him as the embodiment of mental powers which modern civilization has destroyed and as the last possessor of all the ancient grace that has been lost; and there is opinion which holds that Arnold's lectures on Celtic literature were a chief impetus to the Celtic literary revival and the source of many of the most cherished beliefs and postures of that movement. And if, as we should, we make the connection between the cultural adversity of the nineteenth century and that of the twentieth, it is most appropriately done through Arnold because, more than that of any other Victorian, his adverse response to his culture is involved with the depths of his emotional life, with the essence of his temperament; his sadness over the culture and his fatigue with it seem to lead most directly to the disgust, contempt, and rage of Joyce, Eliot, and Yeats.

Of these three great masters of cultural adversity, Yeats was the most personal in his mode of expression. Once Joyce had fulfilled his intention of pointing to the "paralysis" of Irish life in *Dubliners,* he retired into his characteristic manner of detachment and unconcern. Eliot expressed his distastes by means of his ironic ventriloqualization of emotions. But Yeats from the first spoke out *in propria persona* to denounce Philistine culture, first the British variety, then the Irish, talking in his own voice about his own wishes, his own revulsions, his own personality that was hampered and his own career that was thwarted by stupidity and vulgarity. He denounced science and trade (except, of course, the kind of trade his own family engaged in!), complained of an insufficiency of horsemen, and manners, and heroic violence and recklessness, and beauty, and love, and grace, and peasant simplicity. His essays have but one intention—to support in the way of discourse and insistence the preferences that are asserted by his poems in the way of passion. Poems and essays are at one in affirming the necessity of restoring to Western man some earlier instinctual way of being and the mental powers and the joy that are assumed to go with it; the poems make the affirmation with all the intensity and complexity of Yeats's genius, the essays make it rather simply, with an essential modesty and an engaging awkwardness concealed behind a prose manner which is often affected, although inoffensively so; the essays serve not their ostensible subjects but the will of the poems. Here, taken pretty much at random, is the kind of thing Yeats does: "The more a poet rids his verses of heterogeneous knowledge and irrelevant analysis, and purifies his mind with elaborate art, the more does the little ritual of his verse resemble the great ritual of Nature, and become mysterious and inscrutable. He becomes, as all the great mystics have believed, a vessel of the creative power of God; and whether he be a great poet or a small poet, we can praise the poems, which but seem to be his, with the extremity of praise that we give this great ritual which is but copied from the same eternal model. There is poetry that is like the white light of noon, and poetry that has the heaviness of woods . . ." and so on. This was written in 1896, and although the prose becomes rather less purple with the years, Yeats never really works in criticism in any other way than this—near the end of his life we find him praising certain poems because they are the work of a "supreme culture" and yet "appear as much the growth of the common soil as the grass and rushes," or certain poets because they are "not separated individual men" but men who "spoke or tried to speak out of a people to a people." If criticism is presumed to be an exercise of the intellect of the writer and to direct itself to the intellect of the reader, this is not to be called criticism at all, it is propaganda (to use Yeats's own word) for a mode of poetry, for a kind of personality, for a way of life.

But to say this is by no means to denigrate what Yeats does when he writes about literature, it is only to describe the genre in which he works. We can go along with Mr. Eliot in all the strictures that he makes in his famous essay on Imperfect Critics and be as exigent as we please about what is and what is not criticism, but then, if we are honest and simple, we have to say that there are, apart from criticism, ways of writing about literature that give pleasure and illumination. One of these ways is that of Yeats's "propaganda," the great poet telling us what we ought to like because he likes it, what spiritual food we ought to eat because eating it has made him feel fit; and undertaking to communicate his prescription not by means of reason but simply by the authority of his belief. The tastes of genius communicated with the enthusiasm of genius cannot fail to interest and refresh us, and if they now and then seem strange and wrong, they so much the more serve to remind us, as perhaps the best criticism should, that in the response to literature there is no orthodoxy, there is no rightness.

A Comedy of Evil

[A review of *The Short Novels of Dostoevsky*.
The Mid-Century, November 1961]

IT cannot be literally true that, when Dostoevsky died, a million
citizens of St. Petersburg followed his coffin to the grave. But
the figure stays with me from some misremembered account of
Dostoevsky that I read in earliest youth, and it is one of the first
things that come to mind when I think of him. And if that million
must be a number far in excess of the fact, the actual extent of the
public mourning was nevertheless tremendous, and it has become a
part of the Dostoevsky legend. Constance Garnett, in her brief fore-
word to her translation of *The Brothers Karamazov,* refers to the
"vast multitudes" which made up the funeral procession. In Boris
Brasol's preface to his translation of *A Writer's Diary* we read that
"enormous crowds attended his funeral: men and women from all
walks of life—statesmen of high rank and downtrodden prostitutes;
illiterate peasants and distinguished men of letters; army officers and
learned scientists; credulous priests and incredulous students—they
were all there."

Why were they there? Of Dostoevsky's transcendent genius there
cannot be any question, and it seems quite natural that judges as
diverse as J. Dover Wilson and Sigmund Freud should rank it with,
or next to, Shakespeare's. But great as it is, it does not seem, on first
consideration, to be the kind of genius that was likely to have called
forth from "vast multitudes" what was obviously more than an
expression of admiration, what must be comprehended as an impulse

of love. Mr. Brasol, after the passage I have quoted, goes on to ask, "Whom did Russia bury with so great reverence? Was it only one of her famous men of letters?" And he answers, "Indeed not: in that coffin lay a noble and lofty *man*, a prudent teacher, an inspired prophet." A teacher certainly, although "prudent" does seem an odd word to characterize Dostoevsky in this role. A prophet indeed, and of the highest inspiration. But if we are to call him a "lofty and noble *man*," our categories of judgment must be complex indeed and far removed not only from convention but from tradition. Any sense of Dostoevsky's loftiness and nobility as a man can scarcely be drawn from his biography. This informs us of nothing—apart from artistic courage and dedication—which is lovable and of much that is alienating and even repulsive. The critic Nikolai Strakhov, the first biographer of Dostoevsky, wrote to Tolstoy: "In Switzerland, in my presence, he so harassed a waiter that the latter took offence and spoke out: 'But surely I am a man!' I remember how astonished I was that this had been said to the preacher of humanity." The episode does not, to be sure, characterize the whole of Dostoevsky's behavior, but it was by no means unique. As Strakhov goes on to say, "He was drawn to abominations and boasted of them."

But if we cannot see Dostoevsky as a "noble and lofty *man*" in his conduct, we surely can see him so in his work? His thoughts, says Mr. Brasol, "like mountain peaks, were always pointed toward heaven. . . ." He might bully waiters, but in his books "to the meekest he would offer his brotherly compassion—to all who labor and are heavy laden. He would come to them as an equal, laying before them the wisdom of his soul. . . . He would counsel the doubting and soothe the wounds of those afflicted with distress. And many a hope would thus be restored, many a soul resurrected by the grand visions and magic of his genius." This is all too loosely stated, yet no doubt it accurately describes the avowed intention of compassion which is one of the main elements of Dostoevsky's work. Yet even our discovery of the nobility of the man in the nature of his work must be made with reservations. D. H. Lawrence, for all the affinity that may be thought to exist between him and Dostoevsky, hated and feared Dostoevsky's novels for something ghastly and malicious that he perceived in them, exactly in their overt affirmations of loftiness and nobility, exactly in their compassion. Freud, despite his high admiration of Dostoevsky's dramatic power and of his profound psychological insight, which he rated as high as Nietzsche did, was repelled by the personality that the novels implied. In part he was responding to Dostoevsky's political ideas, to his reactionary authoritarian tendency (I believe that he nowhere takes notice of the mystical nationalism and the hysterical xenophobia). But what most repelled Freud was the quality of the love that plays so important a part in the great work, its dependence on the weakness and helplessness of the loved person, its strong charge of masochism and sadism, its asexuality, even its anti-sexuality, its lack of any impulse to pleasure. ("Note," Strakhov wrote to Tolstoy, "that for all his animal sensuality, he had no taste whatever, no feeling whatever, for the beauty and charm of women.")

A good many readers of the present time will go along with Freud in his ambivalence of admiration and revulsion. In my opinion, this division of feeling makes one of the most interesting and fruitful of literary experiences. But of course it was something more than a literary experience that brought the Russian crowds into the great funeral procession. Some of the statesmen and some of the soldiers and some of the priests, even some of the prostitutes, may have been there out of doctrinal solidarity with Dostoevsky's ideas. But we may suppose that the crowd itself—the *people*—walked in the cold out of a love grounded in gratitude. Those unlikely hierophants were grateful for a strange gift that Dostoevsky had made them—the truth of their fallen condition, which was based on Dostoevsky's pitiless confrontation of his own moral repulsiveness. I believe that it is still debated by his biographers whether or not Dostoevsky actually perpetrated the crime—the rape of a ten-year-old girl—which is the substance of Stavrogin's confession in *The*

Possessed, but there can be no doubt that he initiated the belief among his associates that this was an actual episode in his life. This will suggest what pains he was at to destroy, first in himself, then in others, the barrier between good and evil, doing so in the interest of a truth and a freedom which he understood to be as terrible as they were necessary. It is eighty years since Dostoevsky died, and in that time his appalling perceptions have been made into the common coin of modern literature. Any number of writers of the *avant garde,* from Henry Miller and Samuel Beckett down, have appropriated some part of his vision and have been understood and approved by *Mademoiselle, Harper's Bazaar,* and *Esquire.* But at the time when Dostoevsky wrote, before his *epigoni* were born, his subversion of traditional morality and religion was not a *chic* but a revelation, and the more because it affirmed as much as it subverted, because it made the spiritual life—we might almost say the personal life—what it had not been for a long time, an adventure.

And perhaps the element in his work that most accounts for its excitement—I am using the word literally, having in mind the quality that brought the multitudes into the streets—was his sacrifice in himself of all the usual grounds of personal pride and self-respect. It is plain that all the significantly dreadful persons and the shabby or shocking motives of Dostoevsky's fiction are derived from Dostoevsky's sense of himself. No one, I imagine, has ever thought that Tartuffe represented anything of Molière's personality, but nothing is easier than to believe that Foma Fomitch, the superb hypocrite of *The Friend of the Family,* has been drawn by his author from the author himself, from his consciousness of his rage, his aggressive humility, his appetite for spirituality and dominance. No less to be identified with his author is the avowedly repulsive narrator of the most famous of Dostoevsky's short novels, *Notes from Underground,* one of the most astonishing works ever written, indispensable for the understanding not only of Dostoevsky but, as being the essence of the existential vision, of all of modern literature. The freedom from the sanctions of morality and culture, from what he calls "the good and beautiful," which this person discovers in the avowal of his moral and physical debasement, is the ground of the liberation which Dostoevsky was understood to offer, the reason for the love that the great crowds gave him.

My reference to Molière echoes a comparison which Thomas Mann proposes but does not develop in his interesting introduction to the Dial Press's useful and attractive volume of six of Dostoevsky's short novels, and it may serve as the occasion for saying that Dostoevsky is one of the greatest of comic writers. To be sure, he carries comedy, as it were by its own logic, to the verge of its destruction; he makes kinetic the potential force of comedy, which is "positive" only because it holds in check its latent power to destroy, even to destroy itself. In Dostoevsky's great long novels the comic vision runs parallel with the tragic, but in the short novels comedy rules alone. The laughter is ultimate, absolute, and terrible. Like Zarathustra's, it declares the nothingness of human life—and by that declaration requires that the void be made into a cosmos.

Literary Pathology[1]

[Response to a paper on Joseph Conrad by Dr. Bernard Meyer. Read at the meeting of the American Psychoanalytic Association, December 7, 1962]

IF, from the point of view of the student of literature, I under-take to comment on Dr. Meyer's investigation into the path-ology of a literary personality, my first remark must express my admiration of the literary virtues which characterize Dr. Meyer's paper—the lucidity of its exposition and the elegant economy with which it conducts its demonstration.

As for the accuracy of the demonstration, it seems to me that it cannot be denied. Dr. Meyer selects his evidence tellingly, and he draws conclusions from it which are inescapable. For some years now, the scholars and critics who have been concerned with Conrad have recognized that the novelist's imagination was conditioned in decisive ways by a deep and powerful ambiguity in his feelings about women. To this idea Dr. Meyer's identification of Conrad's specific pathology lends added substance and a new specificity.

The student of literature, while accepting the truth of Dr. Meyer's demonstration of the part played by fetishism and sado-masochism in Conrad's psychic structure, might yet wish to complicate the conclusions by regarding them in the light of certain cultural con-siderations.

He might observe, for example, that hair as an object of fetishism is rather different from the other objects which commonly serve

1 Title supplied by the editor of this volume. An extended version of Dr. Meyer's paper appears in *The Journal of the American Psychoanalytic Association*, April 1964.

the fetishist's purposes. Hair, we may say, has a life of its own and holds a salient place in the imagination of the race and in its ritual. We recall the tress of hair which a Greek son placed on his father's tomb; or the Jewish injunction against trimming the man's side-locks, or the late Jewish practice of shaving the bride's head; or the custom of defiling the hair with ashes as a sign of mourning; or the scalp-lock of the Indian brave; or the cherished long hair of the Spartan soldiers, which they combed so carefully before their stand at Thermopylae. The fashion of wearing the hair was once, and to some extent still is, indicative of class position, religious belief, and political opinion—indeed, no part of the body is so available to the symbolic expression of cultural meanings and personal feelings.

Then, too, the force of the erotic significance of hair was in other periods much greater than now. When Milton speaks of the fem-inine seductiveness that threatens man's achievement, he sums it up in "the tangles of Naerea's hair." For Donne it is the symbol of life and love in the very dominion of death: "a bracelet of bright hair about the bone." A lock of hair was once a favorite intimate keepsake. When hair was worn long, for a woman to take down her done-up hair or to permit it to be taken down was a sign of sexual surrender.

Such thoughts do not subvert the truth of Dr. Meyer's conclu-sions about Conrad's preoccupation with hair. But they do some-what mitigate the clinical isolation in which Conrad stands in Dr. Meyer's paper. They tend to connect his particular fantasy with the general fantasy of the race.

And then the student of literature will recall that there was formerly a wider acceptance than now prevails of the idea that female sexual charm constitutes a power and therefore a threat. In the conventional language of love of the eighteenth century, an attractive woman is represented as a soldier in the battle of love— her eyes send forth "arrows" that are fatal, she "wounds," she "conquers," she "ravishes," she binds her lover-enemy in "'chains." In what is perhaps the greatest metaphor in all literature, the lover of *The Song of Songs* says of his beloved that, in her beauty, she is "terrible as an army with banners." Milton's Satan described Eve as "fair, divinely fair, fit love for gods, / Not terrible . . .," and then adds: *"though terror be in love / And beauty. . . ."* The word *mistress* has long lost its old significance, but it serves to remind us of the time when the institutionalized fantasies of love represented the male lover as the servant of his lady. In the conventions of the Courtly Love of the Middle Ages the poet-lover represented his beloved as powerful, and as cruel in her power; and often he addressed her not as "Lady" or "Mistress" but as "Lord" or "Master."

The elaborate fantasy of the imposing woman which haunted European upper-class culture had, we may observe, a new vitality at the time when Conrad wrote. There was at the end of the nineteenth century a very elaborate *mystique* of female power. A leading ideal of womanhood proposed a commanding presence, tallness, a great mass of hair crowning a head held high on shoulders held well back. And, although it may indeed be true that Conrad was influenced by reading Sacher-Masoch's *Venus in Furs,* we must recall that the essential matter of that famous novel was remarkably available to anyone who kept up with the literature of the period. The theme of the male's delight in physical pain inflicted by a beautiful woman was a subject of consuming interest to the *avant garde* writer in England and much more in France. It was Swinburne's obsessive theme; Aubrey Beardsley exploited it in his writings and drawings; it attracted Oscar Wilde. In France it is associated with the names of Mérimée, Eugène Sue, Gautier, Flaubert, Baudelaire, Huysmans, Mallarmé, Barbey d'Aurévilly, and many others. Professor Mario Praz has dealt with the subject in detail in his well-known book, *The Romantic Agony,* giving a full account of the preoccupation with the Fatal Woman, La Belle Dame Sans Merci, and of her attributes—her adored feet, her fierce hair, her often marmoreal body.

In the course of a generalization about the modes of erotic perversity in the literature of the nineteenth century, Professor Praz observes that at the beginning of the century the male was represented as tending to sadism, but at the end of the century to masochism. To which may be added the observation that in the literature of the more respectable emotions an analogous tendency is to be seen—men are represented with increasing frequency as passive, helpless, and defeated, and women as the more active and effectual of the two sexes, often to the point of malevolent domination over men.

The tendency of my remarks has been to suggest that Conrad's pathology is to be understood not only in its particularity, in what I have called its isolate clinical aspect, but also in its relation to a cultural situation of no small complexity.

And now I should like to raise the question of what bearing Dr. Meyer's paper has upon criticism—that is to say, upon the fullest possible response to Conrad's work in its artistic totality. I should say that it has rather more to contribute to critical understanding than psychoanalytical investigations of literary figures usually have. It does not derogate from the merit of Dr. Meyer's paper if I say that this is so partly because of the nature of the case. Conrad, all through his career, was a flawed writer, and at the end of his career he suffered a tragic decline in his creative power. It is very possible, it is, indeed, rather more than probable, that the flaws are to be ascribed to his neurotic constitution, and that the decline is to be ascribed to an acceleration of the neurotic process as Conrad aged and as he fell prey to illness and overwork. What is more, although it seems to me to be usually very difficult to link a highly gifted author's adverse literary traits to particular elements of his neurosis, in the instance of Conrad this connection may be made with relative ease. His love scenes are likely to be embarrassed or extravagant or false by reason of his sexual disposition. His heroes are less interesting than we expect them to be by reason of his own ambiguities.

Yet if the pathology is made to account for the flaws of Conrad's work and for its deterioration, what is to account for his positive achievement? In the context of Dr. Meyer's description of the pathology, the elements of the work figure only as clues to the pathology. The dangerous universe, the jungles of pullulation and decay, the self-defeating heroes, the monastic male societies, the sea like a sheet of steel, the sails like marble—we are led to understand these as the products of neurosis. And so they are. But they are also the elements that make up a great tragic vision. It is possible for a reader to resist and even resent this vision, as D. H. Lawrence did. Lawrence said of a volume of Conrad's stories that it made him "furious." ". . . The stories are *so* good," he said. "But why this giving in before you start . . . I can't forgive Conrad for being so sad and for giving in." It is not hard to understand Lawrence's feeling. And I, for one, share it. But yet—"The stories are *so* good"! Out of what does their goodness arise, out of what comes their power, which enchants the minds of some readers and makes others "furious" in resistance? Not merely, I would submit, out of that degree of health which allowed Conrad to transcend his neurosis and work at his chosen craft, not merely out of what measure of normality he had, but also out of the particular content of the neurosis itself, and the force of the neurosis, which, it may well be, led him into his failures and in the end broke him.

The neurosis of the creative artist may indeed stammer and lie and be silly. But it is the same neurosis that also speaks to the world with an overpowering cogency. For, alas, the imagination of the world is neurotic. Dr. Meyer says of Conrad's love stories that "with very few exceptions [they] are sado-masochistic romances culminating in the destruction or death of the hero." But what love story that the world remembers cannot be thus described? The traditional heroes may be rather more sexually positive than Conrad's, but no less than Conrad's heroes can it be said of Oedipus or Anthony or Tristram or Romeo or Othello that they have willed their own destruction. The neurotic world has insisted that a great love-story must end in the destruction or death of the hero, usually of the heroine too.

For some reason of its neurosis, the world has assigned the highest place in the canon of art to that sado-masochistic genre called tragedy. The world would seem to have an insatiable appetite for the products of neurosis. Civilization may be conceived to be in large part the accretion of the efforts to satisfy that unholy greed. I would suggest that until psychoanalysis reconciles itself to the ineluctable fact of this strange appetite of ours, its investigations will be only peripheral to art and to the understanding of civilization. It may enlighten us about men but not about artists, and not about culture. All that psychoanalysis tells us about Darwin's extreme pathology still does not explain that mind that gave us *The Origin of Species,* although psychoanalysis might possibly have much more to offer in the way of explanation if it did not regard Darwin's neurosis with a pejorative eye. In the same way, all that psychoanalysis tells us about Conrad's pathology does not explain Conrad's creative force. It does not tell us why, say, such a work as Conrad's *Heart of Darkness,* one of the classic works of our time, stands at the very center of the modern literary imagination—it does not say how neurosis put it there. Yet psychoanalysis might do just that, for if Conrad, out of his pathology, fantasied a world of dense, hard, perdurable, virtually indestructible objects—women like statues, a sea like a sheet of steel, sails like marble—surely the densest, hardest, most perdurable, most nearly indestructible of all the objects his imagination conjured up was his own art: *this* was the ultimate object of his fetishism, just as the act of creating it, always for him so painful, was another manifestation of his neurotic character, his obsessive sado-masochistic love.

As, over the years, I have thought about the psychoanalytical study of literature, I have increasingly come to feel that there are two most salient unsatisfactory aspects of the enterprise—the reluctance of psychoanalysis (it seems to grow rather than lessen) to deal with artistic success as being as much implicated in neurosis as is artistic failure, and the limitation of the psychoanalytical purview to the individual artist, without reference to the culture in which he performs. I am most grateful to Dr. Meyer for affording me so pleasant and stimulating an opportunity for making a first general statement on this most interesting subject for investigation.

A Valedictory[1]

[An address by the "valedictorian" of the
recipients of honorary degrees at Northwestern
University, 1964]

THE valedictory address, as it has developed in American
colleges and universities over the years, has become a very
strict form, a literary *genre* which permits very little devia-
tion. We all know what its procedure is. The chosen graduate begins with a conspectus of the world into which he and his classmates
are now about to enter. His view of the world is not calculated to
inspire cheer, it is usually pretty grim. He speaks of the disorder and
violence that prevail in the world, perhaps even close to home. He
speaks of the moral and intellectual inadequacy of society, of the
dominance of personal self-interest, of indifference to the welfare of
others and to all ideal considerations. This constitutes the first movement of the valedictory form.

In the second movement the speaker turns his attention to the
graduating class in whose name he is saying farewell to their college. He remarks on the sheltered life which the members of the
class have been privileged to enjoy for four years. He speaks of the
intellectual and spiritual ideals which have been instilled into them
and goes on to observe how these will be denied and assailed by
that harsh world which is now to be the scene of their new en-
deavors. And then, in a concluding movement, the speaker urges
his fellow graduates to hold fast to the virtues of the educated man

[1] Although "A Valedictory" was first printed in the *Tri-Quarterly Review*, Fall
1964, the text here is reprinted from *Encounter*, March 1965. (D.T.)

and to try to exercise them in the hostile world which, in the degree that it opposes them, has need of them.

In short, the defining characteristic of the valedictory address is its statement of the opposition between the university on the one hand and the world on the other.

How well we know this opposition! For the academic person it may constitute a chief element of his sense of himself and of his position in society. It is charged with a most moving pathos from which the academic man may derive justification and courage. Surely no academic has ever failed to take heart from Matthew Arnold's famous apostrophe to his own university, of which the opposition is of the essence.

"Adorable dreamer," says Arnold to Oxford—"adorable dreamer, whose heart has been so romantic! who has given thyself so prodigally, given thyself to sides and to heroes not mine, only never to the Philistine! home of lost causes, and forsaken beliefs, and unpopular names, and impossible loyalties! what example could ever so inspire us to keep down the Philistine in ourselves, what teacher could ever so save us from that bondage to which we are all prone . . . the bondage of"—and here Arnold quotes Goethe— "'was uns alle bändigt, DAS GEMEINE' ": what binds us all, the narrow, the mundane, the merely practical.

This was, in point of fact, Arnold's actual valedictory to Oxford when he had concluded his term as Professor of Poetry at the university, and it contains the whole *mystique* of the valedictory: it gives ultimate expression to the idea of the opposition between the purity and gentle nobility of the university and the crassness of the world.

And what is a designated valedictorian to do if he finds that he cannot accept this established valedictory *mystique*? I am in just that situation. For some years now, it has seemed to me that the opposition between the university and the world, or at least half the world, is diminishing at a very rapid rate. Gone are the days when H. L. Mencken could laugh a book out of court by referring to its author as Professor, or Dr., or, worst of all, *Herr Professor Dr.*

Gone are the days when middle-class fathers groaned and middle-class mothers wept when their sons announced their intention of making a career in the university—scholarship and teaching now appear to the parental mind as amounting to a profession like another, and throughout the land we hear the low purr of satisfaction that accompanies reference to "my son, the one who's abroad on a Fulbright," "my son, the one who's working on genes."

Perhaps there is no more striking fact in American social life today than the rapid upward social mobility of our academic personnel, the upward movement of the university itself in national esteem. If ever the university was the object of condescension as the place where abstraction consorted most happily with incompetence, it is now, perhaps more than any other American institution, an object of admiring interest and even of desire, as suggesting the possibility of a life of reason and order. I have the sense that the authority the university has over people's minds grows constantly. No less constant is the increase of the university's scope—it seems to be a chief characteristic of our American culture that virtually any aspect of human life can be thought of as an object of study, and that eventually the intellectual discipline that develops around it seeks to find shelter in the university. Nothing is too mundane, nothing is too instinctual, nothing is too spiritual for the university to deal with.

What is a valedictorian to do? How is he to evoke the appropriate valedictory pathos of the opposition that the world shows to the university when so much of the world is trying to crowd itself into the university? And he is the more debarred from the valedictory *mystique* and pathos if his own impression of the state of affairs is supplemented by a reading of Clark Kerr's recent book, *The Uses of the University*. Dr. Kerr is president of the University of California and thus speaks with no small authority about university affairs. He tells us that we are witnessing a *rapprochement* of ever-increasing intimacy between the university and the world.

But this puts it all too mildly. How far things have gone in this new direction is strikingly suggested by Dr. Kerr's statement—it is the statement not only of a university president but of a distinguished economist—that the university has become one of the decisive economic facts of our society. Dr. Kerr speaks of the university as being at the center of what he calls "the knowledge industry," and he is not using a mere figure of speech when he makes that phrase. He does not mean that the university's activity and organization may be thought of as in some ways analogous to the activity and organization of a manufacturing or a processing industry. Nor does he mean that the knowledge that universities develop is a commodity which businessmen are eager to possess. He means that the existence of our universities bears a relation to the national economy that is materially comparable to those enterprises whose achievements are noted in the Dow-Jones averages. He tells us that "the production, distribution, and consumption of 'knowledge' in all forms is said to account for 29 per cent of gross national product . . . ; and knowledge production is growing at about twice the rate of the rest of the economy." And he goes on:

What the railroads did for the second half of the last century and the automobile for the first half of this century may be done for the second half of this century by the knowledge industry: that is, to serve as the focal point of national growth. And the university is at the center of the knowledge process.

Adorable dreamer!—is it this that you were dreaming about all these years: that some day you would "serve as the focal point for national growth"? That so much power could come into your hands?—for economic strength implies political power, and the end of your new economic strength is not yet in sight. Consider Dr. Kerr's plans for the new campus at La Jolla, where a new college to accommodate 2,500 students is to be organized and built every two years for the next twenty years: project these plans sufficiently far into the future and it becomes plain that the Governorship of California will be a mere honorary office, all real authority lying with the President of the University. Push the project yet a little further and we envisage the day when the President of the United States will call his cabinet together and will meet with the

Dean of State, the Dean of Defense, the Dean of the Interior, when the Federal office commanding the greatest patronage will not be that of Postmaster-General but that of Director of Admissions.

It is a splendid vision. We have always said that knowledge is power, and maybe this is going to turn out to be true. The idea of Philosopher-Kings has always haunted the academic mind and perhaps, on Dr. Kerr's showing, we are now on the point of ushering in their reign. And is it not characteristic of an American dream that Dr. Kerr, conceiving a city of the mind, should be so much more catholic, tolerant, and inclusive than Plato?—Dr. Kerr tells us that the fully developed university of the future, which he calls Ideopolis, so far from excluding the poets, as Plato did from his Republic, must find an honored place for all the creative arts. Dr. Kerr speaks of the creative arts as being "hitherto the ugly ducklings or Cinderellas of the academic world," but he is confident that this is a condition which is now to be changed.

America [Dr. Kerr says] is bursting with creativity in painting, music, literature, the theater, with a vigor equaled in few parts of the world today. Italy, France, Spain, Germany, Russia, England, the Low Countries have had great periods of cultural flowering. America is having one now. . . . The universities need to find ways . . . to accommodate pure creative effort if they are also to have places on stage as well as in the wings and in the audience in the great drama of cultural growth now playing on the American stage.

Let us not stop to question Dr. Kerr's belief that the university *should* be on-stage "in the great drama of cultural growth"—let us only investigate what the university must do to "accommodate pure creative effort" in the arts, giving our fullest attention to literature. Let us appoint a Committee for the purpose, and endow it with very considerable powers, of which one is that of choosing its personnel from among the illustrious dead if it wishes to do so, of which another is that of considering the candidate at any point in his career it elects.

And let us suppose the Committee to be a Committee of the faculty of Northwestern University—then, without question, because

of the superb biography by their colleague, Professor Richard Ell-
man, the members will think first of James Joyce as an especially
impressive example of pure creative effort. The Committee considers Mr. Joyce at that moment in his career when he has as yet
published only *Dubliners* and *A Portrait of the Artist as a Young
Man,* but is on the point of bringing out *Ulysses.* The members are
reassured by Mr. Joyce's academic attainments—he commands several romance languages, has a working knowledge of the Scandinavian tongues, and a strong interest in linguistics; he is adept in
Scholastic philosophy, gives signs of being a powerful theorist of
aesthetics. The Committee doesn't want to interfere with his writing,
but it can't help thinking that, in addition to carrying on his pure
creative effort, Mr. Joyce might well turn out to be useful in inter-
disciplinary seminars.

But there are certain personal circumstances which raise questions.
One circumstance is that Mr. Joyce is not married to Mrs. Joyce.
Maybe in spirit but not in church and not in law. Then there is
the probability that Mrs. Joyce will not be happy in an academic
community—she is a lady (but not actually a *lady*) of very simple
education; so far from being of use to her husband in his work, like
a proper academic wife, she never reads what he writes. Mr. Joyce
makes inordinate demands on everyone around him, is never grateful for what people do for him, believes that he is the object of
treachery, even of conspiracy. He drinks too much. It is an aspect
of his pure creative effort that he portrays actual people, including
his literary colleagues, usually satirically, and using their actual
names. The chances are that he will make no exception of his academic colleagues. Is this good for faculty morale? The new book he
is writing, the one that is to be called *Ulysses,* is said to be a work
of genius. But it is full of indecent words and scatological and
sexual details. It is going to be prosecuted, condemned, burned.
Early readers, even very intelligent ones, will find it harsh and cruel.
To be sure, with the passing decades, nobody will be troubled by its
outspokenness, and the judgment of harshness and cruelty will yield
to the opinion that this is a sweet, kind, tender book, almost to the

point of sentimentality. But does the university want to accommodate the decades of scandal it will cause?

With great reluctance the Committee decides against Mr. Joyce and turns its attention to another great creative personality. This one is also salient in Northwestern consciousness—it is Professor Erich Heller's "ironic German," Thomas Mann. He, too, is not only creative but learned—he is encyclopaedic in science, psychology, history, Egyptology, musicology. He is probably the world's leading authority on the work and personality of Thomas Mann—nothing would please him more than to give a course of lectures or a seminar on the development of this genius. His aptness for the academic life is suggested by his fondness for being known as *Dr.* Mann. It is pleasing to note that there can be no doubt that Dr. Mann is married to Frau Dr. Mann. No lives could be more orderly than theirs. In short, everything makes it clear that Dr. Mann should be recommended for appointment. The Committee moves fast, the Deans move fast, the President moves fast, the Trustees move fast—alas, to no avail: Harvard has got to him first. What is more, the University of California is after Dr. Mann, and is likely to snatch him from Harvard itself, for California plans to create a Mann-Goethe Institute which will be an exact replica of Weimar in 1775.

Disappointed but hopeful, the Committee turns to André Gide, an eventual Nobel Prize Winner. There can be no doubt about it: Monsieur Gide is married to Madame Gide. And yet—alas! . . . It is not that the Committee wishes to exclude sexual deviants from academic life; they have been there before. But Monsieur Gide insists on making a point of it, he defends it, he urges it. What is more, he represents the family as a malevolent institution. Who would deny his right to take these positions, yet should they be taken with the university as the forum? The parents of our students cannot be wholly left out of account.

But all these adverse considerations are in a sense irrelevant. For it turns out that Monsieur Gide would not accept the appointment even if it were offered him. For he conceives it to be of the essence of his existence as a writer that he startle and shock and dismay his readers. He cannot help entertaining the idea that the university is an institution, that it is by nature conservative, although not necessarily in any bad sense of that word, and respectable, in whatever sense may be attached to *that* word, and that if his writings were to issue from the university, they would seem certified as virtuous, they would lose much—perhaps all—of their shocking force.

If not Gide, then certainly not Genet. Anyway, with his prison record he would have difficulty with the immigration authorities.

What of Jean-Paul Sartre, not only eminent as a creative but as a speculative mind? We are large-minded enough to overlook his sometimes rather odd political positions and also *his* antagonism to respectable life. But Monsieur Sartre does not want to come to us. He likes to do his writing at a table in a café. Very well, this is one of the ways the university can accommodate creative effort—we will have a café; we need one anyway; we will engage Philip Johnson or Mies van der Rohe to build one as an annex to the Student Union. Monsieur Sartre is touched, but still says no thank you. It isn't only the café, it is all of Paris: all that noise, all that distraction, all those political quarrels—how is a man to write without them?

William Butler Yeats, when approached, returns something of the same answer. Ireland is wearing him out, tries his temper, frays his nerves. The Irish nation disgusts and infuriates him. How can he leave it? Not to mention the great houses, and the beautiful great ladies, and unforgivable England, and the language. How can the university possibly accommodate *these* necessities of Mr. Yeats's creative efforts? Rather to the relief of the Department of History, which was apprehensive that Mr. Yeats might wish to give a course on his theory of history as set forth in *A Vision,* a work which had been dictated to his wife by certain spirits whose academic background is quite vague, Mr. Yeats declines the offer.

The Committee thinks that perhaps its century is wrong. It tries the nineteenth. Dostoevsky? A genius, but his political views are not easily accommodated by a liberal university. A genius, but an utterly impossible person. Count Leo Tolstoy? Without doubt he is married to the Countess, but he is just on the point of his religious conversion and there is trouble in the offing. Charles Dickens? Doesn't want to leave London and young Ellen Ternan.

Perhaps, then, the art is wrong?—Cézanne stares when the Committee approaches him. Why, in the name of everything rational, should he want to leave these old hot southern rocks? As for apples, tablecloths, pitchers, he can find plenty here at home—what need for a university? What would he do there that he does not do here?— he paints and he paints and he paints: what else *is* there to do? Beethoven (a most deficient and maladjusted person—another *impossible* person) replies with a titanic stare, growl, and shrug. It occurs to both of them to ask, in a moment of terrifying geniality, what the Committee means by its talk of *pure creative effort*. "Pure, pure; creative, creative," they say, "what *blague,* what *Quatsch* is this?—we are not making pure creative efforts: we are telling you God's truth." Sometimes, it appears, genius is touched with paranoia. Alas.

Our Committee retires to think things over. Like any Committee, ours will not admit that it has failed. It reports some strange, deeply ingrained resistance of the artists to the university, a resistance that is not to be in the least diminished by all that they are told about a new function the university has, which is that of serving as "the focal point of national growth." Like any Committee, ours looks to the future, to the time when the universities will have discovered the way to rear up a new generation of artists who will be trained to find it possible to accommodate themselves to the accommodation of pure creative effort in the arts that the university will devise.

On Irony: An Addendum[1]

[An addendum to the preface of *Beyond Culture*
in the Viking Compass edition of that volume,
1968]

THE ironic mode has lately become riskier than it formerly was and because I occasionally used it in this book some of the things I say have been understood in a way I did not intend. I take the opportunity of a new edition to make my meaning plain.

One writer, supposing me to have said in my preface that I was happy over the situation predicted by Dr. Kerr, that the creative arts would increasingly find their place in the university, has disputed at length and very cogently what he believed to be my position. The paragraph that begins at the bottom of page xiii and the one that follows led him to conclude as he did, for they do say that the old view of the university as hostile to the arts is no longer tenable and that the arts have every reason to expect that they will be very comfortably accommodated in their new environment. I had meant some wryness to color my description of this state of affairs, bringing it into accord with the opinion which (I hope) is expressed in the preface as a whole, and in several of the essays of the volume, that a certain amount of skepticism ought to qualify our satisfaction over the hospitality that is being shown even to—especially to— radical and subversive art by the established and respectable agencies of our culture. To be quite explicit: I regard with misgivings the growing affinity between the university and the arts. Further:

[1] Title supplied by the editor of this volume.

my uneasiness over the situation arises from my concern for the integrity and right influence of the arts.

On two occasions in the book I speak of advertising in relation to literature, considering both as having an influence on the choices that are made among "life styles," and on one of these occasions I speak of advertising as "the wonderful and terrible art which teaches us that we define ourselves and realize our true being by choosing the right style." Responding to this, one of my reviewers, a critic of eminence, said that I "embrace advertising as a cultural ally" and offered unimpeachable reasons why advertising is not worthy of such trust. My purpose in speaking of literature and advertising in the same breath was to take notice of the excessive concern with the "style" of life which, as I believe, has come to mark our culture: by associating literature with advertising I did not mean to praise the latter (about which I have all the right-minded opinions) but to raise a question about the former.

In the last essay of the volume I refer to a leading article in the *Times Literary Supplement* which expressed the opinion that the growing desire of English undergraduates to have modern literature made a subject of university study is not to be taken seriously, that it is merely a "modish" or "faddish" preference. I say that if the new tendency is rightly to be called a fad, we must consider the part played in history by such fads as this, giving as an example the "fad of Bible-reading and theological radicalism," which, by making the Puritan Revolution, "changed the social and cultural fabric of England and helped create the social and cultural fabric of America." It was not the least distinguished of my reviewers who expressed his shocked surprise over the frivolity of a mind that could give so much importance to fads in the history of culture as I did. "If Oliver Cromwell was the product of a 'fad,'" he said, "then so were Robespierre and Lenin . . . ," meaning to propose the thought that the Puritan Revolution, the French Revolution, and the Russian Revolution were not, in point of fact, the outcome of fads. I am glad to avow my assent to this proposition: the intellectual commitments that led to the Puritan, the French, and the Russian Revolutions were not fads. Neither is the undergraduate commitment to modern literature as a subject of study. This was the opinion I had meant to express.

One other use of the mode of irony that I am aware I made—that on page 196, where Henry James is spoken of as perhaps open to the charge of being a Philistine—was from the first protected by a footnote which explains that the statement is not to be taken literally.

APPENDIX
Lionel Trilling:
A Jew at Columbia

by Diana Trilling

[*Commentary*, March 1979]

I F LIONEL TRILLING had lived to write the autobiographical memoir he had for a long time wanted to write—it was
scarcely begun at his death in 1975—an important section of it
would no doubt have been devoted to his early career at Columbia
and to the difficulties of establishing himself in the English-teaching
profession. In part this would inevitably have been a story of the
Depression of the Thirties, since the decade in which he was chiefly
trying to get his start in the university was also the decade in which
his family, always firm in the middle class so far as its social expectations were concerned but never financially secure, finally lost its
economic foothold and dropped the burden of its support, together
with the responsibility for decision in family affairs, upon his young
shoulders. But it would also have been the story of what it meant
to be a Jew in the American academy before we actually let ourselves
recognize what was happening in Germany and what the casual
anti-Semitism of our own country could portend.

Lionel's situation as a Jew who wished to teach in a college was at
once typical and untypical. Typical was the uncertainty whether the
choice was a possible one—quite apart, that is, from academic qualification. This was not the uncertainty of graduate students today as

they face academic recession and a steadily diminishing job market. In Lionel's time there was no problem of the continuing strength of the universities. The question was, could a Jew realistically plan on a university career? The consensus was that especially in certain fields he could not. Several of Lionel's friends had already given up. Elliot Cohen had been a brilliant student of English at Yale but with university teaching closed to him, or so he was convinced— correctly, I think—he had become editor of the *Menorah Journal,* a magazine of Jewish thought for which Lionel and other of his Columbia contemporaries had begun to write as undergraduates. Another Jewish friend from Columbia days, unable to foresee a job in a college history department, had deserted graduate study to become a taxi driver, until one day his father discovered how his son was occupying himself and persuaded him to become a lawyer.

Of course, there were the usual hindrances to generalization: one knew of exceptions to the ruling proscription of Jews from college teaching. Sidney Hook was at New York University; the physicist I. I. Rabi and several philosophers, including Irwin Edman, whose mother was a friend of Lionel's mother, were at Columbia; Morris R. Cohen was at City College. Even art history, then the most socially fastidious of disciplines, had been forced to make place for a Columbia scholar of Meyer Schapiro's spectacular abilities. But English gave no such promise of breakthrough: university English departments were still under the vigilant protection of something called the Anglo-Saxon tradition.

Untypical were Lionel's tenacity and courage—he was among the most unostentatiously *enduring* of people—and the curious assumptions of his upbringing. The belief that was commonly inculcated in the sons of East European Jewish immigrants, particularly those whose fathers had been deflected from the scholarly lives toward which their own early training had been bent, was that Jews came into a hostile world armed with notably superior intellectual powers. To achieve success, which also meant advancing in Americanization or (much the same thing) moving upward on the class ladder, they had only to deploy their native capacities to advantage.

The message of Lionel's upbringing was of a different order. It seemed not to have occurred to his parents that money was necessary to social mobility; as naturally as they breathed they thought of themselves, and always had, as middle-class people—were they not honest, respectable, committed to the solidity and progress of their adopted country? They were not people who went much into the world. They seldom ate in restaurants or attended the theater, although they occasionally went to an opera or concert. They belonged to no clubs and limited their social life to relatives and a modest group of neighbor-friends. But they never felt excluded from life on the ground of having little money or being Jews. English was always the language of the home, well spoken, and Lionel's mother in particular moved among Gentiles without self-consciousness—when Lionel was not accepted as a freshman in good standing because he had done badly in math, his mother had no hesitation in approaching the Columbia officer who had these matters in charge so that the decision was altered.

Unlike others of his intellectual generation, that is, Lionel had no need to make for himself the strategic leap into the American middle class, with what this so often involves in defensiveness. Also, unlike many first-generation Jewish intellectuals, he had not been taught to think of himself as "smart." It was not his sense that life was a contest of minds or that intellect was a weapon; it was more an instrument of conscience. But his parents had made him feel unusually valuable, or certainly much valued by them. While he had no belief that he possessed outstanding skills—on the contrary, throughout his life he thought that virtually everyone with whom he associated had read more than he had, had a better memory, and was better trained in the use of the basic tools of the intellectual trade—he had grown up with an undefined feeling of personal worth, some secret quality of being to which he could give no name but on which he could ultimately rely. As a child, or perhaps even at birth, he had been proved, as if born with a caul. Just as Jewish intellectual arrogance has its mythic dimension, this curious intuition of whatever it was that Lionel's parents cherished in him also had a magical character.

For example, without truly distancing himself from the incident, not finally, Lionel told me of the day in his childhood when he was the object of an ugly street assault by a group of boys who pelted him with snowballs, possibly with rocks in them. He had not run. He had continued on his way, though frightened, telling himself that, like Baldur, he could not be hurt—and he was not hit.

Casual acquaintances of Lionel's father—these would of course be contemporaries—referred to him as "a perfect gentleman." With more daring, he might once have been a fop. Failed as he perhaps knew himself to be and all too manifestly inferior to his wife in attractiveness and energy, he still didn't entirely conform to the now-established image of the failed father of Jewish-American fiction. His wife said that as a young man he had been a prodigious dancer. And even Lionel described him as having been an excellent swimmer. I found all this hard to imagine—I would have thought him afraid of cold water—but then it was also easy for me to bypass the fact that early in his marriage he had cared for his mother, sisters, and brothers much as he now assumed Lionel would care for him.

A gentleman he was in his manner of speech and in his public stance but his family temper was violent. He was also an overbearing hypochondriac. And he had a most faulty sense of money, quite regularly confusing it with something distinctly less tangible, such as personal due or honor. In the worst years of the Depression, when we had all of us, Lionel's parents, Lionel, I, to apportion our infinitesimal funds among many creditors, he would solicit Lionel for money with which to meet, not the rent or food bills—these were not his concern—but his debt (as he interpreted it) to a porter whom he accused himself of once having unfairly laid off; his tone in these approaches was that of a man the plain plausibility of whose mission must be self-evident. Innocent of guilt or, so far as one could see, pain for shifting his responsibilities to a son who was not yet started in his own career, he lived in great fear of punishment for the neglect of fancied obligations outside the family.

The weak hold that his father had on reality was maddening to

Lionel, especially because of the blandness with which his father met opposition to his conduct or contradiction of his views. While still living with his family as a student, Lionel had returned home one day to find his father rifling his desk and reading his mail. To Lionel's angry protest his father replied, "I'm not reading your mail, son. I'm just interested in your life." He spoke in hurt because his son so misunderstood his motives.

At Lionel's birth his father had been a decently successful custom-tailor but he had given this up to become a wholesale furrier—years later, struggling to maintain two families, Lionel would tell his friends in weary irony the reason that had been given him for the change: his father wanted Lionel to be able to say that he was the son of a manufacturer, not a tailor! I doubt he was meant for any business, but wholesale-fur dealing offered him irresistible temptations to calamity. Probably the most notable, the last, was his decision in the late Twenties to make the most beautifully-matched raccoon coats that had ever been put on the market—they were for chauffeurs. Closed cars had by now come in but he was convinced they were not here to stay; the passengers in open cars could cover themselves with rugs but chauffeurs had no such warmth. When Lionel inquired why, instead of trying to outfit chauffeurs in such expensive coats, he didn't look to the colleges for his customers, his father smiled in pity and explained that obviously it was only rudimentary good sense to know that students couldn't afford such costly garments.

And was it also rudimentary good sense to know that a young man with a salary of $2,400 a year—but this would be considerably later, when Lionel got his first job at Columbia—and with two families to support couldn't afford custom clothes? In 1932 Lionel had just been made an instructor and to meet the occasion he had bought himself a suit at Macy's—the price, as I recall, was $29.99. Lionel's mother liked to have us to dinner on Friday nights—although her husband, eating outside the house in better days, ate ham and even shellfish, she kept a kosher home and lit Sabbath candles. Waiting vainly, irritably, for his father to notice his new suit, Lionel at last asked his opinion. His father sighed: "Get up, son." Lionel tried to restrain his annoyance while his father slowly twirled him about, yanking up the collar of the jacket and hauling at its skirt. Finally he gave his judgment: "Don't you think a young man in your position owes it to himself to have a tailor-made suit?" What position, *what* position, Lionel wanted to shout—but could he attack a pride as perilously rooted as his father's? Around the house there was of course no talk of the determining experience of his father's childhood, but long before 1932 Lionel had learned the story: slated for an intellectual life, probably the rabbinate, in his native city of Bialystok, his father's course had all in a single day been abruptly terminated. He had broken down during his Bar Mitzvah: I suppose he forgot his lines. In consequence, a thirteen-year-old had been shipped off to America, put out of sight. For the rest of his life a cloud of disgrace and of the potential for still-uncharted disaster hovered about him.

Lionel's mother was determined that her husband's tendency to panic, overlaid as it was with disquieting fantasies of conquest, should not be communicated to Lionel—Lionel remembered his initial appearance in a school play, and his confused awareness that his mother didn't want his father in the room when she heard him go through his part. It must have given her singular pleasure (but she kept it to herself) that she lived to see Lionel such a relaxed lecturer. But this is not to say that hers was only a negative capability. Lionel's mother was a vigorous presence for anyone who knew her. Few people I have met have been so educable so long: her character and outlook on life changed radically in her middle and old age, the small-spirited values she could once share with her wealthy, self-imposing brothers and sisters steadily giving place to impulses that weren't validated by the conventions of their segment of the world.

Her parents, too, had been East European but she had been born and schooled in London's East End—without ever saying it, she could somehow suggest that Israel Zangwill had been a neighborhood intimate. But then, in celebration of female sturdiness, she could also speak of her "little English mother" in a way to suggest the natural family resemblance to Queen Victoria! Literary to her fingertips and wistfully envious of younger sisters who had been sent to Hunter College when the family had moved to New York, she was among the best-read people I have known, with critical perceptions that were the more impressive for always being voiced, and only to Lionel or me, with unaffected tentativeness: "Li dear, I never went to college and maybe I'm all wrong but did Stendhal . . . did Thackeray . . . did Tolstoy . . . ?" or "Di dear, you know these things better than I do. Did Henry James . . . did Mann . . . did Lawrence . . . ?" Lionel's father had been a reader too, but not like this. She read incessantly until her eyes gave out in her late eighties.

Lionel's mother had early decided that Lionel was to have an Oxford Ph.D.; he said he couldn't have been more than four or five when she first announced this to him. That it didn't work out as she had planned and that his closest approach to the fulfillment of that particular dream was to become Eastman Professor at Oxford in 1964, a few months before her death, was—I think—troubling to him.

It was to his mother's confident expectations for him that Lionel, following Freud, ascribed his own ambitions and such faith as he had in his intellectual capacities. But in his later years he began to feel that this might not be a just assessment of the situation and that perhaps, if only genetically, he drew more from his father than he might once have liked to admit—this was when he heard of Trillings scattered in many parts of the world, an unusual number of whom were of high professional repute; they all of them traced their lineage to a common ancestor in Bialystok, a rabbi renowned for his learning. (How could one not think of a small boy in Bialystok, fluffing his Bar Mitzvah speech!) To be sure, the Cohens, too, and not Lionel's mother alone but others in her family, had their own demonstrable claim to gift, but among the Cohens as Lionel had known them in his formative years—even his own mother not altogether apart—the line between intellectual seriousness and intellectual chic had not been unblurred. Among the Trillings there seemed to be no such push for status on the basis of "culture."

I had met Lionel in 1927 and we married in June 1929. In October came the stock-market crash. I was not a particularly welcome addition to his family until slowly, very slowly, over the next strenuous years, as she was forced to confront not only the financial callousness but also the emotional isolateness of her Park Avenue brothers and sisters, four of them unmarried and living together in an apartment sealed to life, consecrated only to a remarkable art collection, Lionel's mother transferred much of her loyalty from them to me. My father was wiped out in the crash; anguished by "robbing his children," as he put it, he lived by borrowing on his life insurance. Lionel's father soon lost his fur business; we couldn't carry *his* insurance, it had been taken out too late in life. I became gravely ill with hyperthyroidism; far from being able to contribute to the family income I was an expense—in the next ten years, until I regained my strength, I asked much of Lionel, more than is easily told, in emotional support. The bills mounted. My mother was no longer alive: my sister did my father's laundry and housework; the money this saved they gave us to help Lionel's family. We borrowed from everyone we knew, $50 here, $100 there—the people to whom we were sufficiently close to be able to borrow seldom had more than small sums to lend. When my father died at the end of 1932 and I inherited my third of an insurance trust, all that remained of a once-substantial estate, we owed the capital distributions before they could be made.

Because he looked as he did, so quietly self-possessed; spoke as he did; was as he was, unscarred by grievance, Lionel has been pictured since his death as socially privileged above most intellectuals, someone to whom everything had always been given, nothing exacted: a child of gracious fortune. Surely his students couldn't have known the difficulties of his early career, although a sharp observer might perhaps have read a reminiscence of them in his eyes and in his never-completed smile. "Tell your husband to move over and give *us* a chance," raged a Columbia revolutionary of 1968 who had been busted and was now phoning to vent his fury at the "authority," not any authority but the one who must have been nearest to his own ideal. Lionel was not at home to take the call; the message was to be passed on by me.

Seven years had elapsed between Lionel's graduation from Columbia in 1925, shortly before his twentieth birthday, and his appointment as an English instructor in 1932—there was of course no tenure in an instructorship, but the appointment was an accolade; both families felt very proud. But no one was under the illusion, unless perhaps Lionel's father, that Lionel's professional problems were now permanently solved. My own father was ill, terminally, and I remember a conversation with him that fall in which I tried to divert him with an account of a debate Lionel and I had recently attended between Earl Browder for the Communist party and McAlister Coleman for the Socialists at the Morningside branch of the Socialist party, near the University. My father was upset; "Don't you know that President Butler has his spies at meetings like that?" I pointed out that Lionel was in no danger, I had even seen Corliss Lamont at the meeting. "A Communist like Corliss Lamont Lionel should be!" To the son of a Morgan partner—my father was saying—life offered safer harbors than to an anonymous Jew. But he was reflecting as well the then-prevalent idea of the university, contradictory though it was of his own deep-rooted respect for all institutions of learning, as a bulwark of entrenched political and social values, and in itself a power entity. To all Jews and maybe to most non-Jews, too, certainly in New York, the university had an authority not unlike that of the state: remote, virtually absolute. And this view was fortified at Columbia by the public image of Nicholas Murray Butler, who was known to associate with the great financiers and political leaders of the day and to want the Presidency of the United States. We forget that our picture of the college as a liberal citadel is of recent vintage, post-Roosevelt.

It had not been a calm road Lionel had traveled in the seven years since his graduation in 1925. He had remained at Columbia in 1925–26 to take his M.A., after which he had spent a year as what would now be called a teaching assistant in Alexander Meiklejohn's experimental college at the University of Wisconsin. My knowledge of 1927–29 is not precise: while I know he taught at Hunter under Blanche Colton Williams, I am unsure whether it was in the day or evening session; he regarded the experience as only a degrading one and afterward didn't wish to speak of it. In this area, too, we have to keep in mind the changes that have taken place since that period: the city system was then well locked into the system of Tammany patronage; merit was scarcely the sole ground on which one got a Hunter appointment.

We married in 1929 and during the next year Lionel worked as an assistant editor of the *Menorah Journal* for Elliot Cohen, apparently giving satisfaction neither to Cohen nor himself—it was another experience he preferred not to discuss. Between 1930 and 1932 he taught in the evening session of Hunter; in the second of those two years he also had an $1,800 fellowship from Columbia—he had to appeal for special permission to augment this by his part-time teaching. Evening teaching at Hunter was piece work: one was paid a bit more than $3 an hour for an undergraduate class, something over $5 an hour for graduate teaching. Lionel had one undergraduate and one graduate class. When there was insufficient graduate registration, several of my friends signed up, the investment of the $15 registration fees being justified by our need for the income. But a bout of flu could spell financial catastrophe: on an evening when Lionel was too ill to leave his bed, we could think of no salvation but for me to take his classes for him. As a direct result of that undertaking—I tried to teach his graduate students a book I had never read—I have not again ventured into a classroom.

Accesses of inexplicable power can suddenly come to one—as Lionel would learn a few years later—and sudden beneficences too: the offer to Lionel of an instructorship at Columbia is not readily accounted for. By and large, except for Raymond Weaver, who was outspokenly hostile until a long time afterward when his enmity changed into affection as precipitously as it had appeared, his teachers liked Lionel well enough, but he was far from esteemed above all others—it is even possible that a piece by Mark Van Doren in the *Menorah Journal* in 1927, in which he describes some of his former

Jewish students, reflects more than just his own estimate that Lionel's was one of the less commanding talents of his college generation. (What strikes one, reading the piece today, is surely not any prescience it can boast but its subject. In 1927 only an editor of Elliot Cohen's ironic imaginativeness could have thought to invite a college teacher of English, even in New York, to write about the Jews he had taught!) The person directing Lionel's dissertation was Emery Neff, a scholar of Carlyle and Mill. Neff was personally not unfriendly but Lionel had given him little to go on in judgment of his capacities other than vague gropings toward a book about Matthew Arnold. When the appointment as instructor came, it was from an entirely unexpected source. There was no reason to suspect that Ashley Thorndike, then head of the department, took notice of Lionel, yet it was Thorndike who offered him the job. Did Thorndike, in proposing Lionel for the English department, have a programmatic purpose? Had he caught something about Lionel that others missed? Lionel never learned. Obviously, if it was Thorndike's intention to test a Jew, Lionel made a good gamble in both appearance and name. Had his name been that of his maternal grandfather, Israel Cohen, it is highly questionable whether the offer would have been made. (This was the grandfather whose uncanny resemblance to Freud would in later years capture Lionel's imagination.)

It was a period in which one earned one's keep: for $2,400 an instructor taught four full courses while commonly working for his Ph.D. If, like Lionel, he had ambitions to write elsewhere than only in scholarly periodicals, he also wrote book reviews when he could get them. If he was desperate as Lionel was for money, he added to this schedule such literary odd jobs as came his way—for $10 fees Lionel talked to women's clubs in Staten Island or Westchester; he pasted up anthologies to be given away as bonuses with newspaper subscriptions; at one stage, he tutored a rich young man in novel-writing and, at another, he taught a class at a Junior League. I don't know if the quality of his teaching suffered under the pressure but undoubtedly his thesis did. It would nevertheless be inac-

curate to blame the difficulties he was having with his book wholly
on the strains of such urgent money-earning, severe as these were.
He was depressed, he had a considerable writing block though fortunately not a total one, he didn't know what kind of book he had
undertaken to write: how did you write an intellectual biography of
Matthew Arnold without writing the history of the nineteenth
century? From the start his department had no great enthusiasm for
his dissertation subject; it was too big, too amorphous, and who
cared about Arnold anyway? Yet with no clear notion of what he
was about, which might have persuaded them to take a more cheer-
ful view of his project, Lionel never yielded his determination to
stay with his topic. No one could have worked harder, nor less fruit-
fully—he went out no more than one evening a week, he read, he
brooded, he drafted chapter after chapter. My own recollection of
his early efforts on the Arnold was of a dissertation that, week in
and week out, found yet another way of saying that England had
had an Industrial Revolution and that the roads were bad! Although
Lionel knew better than to show all these versions to Neff, an occasional presentation was unavoidable, and each time Neff read a
chapter he sent Lionel back for a fresh try. Later, when life improved, Lionel confessed to me that he didn't always go to the library
when he told me that that was his destination: things were too bad.
In fact, even earlier in our marriage, assailed by depression, he
would go to the movies, sitting through interminable double features
like someone homeless.

It went this way for four years. In 1936 the Columbia department
dropped him. The way it was done was not harsh. The departmental
spokesman said he would not be reappointed for a next year because
"as a Freudian, a Marxist, and a Jew" he was not happy there.
Lionel said he *was* happy in the department. They said he would be
"more comfortable" elsewhere.

Obviously in the midst of the devastation produced by his dismissal
—what would he do now?—Lionel couldn't grasp the complex truth
of what was involved in this termination of his appointment. But
though not yet formulated with the conviction that would later

come to him, at least one thing was immediately clear: his dismissal
was not any *simple* act of anti-Semitism, any more than it was a
simple act of anti-Freudianism or anti-Marxism—while he had been
known to be a Communist fellow-traveler at the time he got his job
in 1932, in the years since then he had moved steadily away from his
earlier Marxist commitment, although never ceding his interest in
and respect for Marx's thought; as for his Freudian preference, it
could be known only through conversation because in 1936 it had
not yet appeared in his writing. Although over the years the story of
Lionel's dismissal came to be talked about among people we knew
as a gross instance of collegiate anti-Semitism, this was a bargain-
basement version of the actual scenario. What was in fact going on
doesn't make the ready matter of religious polemics; it makes the
more textured matter of fiction. Lionel was a harried, frightened
young man. He proclaimed no confidence in himself—this was true
outside the University as well as within it—and he therefore inspired little confidence in others. In 1936 his dissertation was not yet
visible to the naked eye. His moral and intellectual force, like his
tenaciousness and wit, was visible chiefly to me and a few other
intimates. When his department said he wasn't happy with them
and would be more comfortable elsewhere, what they meant was
that *they* weren't happy with *him* and would be more comfortable if
he went somewhere else. The documentation they produced in evidence of his—their—unease was the aspect of the situation that had
significant social implications, for what it revealed was that Jews
were people who made the Columbia faculty uncomfortable, Freu-
dians were people who made the Columbia faculty uncomfortable,
Marxists were people who made the Columbia faculty uncomfortable. It is in this sense, circumscribed but charged enough, that in
dismissing Lionel, Columbia can be accused of anti-Semitism together with other biases and cautions.

It was a few days before Lionel responded at Columbia to his dismissal: the action he took was the single most decisive move of his
life, undoubtedly its source his mother's insistence that *her* hope for
her son, her certainty of his firm future, must triumph over his

father's long tragic concourse with defeat. One after the other Lionel confronted those members of his department whom he knew best: Van Doren, Weaver, Neff. He didn't reason with them, he didn't argue with them. He told them that they were getting rid of a person who would one day bring great distinction to their department; they would not easily find another as good. It was his habit to speak quietly but now he spoke so loud that Neff was distressed, closed the transom. It wasn't a ploy, it wasn't planned—for the rest of his life Lionel would recur to this deeply uncharacteristic moment. With me or with friends, he would speculate on what had generated conduct this alien to his usual temper and also what lessons about our human workings were to be learned from its outcome. All at once he had presented himself to these people as the opposite of what he had previously been, someone who tempted their aggression, and, as he analyzed it, it was this that had accomplished its miracle: with such high opinion of himself, was it not possible that he deserved their high opinion? At any rate, so it worked out: it was agreed that he was to stay on for another year; the year multiplied because he was now a changed person. He began his book anew; his confusions about the direction it must take seemed overnight to vanish. By 1939 it was published to his department's satisfaction and President Butler's pride. In those days a dissertation had to be published and a hundred copies deposited in the library in order to earn one's degree; it was a last unhappy note to the history of Lionel's *Matthew Arnold* that W. W. Norton required a subsidy to publish it. Somehow—more borrowing!—we found the money.

The role of President Butler in the next stage of Lionel's academic career importantly modifies the image of Butler that has come down to us. Few good words have been written about him; in general he has been made to appear, especially in the recollection of students who were engaged in Communist activities on the campus in the Thirties, a fiercely repressive administrator, indeed a tyrant. I don't know the justice or injustice of these reports. His relation to Lionel, however, was exemplary in an administrative tradition that no longer exists.

One day in early 1939—his book had just been published in England as well as here—Lionel met his old friend and teacher Irwin Edman in the neighborhood. As they chatted, Irwin asked Lionel whether he had thought to send Butler a copy of the *Matthew Arnold*. No, Lionel had not; it had not occurred to him. But Butler *liked* to be sent copies of books written by members of his faculty, Irwin explained; in fact, he considered it a breach of etiquette if this courtesy was denied him. No one was more knowledgeable in such matters than Irwin. He was the only person of our acquaintance who also had acquaintance with the President; his urging of this duty upon Lionel was not to be written off. To Lionel, Butler was a distant, formidable figure, known for his almost comically exalted style of life: how did one even address him? Irwin must be bothered once more. In reply to Lionel's embarrassed phone call, Irwin explained the procedure: addressing him "Dear Mr. President," Lionel must write a letter asking the privilege of sending him his recent book; the book, inscribed "To President Butler, Respectfully . . . ," was to be mailed the next day. Insisting that he could not do it, would not do it, could not be prevailed upon to do it, Lionel followed Irwin's instructions.

That night I had a waking dream in which President Butler got Lionel's book, read it, and rushed into the next office to Frank Fackenthal, Columbia's Provost. "Frank, do you mean to say we have an instructor in this university who can write a book like this? He must be promoted!" I later learned that as nearly as a fantasy can be re-enacted in reality, this one had been.

If President Butler wanted a young man promoted, he had his procedures. Every spring the Association for University Teas gave a reception at the Faculty Club for the President and his wife. Several weeks before the event this spring an engraved invitation arrived at our house: Lionel and I were asked to dinner at the President's the evening of the reception. No one we knew had ever been at the Butlers' for dinner, perhaps not even Irwin Edman—I remember I had to go afield for advice about dress, but that could have been because Irwin had no wife I could consult. I felt I was taking my life in my hands in even calling the Secretary of the University, a white-haired gentleman who suggested a plumper smoother Cordell Hull, to inquire whether it was white or black tie that was indicated for our occasion. "White tie, I should think," said Mr. Hayden in a voice that froze the heart. It was decided: Lionel would hire tails and I would buy a ball gown. A terrible thought came to me: need I wear long white gloves? Who was there to tell me? I called the fashion department of *Vogue* magazine, which assured me that there was no occasion or place that any longer required long white gloves, unless it was the Court of St. James's. This convinced me: long white gloves would be worn at President Butler's. I called the fashion adviser of Bonwit Teller and got the same reply but this time I was more specific: "What about dinner at the home of President Butler of Columbia University?" "Well, yes," came the reply. "That might be a good idea."

Public figures and University people were obviously not to be mixed; on the evening of our dinner the guests were entirely from the faculty, I think there were twenty people present. For dinner at eight, Lionel and I carefully arrived at 8:02. We were the last to arrive and were rather urgently propelled toward the closed drawing-room doors by a footman. The doors were flung open, we were announced by a butler. The receiving line consisted of the President and his wife. "Let me congratulate you, sir, on your splendid English reviews," was the President's greeting to Lionel. "There's only been one," said Lionel. "There have been two, sir," the President corrected him. In the meantime I was being welcomed, if that's the word, by his wife. "Do you know everyone here, my dear?" I made a lightning survey of the room. "I'm afraid I don't know anyone." "That, my dear, is because you never come to any of the teas or receptions." In the dining room it was possible to study the company. All the women but one wore long white kid gloves, the hands now rolled back. Lionel was the obvious purpose of the evening. Dean Hawkes of the College was a guest and so was Ernest Hunter Wright, now head of the University English department. For his communication to be unmistakable, Butler would have had to do no more than invite Lionel, an instructor, in this company. But he had yet another arrow to fire.

Through dinner the President ate nothing; he drank a great deal of Scotch. The food was delicious: his wife was a Frenchwoman of mature years built with the kind of one-piece sloping bosom that made a properly solid armature for a lavender cut-velvet Worth gown, very expensive, elegant, and unbeautiful, that was then in favor among higher-echelon ladies of two continents, and I knew about her table from the grocer we shared. One day when I had been offered a bargain in loose carrots from a corner basket and I had rejected them as "horse carrots," he had confided to me that these were the ones Mrs. Butler bought for the servants' kitchen; nothing was too good for her own table. There were several footmen to serve, so that the meal went swiftly. At its end the women repaired to Mrs. Butler's sitting room upstairs while the men had cigars and brandy in the President's library. The President sat on a bench with his back to the fireplace, Lionel told me, and did all the talking. He was growing old; under any circumstances it would have been easier to talk than listen. In a circle in front of him the men attended what he had to say.

What the prefatory monologue consisted in was of no import; it was where it inescapably led that mattered: Butler recounted the correspondence he had had with the Chancellor of the University of Berlin when the two universities, Berlin and Columbia, had decided on an exchange of philosophy professors. Columbia proposed to send Felix Adler and the Chancellor had written to protest a Jewish visitor. Lionel re-created the scene. Having got this far in his narrative, Butler had put down his brandy glass and firmly planted his hands on his knees, fixing his eyes on Professor Wright as he boomed: "And I, gentlemen, I wrote back: 'At Columbia, sir, we recognize merit, not race.'" Silence. The party rose to join the ladies and move on to the Faculty Club reception. In the summer, "under his summer powers," President Butler appointed Lionel an Assistant Professor of

English, the first Jew of that department to become a member of the faculty.

How much, then, had anti-Semitism actually been a factor in Lionel's dismissal in 1936? Who can say? Certainly it was by Butler's intervention, by fiat of the top authority of the University, that a Jew was first given a post teaching English at Columbia, which in those days implied permanence.

Everyone was easy with him; Lionel felt no hidden tensions. Indeed, the generosity that he met from this point forward in his Columbia career has, for me, a legendary quality—his departmental colleagues could not have taken more pleasure in his academic or critical successes if they had been their own.

One day, however, very soon after his promotion, Lionel had a call from Emery Neff: he wished to come to the house and he hoped that I would be at home too. Although we were mildly on visiting terms with Neff and his wife, a call of this kind was unprecedented.

What Emery Neff came to say was that now that Lionel was a member of the department, he hoped that he would not use it as a wedge to open the English department to more Jews. He made his statement economically and straightforwardly, ungarnished; it must have taken some courage. And he seemed to be speaking for himself alone; he cited no other departmental opinion. Lionel and I just sat and stared. Neither of us spoke. Emery turned to other subjects and soon left.

World War II had started. In the next years the situation of Jews in American universities changed radically. Not only at Columbia, but everywhere, even Harvard, Princeton, Yale, and not only in English departments but in all fields of study and in administration, Jews made their comfortable way. I remember Lionel's grin the day he came home to report: "We hired a new English instructor today. His name is Hyman Kleinman." I also remember, in fact together we remembered, one of his father's wilder—no, wildest—flights of fancy back in the early Thirties when it seemed to us that if we had to endure yet another of his unrealities we might ourselves lose our hold. We had been talking about Jews in college teaching, the failure they almost surely faced. His father, as always unperturbed in his reading of this world we presumably inhabited with him, had fixed his most unbearably pitying look on Lionel. "Why, son, this is America. A Jew could be President of Columbia University."